Weight equivalents

METRIC	IMPERIAL	METRIC	
15g	½oz	150g	5½oz
20g	¾oz	175g	6oz
30g	1oz	200g	7oz
45g	1½oz	225g	8oz
50g	1¾oz	250g	9oz
60g	2oz	300g	10oz
75g	2½oz	450g	1lb
85g	3oz	500g	1lb 2oz
100g	3½oz	675g	1½lb
115g	4oz	900g	2lb
125g	4½oz	1kg	2¼lb
140g	5oz	1.5kg	3lb 3oz

Cake tin equivalents

ROUND TIN	SQUARE TIN
15cm (6in)	12cm (5in)
18cm (7in)	15cm (6in)
19cm (7½in)	16cm (6½in)
20cm (8in)	18cm (7in)
23cm (9in)	20cm (8in)
25cm (10in)	23cm (9in)

Yeast equivalents

1 tsp dried yeast = 5g / ⅕oz fresh yeast
1 cake fresh yeast = 15g / ½oz fresh yeast = 3 tsp dried yeast

Calculating pastry quantities

For basic shortcrust pastry use half the amount of fat to flour.

SIZE OF FLAN TIN	QUANTITY OF FLOUR
15cm (6in)	115g (4oz)
18cm (7in)	140g (5oz)
19cm (7½in)	150g (5½oz)
20cm (8in)	175g (6oz)
23cm (9in)	200g (7oz)
25cm (10in)	225g (8oz)

STEP-BY-STEP
baking

STEP-BY-STEP
baking

Caroline Bretherton

LONDON, NEW YORK,
MUNICH, MELBOURNE, DELHI

Senior Editor Alastair Laing
Project Art Editor Kathryn Wilding
Managing Editor Dawn Henderson
Managing Art Editor Christine Keilty
Senior Jacket Creative Nicola Powling
Production Editor Maria Elia
Senior Production Controller Alice Sykes
Creative Technical Support Sonia Charbonnier
Photographers Howard Shooter, Michael Hart

DK INDIA
Project Editor Charis Bhagianathan
Senior Art Editor Neha Ahuja
Project Designer Divya PR
Assistant Art Editor Mansi Nagdev
Managing Editor Glenda Fernandes
Managing Art Editor Navidita Thapa
DTP Manager Sunil Sharma
Production Manager Pankaj Sharma
DTP Operators Neeraj Bhatia,
Sourabh Challariya, Arjinder Singh

First published in Great Britain in 2011 by
Dorling Kindersley Limited
80 Strand, London WC2R 0RL
Penguin Group (UK)

4 6 8 10 9 7 5 3
009 – 180077 – Sept/2011

A CIP catalogue record for this book
is available from the British Library.
ISBN 978-1-4053-6823-0

Colour reproduction by Alta Image
Printed and bound by Hung Hing, China

Discover more at www.dk.com

Contents

Introduction

My first introduction to baking was at my first birthday party, when family history has it that I launched myself into a cream-laden gâteau head first, a moment carefully preserved forever by my mother's polaroid camera. Years later I have a similarly enthusiastic response to baked goods, albeit tempered by a lifetime of experience.

Getting It Right: Be Patient, Be Precise

Baking is something most people approach with caution, speaking of fallen sponges, soggy bottoms, and crumbling pastry. Yet it is, above all, a science. With a tried-and-tested recipe (as all the recipes in this book are) and careful application to quantities, timing, and temperature, there is little that cannot be achieved by the home baker. The key to competent baking is patience and precision. Read the recipe carefully, follow it unwaveringly, and you will rarely fail.

Must-have Equipment

Having said that, there are a few items of equipment that will help you along the way. Digital scales are an absolute must. Weighing ingredients carefully is vital to most baking. Unlike everyday cooking, where we can rely on taste and personal preference, the correct balance of fat to flour to eggs is always required to make a cake rise.

Beyond the scales a simple set of baking equipment should include: a set of quality, non-stick cake and flan tins and baking sheets. A large mixing bowl, a set of measuring spoons, a spatula, a balloon whisk, electric whisk, and some wooden spoons. Many of the recipes in this book can be achieved with little else, but if you love to bake and would like to attempt the more complex recipes, I would recommend a standing mixer with dough hook. This takes a lot of the hard work out of bread making, for example, and well kneaded dough always produces better bread.

Finally, an oven thermometer. It may seem strange when your oven has a temperature display on it, but the temperature inside some ovens differs significantly from the dial setting. For a small outlay you can buy a simple thermometer that hangs from the oven shelf and accurately reads the temperature inside your oven.

My Essential Tips

Once you have your equipment in place the best thing to do is practise. Carefully follow a new recipe the first couple of times you attempt it and you will soon find your confidence growing. You will start to understand how ingredients respond and work together so that, with time, you will be able to create your own alternative versions.

Cakes should mostly be light and airy. Barring the heavier fruit varieties, most cakes rely on air being whisked into the mixture then carefully preserved by a light touch when folding in the flour, before cooking. Although butter gives a richer taste to the finished cake, baking margarine will produce a lovely, light result too.

Meringues need a scrupulously clean bowl and not a trace of yolk in the egg whites, or they will not whisk well. A long, slow cook always helps. My oven is always too hot to produce a pure white meringue, so I counteract this by propping the door open slightly with the handle of a wooden spoon to allow the temperature to drop. Meringues that are cooled in the oven tend to crack less, too.

Pastry is often seen as more challenging than it should be. "Pastry hands" are basically just cool hands, helpful in preventing the fat from softening too much when preparing and rolling the pastry, which can cause it to end up greasy. If you're a little too warm-blooded, minimize contact by using a food processor to produce pastry crumbs, and even to bind the dough; also try to work in a cool kitchen and with chilled equipment. The real secret to making good pastry, however, is to use good-quality butter and egg yolks (and a little water if necessary) to bind it together. Other than that, pastry must be rested in a cool place before rolling, as this allows the glutens in the flour to relax; otherwise they become springy and cause the pastry to shrink and crack when baked. Do not over-flour surfaces, or the pastry will absorb too much flour. And handle pastry as little as possible, or it will become tough. Simple!

Bread making is the thing that has the average home baker running scared. Many of us rely on a bread maker, but using your hands and really getting to know your dough is the only way to produce top-quality bread at home. Yeast is a living organism and learning how it responds to time and temperature is a revelation. With thoughtful practice, you could be producing quality artisan breads and saving yourself a fortune. If something goes wrong, try to work out why – did you under or over knead the dough? Did it have enough time to rise the first time? Did it rise too quickly? Was it too warm? Was the loaf sufficiently proven before it went into the oven? Was the oven hot enough? These are all questions that may provide the answers to why a loaf came out less than perfect.

Strangely enough, my most common fault is one that is easily rectified. I always want to cut into my loaves as soon as possible. If they have just come out of the oven, the steam created inside them will be continuing to cook the loaf from the inside. Cut into the bread too early and all this steam will escape. The loaf will be compressed by the cutting action, and the crumb will feel damp on first eating, only to go dry and hard afterwards. After all your patience in the process of making the loaf, surely it's worth waiting a little longer to produce a perfect crust and crumb?

About the Recipes

I have divided the recipes into classics, step-by-steps, and variations. The classics are of the "must have" variety, loved by bakers everywhere. The step-by-step spreads will help even the first-time baker get it right, and the variations are exactly that: variations on the theme of the step-by-step recipes, so that once you have mastered the main recipe you can try alternative versions, adding your own touches and developing new variations, to take your baking onto the next level.

Each recipe starts with information about quantity of servings, how long the recipe takes to prepare (including chilling, rising, and proving times), cooking time, and whether it is possible to freeze the finished bake or freeze at an earlier stage of preparation. At the end of recipes, I provide information about whether the baked goods will store well and for how long, and steps you can take to prepare ahead if you are pressed for time or planning a party. I have also included some crucial nuggets of advice from my baking experience in the form of Baker's Tips.

Caroline

Traditional Afternoon Tea

Currant Scones
page 142

15–20 MINS 12–15 MINS

Fondant Fancies
page 120

20–25 MINS 25 MINS

Carrot Cake
page 42

20 MINS 45 MINS

Shortbread
page 220

15 MINS 35–40 MINS

Light Fruit Cake
page 87

25 MINS 1¾ HOURS

English Muffins
page 444

25–30 MINS 13–16 MINS

Chocolate Éclairs
page 165

30 MINS 25–30 MINS

Coffee and Walnut Cake
page 30

20 MINS 20–25 MINS

Bara Brith
page 78

40 MINS 25–40 MINS

Chelsea Buns
page 160

Chocolate Cake
page 54

30 MINS | 25–30 MINS

Pecan and Cranberry Loaf Cake page 76

30 MINS | 50–60 MINS

Cherry and Almond Cake
page 71

20 MINS | 1½–1¾ HOURS

Crumpets
page 516

10 MINS | 20–26 MINS

Strawberry Shortcakes
page 143

15–20 MINS | 12–15 MINS

White Loaf
page 402

20 MINS | 40–45 MINS

Victoria Sponge Cake
page 28

30 MINS | 20–25 MINS

Scones
page 140

15–20 MINS | 12–15 MINS

Weekend Brunch

RECIPE CHOOSERS

Waffles
page 532

10 MINS 20–25 MINS

English Muffins
page 444

25–30 MINS 13–16 MINS

Zweibelkuchen
page 368

30 MINS 60–65 MINS

Almond Crescents
page 156

30 MINS 15–20 MINS

Pão de queijo
page 410

10 MINS 30 MINS

Brioche Nanterre
page 101

30 MINS 30 MINS

Multi-grain Breakfast Bread
page 416

45–50 MINS 40–45 MINS

Buttermilk Biscuits
page 514

10 MINS 15 MINS

Croissants
page 150

1 HOUR 15–20 MINS

anana, Yogurt, and Honey ancake Stack page 512

10 MINS · **15–20 MINS**

Jam Doughnuts page 182

30 MINS · **5–10 MINS**

Hazelnut and Raisin Rye Bread page 465

25 MINS · **40–50 MINS**

Danish Pastries page 154

30 MINS · **15–20 MINS**

Staffordshire Oatcakes page 522

10 MINS · **15 MINS**

Crumpets page 516

10 MINS · **20–26 MINS**

Buckwheat Galettes page 520

25 MINS · **25–30 MINS**

Bagels page 434

40 MINS · **20–25 MINS**

Skillet Bread page 498

5–10 MINS · **30–40 MINS**

Picnic Basket

Feta Filo Pie
page 386

30 MINS   35–40 MINS

Chicken and Ham Raised Pie
page 378

50–60 MINS   1½ HOURS

Cornish Pasties
page 392

20 MINS   40–45 MINS

Forfar Bridie
page 395

15 MINS   20–25 MINS

Spinach and Goat's Cheese Tart page 365

20 MINS   55–65 MINS

Quiche Lorraine
page 363

35 MINS   47–52 MINS

Walnut and Rosemary Loaf
page 403

20 MINS   30–40 MINS

Individual Pork Pies
page 380

40 MINS   1 HOUR

Spiced Lamb Pies
page 482

40–45 MINS   10–15 MINS

Fougasse
page 423

30–35 MINS | 15 MINS

Sausage Rolls
page 384

30 MINS | 10–12 MINS

Chocolate and Hazelnut Brownies page 228

25 MINS | 12–15 MINS

Pissaladière
page 478

20 MINS | 85 MINS

Wholemeal Fennel Seed Rolls
page 409

20 MINS | 25–35 MINS

Pistachio and Cranberry Oat Cookies page 190

20 MINS | 10–15 MINS

Strawberry Tart
page 292

40 MINS | 25 MINS

Apple and Almond Galettes
page 172

25–30 MINS | 20–30 MINS

Almond and Peach Tart
page 289

20 MINS | 30 MINS

Sweet Party Bites

RECIPE CHOOSERS

Whoopie Pies
page 126

40 MINS | 12 MINS

Mince Pies
page 336

20 MINS | 10–12 MINS

Raspberry Cream Meringues
page 242

10 MINS | 1 HOUR

Strawberries and Cream Macarons page 246

30 MINS | 18–20 MINS

Baklava
page 346

50–55 MINS | 1¼–1½ HOURS

Blackberry Focaccia
page 422

30–35 MINS | 15–20 MINS

Fruit Tartlets
page 297

40–45 MINS | 11–13 MINS

Raspberry Macarons
page 251

30 MINS | 18–20 MINS

Cinnamon Palmiers
page 178

45 MINS | 25–30 MINS

Savoury Party Bites

Blinis
page 524

20 MINS · 15 MINS

Prawn and Guacamole Tortilla Stacks page 493

15 MINS · 10–15 MINS

Ciabatta Crostini
page 426

15 MINS · 10 MINS

Pizza Bianca
page 477

25 MINS · 20 MINS

Pane di patate
page 404

50–55 MINS · 40–45 MINS

Spanish Picos
page 432

40–45 MINS · 18–20 MINS

Pita Crisps
page 483

10 MINS · 7–8 MINS

Parmesan and Rosemary Thins page 236

10 MINS · 15 MINS

Pesto-filled Garland Bread
page 414

35–40 MINS · 30–35 MINS

Parma Ham-wrapped Canapés page 433

45 MINS · 15–18 MINS

Chocolate Fix

RECIPE CHOOSERS

Profiteroles
page 162

30 MINS · 22 MINS

Marbled Millionaire's Shortbread page 223

45 MINS · 35–40 MINS

Devil's Food Cake
page 58

30 MINS · 30–35 MINS

Pains au chocolat
page 152

1 HOUR · 15–20 MINS

Chocolate Cupcakes
page 118

20 MINS · 20–25 MINS

White Chocolate and Coconut Snowballs page 125

40 MINS · 25 MINS

Chocolate Fondants
page 132

20 MINS · 5–15 MINS

Chocolate Muffins
page 136

10 MINS · 15 MINS

Chocolate Millefeuilles
page 170

2 HOURS · 25–30 MINS

Raspberry Tart with Chocolate Cream
page 296

40 MINS | 20–25 MINS

Chocolate and Brazil Nut Cake page 50

25 MINS | 45–50 MINS

Chocolate Palmiers
page 180

45 MINS | 25–30 MINS

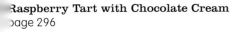

White Chocolate and Macadamia Nut Cookies page 191

25 MINS | 10–15 MINS

Sour Cherry and Chocolate Brownies page 232

15 MINS | 20–25 MINS

Chocolate and Pear Meringue Roulade page 262

25 MINS | 15 MINS

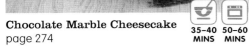

Chocolate Marble Cheesecake
page 274

35–40 MINS | 50–60 MINS

Chocolate Chestnut Roulade
page 104

50–55 MINS | 5–7 MINS

Chocolate Walnut Truffle Tart
page 326

45–50 MINS | 35–40 MINS

Children's Parties

Fondant Fancies
page 120

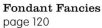 20–25 MINS 25 MINS

Vanilla Cream Cupcakes
page 114

20 MINS 20–25 MINS

Swiss Roll
page 36

20 MINS 12–15 MINS

Sausage Rolls
page 384

30 MINS 10–12 MINS

Chocolate Fudge Cake Balls
page 122

35 MINS 25 MINS

Tarta di nata
page 317

30 MINS 20–25 MINS

Hot Dog Pretzels
page 442

30 MINS 15 MINS

Mini Bagels
page 436

45 MINS 15–20 MINS

Spiced Carrot Cake
page 45

20 MINS 30 MINS

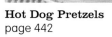

Children's Bake Time

Gingerbread Men
page 196

20 MINS 10–12 MINS

Banana Bread
page 74

20–25 MINS 35–40 MINS

Four Seasons Pizza
page 472

40 MINS 40 MINS

Rock Cakes
page 146

15 MINS 15–20 MINS

Blueberry Cobbler
page 348

15 MINS 30 MINS

**Hazelnut and Raisin
Oat Cookies** page 188

20 MINS 10–15 MINS

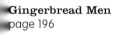

Butter Biscuits
page 192

15 MINS 10–15 MINS

Quick Pumpkin Bread
page 500

20 MINS 50 MINS

Cinnamon and Plum Crumble
page 352

10 MINS 30–40 MINS

Flapjacks
page 224

15 MINS 40 MINS

Prepare Ahead

Tropical Fruit Pavlova
page 255

15 MINS | 65–80 MINS

Pistachio and Orange Biscotti
page 214

15 MINS | 40–45 MINS

Dried Fruit Strudel
page 344

45–50 MINS | 30–40 MINS

Black Forest Gâteau
page 108

55 MINS | 40 MINS

Giant Pistachio Meringues
page 244

15 MINS | 1½ HOURS

Ginger Cheesecake
page 275

40–45 MINS | 50–60 MINS

Sticky Toffee Puddings
page 52

20 MINS | 20–25 MINS

Individual Stuffed Panettones
page 93

1 HOUR | 30–35 MINS

Apple Jalousie
page 174

1¼–1½ HOURS   30–40 MINS

Tarte aux pommes
page 298

20 MINS   50–55 MINS

Cinnamon Rolls
page 158

40 MINS   25–30 MINS

Rich Fruit Cake
page 82

25 MINS   2½ HOURS

Sourdough Rolls
page 456

45–50 MINS   25–30 MINS

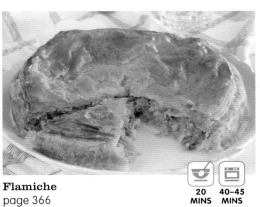

Flamiche
page 366

20 MINS   40–45 MINS

Beef and Ale Cobbler
page 374

40 MINS   2½–3¼ HOURS

Salmon En Croûte
page 385

25 MINS   30 MINS

Chicken Pot Pies
with Herb Crust page 376

25–35 MINS   22–25 MINS

Anadama Cornbread
page 418

25 MINS   45–50 MINS

Fast and Fabulous

Brandy Snaps
page 218

15 MINS 6-8 MINS

Apple Brown Betty
page 354

15 MINS 35-45 MINS

Welsh Cakes
page 144

20 MINS 16-24 MINS

Orange Soufflés
page 264

20 MINS 12-15 MINS

Lemon Cheesecake
page 278

30 MINS

Madeleines
page 138

15-20 MINS 10 MINS

Swedish Spice Biscuits
page 198

20 MINS 10 MINS

Génoise Cake with Raspberries and Cream
page 34

30 MINS 25-30 MINS

Pear and Chocolate Cake
page 57

15 MINS · 30 MINS

Swedish Pancake Stack Cake
page 521

10 MINS · 15 MINS

Macaroons
page 202

10 MINS · 12–15 MINS

American Blueberry Pancakes page 508

10 MINS · 15–20 MINS

Chocolate Amaretti Roulade
page 106

25–30 MINS · 20 MINS

Apple Muffins
page 137

10 MINS · 20–25 MINS

Churros
page 185

10 MINS · 5–10 MINS

Parsnip and Parmesan Bread
page 503

20 MINS · 50 MINS

Southern US-style Cornbread
page 506

10–15 MINS · 25–35 MINS

Stilton and Walnut Biscuits
page 234

10 MINS · 20 MINS

everyday cakes

Victoria Sponge Cake

Probably the most iconic British cake, a good Victoria sponge should be well-risen, moist, and as light as air.

SERVES 6–8 | **30 MINS** | **20–25 MINS** | **4 WEEKS, UNFILLED**

Special equipment
2 x 18cm (7in) round cake tins

Ingredients

175g (6oz) unsalted butter, softened, plus extra for greasing
175g (6oz) caster sugar
3 eggs
1 tsp vanilla extract
175g (6oz) self-raising flour
1 tsp baking powder

For the filling

50g (1¾oz) unsalted butter, softened
100g (3½oz) icing sugar, plus extra to serve
1 tsp vanilla extract
115g (4oz) good-quality seedless raspberry jam

1 Preheat the oven to 180°C (350°F/Gas 4). Grease the tins and line with parchment.

2 Whisk the butter and sugar in a bowl for 2 minutes, or until pale, light, and fluffy.

3 Add the eggs one at a time, mixing well between additions to avoid curdling.

4 Add the vanilla extract and whisk briefly until it is well-blended through the batter.

5 Whisk the mixture for another 2 minutes until bubbles appear on the surface.

6 Remove the whisk, then sift the flour and baking powder into the bowl.

7 With a metal spoon, gently fold in the flour until just smooth; try to keep the mixture light.

8 Divide the mixture evenly between the tins and smooth the tops with a palette knife.

9 Cook for 20–25 minutes or until golden brown and springy to the touch.

10 Test the sponges by inserting a skewer. If it comes out clean, the cakes are cooked.

11 Leave for a few minutes in the tins. Turn out, good side up, onto a wire rack to cool.

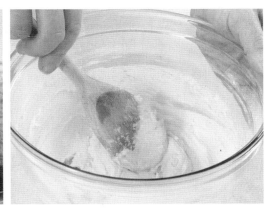

12 For the filling, beat together the butter, icing sugar, and vanilla extract until smooth.

13 Spread the buttercream evenly onto the flat side of a cooled sponge with a palette knife.

14 Gently spread the jam on top of the buttercream using a table knife.

15 Top with the second sponge, flat sides together. Serve dusted with sifted icing sugar.

STORE The filled cake will keep in an airtight container in a cool place for 2 days.
PREPARE AHEAD Unfilled, the sponges will keep for up to 3 days.

Victoria Sponge Cake variations

Coffee and Walnut Cake

A slice of coffee and walnut cake is the perfect accompaniment to morning coffee. Here the cake is made in smaller tins than the classic Victoria sponge to give it extra height and impact.

| SERVES 8 | 20 MINS | 20–25 MINS | 8 WEEKS, UNFILLED |

Special equipment
2 x 17cm (6¾in) round cake tins

Ingredients
175g (6oz) unsalted butter, softened, plus extra for greasing
175g (6oz) soft light brown sugar
3 eggs
1 tsp vanilla extract
175g (6oz) self-raising flour
1 tsp baking powder
1 tbsp strong coffee powder, mixed with 2 tbsp boiling water and cooled

For the icing
100g (3½oz) unsalted butter, softened
200g (7oz) icing sugar
9 walnut halves

Method

1 Preheat the oven to 180°C (350°F/Gas 4). Grease the tins and line the bases with parchment. Cream together the butter and sugar in a bowl, using an electric whisk, until light and fluffy.

2 Add the eggs one at a time, beating well between additions. Add the vanilla, and whisk for 2 minutes until bubbles appear on the surface. Sift in the flour and baking powder.

3 Gently fold in the flour, followed by half the coffee mixture. Divide the batter evenly between the prepared tins, and smooth the tops with a palette knife.

4 Cook for 20–25 minutes or until golden brown and springy to the touch. Test by inserting a skewer; if it comes out clean, the cakes are cooked. Leave for a few minutes, then turn out onto a wire rack to cool.

5 To make the filling, beat the butter and icing sugar together until smooth. Beat in the remaining coffee mixture. Spread half the buttercream evenly onto the flat side of one of the cakes. Top with the second cake, flat sides together, and spread with the remaining buttercream. Decorate with the walnut halves.

STORE The cake will keep in an airtight container in a cool place for 3 days.

Madeira Cake

In this simple cake the flavours of lemon and butter shine through.

| SERVES 8–10 | 20 MINS | 50–60 MINS | UP TO 8 WEEKS |

Special equipment
18cm (7in) round springform cake tin

Ingredients
175g (6oz) unsalted butter, softened,
  plus extra for greasing
175g (6oz) caster sugar
3 eggs
225g (8oz) self-raising flour
finely grated zest of 1 lemon

Method
1 Preheat the oven to 180°C (350°F/Gas 4). Butter the cake tin and line the base and sides with baking parchment.

2 Cream the butter and sugar with an electric whisk for about 2 minutes, until light and fluffy. Add the eggs one at a time, mixing well between additions.

3 Whisk for 2 minutes until bubbles appear on the surface. Sift in the flour and add the lemon zest. Gently fold in the flour and zest until just smooth.

4 Spoon the mixture into the tin. Bake for 50 minutes–1 hour or until a skewer comes out clean. Leave the cake in the tin for a couple of minutes, then turn out onto a wire rack to cool. Remove the parchment.

STORE The cake will keep in an airtight container for 3 days.

BAKER'S TIP
The secret to a good, light Victoria sponge-style cake is to ensure that as little air as possible is lost during the folding-in stage, when the flour is added. For an even lighter finish, use baking margarine; the higher water content seems to bake air into the cake, though butter gives a richer flavour.

Marble Loaf Cake

For a twist on a classic sponge mixture, divide the batter in two and flavour half with cocoa before mixing them together for a wonderful marbled effect.

| SERVES 8–10 | 25 MINS | 45–50 MINS | UP TO 8 WEEKS |

Special equipment
900g (2lb) loaf tin

Ingredients
175g (6oz) unsalted butter, softened,
  plus extra for greasing
175g (6oz) caster sugar
3 eggs
1 tsp vanilla extract
150g (5½oz) self-raising flour
1 tsp baking powder
25g (scant 1oz) cocoa powder

Method
1 Preheat the oven to 180°C (350°F/Gas 4). Grease the loaf tin and line the base with baking parchment.

2 Using an electric whisk on medium speed, cream together the butter and sugar for about 2 minutes, until light and fluffy.

Add the eggs one at a time, beating well between additions. Add the vanilla extract, and whisk for another 2 minutes until bubbles appear on the surface. Sift in the flour and baking powder.

3 Divide the batter evenly between 2 bowls. Sift the cocoa powder into 1 bowl and gently fold in. Pour the vanilla cake batter into the loaf tin, then top with the chocolate batter. Using the end of a wooden spoon, a knife, or a skewer, swirl the 2 mixtures together, creating a marbled effect.

4 Bake for 45–50 minutes or until a skewer comes out clean. Leave to cool slightly, then turn out onto a wire rack. Remove the baking parchment.

STORE The cake will keep in an airtight container for 3 days.

Angel Food Cake

This American classic is named for its almost pure white sponge that is as light as air. Fat-free, it does not keep well and is best eaten the same day.

SERVES 8–12 | **30 MINS** | **35–45 MINS**

Special equipment
1.7-litre (3-pint) ring mould
sugar thermometer

Ingredients
large knob of butter, for greasing
150g (5½oz) plain flour
100g (3½oz) icing sugar

8 egg whites
 (keep the yolks for custards and tart fillings)
pinch of cream of tartar
250g (9oz) caster sugar
few drops of almond or vanilla extract

For the frosting
150g (5½oz) caster sugar
2 egg whites
strawberries (halved), blueberries,
 and raspberries, to decorate
icing sugar, for dusting

Method

1 Preheat the oven to 180°C (350°F/Gas 4). Melt the butter in small pan and use to generously brush the inside of the ring mould. Sift the flour and icing sugar into a bowl (see Baker's Tip).

2 Whisk the egg whites and cream of tartar until stiff, then whisk in the caster sugar, 1 tablespoon at a time. Sift in the flour mixture and gradually fold it in with a metal spoon, then fold in the almond or vanilla extract.

3 Spoon the mixture gently into the ring mould, filling right to the brim, and level the surface with a palette knife. Place the mould on a baking tray and bake for 35–45 minutes or until just firm to the touch.

4 Carefully remove the cake from the oven, and invert the mould onto a wire rack. Leave the cake to cool, then ease it out of the mould.

5 To make the frosting, place the caster sugar in a saucepan with 4 tablespoons of water. Heat gently, stirring, until the sugar dissolves. Boil until the syrup reaches

a soft-ball stage (114–118°C/238–245°F), or until a little of the syrup forms a soft ball when dropped into very cold water.

6 Meanwhile, whisk the egg whites until stiff. As soon as the sugar syrup reaches the correct temperature, plunge the base of the pan into cold water to stop the syrup getting any hotter. Pour the sugar syrup into the egg whites while whisking, pouring in a slow, steady stream into the centre of the bowl. Keep whisking for about 5 minutes, until stiff peaks form.

7 Working quickly, because the frosting will set, spread it thinly all over the inside and outside of the cake with a palette knife, swirling the surface to create texture. Top with strawberries, blueberries, and raspberries, and dust over icing sugar using a fine sieve.

BAKER'S TIP
Sifting the flour twice produces a very light cake. For best results, try to lift the sieve high above the bowl, allowing the flour to come into contact with as much air as possible as it floats down. For an even lighter cake, sift the flour twice before sifting again into the egg mixture.

Génoise Cake with Raspberries and Cream

This delicate, whisked sponge makes an impressive dessert, but is also perfect as the centrepiece for an afternoon tea on a sunny summer's day.

SERVES 8–10	30 MINS	25–30 MINS	4 WEEKS, UNFILLED

Special equipment
20cm (8in) round springform cake tin

Ingredients
40g (1½oz) unsalted butter, plus extra for greasing
4 large eggs

125g (4½oz) caster sugar
125g (4½oz) plain flour
1 tsp vanilla extract
finely grated zest of 1 lemon
75g (2½oz) raspberries, to decorate (optional)

For the filling
450ml (15fl oz) double or whipping cream
325g (11oz) raspberries
1 tbsp icing sugar, plus extra for dusting

Method

1 Melt the butter and reserve. Preheat the oven to 180°C (350°F/Gas 4). Grease the cake tin and line the base with parchment.

2 Bring a pan of water to the boil, remove from the heat and stand a heatproof bowl over the top. Add the eggs and sugar and whisk, using an electric whisk, for 5 minutes until the whisk leaves a trail when lifted; the mixture will expand up to 5 times its original volume. Remove the bowl from the pan and whisk for another minute to cool.

3 Sift in the flour and carefully fold it into the mixture. Fold in the vanilla, lemon zest, and melted butter.

4 Put the mixture into the tin and bake for 25–30 minutes or until the top is springy and light golden brown. A skewer inserted into the middle of the cake should come out clean.

5 Leave the cake to cool in its tin for a few minutes, then turn out onto a wire rack and cool completely. Remove the parchment.

6 When the cake is cold, carefully cut it horizontally into three equal pieces, using a serrated bread knife.

7 In a large bowl, whip the cream until stiff. Lightly crush the raspberries with the icing sugar and fold into the cream, leaving behind any juice so that the cream is not too wet.

8 Place the bottom slice of cake on a serving plate and spread with half the cream mixture. Top with the second slice, spread with the remaining cream, and then place the final slice on top. Decorate with raspberries, if using, and dust the cake with icing sugar. Serve immediately.

PREPARE AHEAD The sponge will keep in an airtight container for 1 day before being cut and filled.

BAKER'S TIP

This is a classic Italian cake that uses only a little melted butter for flavouring. These cakes are infinitely adaptable, and can be filled with anything you like, but should ideally be eaten within 24 hours of baking, since the lack of fat means they do not store as well as other cakes.

Swiss Roll

There is a trick to rolling up a Swiss roll – follow these simple steps and yours will come out perfectly.

SERVES 8–10 **20 MINS** **12–15 MINS** **UP TO 8 WEEKS**

Special equipment
32.5 x 23cm (13 x 9in) Swiss roll tin

Ingredients
3 large eggs
100g (3½oz) caster sugar, plus extra for sprinkling
pinch of salt
75g (2½oz) self-raising flour
1 tsp vanilla extract
6 tbsp raspberry jam (or use any other type of jam, or chocolate-hazelnut spread), for the filling

1 Preheat the oven to 200°C (400°F/Gas 6). Line the base of the tin with baking parchment.

2 Set a bowl over a pan of simmering water; the base of the bowl shouldn't touch the water.

3 Add the eggs, sugar, and salt and whisk with an electric whisk for 5 minutes until thick.

4 Test the egg mixture: drips from the beaters should sit on the surface for a few seconds.

5 Remove the bowl from the pan, place it on a work surface. Whisk for 1–2 minutes until cool.

6 Sift in the flour, add the vanilla extract, and gently fold in, trying to keep the volume.

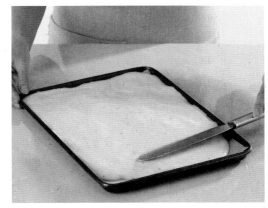

7 Pour into the tin and gently level into all the corners, smoothing the top with a palette knife.

8 Bake for 12–15 minutes in the preheated oven until firm and springy to the touch.

9 Check the cake has shrunk away slightly from the sides of the tin; this shows it is ready.

10 Sprinkle a sheet of baking parchment evenly with a thin layer of caster sugar.

11 Carefully turn the Swiss roll out of its tin onto the caster sugar, so it lies upside down.

12 Leave to cool for 5 minutes, then carefully peel the baking parchment from the cake.

13 For the filling, if the jam is too thick to spread, warm it gently in a small pan.

14 Spread the jam over the top of the cake, spreading to the edge with a palette knife.

15 Make an indent with the back of a knife along one short side, 2cm (¾in) from the edge.

16 Using the indented edge to start it off, gently but firmly roll it up, using the parchment.

17 Use the baking parchment to keep the cake tightly rolled and in shape. Leave to cool.

18 When ready to serve, unwrap the cake and place it, join downwards, on a serving plate. Sprinkle with extra caster sugar. **STORE** The roll will keep in an airtight container for 2 days.

Swiss Roll variations

Orange and Pistachio Swiss Roll

Using the delicate flavours of pistachio nuts and orange flower water gives this classic recipe a slightly more modern twist. It is easily portioned and makes an ideal dessert for large parties and buffets.

SERVES 8 | **20 MINS** | **15 MINS** | **8 WEEKS UNFILLED**

Special equipment
32.5 x 23cm (13 x 9in) Swiss roll tin

Ingredients
3 large eggs
100g (3½oz) caster sugar, plus extra for sprinkling
pinch of salt
75g (2½oz) self-raising flour
finely grated zest of 2 oranges, and 3 tbsp juice
2 tsp orange flower water (optional)
200ml (7fl oz) double cream
75g (2½oz) unsalted pistachio nuts, chopped
icing sugar, for dusting

Method
1 Preheat the oven to 200°C (400°F/Gas 6). Line the tin with baking parchment. Set a bowl over a pan of simmering water. Whisk the eggs, sugar, and salt with an electric whisk for 5 minutes until thick and creamy.

2 Remove the bowl from the pan and whisk for another 1–2 minutes until cool. Sift in the flour, add half the orange zest, and 1 tablespoon of juice. Gently fold together. Pour into the tin and bake for 12–15 minutes until firm to the touch.

3 Sprinkle a sheet of baking parchment with caster sugar. Turn out the cake onto the sugar. Leave to cool for 5 minutes, then peel off the parchment from the cake and discard. Sprinkle with the orange flower water (if using).

4 Make an indent with the back of a knife along one short side, about 2cm (¾in) from the edge. Using the indent to start it off, roll up the cake around the sugared parchment (see Baker's Tip). Leave to cool.

5 Whip the cream and fold in the pistachios, the remaining orange zest, and juice. Unroll the cake, discard the parchment, and spread the cream filling evenly over the surface. Roll up the cake again and place join downwards on a serving plate. Dust with icing sugar just before serving.

ALSO TRY...
Lemon Swiss Roll Instead of orange, fold in lemon zest and juice to the cake mix, then fill with 300g (10oz) lemon curd.

BAKER'S TIP
If a recipe requires a Swiss roll to be completely cool before filling, the cake will need to be rolled into shape while still warm, and then unrolled. Roll the cake around a fresh sheet of parchment paper. This will prevent the layers from sticking and allow the cake to be rolled tightly for a neat shape, and easily unrolled.

Spanish Rolled Sponge Cake

In this sophisticated Spanish take on Swiss roll, a tangy lemon sponge is rolled around a smooth filling of chocolate-rum ganache, forming a pretty spiral for slicing. Impressive as a dinner party dessert. ▶

SERVES 8–10 | **40–45 MINS** | **7–9 MINS** | **8 WEEKS, UNFILLED**

Chilling time
6 hours

Ingredients
butter, for greasing
150g (5½oz) caster sugar
5 eggs, separated
finely grated zest of 2 lemons
45g (1½oz) plain flour, sifted
pinch of salt
125g (4½oz) dark chocolate, coarsely chopped
175ml (6fl oz) double cream
1½ tsp ground cinnamon
1½ tbsp dark rum
60g (2oz) icing sugar
candied lemon zest, to serve (optional)

Method
1 Preheat the oven to 220°C (425°F/Gas 7). Grease and line a baking sheet with parchment. Mix 100g (3½oz) caster sugar with the egg yolks and zest. With an electric whisk, beat for 3–5 minutes until thick. In a separate bowl, whisk the egg whites until stiff. Add the remaining sugar and whisk until glossy. Add salt to the yolk mix, then sift and fold in the flour, and the egg whites.

2 Pour the mixture onto the baking sheet and spread it almost to the edges. Bake near the bottom of the oven for 7–9 minutes until firm and golden brown.

3 Turn out onto another baking sheet and remove the parchment. Make an indent with the back of a knife along one short side, 2cm (¾in) from the edge. Using the indent to start it off, tightly roll the cake up around a piece of parchment (see Baker's Tip). Leave to cool.

4 For the ganache, put the chocolate in a large bowl. Heat the cream with ½ teaspoon of cinnamon in a saucepan until almost boiling. Add to the chocolate and stir until melted. Let cool and add the rum. Beat the ganache with an electric whisk for 5–10 minutes until thick and fluffy.

5 Mix half the icing sugar with 1 teaspoon cinnamon and evenly sieve over a sheet of parchment. Unroll the cake onto the sugared paper. Spread the ganache, then carefully roll up and wrap with parchment. Chill for 6 hours until firm. Unwrap the cake, trim each end, sift over the remaining icing sugar and scatter with candied lemon zest (if using).

Ginger Cake

Deeply flavoured with preserved ginger, this rich and moist ginger cake is a firm favourite, and keeps well for up to a week – should it last that long!

| SERVES 12 | 20 MINS | 35–45 MINS | UP TO 8 WEEKS |

Special equipment
18cm (7in) square cake tin

Ingredients
110g (4oz) unsalted butter, softened, plus extra for greasing
225g (8oz) golden syrup
110g (4oz) soft dark brown sugar
200ml (7fl oz) milk

4 tbsp syrup from preserved ginger jar
finely grated zest of 1 orange
225g (8oz) self-raising flour
1 tsp bicarbonate of soda
1 tsp mixed spice
1 tsp cinnamon
2 tsp ground ginger
4 pieces of preserved stem ginger, finely chopped and tossed in 1 tbsp plain flour
1 egg, lightly beaten

Method
1 Preheat the oven to 170°C (340°F/Gas 3½). Grease the cake tin and line the base with baking parchment.

2 In a saucepan, gently heat the butter, golden syrup, sugar, milk, and ginger syrup until the butter has melted. Add the orange zest and leave to cool for 5 minutes.

3 In a large mixing bowl, sift together the flour, bicarbonate of soda, and ground spices. Pour the warm syrup mixture into the dry ingredients and beat them well, using a balloon whisk. Stir in the preserved ginger and egg.

4 Pour the batter into the tin and cook for 35–45 minutes until a skewer inserted into the middle of the cake comes out clean. Leave to cool in the tin for at least 1 hour before turning out onto a wire rack. Remove the baking parchment before serving.

STORE This cake is very moist and keeps well in an airtight container for up to 1 week.

BAKER'S TIP
The use of golden syrup and dark brown sugar here gives a dense, moist cake that keeps very well. If the cake is beginning to get a little dry with age, try slicing it and spreading with butter as a breakfast snack, or even turning it into a rich version of the Bread and Butter Pudding (see page 92).

EVERYDAY CAKES

Carrot Cake

For a more luxurious cake, double the icing, slice the cake in two, and fill the middle as well.

SERVES 8–10

20 MINS

45 MINS

8 WEEKS, UN-ICED

Special equipment
22cm (9in) round springform cake tin
zester

Ingredients
100g (3½oz) walnuts
225ml (7½fl oz) sunflower oil, plus extra for greasing
3 large eggs
225g (8oz) soft light brown sugar
1 tsp vanilla extract
200g (7oz) carrots, finely grated
100g (3½oz) sultanas

200g (7oz) self-raising flour
75g (2½oz) wholemeal self-raising flour
pinch of salt
1 tsp cinnamon
1 tsp ground ginger
¼ tsp finely grated nutmeg
finely grated zest of 1 orange

For the icing
50g (1¾oz) unsalted butter, softened
100g (3½oz) cream cheese, at room temperature
200g (7oz) icing sugar
½ tsp vanilla extract
2 oranges

1 Preheat the oven to 180°C (350°F/Gas 4). Bake the walnuts for 5 minutes, until light brown.

2 Put the nuts on a clean tea towel and rub them to remove excess skin. Set aside to cool.

3 Pour the oil and eggs into a large bowl, tip in the sugar, and add the vanilla.

4 Using an electric whisk, beat the oil mixture until it is lighter and noticeably thickened.

5 Squeeze the grated carrot thoroughly in a clean tea towel to remove excess liquid.

6 Gently fold the carrot into the cake batter, ensuring it is evenly blended throughout.

7 Chop the cooled walnuts roughly, leaving some large pieces.

8 Add the walnuts to the mixture, along with the sultanas, and gently fold them in.

9 Sift over the 2 types of flour, then tip in any bran remaining in the sieve.

0 Add the salt, spices, and orange zest, and fold all the ingredients together to combine.

11 Oil the tin and line with parchment. Pour in the cake mix and smooth with a palette knife.

12 Bake for 45 minutes. Test by inserting a skewer into the cake; it should come out clean.

13 If not, bake for a few more minutes and test again. Transfer to a wire rack to cool.

14 Combine the butter, cream cheese, icing sugar, and vanilla. Grate in the zest of 1 orange.

15 Using an electric whisk, mix all the ingredients until smooth, pale, and fluffy.

16 Using a palette knife, spread the icing over the cake. Make swirls for texture.

17 For additional decoration, zest the remaining orange using a zester tool.

18 Sprinkle the orange zest over the icing in an attractive pattern and transfer to a serving plate or cake stand. **STORE** The cake will keep in an airtight container for 3 days.

Carrot Cake variations

Courgette Cake

This intriguing alternative to carrot cake is a firm favourite.

SERVES 8–10 | **20 MINS** | **45 MINS** | **UP TO 8 WEEKS**

Special equipment
22cm (9in) round springform cake tin

Ingredients
225ml (7½fl oz) sunflower oil,
  plus extra for greasing
100g (3½oz) hazelnuts
3 large eggs
1 tsp vanilla extract
225g (8oz) caster sugar
200g (7oz) courgettes, finely grated
200g (7oz) self-raising flour
75g (2½oz) wholemeal self-raising flour
pinch of salt
1 tsp cinnamon
finely grated zest of 1 lemon

Method

1 Preheat the oven to 180°C (350°F/Gas 4). Oil the base and sides of the tin and line the base with baking parchment. Spread hazelnuts on a baking tray and cook for 5 minutes until lightly browned. Put the nuts on a clean tea towel and rub them to get rid of excess skin. Roughly chop and set aside.

2 Pour the oil and eggs into a bowl, add the vanilla, and tip in the sugar. Whisk the oil mixture until lighter and thickened. Squeeze moisture from the courgettes and fold in with the nuts. Sift over the flour, tipping any bran left in the sieve. Add the salt, cinnamon, and lemon zest, and fold.

3 Pour the batter into the tin. Bake for 45 minutes or until springy to the touch. Turn out onto a wire rack to cool completely.

STORE The cake will keep in an airtight container for 3 days.

BAKER'S TIP
Don't be put off by the unusual inclusion of courgettes. Courgettes are less sweet than carrots, but add moisture and a fresh flavour. The lack of icing makes this cake healthier.

EVERYDAY CAKES

Quick Carrot Cake

Carrot cakes are perfect for novice bakers as they do not require lengthy whisking or delicate folding. This variation is quick to prepare and guaranteed to disappear even faster.

SERVES 8 | **15 MINS** | **20–25 MINS** | **8 WEEKS, UN-ICED**

Special equipment
20cm (8in) round springform cake tin

Ingredients
75g (2½oz) unsalted butter, melted and cooled, plus extra for greasing
75g (2½oz) wholemeal self-raising flour
1 tsp ground allspice
½ tsp ground ginger
½ tsp baking powder
2 carrots, coarsely grated
75g (2½oz) soft light brown sugar
50g (1¾oz) sultanas
2 eggs, beaten
3 tbsp fresh orange juice

For the icing
150g (5½oz) cream cheese, at room temperature
1 tbsp icing sugar
lemon zest, to decorate

Method
1 Preheat the oven to 190°C (375°F/Gas 5). Grease the cake tin and line the base with baking parchment.

2 Sift the flour, allspice, ginger, and baking powder into a large bowl, tipping in any bran that remains in the sieve. Add the carrots, sugar, and sultanas, then stir to mix. Add the eggs, 1 tablespoon of orange juice, and the butter. Stir until blended.

3 Pour the cake mix into the tin and level with a palette knife. Bake on a baking tray for 20 minutes or until a skewer inserted into the centre of the cake comes out clean. Let it stand in the tin for 10 minutes to cool.

4 Run a knife around the sides, invert onto a wire rack, peel off the paper, and leave to cool completely. Split the cake horizontally into 2 layers with a serrated knife.

5 For the icing, beat the cream cheese with the remaining orange juice and icing sugar. Spread the icing in the centre and over the top of the cake, and decorate with lemon zest.

STORE The cake will keep in an airtight container for 3 days.

Spiced Carrot Cake

This is a fabulous cake for winter, with hints of warming spice. Baking in a square tin allows the cake to be cut into bite-sized pieces, perfect for a party. **PICTURED OVERLEAF**

MAKES 16 SQUARES | **20 MINS** | **30 MINS** | **8 WEEKS, UN-ICED**

Special equipment
20cm (8in) square cake tin

Ingredients
175g (6oz) self-raising flour
1 tsp cinnamon
1 tsp mixed spice
½ tsp bicarbonate of soda
100g (3½oz) light or dark soft brown sugar
150ml (5fl oz) sunflower oil
2 large eggs
75g (2½oz) golden syrup
125g (4½oz) carrots, coarsely grated
finely grated zest of 1 orange

For the icing
75g (2½oz) icing sugar
100g (3½oz) cream cheese, at room temperature
1–2 tbsp orange juice
finely grated zest of 1 orange, plus extra to decorate (optional)

Method
1 Preheat the oven to 180°C (350°F/Gas 4). Line the base and sides of the tin with parchment. In a bowl, mix the flour, spices, bicarbonate of soda, and sugar together.

2 In another bowl, mix the oil, eggs, and syrup, then combine with the dry ingredients. Stir in the carrot and orange zest, transfer to the tin and level the top.

3 Bake for 30 minutes or until firm to the touch. Leave in the tin for a few minutes, then turn out onto a wire rack to cool completely. Remove the baking parchment.

4 For the icing, sift the icing sugar into a bowl, add the cream cheese, orange juice, and orange zest. Beat with an electric whisk until spreadable. Spread the icing over the cake. Decorate with extra orange zest (if using), and cut into 16 squares to serve.

STORE The cake will keep in an airtight container for 3 days.

Lemon Polenta Cake

One of the few wheat-free cakes that work just as well as those made from wheat flour.

SERVES 6–8 | 30 MINS | 50–60 MINS | UP TO 8 WEEKS

Special equipment
22cm (9in) round springform cake tin

Ingredients
175g (6oz) unsalted butter, softened, plus extra for greasing
200g (7oz) caster sugar
3 large eggs, beaten
75g (2½oz) polenta or coarse-ground cornmeal
175g (6oz) ground almonds
finely grated zest and juice of 2 lemons
1 tsp gluten-free baking powder
thick cream or crème fraîche, to serve (optional)

1 Preheat the oven to 160°C (325°F/Gas 3). Grease the tin, lining the base with parchment.

2 With an electric whisk, cream the butter and 175g (6oz) of the sugar until fluffy.

3 Gradually pour in the beaten eggs, a little at a time, whisking well after each addition.

4 Add the polenta and almonds, and gently fold into the mix using a metal spoon.

5 Finally, fold in the lemon zest and baking powder. The batter will seem quite stiff.

6 Scrape the mixture into the prepared tin and smooth the surface with a palette knife.

7 Bake the cake for 50–60 minutes until springy to the touch. It will not rise much.

8 Check the cake is cooked by inserting a skewer. The skewer should emerge clean.

9 Leave the cake in the tin for a few minutes until cool enough to handle.

EVERYDAY CAKES

48

10 Meanwhile, put the lemon juice and the remaining sugar in a small saucepan.

11 Heat the juice over medium heat until the sugar has completely dissolved. Take off heat.

12 Turn the cake out onto a wire rack, baked side upwards. Retain the parchment for now.

13 Using a thin skewer or cocktail stick, poke holes in the top of the cake while still warm.

14 Pour the hot lemon syrup a little at a time over the surface of the cake.

15 Only once the syrup has soaked into the cake, pour more on, until it is all used up.

16 Once cooled, serve the cake at room temperature on its own or with thick cream or crème fraîche. **STORE** The cake will keep in an airtight container for 3 days.

Wheat-free Cake variations

EVERYDAY CAKES

Chocolate and Brazil Nut Cake

This unusual wheat-free cake uses Brazil nuts instead of the typical almond and chocolate combination, to give a moist, rich finish to the cake.

SERVES 6–8 | **25 MINS** | **45–50 MINS** | **UP TO 4 WEEKS**

Special equipment
20cm (8in) round springform cake tin
food processor

Ingredients
75g (2½oz) unsalted butter, cubed,
  plus extra for greasing
100g (3½oz) good-quality dark chocolate,
  broken into pieces
150g (5½oz) Brazil nuts
125g (4½oz) caster sugar
4 large eggs, separated
cocoa powder or icing sugar, to serve
thick cream, to serve (optional)

Method
1 Preheat the oven to 180°C (350°F/Gas 4). Grease the cake tin and line the base with baking parchment. Melt the chocolate in a bowl over a little simmering water, and leave to cool.

2 In a food processor, grind the nuts and sugar finely. Add the butter and pulse until just blended (see Baker's Tip). Continue to blend while adding the egg yolks one at a time. Add the melted chocolate and blend.

3 In a separate bowl, whisk the egg whites to stiff peaks. Turn the chocolate mixture into a large bowl and beat in a few tablespoons of the egg whites to loosen it a little. Now carefully fold in the remaining egg whites with a large metal spoon.

4 Scrape the mixture into the tin and bake for 45–50 minutes until the surface is springy and a skewer inserted into the middle comes out clean. Allow to cool in the tin for a few minutes, then turn out onto a wire rack to cool completely. Remove the parchment. Sift over the cocoa powder or icing sugar. Serve with thick cream if you like.

STORE The cake will keep in an airtight container for 3 days.

> **BAKER'S TIP**
> Care should be taken to pulse the butter into the nut and sugar mixture in short bursts, as prolonged processing will result in the natural oils in the nuts being released, which would give the finished cake an oily flavour.

Torta margherita

This Italian classic is made with potato flour and is as light as air.

SERVES 6–8 | **20 MINS** | **25–30 MINS** | **UP TO 8 WEEKS**

Special equipment
20cm (8in) round springform cake tin

Ingredients
25g (scant 1oz) unsalted butter,
  plus extra for greasing
2 large eggs, plus 1 egg yolk
100g (3½oz) caster sugar
½ tsp vanilla extract
100g (3½oz) potato flour, sifted
½ tsp gluten-free baking powder
finely grated zest of ½ lemon
icing sugar, for dusting

Method
1 Melt the butter and set aside to cool. Preheat the oven to 180°C (350°F/Gas 4). Grease the tin and line the base with baking parchment.

2 In a large bowl, whisk the eggs, egg yolk, sugar, and vanilla extract together for about 5 minutes until thick, pale, and at least doubled in volume. Gently fold in the potato flour, baking powder, and lemon zest, then fold in the melted butter.

3 Scrape the batter into the prepared tin and bake for 25–30 minutes until the surface is golden brown and springy to the touch. A skewer inserted into the middle should come out clean.

4 Leave the cake to cool for 10 minutes in its tin, then turn out to cool completely on a wire rack. Remove the baking parchment. Dust with icing sugar to serve.

STORE The torta will keep in an airtight container for 2 days.

Castagnaccio

Chestnut flour gives this interesting cake a dense yet moist texture.

SERVES 6–8 | **25 MINS** | **50–60 MINS**

Special equipment
20cm (8in) round springform cake tin

Ingredients
1 tbsp olive oil, plus extra for greasing
50g (1¾oz) raisins
25g (scant 1oz) flaked almonds
30g (1oz) pine nuts
300g (10½oz) chestnut flour
25g (scant 1oz) caster sugar
pinch of salt
400ml (14fl oz) milk or water
1 tbsp finely chopped rosemary leaves
1 orange, zested

Method
1 Preheat the oven to 180°C (350°F/Gas 4). Grease the cake tin and line the base with baking parchment. Cover the raisins with warm water and leave for 5 minutes to plump them up. Drain.

2 Put the almonds and pine nuts on a baking tray and bake in the oven for 5–10 minutes until lightly browned. Sift the chestnut flour into a large mixing bowl. Add the sugar and salt.

3 Using a balloon whisk, gradually whisk in the milk or water to produce a thick, smooth batter. Whisk in the olive oil, pour the batter into the tin, and scatter over the raisins, rosemary, orange zest, and nuts.

4 Bake at the centre of the oven for 50–60 minutes until the surface is dry and the edges slightly browned. The cake will not really rise. Leave in the tin for 10 minutes, then carefully turn it out onto a wire rack and leave it to cool completely. Remove the baking parchment and serve.

STORE The cake will keep in an airtight container for 3 days.

NOTE Chestnut flour is available from Italian delis, health food stores, or online.

Sticky Toffee Puddings

A new British classic, said to have been invented in the Lake District in the 1960s, this recipe gets the balance of sweetness just right.

MAKES 8 · **20 MINS** · **20–25 MINS** · **UP TO 8 WEEKS**

Special equipment
8 pudding basins, 200ml (7fl oz) each
food processor or blender

Ingredients
125g (4½oz) unsalted butter, at room
 temperature, plus extra for greasing
200g (7oz) stoned dates (preferably Medjool)
1 tsp bicarbonate of soda
225g (8oz) self-raising flour
175g (6oz) dark or light soft brown sugar
3 large eggs

For the toffee sauce
150g (5½oz) dark or light soft brown sugar
75g (2½oz) unsalted butter, cubed
150ml (5fl oz) double or whipping cream
pinch of salt
single cream, to serve (optional)

Method
1 Preheat the oven to 190°C (375°F/Gas 5). Butter the 8 pudding basins well, including all the corners.

2 In a small pan, simmer the dates with the bicarbonate of soda and 200ml (7fl oz) water for 5 minutes until softened. Purée with the cooking liquid in a food processor or blender.

3 Sift the flour into a mixing bowl. Add the butter, sugar, and eggs, and whisk with an electric hand whisk until well combined, then mix in the date purée. Pour the mixture into the pudding basins and place them on a baking tray.

4 Bake for 20–25 minutes or until firm to the touch. Meanwhile, make the toffee sauce. Heat the sugar, butter, and cream together in a pan, stirring occasionally until the butter and sugar have melted, and everything is smooth and combined. Stir in the salt and allow to boil for a few minutes. Serve the warm puddings with the hot toffee sauce and some single cream, if you like.

PREPARE AHEAD The puddings and sauce can be made up to 2 days ahead and reheated. Place the puddings on a baking tray and warm through in an oven preheated to 180°C (350°F/Gas 4) for 15–20 minutes, and gently warm through the sauce in a small pan. They can also be frozen and reheated in the same way after defrosting.

BAKER'S TIP
This recipe can also be used to make 1 large pudding. Add a few of the simmered dates, roughly chopped, to the bottom of a large pudding basin before topping with the cake mixture, and bake for 40–45 minutes or until firm to the touch. Turn out onto a serving plate and drizzle with the toffee sauce.

EVERYDAY CAKES

Chocolate Cake

Everyone loves a classic chocolate cake, and in this version the yogurt in the mix makes it extra moist.

| SERVES 6–8 | 30 MINS | 20–25 MINS | 8 WEEKS, UNFILLED |

Special equipment
2 x 17cm (6¾in) round cake tins

Ingredients
175g (6oz) unsalted butter, softened, plus extra for greasing
175g (6oz) soft light brown sugar
3 large eggs
125g (4½oz) self-raising flour
50g (1¾oz) cocoa powder
1 tsp baking powder
2 tbsp Greek yogurt or thick plain yogurt

For the chocolate buttercream
50g (1¾oz) unsalted butter, softened
75g (2½oz) icing sugar, sifted, plus extra to serve
25g (scant 1oz) cocoa powder
a little milk, if needed

1 Preheat the oven to 180°C (350°F/Gas 4). Grease the tins and line with parchment.

2 Chop the butter and place it in a large bowl with the sugar.

3 With an electric whisk, cream the butter mixture until light and fluffy.

4 Drop in the eggs one at a time, beating after each addition, until well combined.

5 In a separate large bowl, sift together the flour, cocoa powder, and baking powder.

6 Fold the flour mixture into the cake batter until well blended, trying to keep volume.

7 Gently fold through the thick yogurt. This will help to make the cake moist.

8 Divide the mixture between the 2 cake tins, smoothing the surfaces with a palette knife.

9 Bake in the middle of the oven for 20–25 minutes until risen and springy to the touch.

10 A skewer inserted into the middle should come out clean. If not, bake a little more.

11 Leave the sponges in their tins for a few minutes. Remove the parchment and cool.

12 For the buttercream, place the butter, icing sugar, and cocoa powder in a large bowl.

13 Blend the buttercream together with an electric whisk for 5 minutes or until fluffy.

14 If the cream is stiff, add milk, 1 teaspoon at a time, until it has a spreading consistency.

15 Spread the base of one sponge with the buttercream, then top with the other sponge.

16 Transfer the cake to a serving plate and sift a little icing sugar evenly over the top, to serve.
STORE The cake will keep in an airtight container for 2 days.

CHOCOLATE CAKE

Chocolate Cake variations

Chocolate Almond Cake

Suitable for serving as a torte-style dessert, use the best dark chocolate you can find for this cake – it will make all the difference.

SERVES 6–8 | **30 MINS** | **25 MINS** | **4 WEEKS UN-ICED**

Special equipment
18cm (7in) round loose-bottomed cake tin

Ingredients
175g (6oz) unsalted butter, softened,
  plus extra for greasing
plain flour, for dusting
230g (8oz) good-quality dark chocolate,
  broken into pieces (see Baker's Tip)
140g (5oz) caster sugar
3 eggs, separated
60g (2oz) ground almonds
30g (1oz) white breadcrumbs
½ tsp baking powder
1 tsp almond extract
1 tbsp brandy or rum (optional)

Method
1 Preheat the oven to 180°C (350°F/Gas 4). Grease the tin and line the base with baking parchment, then dust with plain flour.

2 Melt half the chocolate in a bowl over a pan of simmering water. Leave to cool slightly. In a separate bowl, beat 115g (4oz) of the butter and the sugar until creamy. Add the egg yolks one at a time, and beat well. Beat in the chocolate. Fold in the remaining ingredients with a metal spoon.

3 Whisk the egg whites until soft peaks form. Fold into the mixture, spoon into the tin, and bake for 25 minutes. Remove and cool on a wire rack. Melt the remaining chocolate and butter in a bowl over a pan of simmering water. Cool and spread over the cake.

STORE The cake will keep for 3 days.

> ### BAKER'S TIP
> Choose dark chocolate with a high cocoa solids content of more than 60 per cent. Do not melt this kind of chocolate in a microwave as the high cocoa solids cause it to burn easily.

Chocolate Cake with Fudge Icing

Always a popular choice, this one is a must for your cake repertoire.

SERVES 8–12 | **20 MINS** | **40 MINS** | **8 WEEKS, UN-ICED**

Special equipment
2 x 20cm (8in) round cake tins

Ingredients
225g (8oz) unsalted butter, softened,
  plus extra for greasing
200g (7oz) self-raising flour
25g (scant 1oz) cocoa powder
4 large eggs
225g (8oz) caster sugar
1 tsp vanilla extract
1 tsp baking powder

For the icing
45g (1½oz) cocoa powder
150g (5½oz) icing sugar
45g (1½oz) unsalted butter, melted
3 tbsp milk, plus extra to slacken the mixture

Method
1 Preheat the oven to 180°C (350°F/Gas 4). Grease the tins, then line the bases with baking parchment. Sift the flour and cocoa powder into a bowl, and add all the other cake ingredients. Whisk together with an electric whisk for a few minutes until well combined. Whisk in 2 tablespoons of warm water so the mixture is soft. Divide evenly between the tins, and smooth the tops.

2 Bake for 35–40 minutes or until risen and firm to the touch. Leave to cool for a few minutes before turning out onto wire racks to cool completely. Remove the parchment.

3 For the icing, sift the cocoa powder and icing sugar into a bowl, add the butter and milk, and whisk until smooth and well combined. Add a little extra milk if the mixture is too thick; you need to be able to spread it easily. Spread over the tops of the cooled cakes, then sandwich together.

STORE The cake will keep for 2 days in an airtight container.

Pear and Chocolate Cake

This rich, luscious cake is a good choice when you want to impress.

SERVES 6–8 | **15 MINS** | **30 MINS**

Special equipment
20cm (8in) round springform cake tin

Ingredients
125g (4½oz) unsalted butter, softened,
  plus extra for greasing
175g (6oz) golden caster sugar
4 large eggs, lightly beaten
250g (9oz) wholemeal self-raising flour, sifted
50g (1¾oz) cocoa powder, sifted
50g (1¾oz) good-quality dark chocolate,
  broken into pieces (see Baker's Tip)
2 pears, peeled, cored, and chopped
150ml (5fl oz) milk
icing sugar, for dusting

Method
1 Preheat the oven to 180°C (350°F/Gas 4). Line the base of the cake tin with baking parchment and grease the sides with butter.

2 Cream the butter with the sugar using an electric whisk until pale and creamy. Beat the eggs in gradually, adding a little of the flour each time until all of it is combined. Fold in the cocoa powder, chocolate, and pears. Add the milk to the mixture and combine.

3 Pour the cake mixture into the prepared tin, place it in the oven, and bake for about 30 minutes or until firm and springy to the touch. Allow to cool in the tin for 5 minutes, then remove the tin, and transfer the cake to a wire rack to cool completely. Remove the baking parchment. Sift over icing sugar before serving.

STORE The cake will keep in an airtight container for 2 days.

Devil's Food Cake

This American classic uses the flavour of coffee to enhance the richness of the chocolate, adding a wonderful depth of flavour to the finished cake.

SERVES 8–10 | **30 MINS** | **30–35 MINS** | **8 WEEKS, UNFILLED**

Special equipment
2 x 20cm (8in) round cake tins

Ingredients
100g (3½oz) unsalted butter, softened, plus extra for greasing
275g (9½oz) caster sugar
2 large eggs
200g (7oz) self-raising flour
75g (2½oz) cocoa powder
1 tsp baking powder
1 tbsp coffee powder mixed with 125ml (4fl oz) boiling water, or equivalent cooled espresso
125ml (4fl oz) milk
1 tsp vanilla extract

For the frosting
125g (4½oz) unsalted butter, diced
25g (scant 1oz) cocoa powder
125g (4½oz) icing sugar
2–3 tbsp milk
dark or milk chocolate, for the shavings

Method

1 Preheat the oven to 180°C (350°F/Gas 4). Grease the cake tins and line the bases with baking parchment. Using an electric whisk, cream together the butter and sugar until light and fluffy.

2 Beat in the eggs one at a time, whisking well after each addition, until well mixed. In a separate bowl, sift together the flour, cocoa powder, and baking powder. In another bowl, mix together the cooled coffee, milk, and vanilla extract.

3 Beat alternate spoonfuls of the dry and liquid ingredients into the cake batter. Once the mixture is well blended, divide it between the tins.

4 Bake for 30–35 minutes until the cakes are springy to the touch and a skewer inserted into the middle comes out clean. Leave to cool in the tins for a few minutes, then turn out onto a wire rack to cool completely. Remove the baking parchment.

5 For the frosting, melt the butter in a pan over low heat. Add the cocoa powder and continue to cook for a minute or two, stirring frequently. Allow to cool slightly.

6 Sift in the icing sugar, beating thoroughly to combine. Blend in the milk 1 tablespoon at a time, until smooth and glossy. Allow to cool (it will thicken) and then use half to sandwich the cakes together, and the remainder to decorate the top and sides of the cake. Finally, use a vegetable peeler to create chocolate shavings and scatter them evenly over the top of the cake.

STORE This cake will keep in an airtight container in a cool place for 5 days.

BAKER'S TIP
Don't be put off by the inclusion of coffee in this recipe. Even if you don't normally like coffee-flavoured cakes, you should use it here. It results in a deep, dark fudgy texture and also subtly enhances the chocolate flavour, rather than giving an overt coffee taste.

Chocolate Fudge Cake

Everyone should have a chocolate fudge cake recipe, and this one is a winner. The oil and syrup keep it moist, and the icing is a classic.

SERVES 6–8 | **40 MINS** | **30 MINS** | **8 WEEKS, UNFILLED**

Special equipment
2 x 17cm (6¾in) round cake tins

Ingredients
150ml (5fl oz) sunflower oil,
  plus extra for greasing
175g (6oz) self-raising flour
25g (scant 1oz) cocoa powder
1 tsp baking powder
150g (5½oz) soft light brown sugar
3 tbsp golden syrup
2 eggs
150ml (5fl oz) milk

For the icing
125g (4½oz) unsalted butter
25g (scant 1oz) cocoa powder
125g (4½oz) icing sugar
2 tbsp milk, if necessary

Method

1 Preheat the oven to 180°C (350°F/Gas 4). Grease the tins and line the bases with baking parchment. In a large bowl, sift together the flour, cocoa, and baking powder. Mix in the sugar.

2 Gently heat the golden syrup until runny and leave to cool. In a separate bowl, beat the eggs, sunflower oil, and milk together using an electric whisk.

3 Whisk the egg mixture into the flour mixture until well combined. Gently fold in the syrup and divide the batter between the cake tins.

4 Bake the cakes in the middle of the oven for 30 minutes or until springy to the touch, and a skewer inserted into the middle comes out clean. Leave to cool slightly in the tins, then turn out onto a wire rack to cool completely. Remove the parchment.

5 To make the icing, melt the butter over low heat. Stir in the cocoa powder and cook gently for 1–2 minutes, then leave to cool completely. Sift the icing sugar into a bowl.

6 Pour the melted butter and cocoa into the icing sugar and beat together to combine. If the mixture seems a little dry, add the milk, 1 tablespoon at a time, until the icing is smooth and glossy. Leave to cool for up to 30 minutes. It will thicken as it cools.

7 When thick, use half the icing to fill the cake and the other half to top it.

STORE This cake will keep in an airtight container for 3 days.

BAKER'S TIP
The icing used here is a real staple, and can be used to finish many chocolate recipes. Leftovers that are slightly old can be heated for 30 seconds in a microwave. The icing will melt into a rich, fudgy sauce, and the cake can be served with vanilla ice cream for a delicious, quick dessert.

EVERYDAY CAKES

Baked Chocolate Mousse

This classic mousse is easy to make, even for a novice. Slice the moist mousse with a sharp knife dipped in hot water, and wipe between cuts.

SERVES 8–12
20 MINS
1 HOUR

Special equipment
23cm (9in) round springform cake tin

Ingredients
250g (9oz) unsalted butter, cubed
350g (12oz) good-quality dark chocolate, broken into pieces
250g (9oz) light soft brown sugar
5 large eggs, separated
pinch of salt
cocoa powder or icing sugar, for dusting
thick cream, to serve (optional)

Method

1 Preheat the oven to 180°C (350°F/Gas 4). Line the base of the tin with parchment. Set a heatproof bowl over a pan of simmering water (make sure the base of the bowl does not touch the water), and melt the butter and chocolate together until smooth and glossy, lightly stirring to combine.

2 Remove from the pan and allow to cool slightly, then stir in the sugar, followed by the egg yolks, one at a time.

3 Put the egg whites in a mixing bowl with the salt, and beat with an electric whisk until soft peaks form. Gradually fold into the chocolate mixture, then pour into the cake tin, and smooth the top.

4 Bake for 1 hour, or until the top is firm but the middle still wobbles slightly when you shake the tin. Leave to cool completely in the tin. Remove the baking parchment. Dust with cocoa powder or icing sugar before serving with a dollop of thick cream.

> **BAKER'S TIP**
> To give a deliciously moist, almost gooey finish to this recipe, take care not to overcook the cake. The centre should be only just set when it is taken out of the oven, and when the mousse is pressed gently with a finger it should hold the impression and not spring back.

German Apple Cake

This simple apple cake is transformed into something special with a delicious, crumbly streusel topping.

SERVES 6–8 | **30 MINS** | **45–50 MINS**

Chilling time
30 mins

Special equipment
20cm (8in) loose-bottomed cake tin

Ingredients
175g (6oz) unsalted butter, softened, plus extra for greasing
175g (6oz) light muscovado sugar
finely grated zest of 1 lemon
3 eggs, lightly beaten
175g (6oz) self-raising flour
3 tbsp milk
2 tart dessert apples, peeled, cored, and cut into even, slim wedges

For the streusel topping
115g (4oz) plain flour
85g (3oz) light muscovado sugar
2 tsp ground cinnamon
85g (3oz) unsalted butter, diced

1 To make the topping, put the flour, sugar, and cinnamon in a mixing bowl.

2 Rub in the butter gently with your fingertips to form a crumbly ball of dough.

3 Wrap the streusel dough in cling film and chill in the refrigerator for 30 minutes.

4 Preheat the oven to 190°C (375°F/Gas 5). Grease the tin and line with baking parchment.

5 Put the butter and sugar in a bowl, and whisk until pale and creamy.

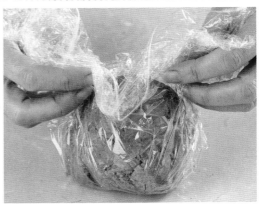

6 Add the lemon zest and whisk slowly until well dispersed through the batter.

7 Beat in the eggs, a little at a time, mixing well after each addition to avoid curdling.

8 Sift the flour into the batter and gently fold in with a metal spoon.

9 Finally, add the milk to the batter and gently mix it in.

10 Spread half the mixture in the prepared tin and smooth the surface with a palette knife.

11 Arrange half the apple wedges over the batter, reserving the best pieces for the top.

12 Spread the rest of the mixture over the apples. Smooth once more with a palette knife.

13 Arrange the remaining apple wedges on top of the cake in an attractive pattern.

14 Remove the streusel dough from the refrigerator and coarsely grate it.

15 Sprinkle the grated streusel evenly over the top of the cake.

16 Bake in the centre of the oven for 45 minutes. Insert a skewer into the centre.

17 If the skewer emerges coated in batter, cook for a few minutes more and test again.

18 Leave the cake in the tin for 10 minutes. Keeping the streusel on top, carefully remove the cake from the tin and cool on a wire rack. Serve warm.

Apple Cake variations

Apple, Sultana, and Pecan Cake

Sometimes I like a healthier cake. This cake uses little fat and is stuffed full of fruit and nuts, making it a virtuous yet delicious choice.

SERVES 10–12 | 25 MINS | 30–35 MINS

Special equipment
23cm (9in) round springform cake tin

Ingredients
butter, for greasing
50g (1¾oz) shelled pecan nuts
200g (7oz) apples, peeled, cored, and finely diced
150g (5½oz) soft light brown sugar
250g (9oz) self-raising flour
1 tsp baking powder
2 tsp cinnamon
pinch of salt
3½ tbsp sunflower oil
3½ tbsp milk, plus extra if necessary
2 eggs
1 tsp vanilla extract
50g (1¾oz) sultanas
whipped cream or icing sugar, to serve (optional)

Method
1 Preheat the oven to 180°C (350°F/Gas 4). Grease the tin and line the base with baking parchment. Place the nuts on a baking sheet and toast them in the oven for 5 minutes until crisp. Cool and roughly chop.

2 In a large bowl, mix the apples and sugar together. Sift over the flour, baking powder, cinnamon, and salt, and fold in. In a jug, whisk together the oil, milk, eggs, and vanilla extract.

3 Pour the milk into the cake mixture and stir until well combined. Fold in the pecans and sultanas, and pour into the prepared tin.

4 Bake in the centre of the oven for 30–35 minutes, until a skewer comes out clean. Leave to cool for a few minutes in the tin, then turn out onto a wire rack. Remove the baking parchment. Serve warm with whipped cream as a dessert, or cooled and dusted with icing sugar.

STORE The cake will keep in an airtight container for 3 days.

Torta di mela

A firm dessert apple is best for this moist and dense Italian cake.

SERVES 8 | 20–25 MINS | 1¼–1½ HOURS | UP TO 8 WEEKS

Special equipment
23–25cm (9–10in) round springform cake tin

Ingredients
175g (6oz) unsalted butter, softened, plus extra for greasing
175g (6oz) plain flour, plus extra for dusting
½ tsp salt
1 tsp baking powder
finely grated zest and juice of 1 lemon
625g (1lb 5oz) apples, peeled, cored, and sliced
200g (7oz) caster sugar, plus 60g (2oz) for glazing
2 eggs
4 tbsp milk

Method
1 Preheat the oven to 180°C (350°F/Gas 4). Grease the tin and sprinkle with a little flour. Sift the flour with the salt and baking powder. Pour the lemon juice over the apple slices.

2 With an electric whisk, beat the butter in a large bowl until soft and creamy. Add the sugar and zest, and beat until light and fluffy. Add the eggs one at a time, beating well after each addition. Gradually whisk in the milk until the batter is smooth.

3 Fold in the flour mix and half the apples, spoon into the tin, and smooth the top. Place the remaining apple slices in concentric circles on top. Bake for 1¼–1½ hours, until a skewer comes out clean; it will still be moist.

4 Meanwhile, make the glaze. Heat 4 tablespoons of water and the remaining sugar in a pan over low heat until the sugar has dissolved. Bring to a boil and simmer for 2 minutes, without stirring. Let it cool.

5 Brush the glaze over the top of the cake as soon as it comes out of the oven. Let the cake cool in the tin, then transfer to a serving plate.

STORE The cake will keep in an airtight container for 2 days.

Toffee Apple Cake

Caramelizing the apples in this cake gives them a wonderful toffee apple taste, and soaking the cake in the buttery cooking juices after baking makes it especially moist and flavoursome.

| SERVES 8–10 | 40 MINS | 40–45 MINS | UP TO 4 WEEKS |

Special equipment
22cm (9in) round springform cake tin

Ingredients
200g (7oz) unsalted butter, softened, plus extra for greasing
50g (1¾oz) caster sugar
250g (9oz) apples, peeled, cored, and diced
150g (5½oz) soft light brown sugar
3 eggs
150g (5½oz) self-raising flour
1 heaped tsp baking powder
whipped cream or icing sugar, to serve (optional)

Method

1 Preheat the oven to 180°C (350°F/Gas 4). Grease the tin and line the base with baking parchment. In a large frying pan, gently heat 50g (1¾oz) of the butter and the caster sugar until melted and golden brown. Add the diced apple and fry gently for 7–8 minutes until they start to soften and caramelize.

2 With an electric whisk, cream together the remaining butter and brown sugar in a bowl until light and fluffy. Add the eggs one at a time, beating well after each addition. Sift the flour and baking powder together, and gently fold into the mixture.

3 Remove the apples from the pan with a slotted spoon and set aside the pan with the juices to use later. Scatter the apples over the base of the tin. Spoon the batter on top, then place the tin on a baking tray, with sides to catch any drips, and bake in the centre of the oven for 40–45 minutes. Leave to cool for a few minutes, then turn out onto a wire rack.

4 Put the frying pan with the leftover juices back on low heat, and heat gently until warmed through. With a fine skewer or wooden cocktail stick, make holes over the surface of the cake. Put the cake on a plate and pour over the apple syrup, letting it soak in. Serve warm with whipped cream, or cooled and dusted with icing sugar.

STORE The cake will keep in an airtight container for 3 days.

67

Rhubarb and Ginger Upside Down Cake

Young rhubarb is cooked into a simple upside down cake to give a modern twist on a classic dessert.

SERVES 6-8 | **40 MINS** | **40-45 MINS**

Special equipment
22cm (9in) round springform cake tin

Ingredients
150g (5½oz) unsalted butter,
   softened, plus extra for greasing
500g (1lb 2oz) young, pink rhubarb
150g (5½oz) soft dark brown sugar
4 tbsp finely chopped, preserved
   stem ginger
3 large eggs
150g (5½oz) self-raising flour

2 tsp ground ginger
1 tsp baking powder
double cream, whipped, or
   crème fraîche, to serve (optional)

1 Preheat the oven to 180°C (350°F/Gas 4). Melt a little butter and brush to grease the tin.

2 Line the base and sides of the cake tin with baking parchment.

3 Wash the rhubarb, removing discoloured pieces and the dry ends of the stalks.

4 Cut the rhubarb into 2cm (¾in) lengths with a sharp knife that will cut through the strings.

5 Scatter a little of the sugar evenly over the base of the cake tin.

6 Now scatter half the chopped ginger evenly over the base of the tin.

7 Lay the rhubarb in the tin, tightly packed, making sure the base is well covered.

8 Place the butter and remaining sugar into a large bowl.

9 With an electric whisk, cream the butter and sugar until light and fluffy.

10 Beat in the eggs one at a time, whisking as much air as possible into the mixture.

11 Gently fold the remaining chopped ginger into the batter, until well dispersed.

12 Sift together the flour, ground ginger, and baking powder into a separate bowl.

13 Add the sifted ingredients to the bowl containing the cake batter.

14 Gently fold the dry ingredients into the cake batter, keeping volume in the batter.

15 Spoon the cake batter over the base, being careful not to disturb the rhubarb.

16 Bake the cake in the centre of the oven for 45 minutes until springy to the touch.

17 Leave the cake to cool in its tin for 20–30 minutes, before carefully turning it out.

18 Serve warm as a dessert with whipped cream or crème fraîche. **STORE** The cake is also good cold and will keep in a cool place in an airtight container for 2 days.

Fresh Fruit Cake variations

Blueberry Upside Down Cake

This is an unusual yet delicious way of turning a punnet of blueberries and a few storecupboard essentials into a quick and delicious dessert for a crowd.

SERVES 8–10 | 15 MINS | 40 MINS

Special equipment
22cm (9in) round springform cake tin

Ingredients
150g (5½oz) unsalted butter, softened, plus extra for greasing
150g (5½oz) caster sugar
3 eggs
1 tsp vanilla extract
100g (3½oz) self-raising flour
1 tsp baking powder
50g (1¾oz) ground almonds
250g (9oz) fresh blueberries
cream or vanilla custard, or icing sugar, to serve (optional)

Method

1 Preheat the oven to 180°C (350°F/Gas 4) and place a baking sheet inside. Grease the cake tin and line the base with baking parchment. Cream together the butter and sugar using an electric whisk, until light and fluffy.

2 Gradually beat in the eggs and vanilla extract, whisking well between each addition, until well combined. Sift together the flour and baking powder, add the ground almonds, and fold into the batter.

3 Tip the blueberries into the tin and spread the batter gently over them. Bake the cake on the baking sheet in the centre of the oven for 35–40 minutes until golden brown and springy to the touch; a skewer should come out clean. Leave to cool for a few minutes, before removing from the tin.

4 Place the cake on a serving plate. Serve warm as a dessert, topped with cream or light vanilla custard; or serve cold, dusted with icing sugar.

STORE The cake will keep for 2 days in an airtight container.

Pear Cake

Fresh pear, yogurt, and almonds make this a very moist cake.

SERVES 6–8 | 40 MINS | 45–50 MINS | UP TO 8 WEEKS

Special equipment
18cm (7in) round springform cake tin

Ingredients
100g (3½oz) unsalted butter, softened, plus extra for greasing
75g (2½oz) soft light brown sugar
1 egg, lightly beaten
125g (4½oz) self-raising flour
1 tsp baking powder
½ tsp ground ginger
½ tsp cinnamon
finely grated zest and juice of ½ orange
4 tbsp Greek yogurt or soured cream
25g (scant 1oz) ground almonds
1 large or 2 small pears, peeled, cored, and sliced

For the topping
2 tbsp flaked almonds, lightly toasted
2 tbsp demerara sugar

Method

1 Preheat the oven to 180°C (350°F/Gas 4). Grease the cake tin and line the base with baking parchment. Whisk together the butter and sugar until light and fluffy. Beat the egg into the creamed mixture.

2 Sift together the flour, baking powder, ginger, and cinnamon, and very gently fold into the batter mixture. Fold in the orange zest and juice, yogurt or soured cream, and the ground almonds. Pour half the batter into the tin. Top with the pears and cover with rest of the batter.

3 In a small bowl, toss together the flaked almonds and demerara sugar. Sprinkle the mixture over the top of the cake and bake in the centre of the oven for 45–50 minutes until a skewer comes out clean.

4 Leave the cake to cool in its tin for about 10 minutes, then turn it out onto a wire rack to cool. Serve warm or at room temperature.

STORE The cake will keep in a cool place in an airtight container for 3 days.

Cherry and Almond Cake

A classic combination of flavours, and always popular with guests.

| SERVES 8–10 | 20 MINS | 1½–1¾ HOURS | UP TO 4 WEEKS |

Special equipment
20cm (8in) deep round springform cake tin

Ingredients
150g (5½oz) unsalted butter, softened, plus extra for greasing
150g (5½oz) caster sugar
2 large eggs, lightly beaten
250g (9oz) self-raising flour, sifted
1 tsp baking powder
150g (5½oz) ground almonds
1 tsp vanilla extract
75ml (2½fl oz) whole milk
400g (14oz) pitted cherries
25g (scant 1oz) blanched almonds, chopped

Method
1 Preheat the oven to 180°C (350°F/Gas 4). Grease the tin and line the base with baking parchment. In a bowl, whisk the butter and sugar until creamy. Beat in the eggs one at a time, adding a tablespoon of flour to the mixture before adding the second egg.

2 Mix in the remaining flour, baking powder, ground almonds, vanilla extract, and milk. Mix in half the cherries, then spoon the mixture into the tin and smooth the top. Scatter the remaining cherries and almonds over the surface.

3 Bake for 1½–1¾ hours or until golden brown and firm to the touch. A skewer inserted into the cake should come out clean. If the surface of the cake starts to brown before it is fully cooked, cover with foil. When cooked, leave to cool in the tin for a few minutes, then remove the foil and parchment, and transfer to a wire rack to cool completely before serving.

STORE This cake will keep in an airtight container for 2 days.

Bavarian Plum Cake

Bavaria is famous for its sweet baking. This unusual cake is a cross between a sweet bread and a custardy fruit tart.

| SERVES 8–10 | 35–40 MINS | 50–55 MINS | UP TO 4 WEEKS |

Rising and proving time
2–2¾ hrs

Special equipment
28cm (11in) tart tin

Ingredients
1½ tsp dried yeast
vegetable oil, for greasing
375g (13oz) plain flour, plus extra for dusting

2 tbsp caster sugar
1 tsp salt
3 eggs
125g (4½oz) unsalted butter, softened,
  plus extra for greasing

For the filling
2 tbsp dried breadcrumbs
875g (1lb 12½oz) purple plums,
  stoned and quartered
2 egg yolks
100g (3½oz) caster sugar
60ml (2fl oz) double cream

Method

1 Sprinkle the yeast over 60ml (2fl oz) lukewarm water in a small bowl. Let stand for 5 minutes until dissolved. Lightly oil another bowl. Sift the flour onto a work surface. Make a well in the centre and add the sugar, salt, yeast mixture, and eggs.

2 Work the flour to form a soft dough; adding more flour if it is very sticky. Knead on a floured work surface for 10 minutes until elastic. Work in more flour as needed so that the dough is slightly sticky but peels away easily from the work surface.

3 Add the butter to the dough; pinch and squeeze to mix it in, then knead until smooth. Shape into a ball and put it into the oiled bowl. Cover, and let rise in the refrigerator for 1½–2 hours, or overnight, until doubled in size.

4 Grease the tart tin. Knead the chilled brioche dough lightly to knock out the air. Flour the work surface; roll out the dough into a 32cm (13in) round. Wrap the dough around the rolling pin and loosely drape it over the dish. Press the dough into the dish and cut off any excess.

5 Sprinkle the breadcrumbs over the dough. Arrange the plum wedges, cut side up, in concentric circles on the brioche shell. Let stand at room temperature for 30–45 minutes until the edge of the dough is puffed. Meanwhile, preheat the oven to 220°C (425°F/Gas 7) and put a baking sheet in the oven to heat up.

6 For the custard mixture, place the egg yolks and two-thirds of the sugar into a bowl. Pour in the double cream, whisk together, and set aside.

7 Sprinkle the plums with the remaining sugar. Transfer the tart to the warmed baking sheet and cook in the oven for 5 minutes. Remove from the oven and reduce the heat to 180°C (350°F/Gas 4).

8 Ladle the custard mixture over the fruit and return to the oven. Continue baking for about 45 minutes until the dough is browned, the fruit tender, and the custard is just set. Let it cool on a wire rack. Serve warm or at room temperature.

STORE The cake will keep in an airtight container in the refrigerator for 2 days.

BAKER'S TIP
Baked custard should never be completely set when it is taken from the oven. Instead, there should always be a slight wobble in the middle when the tin is shaken, or the custard will be rubbery and hard, rather than unctuous and yielding.

Banana Bread

A mash of ripe bananas is delicious baked in this sweet quick bread. Spices and nuts add flavour and crunch.

MAKES 2 LOAVES | 20–25 MINS | 35–40 MINS | UP TO 8 WEEKS

Special equipment
2 x 450g (1lb) loaf tins

Ingredients
unsalted butter, for greasing
375g (13oz), strong white bread flour, plus extra for dusting
2 tsp baking powder
2 tsp cinnamon
1 tsp salt
125g (4½oz) walnut pieces, coarsely chopped

3 eggs
3 ripe bananas, peeled and chopped
finely grated zest and juice of 1 lemon
125ml (4fl oz) vegetable oil
200g (7oz) granulated sugar
100g (3½oz) soft brown sugar
2 tsp vanilla extract
cream cheese or butter, to serve (optional)

1 Preheat the oven to 180°C (350°F, Gas 4). Grease each of the loaf tins thoroughly.

2 Sprinkle 2–3 tablespoons of flour into each tin. Turn to coat and tap to remove excess flour.

3 Sift the flour, baking powder, cinnamon, and salt into a large bowl. Mix in the walnuts.

4 Make a well in the centre of the flour mixture for the wet ingredients.

5 Beat the eggs in a separate bowl with a fork or hand whisk.

6 Mash the bananas with a fork in another bowl, until they form a smooth paste.

7 Stir the bananas into the egg mixture until well blended. Add the lemon zest and mix.

8 Add the oil, granulated and brown sugars, vanilla, and lemon juice. Stir until combined.

9 Pour three-quarters of the banana mixture into the well in the flour, and stir well.

10 Gradually blend in the dry ingredients, adding the remaining banana mixture.

11 Stir until just smooth; if the batter is over-mixed, the banana bread will be tough.

12 Spoon the batter into the tins, dividing it equally. The tins should be about half full.

13 Bake for 35–40 minutes until the loaves start to shrink away from the sides of the tins.

14 Test each loaf with a skewer inserted into the centre; it should come out clean.

15 Let the loaves cool slightly, then transfer to a wire rack to cool completely.

16 Serve the banana bread sliced and spread with cream cheese or butter. It is also good toasted. **STORE** This bread will keep in an airtight container for 3–4 days.

Loaf Cake variations

Apple Loaf Cake

Here apples and wholemeal flour make for a healthier cake.

| MAKES 1 LOAF | 30 MINS | 40–50 MINS | UP TO 8 WEEKS |

Special equipment
900g (2lb) loaf tin

Ingredients
120g (4oz) unsalted butter, softened, plus extra for greasing
60g (2oz) soft light brown sugar
60g (2oz) caster sugar
2 eggs
1 tsp vanilla extract
60g (2oz) self-raising flour, plus extra for tossing
60g (2oz) wholemeal self-raising flour
1 tsp baking powder
2 tsp cinnamon
2 apples, peeled, cored, and diced

Method
1 Preheat the oven to 180°C (350°F/Gas 4). Grease the tin and line the base with baking parchment. In a bowl, whisk together the butter and the sugars.

2 Beat in the eggs, one at a time. Add the vanilla extract. In a separate bowl, sift together the flours, baking powder, and cinnamon. Fold the dry ingredients into the batter, mixing well.

3 Toss the apples in a little self-raising flour, then fold them into the batter. Pour the mixture into the tin. Bake in the centre of the oven for 40–50 minutes until the cake is golden brown. Leave to cool slightly, then turn out onto a wire rack.

STORE The cake will keep in an airtight container for 3 days.

BAKER'S TIP
When baking with any dried or fresh fruit, toss it lightly in flour before adding it to the wet ingredients. This floury coating will help stop the fruit from sinking to the bottom of the cake while cooking, ensuring it stays evenly distributed throughout.

Pecan and Cranberry Loaf Cake

Dried cranberries make a novel alternative to the more usual sultanas or raisins, adding sweet and sharp notes to this wholesome cake. ▶

| MAKES 1 LOAF | 30 MINS | 50–60 MINS | UP TO 4 WEEKS |

Special equipment
900g (2lb) loaf tin

Ingredients
100g (3½oz) unsalted butter, plus extra for greasing
100g (3½oz) soft light brown sugar
75g (2½oz) dried cranberries, roughly chopped
50g (1¾oz) pecans, roughly chopped
finely grated zest of 2 oranges and juice of 1 orange
2 eggs
125ml (4fl oz) milk
225g (8oz) self-raising flour
½ tsp baking powder
½ tsp cinnamon
100g (3½oz) icing sugar, sifted

Method
1 Preheat the oven to 180°C (350°F/Gas 4). Grease the tin and line with parchment. In a pan, melt the butter. Leave to cool slightly, then stir in the sugar, cranberries, pecans, and zest of 1 orange. Whisk together the eggs and milk, then stir them in as well.

2 In a separate bowl, sift together the flour, baking powder, and cinnamon. Fold into the batter, mixing well. Tip into the tin. Bake in the centre of the oven for 50–60 minutes. Leave to cool slightly, then turn out.

3 Mix the icing sugar and remaining zest. Add enough orange juice for a drizzling consistency. Drizzle the frosting over the cooled cake and leave to dry before slicing.

STORE Will keep in a container for 3 days.

Sweet Potato Bread

Savoury sounding, this is very much a sweet cake and similar to a banana bread in looks and texture.

| MAKES 1 LOAF | 10 MINS | 1 HOUR | UP TO 4 WEEKS |

Special equipment
900g (2lb) loaf tin

Ingredients
100g (3½oz) unsalted butter, softened, plus extra for greasing
175g (6oz) sweet potatoes, peeled and diced
200g (7oz) plain flour
2 tsp baking powder
pinch of salt
½ tsp mixed spice
½ tsp cinnamon
125g (4½oz) caster sugar
50g (1¾oz) pecans, roughly chopped
50g (1¾oz) chopped dates
100ml (3½fl oz) sunflower oil
2 eggs

Method
1 Grease and line the tin with parchment. Place the sweet potato in a pan, cover with water, and bring to a boil, then simmer for about 10 minutes until tender. Mash and set aside to cool.

2 Preheat the oven to 170°C (335°F/Gas 3½). In a large bowl, sift together the flour, baking powder, salt, spices, and sugar. Add the pecans and dates and mix in thoroughly. Make a well in the centre.

3 In a jug, whisk the eggs with the oil until emulsified. Add the potato and stir until smooth. Pour into the flour mix and stir together until well combined and smooth.

4 Pour the batter into the tin and smooth the top with a palette knife. Bake in the centre of the oven for 1 hour until well risen and a skewer comes out clean. Leave to cool for 5 minutes before turning out.

STORE The cake will keep in an airtight container for 3 days.

Bara Brith

This sweet Welsh "speckled bread" is at its best eaten the same day it is made, ideally while still warm and spread with butter.

| MAKES 2 LOAVES | 40 MINS | 25–40 MINS | UP TO 8 WEEKS |

Rising and proving time
3–4 hrs

Special equipment
2 x 900g (2lb) loaf tins (optional)

Ingredients
2 tsp dried yeast
250ml (8fl oz) warm milk
60g (2oz) caster sugar,
   plus 2 tbsp for sprinkling
1 egg, beaten
500g (1lb 2oz) strong white bread flour,
   plus extra for dusting
1 tsp salt
60g (2oz) unsalted butter, softened and diced
1 tsp mixed spice
oil, for greasing
225g (8oz) dried mixed fruit
   (raisins, sultanas, and mixed peel)

Method

1 Whisk the yeast into the milk with 1 teaspoon of caster sugar, and leave in a warm place for 10 minutes until the mixture froths. Add most of the beaten egg, reserving a little for glazing.

2 Rub the flour, salt, and butter together until the mixture resembles fine breadcrumbs. Stir in the mixed spice and remaining sugar. Make a well in the centre of the dry ingredients. Pour in the milk mixture, and mix it together with your hands to form a sticky dough.

3 Turn it out onto a lightly floured work surface and knead for up to 10 minutes until soft and pliable but still quite sticky. Add more flour, 1 tablespoon at a time, if it's not forming a ball. Place the dough in a lightly oiled bowl and cover with cling film. Leave it to rise in a warm place for 1½–2 hours until doubled in size.

4 Turn out onto a lightly floured work surface, punch the air out with your fists, and gently stretch to around 2cm (¾in) thick. Scatter the dried fruit over the surface of the dough, and bring it together from the sides into the middle to form a ball again.

5 Now either shape the dough into your desired shape and transfer to a greased baking sheet, or halve and put into the greased loaf tins. Cover with oiled cling film or a clean tea towel, and leave in a warm place to prove for another 1½–2 hours until doubled in size again.

6 Meanwhile, preheat the oven to 190°C (375°F/Gas 5). Brush the bread with a little egg wash and sprinkle it with 1 tablespoon of sugar. Bake for 25–30 minutes for loaf tins, or 35–40 minutes for a large free-form loaf. Cover halfway through cooking time with a piece of foil or baking parchment if it browns too much.

7 The bread is done when it is golden brown, firm to the touch, and the bottom is hollow when tapped. Leave to cool for 20 minutes before cutting, as it will continue to cook after being removed from the oven. Cutting too early causes the steam to escape and the loaf to harden.

STORE The bread will keep in an airtight container for 2 days (see Baker's Tip).

BAKER'S TIP

Baking two loaves at a time and freezing one of them makes good sense when there is lengthy rising and proving to be done. Leftover bread can be toasted for a couple of days after baking, or sliced and used in Bread and Butter Pudding (see page 92).

EVERYDAY CAKES

celebration cakes

Rich Fruit Cake

This recipe makes a wonderfully moist, rich fruit cake, ideal for Christmas, weddings, christenings, or birthdays.

SERVES 16   **25 MINS**   **2½ HOURS**

Soaking time
overnight

Special equipment
20–25cm (8–10in) deep round cake tin

Ingredients
200g (7oz) sultanas
400g (14oz) raisins
350g (12oz) prunes, chopped
350g (12oz) glacé cherries
2 small dessert apples, peeled, cored, and diced
600ml (1 pint) cider
4 tsp mixed spice
200g (7oz) unsalted butter, softened
175g (6oz) dark brown sugar
3 eggs, beaten
150g (5½oz) ground almonds
280g (10oz) plain flour
2 tsp baking powder
400g (14oz) ready-made marzipan
2–3 tbsp apricot jam
3 large egg whites
500g (1lb 2oz) icing sugar

1 Place the sultanas, raisins, prunes, cherries, apple, cider, and spice in a saucepan.

2 Simmer over medium-low heat and cover for 20 minutes until most of the liquid is absorbed.

3 Remove from the heat. Leave overnight at room temperature; the fruits will absorb liquid.

4 Preheat the oven to 160°C (325°F/Gas 3). Double-line the tin with baking parchment.

5 With an electric whisk, cream the butter and sugar in a large bowl until fluffy.

6 Add the eggs, a little at a time, beating very well after each addition to avoid curdling.

7 Gently fold in the fruit mix and ground almonds, trying to keep volume in the batter.

8 Sift the flour and baking powder into the bowl, and gently fold into the mixture.

9 Spoon the batter into the prepared tin, cover with foil, and bake for 2½ hours.

10 Test the cake is ready: a skewer inserted into the centre should come out clean.

11 Leave to cool, then turn out onto a wire rack to cool completely. Remove the parchment.

12 Trim the cake to level it. Transfer to a stand and hold in place with some marzipan.

13 Warm the jam and brush thickly over the whole cake. This will help the marzipan stick.

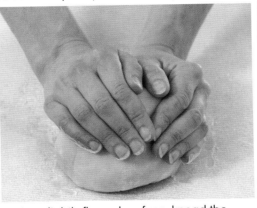

14 On a lightly floured surface, knead the remaining marzipan until softened.

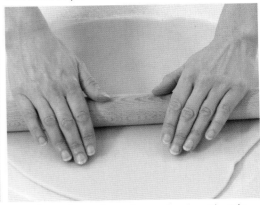

15 Roll out the softened marzipan until wide enough to cover the cake.

16 Drape the marzipan over the rolling pin and lift it over the cake.

17 With your hands, gently ease the marzipan into place, smoothing out any bumps.

18 With a small sharp knife, cut away any excess marzipan from the base of the cake.

19 Place the egg whites in a bowl and sift in the icing sugar, stirring well to combine.

20 With an electric whisk, beat the icing sugar mixture for 10 minutes until stiff.

21 Spread the icing with a palette knife.
PREPARE AHEAD Will keep, un-iced, for 8 weeks.

Fruit Cake variations

Prune Chocolate Dessert Cake

Soaked prunes give this rich, dark cake a warming depth of flavour, making it a perfect dessert for the winter months.

| SERVES 8–10 | 30 MINS | 40–45 MINS | UP TO 8 WEEKS |

Soaking time
overnight

Special equipment
22cm (9in) round springform cake tin

Ingredients
100g (3½oz) ready-to-eat prunes, chopped
100ml (3½fl oz) brandy or cold black tea
125g (4½oz) unsalted butter,
  plus extra for greasing
250g (9oz) good-quality dark chocolate,
  broken into pieces
3 eggs, separated
150g (5½oz) caster sugar
100g (3½oz) ground almonds
cocoa powder, sifted, for dusting
double cream, whipped, to serve (optional)

Method
1 Soak the prunes in the brandy or tea overnight. When ready to bake, preheat the oven to 180°C (350°F/Gas 4). Grease the tin and line the base with baking parchment.

2 Gently melt the chocolate and butter in a heatproof bowl over a pan of simmering water, and then cool. Beat the egg yolks and sugar together with an electric whisk. Whisk the egg whites separately into soft peaks.

3 Mix the cooled chocolate into the egg yolk mixture. Fold in the ground almonds, prunes, and soaking liquid, mixing till well combined. Beat 2 tablespoons of the egg white into the batter to loosen the mixture slightly. Gently fold in the remaining egg white.

4 Pour the mixture into the tin and bake for 40–45 minutes until the surface is springy; the centre will be slightly soft. Leave the cake to cool in its tin for a while, then turn it out onto a wire rack to cool. Remove the parchment.

5 Serve the cake upside down, as this will give a smoother finish to the top. Dust with cocoa powder and serve with the cream.

PREPARE AHEAD This will keep in an airtight container for up to 5 days.

Tea Bread

A simple recipe; don't forget to use the soaking water as well as the fruit.

| SERVES 8–10 | 20 MINS | 1 HOUR | UP TO 4 WEEKS |

Soaking time
overnight

Special equipment
900g (2lb) loaf tin

Ingredients
250g (9oz) mixed dried fruit (sultanas, raisins,
  currants, and mixed peel)
100g (3½oz) soft light brown sugar
250ml (8fl oz) cold black tea
unsalted butter, for greasing
50g (1¾oz) walnuts or hazelnuts, roughly chopped
1 egg, beaten
200g (7oz) self-raising flour

Method
1 Mix the dried fruit and sugar together, and leave to soak in the cold tea overnight. When ready to bake, preheat the oven to 180°C (350°F/Gas 4). Grease the loaf tin and line the base with baking parchment.

2 Add the nuts and the egg to the soaked fruit, and mix well to combine. Sift over the flour, and fold it in, mixing thoroughly.

3 Bake in the centre of the oven for 1 hour or until the top is dark golden brown and springy to the touch.

4 Leave to cool slightly in its tin, then turn out onto a wire rack to cool completely. Remove the baking parchment. This is best served sliced or toasted with butter.

STORE The bread will keep in an airtight container for 5 days.

Light Fruit Cake

Not everyone enjoys a classic rich fruit cake, especially after a hearty celebration meal. This lighter version is a quick and easy alternative that's less heavy on the fruit.

SERVES
8–12

25
MINS

1¾
HOURS

UP TO 8
WEEKS

Special equipment
20cm (8in) deep round cake tin

Ingredients
175g (6oz) unsalted butter, softened
175g (6oz) light soft brown sugar
3 large eggs
250g (9oz) self-raising flour, sifted
2–3 tbsp milk
300g (10½oz) mixed dried fruit (sultanas, raisins, glacé cherries, and mixed peel)

Method
1 Preheat the oven to 180°C (350°F/Gas 4). Line the tin with baking parchment.

2 In a bowl, beat the butter and sugar together with an electric hand whisk until pale and creamy. Then beat in the eggs, one at a time, adding a little of the flour after each one. Fold in the remaining flour and the milk. Add the dried fruit and fold in until well combined.

3 Spoon the mixture into the tin, level the top, and bake for 1½–1¾ hours until firm to the touch and a skewer inserted into the middle of the cake comes out clean. Leave in the tin to cool completely. Remove the baking parchment.

STORE The cake will keep in an airtight container for 3 days.

Plum Pudding

So-named because it contains prunes, this is a classic Christmas dish, here using butter instead of the traditional beef suet.

| SERVES 8–10 | 45 MINS | 8–10 HOURS | UP TO 1 YEAR |

Soaking time
overnight

Special equipment
1kg (2¼lb) pudding bowl

Ingredients
85g (3oz) raisins
60g (2oz) currants
100g (3½oz) sultanas
45g (1½oz) mixed peel, chopped
115g (4oz) mixed dried fruit,
  such as figs, dates, and cherries
150ml (5fl oz) beer

1 tbsp whisky or brandy
finely grated zest and juice of 1 orange
finely grated zest and juice of 1 lemon
85g (3oz) ready-to-eat prunes, chopped
150ml (5fl oz) cold black tea
1 dessert apple, peeled, cored, and grated
115g (4oz) unsalted butter, melted,
  plus extra for greasing
175g (6oz) dark soft brown sugar
1 tbsp black treacle
2 eggs, beaten
60g (2oz) self-raising flour
1 tsp mixed spice
115g (4oz) fresh white breadcrumbs
60g (2oz) chopped almonds
brandy butter, cream, or custard,
  to serve (optional)

Method

1 Place the first 9 ingredients into a large bowl and mix well. Put the prunes in a small bowl and pour in the tea. Cover the bowls and leave to soak overnight.

2 Drain the prunes and discard any remaining tea. Add the prunes and the apple to the rest of the fruit, followed by the butter, sugar, treacle, and eggs, stirring well.

3 Sift in the flour along with the mixed spice, then stir in the breadcrumbs and almonds. Mix until all the ingredients are well combined.

4 Grease the pudding bowl and pour in the mixture. Cover the top of the bowl with 2 layers of baking parchment and 1 layer of foil. Tie the layers to the bowl with string, then put the bowl into a pan of simmering water that comes at least halfway up the side of the bowl. Steam for 8–10 hours.

5 Check regularly to make sure that the water level does not drop too low. Serve with brandy butter, cream, or custard.

PREPARE AHEAD If well sealed, the pudding will keep for up to 1 year in a cool place.

BAKER'S TIP

When steaming a pudding for an extended time, it is very important that the water level in the pan should not drop too low. There are a couple of easy ways to avoid this. Either set a timer every hour, to remind you to check the water level, or put a marble in the pan so it rattles when the water level drops.

CELEBRATION CAKES

Panettone

A sweet bread eaten all over Italy at Christmas. Making one is not as hard as it seems and the results are delicious.

SERVES 8

30 MINS

40–45 MINS

UP TO 4 WEEKS

Rising and proving time
4 hrs

Special equipment
15cm (6in) round springform cake tin
or high-sided panettone tin

Ingredients
2 tsp dried yeast
125ml (4fl oz) milk, warmed in a pan
and left to cool to lukewarm
50g (1¾oz) caster sugar

425g (15oz) strong white bread flour,
plus extra for dusting
large pinch of salt
75g (2½oz) unsalted butter, melted
2 large eggs, plus 1 small egg,
beaten, for brushing
1½ tsp vanilla extract
175g (6oz) mixed dried fruit
(apricots, cranberries, sultanas,
mixed peel)

finely grated zest of 1 orange
vegetable oil, for greasing
icing sugar, for dusting

CELEBRATION CAKES

1 Add the yeast to the warm milk in a jug. Mix the sugar, flour, and salt in a large bowl.

2 Once the yeasted milk is frothy (5 minutes), whisk in the butter, large eggs, and vanilla.

3 Mix the liquid and dry ingredients to form a soft dough; it will be stickier than bread dough.

4 On a lightly floured surface, knead the dough for about 10 minutes until elastic.

5 Form the dough into a loose ball and stretch it out flat onto a floured work surface.

6 Scatter the dried fruit and orange zest on top and knead again until well combined.

7 Form the dough into a loose ball and put it in a lightly oiled bowl.

8 Cover the bowl with a damp, clean tea towel or place inside a large plastic bag.

9 Leave the dough to prove in a warm place for up to 2 hours until doubled in size.

10 Line the tin with a double layer of baking parchment or a single layer of silicone paper.

11 If using a cake tin, form a collar with the paper, 5–10cm (2–4in) higher than the tin.

12 Knock the air out of the dough with your fist and turn out onto a lightly floured surface.

13 Knead the dough into a round ball just big enough to fit into the tin.

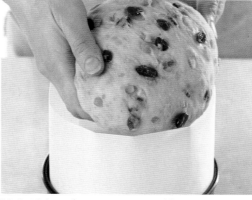

14 Put it into the tin, cover, and leave to prove for another 2 hours until doubled in size.

15 Preheat the oven to 190°C (375°F/Gas 5). Brush the top of the dough with eggwash.

16 Bake in the middle of the oven for 40–45 minutes. If it's browning fast, cover with foil.

17 The bottom will sound hollow when ready. Leave to cool for 5 minutes, then turn out.

18 Remove the parchment and cool completely on a wire rack before dusting with icing sugar to serve. **STORE** The panettone will keep in an airtight container for 2 days.

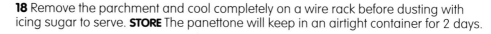

Panettone variations

Chocolate and Hazelnut Panettone

This variation of the classic panettone is a sure-fire winner with children and any leftovers can be used to make a particularly delicious Bread and Butter Pudding (see recipe below).

| SERVES 8 | 30 MINS | 45–50 MINS | UP TO 4 WEEKS |

Rising and proving time
3 hrs

Special equipment
15cm (6in) round springform cake tin or high-sided panettone tin

Ingredients
2 tsp dried yeast
125ml (4fl oz) milk, warmed in a pan and left to cool to lukewarm
50g (1¾oz) caster sugar
425g (15oz) strong white bread flour, plus extra for dusting
large pinch of salt
75g (2½oz) unsalted butter, melted
2 large eggs, plus 1 small egg, beaten, for glazing
1 tsp vanilla extract
75g (2½oz) hazelnuts, roughly chopped
finely grated zest of 1 orange
vegetable oil, for greasing
100g (3½oz) dark chocolate chunks, chopped
icing sugar, for dusting

Method

1 In a jug, add the yeast to the warm milk and leave for about 5 minutes, stirring once, until frothy. Combine the sugar, flour, and salt in a mixing bowl. Add the butter, large eggs, and vanilla extract to the yeasted milk, and whisk to combine.

2 Mix the milk mixture with the dry ingredients to form a soft dough. Knead for 10 minutes until smooth and elastic.

3 Stretch out the dough on a floured surface. Scatter the hazelnuts and zest on top of the stretched dough and knead the dough until well combined. Form the dough into a loose ball and put it in a lightly oiled bowl.

4 Cover the bowl with a damp tea towel and leave it to prove in a warm place for up to 2 hours until doubled in size. Meanwhile, line the tin with silicone paper or a double layer of parchment. If using a cake tin, form a collar with the paper 5–10cm (2–4in) higher than the tin.

5 When the dough has doubled in size, knock it back, and stretch it out again. Scatter the chocolate over the surface and bring together, kneading it before shaping it into a round ball. Put it into the tin, cover it again, and leave it to prove for another 2 hours until doubled in size.

6 Preheat the oven to 190°C (375°F/Gas 5). Brush the top of the panettone with beaten egg. Bake in the middle of the oven for 45–50 minutes. Cover the top with foil if it's browning too quickly.

7 Leave to cool in the tin for a few minutes before turning out onto a wire rack to cool completely. The bottom should sound hollow when tapped. Dust with icing sugar to serve.

STORE The panettone will keep in an airtight container for 2 days.

Panettone Bread and Butter Pudding

Any leftover panettone can be turned into this quick and easy dessert. Try introducing different flavours such as orange zest, chocolate, or dried cherries to the dish before baking.

| SERVES 4–6 | 10 MINS | 30–40 MINS |

Ingredients
50g (1¾oz) unsalted butter, softened
250g (9oz) panettone
350ml (12fl oz) single cream or 175ml (6fl oz) double cream and 175ml (6fl oz) milk
2 large eggs
50g (1¾oz) caster sugar
1 tsp vanilla extract

Method

1 Preheat the oven to 180°C (350°F/Gas 4). Use a little of the softened butter to grease a medium sized, shallow baking dish.

2 Slice the panettone into 1cm (½in) thick slices. Butter each slice with a little of the butter and lay them, overlapping slightly, into the baking dish. Whisk together the cream, or cream and milk, eggs, sugar, and vanilla extract. Pour the liquid over the panettone and then gently press down on top to make sure it has all been soaked in the liquid.

3 Bake in the centre of the oven for 30–40 minutes until it is just set, golden brown and puffed up. Serve warm with thick pouring cream.

PREPARE AHEAD Once cooked, this can be stored in the fridge for 3 days. Reheat thoroughly before eating.

ALSO TRY...
Festive Panettone Pudding
Plain panettone can also be spread with a little good-quality marmalade and the cream enriched with 1–2 tbsp whisky and a grating of orange zest and nutmeg, for a festive alternative.

Individual Stuffed Panettones

Try these as an alternative dessert at a Christmas meal.

SERVES 6   **1 HOUR**   **30–35 MINS**

Rising, proving, and chilling time
3 hrs rising and proving and 3 hrs chilling

Special equipment
6 x 220g empty food cans, well cleaned
food processor with blade attachment

Ingredients
butter, for greasing
1 quantity panettone dough,
   see page 90, steps 1–9
300g (10oz) mascarpone cheese
300g (10oz) crème fraîche
2 tbsp Kirsch or other fruit liqueur (optional)
12 glacé cherries, quartered
50g (1¾oz) unsalted, shelled pistachio nuts,
   roughly chopped
3 tbsp icing sugar, plus extra for dusting

Method
1 Grease the cans and line them with baking parchment. The parchment should rise to double the height of the cans.

2 Cut the dough into 6 pieces, and place a piece in each can. Cover and leave to rise for 1 hour or until doubled in size. Preheat the oven to 190°C (375°F/Gas 5).

3 Bake for 30–35 minutes. The panettones will be golden-brown. Remove one from its can and tap the base. It should sound hollow. If it does not, remove all of them from their cans, place on a baking tray and bake for 5 minutes. Place on a wire rack and cool.

4 Hollow out the panettones by laying each one on its side and, using a sharp knife and a sawing action, cut a circle in the base 1cm (½in) from the edge. Reserve the disks.

5 Now take the knife and cut down along the insides of the rim nearly to the bottom of the upside down panettone. Neatly hollow out the panettone with your fingers.

6 Put the extracted pieces of the panettone into a food processor and reduce them

to fine breadcrumbs. In a bowl, cream together the mascarpone and crème fraîche with the liqueur (if using). Mix in the breadcrumbs and beat well to combine.

7 Fold through the cherries, pistachios, and icing sugar. Divide the filling between the panettones, pressing it in with the back of a spoon, and cover with the reserved disks.

8 Wrap, and refrigerate for at least 3 hours. Unwrap and dust with icing sugar to serve.

PREPARE AHEAD These will keep overnight in the refrigerator.

BAKER'S TIP
Panettone is an Italian sweet bread traditionally baked for Christmas. Although the process is lengthy, the time taken is mostly for the bread to rise twice. It is not complicated to make and gives a marvellously light result quite unlike a shop-bought panettone.

Stollen

This rich, fruity sweet bread, originally from Germany, is traditionally served at Christmas and makes a great alternative to Christmas cake or mince pies.

SERVES 12 | **30 MINS** | **50 MINS** | **UP TO 4 WEEKS**

Soaking time
overnight

Rising and proving time
2–3 hours

Ingredients
200g (7oz) raisins
100g (3½oz) currants
100ml (3½fl oz) rum

400g (14oz) strong white bread flour,
   plus extra for dusting
2 tsp dried yeast
60g (2oz) caster sugar
100ml (3½fl oz) milk
½ tsp vanilla extract
pinch of salt
½ tsp mixed spice
2 large eggs
175g (6oz) unsalted butter,
   softened and diced
200g (7oz) mixed peel
100g (3½oz) ground almonds
icing sugar, for dusting

Method

1 Put the raisins and currants into a large bowl, pour over the rum, and leave to soak overnight.

2 The following day, sift the flour into a large bowl. Make a well in the centre, sprinkle in the yeast, and add a teaspoon of sugar. Gently heat the milk until lukewarm and pour on top of the yeast. Leave to stand at room temperature for 15 minutes or until it turns frothy.

3 Add the rest of the sugar, vanilla extract, salt, mixed spice, eggs, and butter. Mix everything together with a wooden spoon and then knead the dough for 5 minutes until smooth.

4 Transfer to a lightly floured surface. Add the mixed peel, raisins and currants, and almonds, kneading for a few minutes until mixed. Return the dough to the bowl, cover loosely with cling film, and leave to rise in a warm place for 1–1½ hours until doubled.

5 Preheat the oven to 160°C (325°F/Gas 3). Line a baking tray with baking parchment. On a floured surface, roll out the dough to make a 30 x 25cm (12 x 10in) rectangle. Fold one long side over, just beyond the middle, then fold over the other long side to overlap the first, curving it slightly on top to create the stollen shape. Transfer to the baking tray and put in a warm place for 1–1½ hours to prove until doubled in size.

6 Bake in the oven for 50 minutes or until risen and pale golden. Check after 30–35 minutes and if browning too much, cover loosely with foil. Transfer to a wire rack to cool completely, then generously dust with icing sugar.

STORE The stollen will keep in an airtight container for 4 days.

BAKER'S TIP

Stollen can be made with any combination of dried fruits. It can be plain as in this recipe, or stuffed with a marzipan or frangipane layer. Any leftovers are great for breakfast, lightly toasted, with butter.

Bienenstich

The name of this German recipe translates as "bee sting cake". Legend has it that the honey attracts bees who sting the baker!

SERVES 8–10

20 MINS

20–25 MINS

Rising and proving time
1 hr 5 mins–1 hr 20 mins

Special equipment
20cm (8in) round cake tin

Ingredients
140g (5oz) plain flour, plus extra for dusting
15g (½oz) unsalted butter, softened and diced, plus extra for greasing
½ tbsp caster sugar
1½ tsp dried yeast
pinch of salt
1 egg
oil, for greasing

For the glaze
30g (1oz) butter
20g (¾oz) caster sugar
1 tbsp clear honey
1 tbsp double cream
30g (1oz) flaked almonds
1 tsp lemon juice

For the crème pâtissière
250ml (8fl oz) full-fat milk
25g (scant 1oz) cornflour
2 vanilla pods, split lengthways, deseeded, pods and seeds retained
60g (2oz) caster sugar
3 egg yolks
25g (scant 1oz) unsalted butter, diced

Method

1 Sift the flour into a bowl. Quickly rub in the butter, then add the sugar, yeast, and salt, and mix well. Beat in the egg and add just enough water to make a soft dough.

2 Knead on a floured surface for 5–10 minutes or until smooth, elastic, and shiny. Put in a clean, oiled bowl, cover with cling film, and leave to rise in a warm place for 45–60 minutes or until doubled in size.

3 Grease the cake tin and line the base with baking parchment. Knock back the dough and roll it out into a circle to fit the tin. Push it into the tin and cover with cling film. Leave to prove for 20 minutes.

4 To make the glaze, melt the butter in a small pan, then add the sugar, honey, and cream. Cook over low heat until the sugar has dissolved, then increase the heat and bring to a boil. Allow to simmer

for 3 minutes, then remove the pan from the heat, and add the almonds and lemon juice. Allow to cool.

5 Preheat the oven to 190°C (375°F/Gas 5). Carefully spread the glaze over the dough, leave to rise for another 10 minutes, then bake for 20–25 minutes; if it starts to brown too quickly, cover loosely with foil. Allow to cool in the tin for 30 minutes, then transfer to a wire rack.

6 Meanwhile, make the crème pâtissière. Pour the milk into a heavy saucepan and add the cornflour, vanilla seeds and pods, and half the sugar. Place over low heat. Whisk the egg yolks with the remaining sugar in a bowl. Continue whisking and slowly pour in the hot milk. Transfer to the pan and whisk until it just comes to a boil, then remove from the heat.

7 Immediately place the whole saucepan into a bowl of iced water and remove the vanilla pods. Once the sauce has cooled, add the butter, and briskly whisk into the sauce until it is smooth and glossy.

8 Slice the cake in half. Spread a thick layer of crème pâtissière on the bottom half, then place the almond layer on top. Transfer to a serving plate.

BAKER'S TIP
This German classic is traditionally filled with crème pâtissière, as in this recipe. It makes a smooth, luxurious filling which these days is a real treat. However, if you are pushed for time, an easier option would be to fill the cake with whipped double cream, lightly scented with ½ teaspoon vanilla extract.

Brioche des rois

This French bread is traditionally eaten at Epiphany, 6th January. The *fève* represents the gifts of the Three Kings.

SERVES 10–12

25 MINS

25–30 MINS

UP TO 4 WEEKS

Rising and proving time
4–6 hrs

Special equipment
25cm (10in) ring mould (optional)
fève porcelain or metal trinket
(optional; see Baker's Tip, page 101)

Ingredients

For the brioche
2½ tsp dried yeast
2 tbsp caster sugar

5 eggs, beaten
375g (13oz) strong white bread
   flour, plus extra for dusting
1½ tsp salt
oil, for greasing
175g (6oz) unsalted butter,
   cubed and softened

For the topping
1 egg, lightly beaten
50g (1¾oz) mixed candied fruit
   (orange and lemon zest, glacé
   cherries, and angelica), chopped
25g (scant 1oz) coarse sugar
   crystals (optional)

1 Whisk the yeast, 2 tablespoons warm water, and sugar. Leave for 10 minutes. Add eggs.

2 In a large bowl, sift together the flour and salt, and add the remaining sugar.

3 Make a well in the flour and pour in the eggs and yeast mixture.

  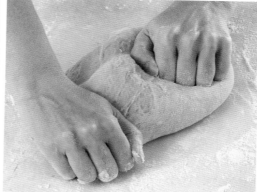

4 Use a fork and then your hands to bring the dough together; it will be quite sticky.

5 Turn out the dough onto a lightly floured work surface.

6 Knead the dough for 10 minutes until elastic but still sticky.

7 Put in an oiled bowl and cover with cling film. Leave to rise in a warm place for 2–3 hours.

8 Gently knock the dough back on a lightly floured work surface.

9 Scatter one-third of the cubed butter over the surface of the dough.

CELEBRATION CAKES

10 Fold the dough over the butter and knead gently for 5 minutes.

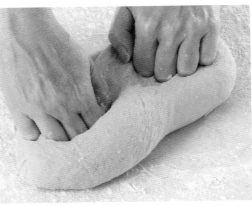

11 Repeat until all the butter is absorbed. Keep kneading until no streaks of butter show.

12 Form into a round and work it into a ring. Bury the *fève*, if using (see Baker's Tip, page 101).

13 Transfer to an oiled baking sheet or fill an oiled ring mould (if using).

14 If you don't have a ring mould, use a ramekin to keep the shape of the hole.

15 Cover with cling film and a tea towel. Leave to prove for 2–3 hours until doubled in size.

16 Brush the brioche with beaten egg. Sprinkle over candied fruit and sugar crystals (if using).

17 Preheat the oven to 200°C (400°F/Gas 6). Bake for 25–30 minutes until golden brown.

18 Leave to cool slightly, then turn out onto a wire rack, without dislodging the toppings.
STORE This will keep in an airtight container for 3 days.

Brioche variations

Brioche Buns

These bite-sized little buns are known in French as *brioche à tête*, for obvious reasons.

MAKES 10 BUNS · **45–50 MINS** · **15–20 MINS** · **UP TO 8 WEEKS**

Rising and proving time
1½–2 hrs

Special equipment
10 x 7.5cm (3in) brioche moulds

Ingredients
butter, melted, for greasing
1 quantity brioche dough,
  see pages 98–99, steps 1–11
flour, for dusting
1 egg, beaten, for glazing
½ tsp salt, for glazing

Method

1 Brush the brioche moulds with melted butter and set them on a baking sheet.

2 Divide the dough in half. Roll 1 piece of dough into a cylinder, 5cm (2in) in diameter, and cut it into 5 pieces. Repeat with the remaining dough. Roll each piece of dough into a smooth ball.

3 Pinch one-quarter of each ball, almost dividing it from the remaining dough, to form the head. Holding the head, lower each ball into a mould, twisting and pressing the head onto the base. Cover with a dry tea towel and leave to prove in a warm place for 30 minutes.

4 Preheat the oven to 220°C (425°F/Gas 7). Mix the egg and salt for glazing. Brush the brioches with egg glaze. Bake for 15–20 minutes until brown and hollow sounding when tapped; unmould and cool on a wire rack.

STORE These will keep in an airtight container for 3 days.

Rum Babas

Boozy, cake-like versions of brioche buns – perfect for a dinner party.

MAKES 4 BABAS · **20 MINS** · **20 MINS**

Rising time
30 mins

Special equipment
4 x 7.5cm (3in) brioche moulds or baba tins

For the babas
60g (2oz) butter, melted, plus extra for greasing
150g (5½oz) strong plain flour
60g (2oz) raisins
1½ tsp fast-action dried yeast
155g (5½oz) caster sugar
pinch of salt
2 eggs, lightly beaten
4 tbsp milk, warmed
vegetable oil, for greasing
3 tbsp rum
300ml (10fl oz) whipping cream
2 tbsp icing sugar
grated chocolate, to serve

Method

1 Grease the moulds with butter. Place the flour in a bowl and stir in the raisins, yeast, 30g (1oz) sugar, and salt. Beat together the egg and milk, and add to the flour mixture. Stir in the butter. Beat well for 3–4 minutes, then pour into the moulds to half fill them.

2 Place the moulds on a baking tray and cover with a sheet of oiled cling film. Leave to rise in a warm place for 30 minutes, or until doubled in size and filling the moulds. Preheat the oven to 200°C (400°F/Gas 6). Bake for 10–15 minutes until golden. Leave to cool on a wire rack. If freezing, do so at this stage.

3 Heat 120ml (4fl oz) of water in a pan with the remaining sugar, boiling rapidly for 2 minutes. Remove from the heat and cool. Stir in the rum. Pierce holes in the babas using a skewer, then dip them in the syrup.

4 Before serving, pour the cream into a bowl, add the icing sugar, and whisk until peaks form. Place a dollop of cream on each baba, sprinkle over chocolate, and serve.

Brioche Nanterre

Basic brioche dough can be baked into rings, buns, or loaves. This classic brioche loaf is best for slicing and fantastic toasted.

MAKES 1 LOAF | **30 MINS** | **30 MINS** | **UP TO 4 WEEKS**

Rising and proving time
4–6 hrs

Special equipment
900g (2lb) loaf tin

Ingredients
1 quantity brioche dough,
  see pages 98–99, steps 1–11
1 egg, beaten, for glazing

Method

1 Line the bottom and sides of the tin with parchment. Put a double layer on the base. Divide the dough into 8 pieces, and roll them up to form small balls. They should fit in pairs, side by side, in the base of the prepared tin.

2 Cover with cling film and a tea towel, and leave to prove for a further 2–3 hours until the dough has again doubled in size.

3 Preheat the oven to 200°C (400°F/Gas 6). Brush the top of the brioche loaf with a little beaten egg, and bake near the top of the oven for 30 minutes or until the bottom of the loaf sounds hollow when tapped. Check the loaf after 20 minutes and cover the top with a piece of loose-fitting parchment if it is in danger of becoming too brown.

4 Leave to cool in the tin for a few minutes, then turn out onto a wire rack to cool. This brioche is delicious toasted and buttered.

STORE The loaf will keep in an airtight container for 3 days.

BAKER'S TIP

Brioche originated in France and was baked to celebrate Epiphany on 6 January. Traditionally, a *fève* is hidden in the dough, and the finder is guaranteed luck for the coming year. In the past, a dried bean or *fève* was used, but these days small decorative ceramic figures are more common.

Kugelhopf

Dark raisins and chopped almonds are baked into this classic kugelhopf, an Alsatian favourite. A dusting of icing sugar hints at the sweet filling.

| MAKES 1 RING | 45–50 MINS | 45–50 MINS | UP TO 8 WEEKS |

Rising and proving time
2–2½ hrs

Special equipment
1-litre (1¾-pint) ring mould or see page 99, steps 12–14, for how to shape without a mould

Ingredients
150ml (5fl oz) milk
2 tbsp granulated sugar
150g (5½oz) unsalted butter, diced, plus extra for greasing
1 tbsp dried yeast
500g (1lb 2oz) strong white bread flour
1 tsp salt
3 eggs, beaten
90g (3oz) raisins
60g (2oz) blanched almonds, chopped, plus 7 whole blanched almonds
icing sugar, for dusting

Method

1 Bring the milk to the boil in a saucepan. Add 4 tablespoons to a bowl and leave to cool till it is lukewarm. Add the sugar and butter to the remaining milk in the pan, and stir until melted. Allow it to cool.

2 Sprinkle the yeast over the milk in the bowl and let stand for 5 minutes until dissolved, stirring once. Sift the flour and salt into a bowl and add the dissolved yeast, eggs, and the milk mixture from the pan.

3 Gradually draw in the flour and work it into the other ingredients to form a smooth dough. Knead for 5–7 minutes, until very elastic and sticky. Cover with a damp tea towel and let rise in a warm place for 1–1½ hours or until doubled .

4 Meanwhile, grease the mould with butter. Freeze the mould until the butter is hard (about 10 minutes), then butter it again. Pour boiling water over the raisins and allow them to plump up.

5 Knock back the dough lightly with your hand to push out the air. Drain the raisins, reserving 7 of them, and knead the rest into the dough with the chopped almonds. Arrange the reserved raisins and whole almonds at the bottom of the mould.

6 Shape the dough into the mould, cover with a tea towel, and leave to prove in a warm place for 30–40 minutes until it comes just above the top of the mould. Preheat the oven to 190°C (375°F/Gas 5).

7 Bake the kugelhopf until puffed and brown, and the bread starts to shrink from the side of the mould. It should take 45–50 minutes. Let it cool slightly. Turn out onto a wire rack and let cool completely. Just before serving, dust with icing sugar.

STORE The kugelhopf will keep in an airtight container for 3 days.

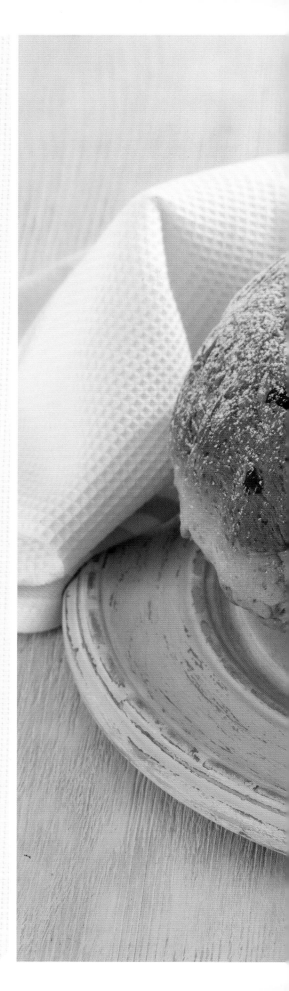

BAKER'S TIP

The dough of kugelhopf is very sticky. It is natural to want to add more flour, in order to make it look more like conventional dough. However, resist the temptation, as it would make the kugelhopf tough.

Chocolate Chestnut Roulade

Perfect for a winter celebration, this rolled sponge is filled with a rich chestnut purée mixed with whipped cream.

SERVES 8–10 | **50–55 MINS** | **5–7 MINS** | **8 WEEKS, UNFILLED**

Special equipment
30 x 37cm (12 x 15in) Swiss roll tin
piping bag and star nozzle

Ingredients
butter, for greasing
35g (1¼oz) cocoa powder
1 tbsp plain flour
pinch of salt
5 eggs, separated
150g (5½oz) caster sugar

For the filling
125g (4½oz) chestnut purée
2 tbsp dark rum
175ml (6fl oz) double cream
30g (1oz) good-quality dark
  chocolate, broken into pieces
caster sugar to taste (optional)

For decoration
50g (1¾oz) caster sugar
2 tbsp dark rum
125ml (4fl oz) double cream
dark chocolate, grated with
  a vegetable peeler,
  to produce shavings

1 Preheat the oven to 220°C (425°F/Gas 7). Grease a baking sheet. Line with parchment.

2 Sift the cocoa powder, flour, and salt into a large bowl and set aside.

3 Beat the egg yolks with two-thirds of the sugar; it should leave a ribbon trail.

4 Whisk the egg whites until stiff. Sprinkle in the remaining sugar and whisk again until glossy.

5 Sift one-third of the cocoa mixture over the yolk mixture. Add one-third of the egg whites.

6 Fold together lightly. Add the remaining cocoa mixture and egg white in 2 batches.

7 Pour the batter onto the prepared baking sheet. Spread the batter almost to the edges.

8 Bake in the bottom of the oven for 5–7 minutes. The cake will be risen and just firm.

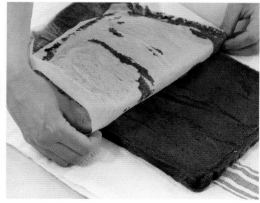

9 Remove the cake from the oven, invert onto a damp tea towel and peel off the parchment.

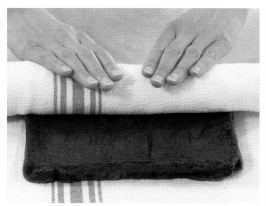  

10 Tightly roll up the cake around the damp tea towel and leave to cool.

11 Put the chestnut purée in a bowl with the rum. Whip the cream until it forms soft peaks.

12 Melt the chocolate in a bowl over a pan of simmering water. Stir into the chestnut mixture.

13 Fold the chocolate and chestnut mixture into the whipped cream. Add sugar to taste.

14 Simmer 50g (1¾oz) in 4 tablespoons of water for 1 minute. Cool and stir in rum.

15 Unroll the cake on fresh parchment. Brush with syrup and spread the chestnut mix.

16 Using the parchment underneath, carefully roll up the filled cake as tightly as possible.

17 Whip the cream and remaining sugar until stiff. Fill the piping bag with the cream.

18 Trim the edges with a serrated knife. Transfer the roulade to a serving plate. Decorate with the whipped cream and chocolate shavings. The roulade is best eaten on the day.

Chocolate Roulade variations

Chocolate Log

The Christmas classic, pairing dark chocolate with raspberry.

SERVES 10 | **30 MINS** | **15 MINS** | **UP TO 24 WEEKS**

Special equipment
20 x 28cm (8 x 11in) Swiss roll tin

Ingredients
3 eggs
85g (3oz) caster sugar
85g (3oz) plain flour
3 tbsp cocoa powder
½ tsp baking powder
icing sugar, for dusting
200ml (7fl oz) double cream
140g (5oz) dark chocolate, chopped
3 tbsp raspberry jam

Method
1 Preheat the oven to 180°C (350°F/Gas 4). Line the Swiss roll tin with parchment.

2 Whisk the eggs with the sugar and a tablespoon of water for 5 minutes or until pale and light. Sift the flour, cocoa powder, and baking powder into the beaten eggs, then carefully and quickly fold in.

3 Pour the mixture into the tin, and bake for 12 minutes until springy to the touch. Turn it out onto a piece of baking parchment. Peel the paper from the base of the cake and discard. Roll the sponge up around the fresh parchment. Leave to cool.

4 To make the icing, pour the cream into a small pan, bring to a boil, then remove from the heat. Add the chopped chocolate and leave it to melt, stirring occasionally. Allow the mixture to cool and thicken.

5 Unroll the cake and spread raspberry jam over the surface. Spread one-third of the icing on the jam and roll it. Place the cake seam-side down. Spread the rest of the icing all over the cake. Use a fork to create ridges down the length and ends of the cake. Transfer to a serving plate and dust with icing sugar.

STORE The cake will keep, chilled, for 2 days.

Chocolate Amaretti Roulade

Crushed Amaretti biscuits add texture and crunch to this beautiful and indulgent roulade. ▶

SERVES 6–8 | **25–30 MINS** | **20 MINS** | **8 WEEKS, UNFILLED**

Special equipment
20 x 28cm (8 x 11in) Swiss roll tin

Ingredients
6 large eggs, separated
150g (5½oz) caster sugar
50g (1¾oz) cocoa powder, plus extra for dusting
icing sugar, for dusting
300ml (10fl oz) double cream or whipping cream
2–3 tbsp Amaretto or brandy
20 Amaretti biscuits, crushed, plus 2 for topping
50g (1¾oz) dark chocolate

Method
1 Preheat the oven to 180°C (350°F/Gas 4). Line the tin with parchment. Put the egg yolks and sugar in a bowl set over a pan of simmering water and beat with an electric whisk for 10 minutes until creamy. Remove from the heat. In another bowl, beat the egg whites with a clean whisk till soft peaks form.

2 Sift the cocoa powder into the egg yolk mixture and gently fold in, along with the egg whites. Pour into the tin and smooth into the corners. Bake for 20 minutes or until just firm to the touch. Cool slightly before carefully turning the cake out, face down, onto a sheet of baking parchment well dusted with icing sugar. Cool for 30 minutes.

3 Whisk the cream with an electric whisk until soft peaks form. Trim the sides of the cake to neaten them, then drizzle over the Amaretto or brandy. Spread with the cream, scatter with the crushed Amaretti biscuits, then grate over most of the chocolate.

4 Starting from one of the short sides, roll the roulade up, using the parchment to help keep it tightly together. Place on a serving plate with the seam underneath. Crumble over the extra biscuits, grate over the remaining chocolate, and dust with a little icing sugar and cocoa powder. The roulade is best eaten on the same day.

Chocolate and Buttercream Roll

This chocolatey variation on a Swiss roll is simple to make and always a hit with kids – perfect for a children's party.

SERVES 8–10 | **20–25 MINS** | **10 MINS**

Special equipment
20 x 28cm (8 x 11in) Swiss roll tin

Ingredients
3 large eggs
75g (2½oz) caster sugar
50g (1¾oz) plain flour
25g (scant 1oz) cocoa powder, plus extra for dusting
75g (2½oz) butter, softened
125g (4½oz) icing sugar

Method
1 Preheat the oven to 200°C (400°F/Gas 6) and line the tin with parchment. Set a bowl over a pan of simmering water, add the eggs and sugar, and whisk for 5–10 minutes until thick and creamy. Remove from the heat, sift in the flour and cocoa, and fold in.

2 Pour the mixture into the tin and bake for 10 minutes or until springy to the touch. Cover with a damp tea towel and cool. Turn the sponge out, face down, onto a sheet of parchment dusted with cocoa powder. Peel off the parchment it was baked on.

3 Whisk the butter until creamy. Beat in the icing sugar, a little at a time, then spread the mixture over the sponge. Using the parchment to help you, roll the sponge up.

STORE The cake will keep, chilled, for 3 days.

Black Forest Gâteau

Newly resurrected to its glorious best, this classic German cake deserves its place on a celebration table.

SERVES 8	55 MINS	40 MINS	UP TO 4 WEEKS

Special equipment
23cm (9in) round springform cake tin
piping bag and star nozzle

Ingredients
85g (3oz) butter, melted,
  plus extra for greasing
6 eggs
175g (6oz) golden caster sugar
125g (4½oz) plain flour
50g (1¾oz) cocoa powder
1 tsp vanilla extract

For the filling and decoration
2 x 425g cans pitted black cherries,
  drained, 6 tbsp juice reserved, and
  cherries from 1 can roughly chopped
4 tbsp Kirsch
600ml (1 pint) double cream
150g (5½oz) dark chocolate, grated

CELEBRATION CAKES

1 Preheat the oven to 180°C (350°F/Gas 4). Grease and line the tin with baking parchment.

2 Put the eggs and sugar into a large heatproof bowl that will fit over a saucepan.

3 Place the bowl over a pan of simmering water. Don't let the bowl touch the water.

4 Whisk until the mixture is pale and thick, and will hold a trail from the beaters.

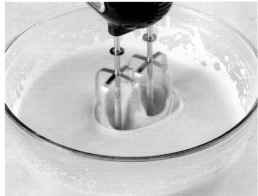

5 Remove from the heat and whisk for another 5 minutes or until cooled slightly.

6 Sift the flour and cocoa together, and gently fold into the egg mixture using a spatula.

7 Fold in the vanilla and butter. Transfer to the prepared tin and level the surface.

8 Bake in the oven for 40 minutes or until risen and just shrinking away from the sides.

9 Turn out onto a wire rack, discard the paper, and cover with a clean cloth. Let it cool.

10 Carefully cut the cake into 3 layers. Use a serrated knife and long sweeping strokes.

11 Combine the reserved cherry juice with the Kirsch, and drizzle a third over each layer.

12 Whip the cream in a separate bowl until it just holds shape; it should not be too stiff.

13 Place a layer of cake on a plate. Spread with cream and half the chopped cherries.

14 Repeat with the second sponge. Top with the final sponge, baked side up. Press down.

15 Cover the side with a layer of cream. Put the remaining cream in the piping bag.

16 Press grated chocolate onto the creamy sides with a palette knife.

17 Pipe a ring of cream swirls around the cake and place the whole cherries inside.

18 Sprinkle any remaining chocolate evenly over the peaks of piped cream, to serve.
PREPARE AHEAD The cake can be covered and chilled for up to 3 days.

Gâteau variations

German Cream Cheese Torte

This German dessert is a cross between a cheesecake and a sponge cake. It makes a good party dessert as it can be prepared well in advance.

SERVES 8–10 | **40 MINS** | **30 MINS**

Chilling time
3 hrs, or overnight

Special equipment
22cm (9in) round springform cake tin

Ingredients
150g (5½oz) unsalted butter, softened,
  or soft margarine, plus extra for greasing
225g (8oz) caster sugar
3 eggs
150g (5½oz) self-raising flour
1 tsp baking powder
juice and finely grated zest of 2 lemons,
  plus 1 extra lemon for zesting to decorate
5 sheets of gelatine (8.5g/¼oz)
250ml (8fl oz) double cream
250g (9oz) quark, or see Baker's Tip
icing sugar, for dusting

Method

1 Preheat the oven to 180°C (350°F/Gas 4). Grease the tin and line with parchment.

2 Cream together the butter or margarine and 150g (5½oz) sugar. Beat in the eggs, one at a time, until smooth and creamy. Sift together the flour and baking powder, and fold into the batter with half the zest. Spoon into the tin and bake for 30 minutes or until well risen. Turn the cake out onto a wire rack. Slice it in half horizontally with a serrated knife. Leave to cool completely.

3 For the filling, put the gelatine in a bowl of cold water for a few minutes until it is soft and pliable. Heat the lemon juice in a pan, then remove from the heat. Squeeze out any excess water from the gelatine and add to the lemon juice. Stir until dissolved, and cool.

4 Whisk the cream until firm. Beat together the quark and remaining zest and sugar. Beat in the lemon juice. Fold in the cream.

5 Spoon the filling onto a cake half. Slice the second half into 8 pieces and arrange on top of the filling; pre-cutting the top layer makes it easier to serve. Chill for at least 3 hours or overnight. Sift over icing sugar and sprinkle with the extra lemon zest.

PREPARE AHEAD Can be made up to 3 days ahead and kept in the refrigerator.

BAKER'S TIP
If you cannot find any quark it can easily be substituted with low-fat cottage cheese, processed to a paste in a food processor with blade attachment.

Bavarian Raspberry Gâteau

When raspberries are not in season, you can use frozen berries.

SERVES 8   **55–60 MINS**   **20–25 MINS**

Chilling time
4 hrs

Special equipment
22cm (9in) round springform cake tin
blender

Ingredients
60g (2oz) unsalted butter, plus extra for greasing
125g (4½oz) plain flour, plus extra for dusting
pinch of salt
4 eggs, beaten
135g (5oz) caster sugar
2 tbsp Kirsch

For the raspberry cream
500g (1lb 2oz) raspberries
3 tbsp Kirsch
200g (7oz) caster sugar
250ml (8fl oz) double cream
1 litre (1¾ pints) milk
1 vanilla pod, split, or 2 tsp vanilla extract
10 egg yolks
3 tbsp cornflour
10g (¼oz) powdered gelatine

Method

1 Preheat the oven to 220°C (425°F/Gas 7). Grease the tin with butter and line the base with buttered parchment. Sprinkle in 2–3 tablespoons flour. Melt the butter and let it cool. Sift the flour and salt into a bowl. Put the eggs in a separate bowl and beat in the sugar, using an electric whisk, for 5 minutes.

2 Sift one-third of the flour mixture over the egg mixture and fold in. Add the remaining flour in 2 batches. Pour in the butter and fold in. Pour into the tin and bake for 20–25 minutes until the cake has risen.

3 Turn out the cake onto a wire rack. Let cool. Remove the parchment. Trim the top and bottom so that they are flat. Cut the cake horizontally in half. Clean, dry, and re-grease the tin. Put a cake round in the tin and sprinkle it with 1 tablespoon of Kirsch.

4 Purée three-quarters of the berries in a blender, then work through a sieve to remove the pips. Stir in 1 tablespoon of Kirsch with 100g (3½oz) of the sugar. Whip the cream until it forms soft peaks.

5 Put the milk in a pan. Add the vanilla pod (if using). Bring to a boil. Remove the pan from the heat, cover, and let stand in a warm place for 10–15 minutes. Remove the pod. Set aside one-quarter of the milk. Stir the remaining sugar into the milk in the pan.

6 Beat the egg yolks and cornflour in a bowl. Add the hot milk and whisk until smooth. Pour the yolk mixture back into the pan and cook over medium heat, stirring, just until the custard comes to a boil. Stir in the reserved milk and the vanilla extract (if using).

7 Strain the custard equally into 2 bowls. Let cool. Stir 2 tablespoons of Kirsch into 1 bowl. Set this custard aside to serve with the finished dessert. Sprinkle the powdered gelatine over 4 tablespoons of water in a small pan and let soften for 5 minutes.

Heat until the gelatine is melted and pourable. Stir into the bowl of unflavoured custard, along with the raspberry purée.

8 Set the bowl in a pan of iced water. Stir the mixture until it thickens. Remove the bowl from the water. Fold the raspberry custard into the whipped cream. Pour half into the cake tin. Sprinkle a few reserved whole raspberries. Pour the remaining Bavarian cream on the berries. Sprinkle 1 tablespoon of Kirsch over the second cake round.

9 Lightly press the cake round, sprinkled-side down, on the cream. Cover with cling film and refrigerate for at least 4 hours until firm. To serve, remove the side of the tin and place on a serving plate. Decorate the top of the cake with the reserved raspberries, and serve the Kirsch custard sauce separately.

PREPARE AHEAD The gâteau can be made up to 2 days ahead and kept in the refrigerator; remove 1 hour before serving.

small cakes

Vanilla Cream Cupcakes

Cupcakes are denser than fairy cakes, which enables them to carry more elaborate types of icing.

MAKES 24 | **20 MINS** | **20–25 MINS** | **4 WEEKS, UN-ICED**

Special equipment
2 x 12-hole cupcake trays
piping bag and star nozzle (optional)

Ingredients
200g (7oz) plain flour, sifted
2 tsp baking powder
200g (7oz) caster sugar
½ tsp salt
100g (3½oz) unsalted butter, softened
3 eggs
150ml (5fl oz) milk
1 tsp vanilla extract

For the icing
200g (7oz) icing sugar
1 tsp vanilla extract
100g (3½oz) unsalted butter, softened
sugar sprinkles (optional)

SMALL CAKES

1 Preheat the oven to 180°C (350°F/Gas 4). Place the first 5 ingredients in a bowl.

2 Mix together with your fingertips until it resembles fine breadcrumbs.

3 In another bowl, whisk the eggs, milk, and vanilla extract together until well blended.

4 Slowly pour the egg mixture into the dry ingredients, whisking all the time.

5 Whisk gently until smooth, being careful not to over-mix. Too much beating toughens cakes.

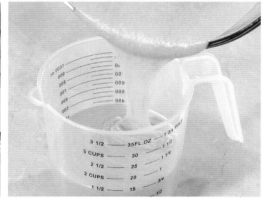

6 Pour all the cake batter into a jug to make it easier to handle.

7 Place the cupcake paper cases into the holes in the cupcake trays.

8 Carefully pour the cake mixture into the papers, filling each one only half full.

9 Bake in the preheated oven for 20–25 minutes until springy to the touch.

10 Test the cakes are done by inserting a skewer into the centre of one cupcake.

11 If traces of cake batter remain on the skewer, cook for a minute more, then test again.

12 Leave for a few minutes, then transfer the cupcakes to a wire rack to cool completely.

13 To make the icing, combine the icing sugar, vanilla extract, and butter in a bowl.

14 Beat with an electric whisk for 5 minutes until very light and fluffy.

15 Check the cakes have completely cooled, or they will melt the frosting.

16 If icing by hand, add a teaspoonful of the frosting mix to the top of each cake.

17 Then use the back of a spoon, dipped in warm water to smooth the surface.

To pipe the icing for a more professional finish, transfer the icing to the piping bag.

Pipe by squeezing out the icing with one hand, while holding the cake with the other.

Starting from the edge, pipe a spiral of icing that comes to a peak in the centre.

18 Decorate with sprinkles. **STORE** The cakes will keep in an airtight container for 3 days.

VANILLA CREAM CUPCAKES

Cupcake variations

Chocolate Cupcakes

Classic chocolate cupcakes are another must-have recipe. A guaranteed winner at children's parties!

MAKES 24 · **20 MINS** · **20–25 MINS** · **4 WEEKS, UN-ICED**

Special equipment
2 x 12-hole cupcake trays
piping bag and star nozzle (optional)

Ingredients
200g (7oz) plain flour
2 tsp baking powder
4 tbsp cocoa powder
200g (7oz) caster sugar
½ tsp salt
100g (3½oz) unsalted butter, softened
3 eggs
150ml (5fl oz) milk
1 tsp vanilla extract
1 tbsp Greek yogurt

For the icing
100g (3½oz) unsalted butter, softened
175g (6oz) icing sugar
25g (scant 1oz) cocoa powder

Method
1 Preheat the oven to 180°C (350°F/Gas 4). Sift the flour, baking powder, and cocoa into a bowl. Add the sugar, salt, and butter. Mix until it resembles fine breadcrumbs. In a bowl, whisk the eggs, milk, vanilla extract, and yogurt together until well blended.

2 Slowly pour in the egg mixture to combine. Gently whisk until smooth. Place the cupcake cases into the trays. Carefully spoon the cake mixture into the cases, filling each one only half full.

3 Bake for 20–25 minutes until lightly coloured and springy to the touch. Leave for a few minutes, then transfer the cupcakes in their cases to a wire rack to cool completely.

4 For the icing, beat together the butter, icing sugar, and cocoa powder until smooth.

5 Ice by hand, using the back of a spoon dipped in warm water to smooth the surface, or transfer the icing to the piping bag and pipe onto the cakes.

STORE These cupcakes keep in an airtight container for 3 days.

Lemon Cupcakes

For a delicate taste, try flavouring the basic cupcake batter with lemon.

MAKES 24 · **20 MINS** · **20–25 MINS** · **4 WEEKS, UN-ICED**

Special equipment
2 x 12-hole cupcake trays
piping bag and star nozzle (optional)

Ingredients
200g (7oz) plain flour
2 tsp baking powder
200g (7oz) caster sugar
½ tsp salt
100g (3½oz) unsalted butter, softened
3 eggs
150ml (5fl oz) milk
finely grated zest and juice of 1 lemon

For the icing
200g (7oz) icing sugar
100g (3½oz) unsalted butter, softened

Method
1 Preheat the oven to 180°C (350°F/Gas 4). Sift the flour and baking powder into a bowl. Add the sugar, salt, and butter. Mix until it resembles fine breadcrumbs. In a bowl, whisk the eggs and milk until well blended.

2 Pour in the egg mixture to combine. Add half the lemon zest and all the lemon juice. Gently whisk until smooth. Place the cupcake paper cases into the cupcake trays. Spoon the mixture into the papers, filling each one only half full. Bake for 20–25 minutes until springy. Cool completely.

3 To make the icing, beat the icing sugar, butter, and remaining lemon zest until smooth. Ice by hand, with a teaspoon, or with the piping bag and star nozzle.

STORE These cupcakes keep in an airtight container for 3 days.

BAKER'S TIP
Due to their fairly dense texture, all these classic American cupcakes will keep well for a few days. If you prefer them well risen, replace the plain flour with self-raising flour but reduce the baking powder to 1 teaspoon, accordingly.

SMALL CAKES

Coffee and Walnut Cupcakes

Definitely one for adults, coffee and nuts add depth to these cupcakes.

MAKES 24	20 MINS	20–25 MINS	4 WEEKS, UN-ICED

Special equipment
2 x 12-hole cupcake trays
piping bag and star nozzle (optional)

Ingredients
200g (7oz) plain flour, plus extra for dusting
2 tsp baking powder
200g (7oz) caster sugar
½ tsp salt
100g (3½oz) unsalted butter, softened
3 eggs
150ml (5fl oz) milk
1 tbsp strong coffee powder mixed with 1 tbsp
  boiling water, and cooled, or 1 cooled espresso
100g (3½oz) halved walnuts, plus extra to decorate

For the icing
200g (7oz) icing sugar
100g (3½oz) unsalted butter, softened
1 tsp vanilla extract

Method
1 Preheat the oven to 180°C (350°F/Gas 4). Sift the flour and baking powder into a bowl. Add the sugar, salt, and butter. Mix until it resembles fine breadcrumbs. In a bowl, whisk the eggs and milk until well blended.

2 Pour in the egg mixture, add half the coffee, and whisk until smooth. Roughly chop the walnuts and toss them in a bowl with a little flour, then fold them into the batter. Place the cupcake cases in the trays. Spoon the mixture into the cases, filling each one only half full. Bake for 20–25 minutes until springy, then cool completely.

3 To make the icing, beat the icing sugar, butter, vanilla extract, and remaining coffee until smooth. Ice by hand, with a teaspoon, or with the piping bag and star nozzle. Top each cake with a walnut half.

STORE These cupcakes keep in an airtight container for 3 days.

Fondant Fancies

Dainty in size, gorgeous to look at, and delectable to eat, these little cakes are perfect for a party or as a special teatime treat.

MAKES 16   20–25 MINS   25 MINS

Special equipment
20cm (8in) square cake tin

Ingredients
175g (6oz) unsalted butter, softened, plus extra for greasing
175g (6oz) caster sugar
3 large eggs
1 tsp vanilla extract
175g (6oz) self-raising flour, sifted
2 tbsp milk
2–3 tbsp raspberry or red cherry conserve

For the buttercream
75g (2½oz) unsalted butter, softened
150g (5½oz) icing sugar

For the icing
juice of ½ lemon
450g (1lb) icing sugar
1–2 drops natural pink food colouring
icing flowers, to decorate (optional)

Method

1 Preheat the oven to 190°C (375°F/Gas 5). Grease the cake tin and line the base with baking parchment. Place the butter and sugar in a large bowl and beat until pale and fluffy. Set aside.

2 Lightly beat the eggs and vanilla extract in another large bowl. Add about one-quarter of the egg mixture and a tablespoon of the flour to the butter mixture and beat well. Add the rest of the egg mixture, a little at a time, beating as you go. Add the remaining flour and the milk, and gently fold in.

3 Transfer the mixture to the prepared tin and bake in the middle of the oven for about 25 minutes or until lightly golden and springy to the touch. Remove from the oven, leave to cool in the tin for about 10 minutes, then remove from the tin and cool upside down on a wire rack. Remove the baking parchment.

4 To make the buttercream, beat the butter with the icing sugar until smooth. Set aside. Slice the cake horizontally with a serrated knife and spread the fruit conserve on one half and the buttercream on the other. Sandwich the layers together, then cut the cake into 16 equal squares.

5 To make the icing, put the lemon juice in a measuring jug and fill it up to 60ml (2fl oz) with hot water. Mix this with the icing sugar, stirring continuously and adding more hot water as required until the mixture is smooth. Add the pink food colouring and stir well.

6 Use a palette knife to transfer the cakes to a wire rack placed over a board or plate (to catch the drips). Drizzle with the icing to cover the cakes completely, or just cover the tops, and allow the icing to drip down the sides so the sponge layers are visible. Decorate with icing flowers (if using), then leave to set for about 15 minutes. Use a clean palette knife to transfer each cake carefully to a paper case.

STORE These fancies will keep in the refrigerator for 1 day.

BAKER'S TIP
For a chocolate version, chill the filled squares well, then pierce each with a cocktail stick. Holding the stick, dip each cake into a bowl of melted dark chocolate (250g/9oz), then set on a wire rack. Once set, drizzle with melted white chocolate (50g/1¾oz) for a contrasting pattern.

Chocolate Fudge Cake Balls

The new must-have cakes to come out of the US. Deceptively simple to make, packet or leftover cake can also be used.

| MAKES 20–25 | 35 MINS | 25 MINS | 4 WEEKS, UNDIPPED |

Chilling time
3 hrs, or 30 mins freezing

Special equipment
18cm (7in) round cake tin
food processor with blade attachment

Ingredients
100g (3½oz) unsalted butter, softened, or soft margarine, plus extra for greasing
100g (3½oz) caster sugar

2 eggs
80g (3oz) self-raising flour
20g (¾oz) cocoa powder
1 tsp baking powder
1 tbsp milk, plus extra if needed
150g (5½oz) ready-made chocolate fudge frosting (or use recipe for Chocolate Fudge Cake icing, see page 60)

250g (9oz) dark chocolate cake covering
50g (1¾oz) white chocolate

1 Preheat the oven to 180°C (350°F/Gas 4). Grease the tin and line with baking parchment.

2 With an electric whisk, cream the butter and sugar until fluffy.

3 Beat in the eggs one at a time, mixing well between additions, until smooth and creamy.

4 Sift together the flour, cocoa, and baking powder, and fold into the cake batter.

5 Mix in enough milk to loosen the batter to a dropping consistency.

6 Spoon into the tin and bake for 25 minutes until the surface is springy to the touch.

7 Test with a skewer and then turn out onto a wire rack to cool completely.

8 Whiz the cake in a processor until it looks like breadcrumbs. Put 300g (10½oz) in a bowl.

9 Add the frosting and blend together to a smooth, uniform mix.

SMALL CAKES

10 Using dry hands, roll the cake mix into balls, each the size of a walnut.

11 Put the balls on a plate and refrigerate for 3 hours or freeze for 30 minutes until firm.

12 Line 2 trays with parchment. Melt the cake covering according to directions on the packet.

13 Coat the balls in chocolate. Work quickly and if they start to break up, coat one at a time.

14 Using 2 forks, turn the balls in the chocolate until covered. Remove, allowing excess to drip.

15 Transfer the coated cake balls to the baking trays to dry. Continue to coat all the balls.

16 Melt the white chocolate in a bowl placed over a pan of boiling water.

17 Drizzle the white chocolate over the balls with a spoon, to decorate.

18 Leave the white chocolate to dry completely before transferring to a serving plate.
STORE The cake balls can be kept in an airtight container for 3 days.

Cake Ball variations

Strawberries and Cream Cake Pops

These are a fantastically impressive treat to serve at a children's party. You could even decorate a whole birthday cake with them.

**MAKES
20–25**   **20
MINS**   **25
MINS**   **4 WEEKS,
UNDIPPED**

Chilling time
3 hrs, or 30 mins freezing

Special equipment
18cm (7in) round cake tin
food processor with blade attachment
25 pieces of bamboo skewer, cut to
    approximately 10cm (4in) lengths,
    to resemble lollipop sticks

Ingredients
100g (3½oz) unsalted butter, softened,
    or soft margarine, plus extra for greasing
100g (3½oz) caster sugar
2 eggs
100g (3½oz) self-raising flour
1 tsp baking powder
150g (5½oz) ready-made buttercream frosting, or
    see vanilla buttercream, page 127, steps 13–15
2 tbsp good quality, smooth strawberry jam
250g (9oz) white chocolate cake covering

Method

1 Preheat the oven to 180°C (350°F/Gas 4). Grease the tin and line with parchment. Cream the butter or margarine, and sugar. Beat in the eggs one at a time, until the mixture is smooth. Sift the flour and baking powder together, and fold into the batter.

2 Pour the batter into the tin and bake for 25 minutes until the surface is springy to the touch. Turn out onto a wire rack to cool. Remove the parchment.

3 When the cake is cool, process it until it resembles breadcrumbs. Weigh out 300g (10½oz) of the crumbs and place in a bowl. Add the frosting and the jam, and mix thoroughly. Using dry hands, roll the mix into balls the size of a walnut. Put the balls on a plate and stick a skewer into each. Refrigerate for 3 hours or freeze for 30 minutes. Line 2 baking trays with parchment.

4 Melt the cake covering in a bowl set over simmering water. Dip the chilled balls one at a time into the molten chocolate, turning until completely covered, right up to the stick.

5 Gently take them out of the chocolate mixture and allow any excess to drip back into the bowl before transferring them to the baking trays to dry. The pops should be eaten on the same day.

> **BAKER'S TIP**
> To ensure a smooth, round finish to cake pops, cut an apple in half and place the halves cut side down on the lined baking tray. Dip the cake pops, then stick their bamboo skewers into the apple. This will help the cake pops dry without any marks to the surface.

Christmas Pudding Balls

I love to serve these cute little puddings at Christmas parties. An easy and delicious way to use up leftover Christmas pudding.

**MAKES
15–20**   **20
MINS**   **25
MINS**   **4 WEEKS,
UNDIPPED**

Chilling time
3 hrs, or 30 mins freezing

Special equipment
food processor with blade attachment

Ingredients
400g (14oz) leftover cooked Christmas Pudding,
    or Plum Pudding, see page 88
200g (5½oz) dark chocolate cake covering
50g (1¾oz) white chocolate cake covering
glacé cherries and candied angelica (optional)

Method

1 Whizz up the Christmas pudding in the processor until thoroughly broken up. Using dry hands roll the Christmas pudding mix into balls the size of a walnut. Put the balls on a plate and refrigerate them for 3 hours or freeze for 30 minutes until firm.

2 Line 2 baking trays with parchment paper. In a small, microwaveable bowl, heat the dark chocolate cake covering in bursts of 30 seconds for up to 2 minutes until melted, but not too hot. Alternatively, melt it in a small heatproof bowl over a saucepan of barely simmering water.

3 Take the balls out of the refrigerator a few at a time. Dip them into the molten chocolate, turning them with 2 forks until covered. Take them out of the chocolate mixture and transfer them to the lined baking sheets to dry.

4 Continue the process until all of the balls are coated. You will have to work quickly at this stage, as the chocolate can harden quite quickly, and the cake balls can disintegrate if left in the warm chocolate for too long.

5 Melt the white chocolate cake covering as above. Using a teaspoon drop a little of the white chocolate mixture on to the top of the Christmas pudding balls, so that it looks as if they have been drizzled with icing, or snow! The white chocolate should drip down the sides, but not cover the dark chocolate.

6 If you are feeling ambitious, slivers of glacé cherries and candied angelica can be cut to resemble holly leaves and berries, and stuck to the still molten white chocolate. Leave the balls until the white chocolate is hard.

STORE The pudding balls will keep in the refrigerator for 5 days.

White Chocolate and Coconut Snowballs

These coconut balls are sophisticated enough to serve as canapés.

MAKES 25–30 | **40 MINS** | **25 MINS** | **4 WEEKS, UNDIPPED**

Chilling time
3 hrs, or 30 mins freezing

Special equipment
18cm (7in) round cake tin
food processor with blade attachment

Ingredients
100g (3½oz) unsalted butter, softened,
  or soft margarine, plus extra for greasing
100g (3½oz) caster sugar
2 eggs
100g (3½oz) self-raising flour
1 tsp baking powder
225g (8oz) ready-made buttercream frosting, or
  see vanilla buttercream, page 127, steps 13–15
225g (8oz) desiccated coconut
250g (9oz) white chocolate cake covering

Method
1 Preheat the oven to 180°C (350°F/Gas 4). Grease the tin and line the base with parchment. Cream the butter or margarine, and sugar until pale and fluffy. Beat in the eggs one at a time, beating well between each addition. Sift together the flour and baking powder, and fold into the cake batter.

2 Pour the batter into the tin and bake for 25 minutes. Turn out onto a wire rack to cool. Remove the baking parchment.

3 When the cake is cool, process until it resembles fine breadcrumbs. Weigh out 300g (10½oz) of the crumbs and put them in a bowl. Add the frosting and 75g (2½oz) of the desiccated coconut, and mix together.

4 Using dry hands, roll the mix into balls the size of a walnut. Refrigerate for 3 hours or freeze for 30 minutes. Line 2 baking trays with parchment and put the remaining coconut on a plate.

5 Melt the cake covering in a heatproof bowl over a pan of barely simmering water. Place the chilled cake balls, one at a time, into the melted chocolate mixture, using 2 forks to turn them until covered.

6 Transfer them to the plate of coconut. Roll them around in the coconut, then transfer to the baking tray to dry. You will have to work fast, as the chocolate can harden quickly, and the balls start to disintegrate if they are left in the chocolate too long.

STORE The cake balls will keep in a cool place in an airtight container for 2 days.

Whoopie Pies

Fast becoming a modern classic, whoopie pies are a quick and easy way to please a crowd.

| MAKES 10 PIES | 40 MINS | 12 MINS | 4 WEEKS, UNFILLED |

Ingredients

175g (6oz) unsalted butter, softened
150g (5½oz) soft light brown sugar
1 large egg
1 tsp vanilla extract
225g (8oz) self-raising flour
75g (2½oz) cocoa powder
1 tsp baking powder

150ml (5fl oz) whole milk
2 tbsp Greek yogurt or thick plain yogurt

For the vanilla buttercream

100g (3½oz) unsalted butter, softened
200g (7oz) icing sugar
2 tsp vanilla extract
2 tsp milk, plus extra if needed

To decorate

white and dark chocolate
200g (7oz) icing sugar

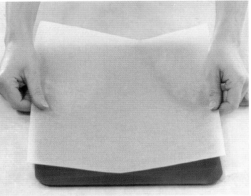

1 Preheat the oven to 180°C (350°F/Gas 4). Line several baking sheets with baking parchment.

2 With a whisk, cream together the butter and brown sugar until light and fluffy.

3 Add the egg and vanilla extract to the creamed mixture and beat in.

4 Beat the egg well to prevent curdling. The batter should appear smooth.

5 In a separate large bowl, sift together the flour, cocoa powder, and baking powder.

6 Gently fold a spoonful of the dry ingredients into the cake batter.

7 Add a little of the milk, mixing. Repeat until all the milk and dry ingredients are combined.

8 Blend in the thick yogurt, gently folding until well combined; this will moisten the pies.

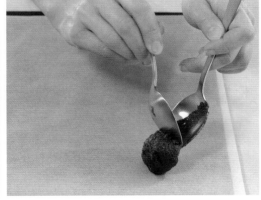

9 Place 20 heaped tablespoons of mixture on the lined baking sheets.

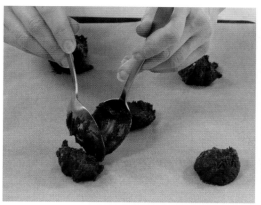

10 Leave space for the mixture to spread out; each half will spread to 8cm (3in).

11 Dip a clean tablespoon in warm water and use it to smooth the surface of the halves.

12 Bake for around 12 minutes until a skewer comes out clean. Cool on a wire rack.

13 Using a wooden spoon, mix together the buttercream ingredients, except the mik.

14 Changing to a whisk, beat the mix for about 5 minutes until light and fluffy.

15 If the mixture seems stiff, loosen with extra milk to make the buttercream spreadable.

16 Spread a tablespoon of the buttercream onto each of the flat sides of half the cakes.

17 Sandwich together the iced with the un-iced halves to form the pies, pressing gently.

18 To decorate, use a vegetable peeler to produce white and dark chocolate shavings.

19 Place the icing sugar in a bowl and add 1–2 tablespoons water to form a thick paste.

20 Spoon the icing onto the top each pie, spreading it out for an even covering.

21 Lightly press the chocolate shavings onto the wet icing. **STORE** Will keep for 2 days.

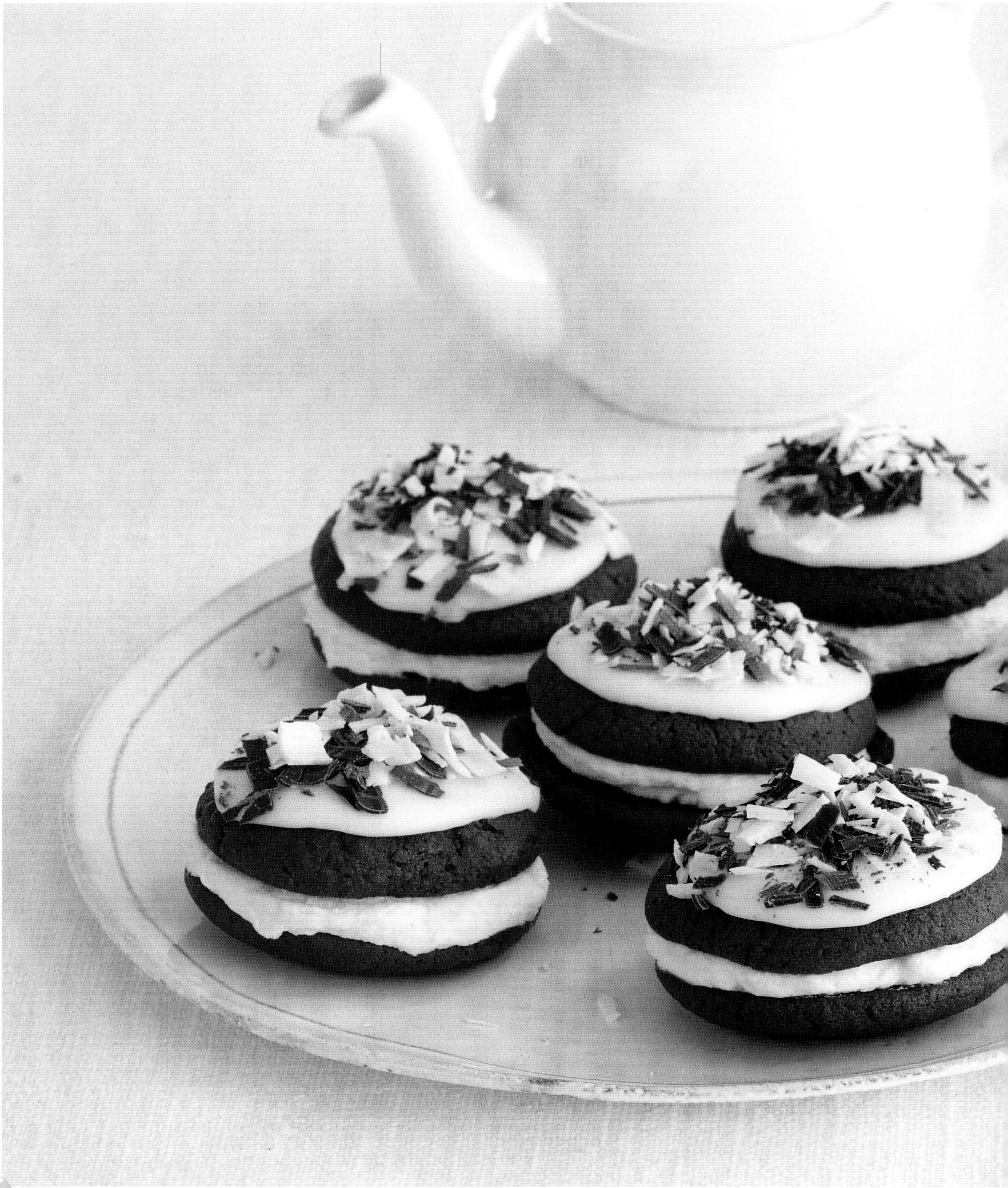

Whoopie Pie variations

Peanut Butter Whoopie Pies

Sweet, salty, and creamy, these whoopie pies are addictive.

MAKES 10 PIES | **40 MINS** | **12 MINS** | **4 WEEKS, UNFILLED**

Ingredients
175g (6oz) unsalted butter, softened
150g (5½oz) soft light brown sugar
1 large egg
1 tsp vanilla extract
225g (8oz) self-raising flour
75g (2½oz) cocoa powder
1 tsp baking powder
150ml (5fl oz) whole milk, plus extra for the filling
2 tbsp Greek yogurt or thick plain yogurt
50g (1¾oz) cream cheese
50g (1¾oz) smooth peanut butter
200g (7oz) icing sugar, sifted

Method
1 Preheat the oven to 180°C (350°F/Gas 4). Line several large baking sheets with baking parchment. Place the butter and sugar in a bowl, and cream together until fluffy. Beat in the egg and vanilla extract.

2 In another bowl, sift in the flour, cocoa powder, and baking powder. Mix the dry ingredients and the milk into the batter a spoonful at a time. Fold in the yogurt.

3 Put heaped tablespoons of the batter onto the baking sheets, leaving space for the mixture to spread. Dip a tablespoon in warm water and use the back to smooth over the surface of the pies. Bake for 12 minutes, until well risen. Turn out on a wire rack to cool.

4 For the filling, beat the cream cheese and peanut butter until smooth. Cream in the sugar, adding a little milk if necessary to make a spreadable consistency. Spread onto each of the flat sides of half the cakes. Sandwich together with the un-iced cakes.

STORE The whoopie pies will keep in the refrigerator for 1 day.

Chocolate Orange Whoopie Pies

Rich, dark chocolate combined with the zesty tang of orange is a classic combination, used here to full advantage in these delicious little cakes.

MAKES 10 PIES | **40 MINS** | **12 MINS** | **4 WEEKS, UNFILLED**

Ingredients
275g (9½oz) unsalted butter, softened
150g (5½oz) soft light brown sugar
1 large egg
2 tsp vanilla extract
finely grated zest and juice of 1 orange
225g (8oz) self-raising flour
75g (2½oz) cocoa powder
1 tsp baking powder
150ml (5fl oz) whole milk or buttermilk
2 tbsp Greek yogurt or thick plain yogurt
200g (7oz) icing sugar

Method
1 Preheat the oven to 180°C (350°F/Gas 4). Line several baking sheets with parchment. Cream 175g (6oz) butter and brown sugar until fluffy. Beat in the egg and 1 teaspoon vanilla, and add the zest. In a bowl, sift the flour, cocoa, and baking powder. Mix the dry ingredients and the milk into the batter, in alternate spoonfuls. Fold in the yogurt.

2 Place heaped tablespoons onto the baking sheets, leaving space between them. Dip a spoon in warm water and use the back to smooth the surface of the cake mounds. Bake for 12 minutes until risen. Leave to cool slightly, then transfer to a wire rack.

3 For the buttercream, blend the remaining butter, icing sugar, 1 teaspoon vanilla extract, and orange juice, loosening with a little water. Spread 1 tablespoon of the filling onto the flat side of each cake half, and sandwich together with the remaining halves.

STORE The whoopie pies will keep in an airtight container for 2 days.

Coconut Whoopie Pies

This simple yet delicious variation uses the natural affinity between coconut and chocolate to great effect.

MAKES 10 PIES | **40 MINS** | **12 MINS** | **4 WEEKS, UNFILLED**

Ingredients
275g (9½oz) unsalted butter, softened
150g (5½oz) soft light brown sugar
1 large egg
2 tsp vanilla extract
225g (8oz) self-raising flour
75g (2½oz) cocoa powder
1 tsp baking powder
150ml (5fl oz) whole milk, plus extra for filling
2 tbsp Greek yogurt or thick plain yogurt
200g (7oz) icing sugar
5 tbsp desiccated coconut

Method
1 Preheat the oven to 180°C (350°F/Gas 4). Line several baking sheets with parchment. Cream 175g (6oz) butter and sugar until fluffy, and beat in the egg and 1 teaspoon vanilla extract. In a bowl, sift the flour, cocoa powder, and baking powder. Mix the dry ingredients and the milk into the batter alternately, a spoonful at a time. Fold in the yogurt.

2 Put tablespoons of batter onto the sheets. Dip a tablespoon in warm water and use the back to smooth over the surface of the pies. Bake for 12 minutes, until risen. Leave to cool slightly, then transfer to a wire rack. Soak the coconut in enough milk to cover it, for 10 minutes until softened. Drain in a sieve.

3 For the buttercream, whisk the remaining butter, icing sugar, vanilla, and 2 teaspoons milk until fluffy. Beat in the coconut. Spread the icing on half the cakes and sandwich with the remaining halves.

STORE The whoopie pies will keep in an airtight container for 2 days.

Black Forest Whoopie Pies

A modern imitation of the famous gâteau, using tinned cherries.

MAKES 10 PIES	40 MINS	12 MINS	4 WEEKS, UNFILLED

Ingredients

175g (6oz) unsalted butter, softened
150g (5½oz) soft light brown sugar
1 large egg
1 tsp vanilla extract
225g (8oz) self-raising flour
75g (2½oz) cocoa powder
1 tsp baking powder
150ml (5fl oz) whole milk or buttermilk
2 tbsp Greek yogurt or thick plain yogurt
225g (8oz) tinned black cherries, drained, or use frozen, defrosted
250g (9oz) mascarpone cheese
2 tbsp caster sugar

Method

1 Preheat the oven to 180°C (350°F/Gas 4). Line several baking sheets with parchment. Cream 175g (6oz) butter and brown sugar until fluffy. Beat in the egg and vanilla extract.

2 In a bowl, sift the flour, cocoa, and baking powder. Mix the dry ingredients and the milk into the batter, in alternate spoonfuls. Fold in the yogurt. Chop 100g (3½oz) of the cherries and fold these in too.

3 Place heaped tablespoons onto the baking sheets, leaving space between them. Dip a spoon in warm water and use the back to smooth the surface of the cakes. Bake for 12 minutes until well risen. Leave to cool slightly, then transfer to a wire rack.

4 Purée the remaining cherries until smooth. Mix the blended cherries and sugar into the mascarpone until well mixed; alternatively, leave a ripple effect in the filling. Spread 1 tablespoon of the filling onto the flat side of each cooled cake half, and sandwich together with the remaining halves.

STORE Best eaten the day of baking but can be stored for 1 day in the refrigerator.

Strawberries and Cream Whoopie Pies

Best served immediately, these strawberry layered whoopie pies make a lovely addition to a traditional afternoon tea.

MAKES 10 PIES	40 MINS	12 MINS	4 WEEKS, UNFILLED

Ingredients

175g (6oz) unsalted butter, softened
150g (5½oz) soft light brown sugar
1 large egg
1 tsp vanilla extract
225g (8oz) self-raising flour
75g (2½oz) cocoa powder
1 tsp baking powder
150ml (8fl oz) whole milk
2 tbsp Greek yogurt or thick plain yogurt
150ml (5fl oz) double cream, whipped
250g (9oz) strawberries, thinly sliced
icing sugar, for dusting

Method

1 Preheat the oven to 180°C (350°F/Gas 4). Line several baking sheets with parchment. Cream the butter and sugar until fluffy. Beat in the egg and vanilla extract. In a bowl, sift together the flour, cocoa, and baking powder. Mix the dry ingredients and the milk into the batter alternately, a spoonful at a time. Fold in the yogurt.

2 Put heaped tablespoons of the batter onto the baking sheets, leaving space for the mixture to spread. Dip a tablespoon in warm water and use the back to smooth over the surface of the pies.

3 Bake for 12 minutes, until well risen. Leave the pies for a few minutes, then turn out onto a wire rack to cool.

4 Spread the cream onto half the cakes. Top with a layer of strawberries and a second cake. Dust with icing sugar and serve. These do not store and should be eaten on the day.

Chocolate Fondants

Usually thought of as a restaurant dessert, chocolate fondants are actually surprisingly easy to prepare at home.

Special equipment
4 x 150ml (5fl oz) dariole moulds
or 10cm (4in) ramekins

Ingredients
150g (5½oz) unsalted butter, cubed,
plus extra for greasing

1 heaped tbsp plain flour, plus extra for sprinkling
150g (5½oz) good-quality dark chocolate,
broken into pieces
3 large eggs
75g (2½oz) caster sugar
cocoa powder or icing sugar, for dusting (optional)
cream or ice cream, to serve (optional)

Method

1 Preheat the oven to 200°C (400°F/Gas 6). Thoroughly grease the sides and base of each dariole mould or ramekin. Sprinkle the insides with a little flour, then turn the flour around in the dish until all the butter is covered with a thin layer of flour. Tip out the excess flour. Line the bases of the moulds with small discs of baking parchment.

2 Gently melt together the chocolate and butter in a heatproof bowl over simmering water, stirring occasionally. Make sure the base of the bowl does not touch the water. Cool slightly.

3 In a separate bowl, whisk together the eggs and sugar. Once the chocolate mixture has cooled slightly, beat it into the eggs and sugar until thoroughly combined. Sift the flour over the top of the mixture and gently fold it in.

4 Divide the mixture between the moulds, making sure that the mixture does not come right up to the top. At this stage the

fondants can be refrigerated for several hours or overnight, as long as they are brought back to room temperature before cooking.

5 Cook the fondants in the middle of the oven for 5–6 minutes if using moulds, 12–15 minutes for ramekins. The sides should be firm, but the middles soft to the touch. Run a sharp knife around the edge of the moulds or ramekins. Turn the fondants out onto individual serving plates by putting a plate on top and inverting the whole thing. Gently remove each mould or ramekin and peel off the parchment.

6 Dust with cocoa powder or icing sugar, if desired, and serve immediately with cream or ice cream.

PREPARE AHEAD The uncooked mixture in the moulds or ramekins can be refrigerated overnight (see Baker's Tip).

BAKER'S TIP

Chocolate fondants are surprisingly simple to get right. They can be prepared up to a day in advance, which makes them a great dinner party dessert. Be sure to bring them back to room temperature before putting into the oven, or they may need cooking for slightly longer.

SMALL CAKES

Lemon and Blueberry Muffins

These featherlight muffins are glazed with lemon juice for an extra burst of flavour. Best served warm.

MAKES 12 **20–25 MINS** **15–20 MINS** **UP TO 4 WEEKS**

Special equipment
12-hole muffin tin

Ingredients
60g (2oz) unsalted butter
280g (10oz) plain flour
1 tbsp baking powder
pinch of salt
200g (7oz) caster sugar
1 egg
finely grated zest and juice of 1 lemon
1 tsp vanilla extract
250ml (8fl oz) milk
225g (8oz) blueberries

SMALL CAKES

1 Preheat the oven to 220°C (425°F/Gas 7). Melt the butter in a pan over a medium-low heat.

2 Sift the flour, baking powder, and salt into a bowl (do not make muffins in a food mixer).

3 Set 2 tablespoons sugar aside and stir the rest into the flour. Make a well in the centre.

4 In a separate bowl, beat the egg lightly until just broken down and mixed together.

5 Add the melted butter, lemon zest, vanilla, and milk. Beat the egg mixture until foamy.

6 In a slow, steady stream, pour the egg mixture into the well in the flour.

7 Stir with a rubber spatula, gradually drawing in the dry ingredients to make a smooth batter.

8 Gently fold in all the blueberries, taking care not to bruise any of the fruits.

9 Do not over-mix, or the muffins will be tough. Stop when the ingredients are blended.

10 Place the muffin cases in the tin. Spoon in the batter, filling to three-quarters full.

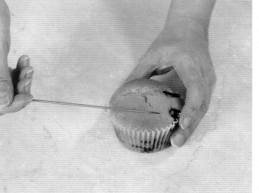

11 Bake for 15–20 minutes until a skewer inserted in the centre comes out clean.

12 Let the muffins cool slightly, then transfer them to a wire rack.

13 In a small bowl, stir the reserved sugar with the lemon juice until the sugar dissolves.

14 While the muffins are warm, dip the crown of each into the sugar and lemon mixture.

15 Set the muffins upright back on the wire rack and brush with any remaining glaze.

16 The warm muffins will absorb the maximum amount of the lemony glaze.
STORE Best served warm but will keep in an airtight container for 2 days.

Muffin variations

Chocolate Muffins

These muffins will fix chocolate cravings, and the buttermilk lends a delicious lightness.

| MAKES 12 | 10 MINS | 15 MINS | UP TO 8 WEEKS |

Special equipment
12-hole muffin tin

Ingredients
225g (8oz) plain flour
60g (2oz) cocoa powder
1 tbsp baking powder
pinch of salt
115g (4oz) soft light brown sugar
150g (5½oz) chocolate chips
250ml (8fl oz) buttermilk
6 tbsp sunflower oil
½ tsp vanilla extract
2 eggs

Method
1 Preheat the oven to 200°C (400°F/Gas 6). Line the muffin tin with the paper cases and set aside. Sift the flour, cocoa powder, baking powder, and salt into a large bowl. Stir in the sugar and chocolate chips, and then make a well in the centre of the dry ingredients.

2 Beat together the buttermilk, oil, vanilla, and eggs, and pour the mixture into the centre of the dry ingredients. Mix together lightly to make a lumpy batter. Spoon the mixture into the paper cases, filling each three-quarters full.

3 Bake for 15 minutes or until well risen and firm to the touch. Immediately transfer the muffins to a wire rack and leave to cool.

STORE The muffins will keep in an airtight container for 2 days.

BAKER'S TIP
The use of liquid in these muffins, whether soured cream, buttermilk, or oil, will ensure a moist, longer-lasting cake. If a recipe calls for oil, make sure that you use a light, flavourless one such as sunflower or groundnut, to ensure that the delicious flavours of the muffins are not masked by the taste of the oil.

Lemon and Poppy Seed Muffins

Poppy seeds add a pleasing crunch to these delicate muffins.

| MAKES 12 | 20–25 MINS | 15–20 MINS | UP TO 4 WEEKS |

Special equipment
12-hole muffin tin

Ingredients
60g (2oz) unsalted butter
280g (10oz) plain flour
1 tbsp baking powder
pinch of salt
200g (7oz) caster sugar, plus 2 tsp for sprinkling
1 egg, beaten
1 tsp vanilla extract
250ml (8fl oz) milk
2 tbsp poppy seeds
finely grated zest and juice of 1 lemon

Method
1 Preheat the oven to 220°C (425°F/Gas 7). Melt the butter in a pan over medium-low heat, then leave to cool slightly. Sift the flour, baking powder, and salt into a bowl. Stir in the sugar and make a well in the centre.

2 Put the egg in a separate bowl. Add in the melted butter, vanilla, and milk, and beat the mixture until foamy. Stir in the poppy seeds, and the lemon zest and juice.

3 Pour the egg mixture into the well in the flour. Stir to make a smooth batter, but do not over-mix. Stop as soon as the ingredients are blended.

4 Place muffin cases in the muffin tin. Spoon the batter evenly between the cases and sprinkle with 2 teaspoons of sugar.

5 Bake for 15–20 minutes until a skewer inserted in the centre of a muffin comes out clean. Let the muffins cool slightly, then transfer them (in their cases) to a wire rack to cool completely.

STORE The muffins will keep in an airtight container for 2 days.

Apple Muffins

These healthy muffins are best served straight from the oven.

| MAKES 12 | 10 MINS | 20–25 MINS | UP TO 8 WEEKS |

Special equipment
12-hole muffin tin

Ingredients
1 Golden Delicious apple, peeled, cored, and chopped
2 tsp lemon juice
115g (4oz) light demerara sugar, plus extra for sprinkling
200g (7oz) plain flour
85g (3oz) wholemeal flour
4 tsp baking powder
1 tbsp ground mixed spice
½ tsp salt
60g (2oz) pecan nuts, chopped
250ml (8fl oz) milk
4 tbsp sunflower oil
1 egg, beaten

Method
1 Preheat the oven to 200°C (400°F/Gas 6). Line the muffin tin with the paper cases and set aside. Put the apple in a bowl, add the lemon juice, and toss. Add 4 tablespoons of the sugar and set aside for 5 minutes.

2 Sift both the flours, baking powder, mixed spice, and salt into a large bowl, tipping in any bran left in the sieve. Stir in the sugar and pecans, then make a well in the centre of the dry ingredients.

3 Beat the milk, oil, and egg well, then add the apple. Tip the wet ingredients into the well of the flour and mix to a lumpy batter.

4 Spoon the mixture into the paper cases, filling each case three-quarters full. Bake the muffins for 20–25 minutes or until the tops are peaked and brown. Transfer all the muffins to a wire rack and sprinkle with extra sugar. Eat warm or cooled.

STORE The muffins will keep in an airtight container for 2 days.

Madeleines

These elegant treats were made famous by French writer Marcel Proust, who took a bite and was transported back to his childhood.

| MAKES 12 | 15–20 MINS | 10 MINS | UP TO 4 WEEKS |

Special equipment
madeleine tin, or small 12-hole bun tin

Ingredients

60g (2oz) unsalted butter, melted and cooled,
   plus extra for greasing
60g (2oz) self-raising flour, sifted,
   plus extra for dusting
60g (2oz) caster sugar
2 eggs
1 tsp vanilla extract
icing sugar, for dusting

Method

1 Preheat the oven to 180°C (350°F/Gas 4). Carefully brush the tin with melted butter and dust with a little flour. Invert the tin and tap to remove excess flour.

2 Put the sugar, eggs, and vanilla into a mixing bowl. Using an electric whisk, mix for 5 minutes until the mixture is pale, thick, and holds a trail.

3 Sift the flour over the top and pour the melted butter down the side of the mixture. Using a large metal spoon, fold them in carefully and quickly, being careful not to knock out too much air.

4 Fill the moulds with the mixture and bake in the oven for 10 minutes. Remove from the oven and transfer to a wire rack to cool, before dusting with icing sugar.

STORE The madeleines will keep in an airtight container for 1 day.

> **BAKER'S TIP**
> These delightful little treats are meant to be as light as air. Care should be taken to incorporate as much air as possible into the batter at the whisking stage, and to lose as little volume from the batter when folding in the flour.

SMALL CAKES

Scones

Home-made scones are one of the simplest and best teatime treats. Buttermilk makes the lightest scones.

MAKES 6–8 | **15–20 MINS** | **12–15 MINS** | **UP TO 4 WEEKS**

Special equipment
7cm (2¾in) pastry cutter

Ingredients
60g (2oz) unsalted butter, chilled and cut into pieces, plus extra for greasing
250g (9oz) strong white bread flour, plus extra for dusting
2 tsp baking powder

½ tsp salt
175ml (6fl oz) buttermilk
butter, jam, and clotted or thick double cream, to serve (optional)

1 Preheat the oven to 220°C (425°F/Gas 7). Line a baking sheet with parchment and grease.

2 Sift the flour, baking powder, and salt into a large chilled bowl.

3 Put the butter in the bowl, keeping all ingredients as cold as possible.

4 Rub with your fingertips until it forms fine crumbs, working quickly, lifting to aerate it.

5 Make a well in the centre and in a slow, steady stream, pour the buttermilk into it.

6 Quickly toss the flour mixture and buttermilk with a fork. Do not over-mix.

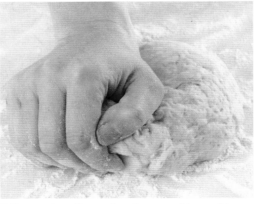

7 Stir the mixture till the crumbs form a dough. Add a little more buttermilk if it seems dry.

8 Turn onto a floured surface and knead for a few seconds. Keep it rough, not smooth.

9 Pat the dough out to a round 2cm (¾in) thick, keeping it as cool and unworked as you can.

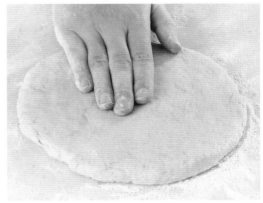

SMALL CAKES

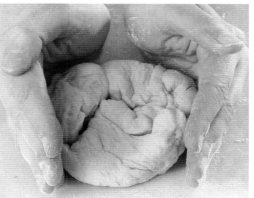

10 Cut out rounds with the pastry cutter; see Baker's Tip, page 142.

11 Pat out the trimmings and cut additional rounds until all the dough has been used.

12 Arrange the scones so they are about 5cm (2in) apart on the prepared baking sheet.

13 Bake in the preheated oven for 12–15 minutes until lightly browned and risen. Scones should be eaten the day they are baked, ideally still warm from the oven. Spread with butter, jam, and clotted cream or thick double cream.

Scone variations

Currant Scones

Serve these currant-studded scones straight from the oven, spread with butter or clotted cream.

| MAKES 6 | 15–20 MINS | 12–15 MINS | UP TO 4 WEEKS |

Ingredients

60g (2oz) unsalted butter, chilled and diced, plus extra for greasing
1 egg yolk, for glazing
175ml (6fl oz) buttermilk, plus 1 tbsp for glazing
250g (9oz) strong white bread flour, plus extra for dusting
2 tsp baking powder
½ tsp salt
¼ tsp bicarbonate of soda
2 tsp caster sugar
2 tbsp currants

Method

1 Preheat the oven to 220°C (425°F/Gas 7), and grease a baking sheet with butter. Beat the egg yolk and a tablespoon of buttermilk together, and set aside.

2 Sift the flour, baking powder, salt, and bicarbonate of soda into a bowl, and add the sugar. Add the butter and rub the mixture with your fingertips until it forms fine crumbs. Stir in the currants. Pour in the buttermilk and quickly toss the mixture with a fork to form crumbs. Stir just until the crumbs hold together and form a dough.

3 Transfer the dough to a floured work surface. Cut it in half and pat each half into a 15cm (6in) round, about 2cm (¾in) thick. With a sharp knife, cut each round into 4 wedges. Arrange the wedges about 5cm (2in) apart on the baking sheet, and brush with glaze.

4 Bake for 12–15 minutes, until lightly browned. Leave for a few minutes on the baking sheet, then transfer to a wire rack to cool. Best eaten warm the same day.

BAKER'S TIP

One of the secrets to well-risen scones is in the way they are cut. It is best to use a sharp pastry cutter, preferably made of metal, or sharp knife as here. They should be cut with a strong downward motion, and the cutter should not be twisted at all when cutting. This ensures a high, even rise on cooking.

Cheese and Parsley Scones

Basic scone mix is easily adapted for a tasty savoury variation.

| 20 SMALL OR 6 BIG | 20 MINS | 8–10 MINS | UP TO 12 WEEKS |

Special equipment

4cm (1½in) pastry cutter for small scones, or 6cm (2½in) pastry cutter for large scones

Ingredients

oil, for greasing
225g (8oz) plain flour, sifted, plus extra for dusting
1 tsp baking powder
pinch of salt
50g (1¾oz) unsalted butter, chilled and cubed
1 tsp dried parsley
1 tsp black peppercorns, crushed
50g (1¾oz) mature Cheddar cheese, grated
110ml (3½fl oz) milk

Method

1 Preheat the oven to 220°C (425°F/Gas 7). Lightly oil a medium-sized baking sheet. In a large bowl, mix together the flour, baking powder, and salt. Add the butter, and using your fingertips, rub it in until the mixture resembles fine breadcrumbs.

2 Stir in the parsley, pepper, and half the cheese. Then add enough milk to bind and make the dough come together (reserve the rest for brushing the tops of the scones). Lightly mix into a soft dough.

3 Roll out the dough on a lightly floured surface to a thickness of about 2cm (¾in). Using your chosen pastry cutter, cut out rounds (see Baker's Tip). Sit them on the prepared baking sheet, brush with the remaining milk, and sprinkle over the remaining cheese.

4 Bake on the top shelf of the oven for 8–10 minutes until golden. Leave on the baking sheet for a couple of minutes to cool a little, then either serve warm or cool completely on a wire rack. These scones are best eaten the same day.

Strawberry Shortcakes

These shortcakes are perfect served as a light summer dessert.

MAKES 6 | **15–20 MINS** | **12–15 MINS** | **4 WEEKS, UNFILLED**

Special equipment
8cm (3in) pastry cutter

Ingredients
60g (2oz) unsalted butter, plus extra for greasing
250g (9oz) plain flour, sifted, plus extra for dusting
1 tbsp baking powder
½ tsp salt
45g (1½oz) caster sugar
175ml (6fl oz) double cream, plus extra if needed

For the coulis
500g (1lb 2oz) strawberries, hulled
2–3 tbsp icing sugar
2 tbsp Kirsch (optional)

For the filling
500g (1lb 2oz) strawberries, hulled and sliced
45g (1½oz) caster sugar, plus 2–3 tbsp
250ml (8fl oz) double cream
1 tsp vanilla essence

Method

1 Preheat the oven to 220°C (425°F/Gas 7). Butter a baking sheet. In a bowl, mix the flour, baking powder, salt, and sugar. Rub to form crumbs. Add cream, tossing; add more, if dry. Add the butter and rub in with your fingertips to form crumbs.

2 Press the crumbs together to form a ball of dough. On a floured surface, lightly knead the dough. Pat out a round, 1cm (½in) thick, and cut out 6 rounds with the cutter (see Baker's Tip). Transfer to the baking sheet and bake for 12–15 minutes. Cool on a wire rack.

3 For the coulis, purée the strawberries, then stir in the icing sugar and Kirsch (if using).

4 For the filling, mix the strawberries and sugar. Whip the cream until soft peaks form. Add 2–3 tablespoons of sugar and the vanilla. Whip until stiff. Cut the cakes in half. Put the strawberries on the bottom halves, followed by the cream. Top each with its lid. Pour the coulis around. Serve immediately.

Welsh Cakes

These traditional small cakes from Wales take minutes to prepare and cook, and you don't even have to remember to preheat the oven.

24 SMALL CAKES | **20 MINS** | **16–24 MINS** | **UP TO 4 WEEKS**

Special equipment
5cm (2in) pastry cutter

Ingredients
200g (7oz) self-raising flour,
    plus extra for dusting
100g (3½oz) unsalted butter,
    chilled and diced, plus extra for frying
75g (2½oz) caster sugar, plus extra for dusting
75g (2½oz) sultanas
1 large egg, beaten
a little milk, if needed

Method

1 Sift the flour into a large bowl. Rub the butter into the flour until the mixture resembles fine breadcrumbs. Mix in the sugar and the sultanas. Pour in the egg.

2 Mix the ingredients together, bringing the mixture into a ball using your hands. This should be firm enough to roll out, but if it seems too stiff add a little milk.

3 On a floured work surface, roll out the dough to about 5mm (¼in) thick and cut out disks, using the pastry cutter.

4 Heat a large, heavy frying pan, cast iron skillet, or flat griddle over medium-low heat. Fry the cakes, in batches, in a little melted butter for 2–3 minutes on each side, until they puff up, are golden brown, and cooked through.

5 While still warm, generously dust the cakes with a little caster sugar, before serving. Welsh cakes are best eaten immediately. If you freeze them, reheat in the oven after defrosting.

BAKER'S TIP
Welsh cakes are an easy afternoon treat, and can be ready to eat within minutes. Cook them over fairly low heat, and be extremely careful when turning them over to cook on the second side as the self-raising flour makes them very fragile at this stage. Delicious eaten immediately with butter.

SMALL CAKES

Rock Cakes

It's high time these classic British buns enjoyed a renaissance. Correctly cooked, they are light, crumbly, and incredibly simple to make.

| MAKES 12 | 15 MINS | 15–20 MINS | UP TO 4 WEEKS |

Ingredients

200g (7oz) self-raising flour
pinch of salt
100g (3½oz) unsalted butter, chilled and diced
75g (2½oz) caster sugar
100g (3½oz) mixed dried fruit
   (raisins, sultanas, and mixed peel)
2 eggs
2 tbsp milk, plus extra if needed
½ tsp vanilla extract
butter or jam, to serve (optional)

Method

1 Preheat the oven to 190°C (375°F/Gas 5). In a large bowl, rub together the flour, salt, and butter until the mixture resembles fine breadcrumbs. Mix in the sugar. Add the dried fruit and mix throughly.

2 In a jug, whisk together the eggs, milk, and vanilla extract. Make a well in the centre of the flour mixture and pour the egg mixture into it. Combine thoroughly to produce a firm mixture. Use a little more milk if the mixture seems too stiff.

3 Line 2 baking sheets with parchment. Place large heaped tablespoons of the mixture onto the baking sheets, leaving space for the cakes to spread. Bake in the centre of the oven for 15–20 minutes until golden brown.

4 Remove to a wire rack to cool slightly. Split and serve warm, split. Spread with butter or jam. Rock cakes should be eaten the day they are baked as they do not store well.

BAKER'S TIP

These easy-to-make cakes are named after their classic, rugged shape, rather than their texture! Make sure that the mixture is piled at least 5–7cm (2–3in) high on the baking sheet, which will ensure the classic rough edges even after they have spread out on baking.

SMALL CAKES

patisserie

Croissants

Although these take some time to make, the final result is well worth the effort. Start a day ahead.

MAKES 12 · **1 HOUR** · **15–20 MINS** · **4 WEEKS, UNBAKED**

Chilling time
5 hrs, plus overnight

Rising time
1 hr

Ingredients
300g (10½oz) strong white bread
  flour, plus extra for dusting
½ tsp salt
30g (1oz) caster sugar
2½ tsp dried yeast
vegetable oil, for greasing
250g (9oz) unsalted butter, chilled
1 egg, beaten
butter or jam, to serve (optional)

1 Place the flour, salt, sugar, and yeast in a large bowl, and stir to blend well.

2 Using a table knife, mix in enough warm water, a little at a time, to form a soft dough.

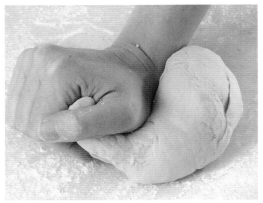

3 Knead on a lightly floured surface until the dough becomes elastic under your hands.

4 Place back in the bowl, cover with lightly oiled cling film, and chill for 1 hour.

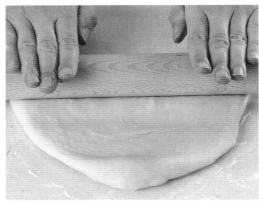

5 Roll the dough out into a rectangle that measures 30 x 15cm (12 x 6in).

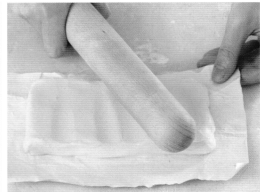

6 Squash the chilled butter with a rolling pin, keeping the pat shape, until 1cm (½in) thick.

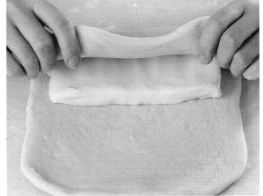

7 Place the butter in the centre of the dough. Fold the dough over it. Chill for 1 hour.

8 Roll out the dough on a lightly floured surface to a 30 x 15cm (12 x 6in) rectangle.

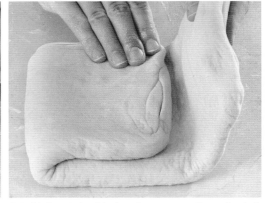

9 Fold the right third to the centre, then the left third over the top. Chill for 1 hour until firm.

PATISSERIE

10 Repeat the rolling, folding, and chilling twice. Wrap in cling film and chill overnight.

11 Cut the dough in half and roll out 1 half to a 12 x 36cm (5 x 14½in) rectangle.

12 Cut into 3 x 12cm (1 x 5in) squares, then cut diagonally to make 6 triangles. Repeat.

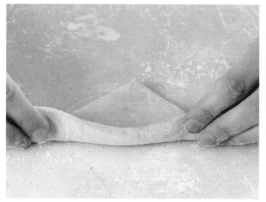

13 Holding the ends of the longest side, roll it towards you. Curve into cresent shapes.

14 Place on baking trays lined with baking parchment, leaving space between each.

15 Cover with lightly oiled cling film. Leave for 1 hour until doubled in size. Remove the film.

16 Preheat the oven to 220°C (425°F/Gas 7). Brush them with egg, then bake for 10 minutes.

17 Reduce the temperature to 190°C (375°F/Gas 5) and bake for another 5–10 minutes.

STORE The croissants are best served when still warm, with butter and jam, but will keep in an airtight container for 2 days; gently reheat to serve.

Croissant variations

Pains au chocolat

Fresh pains au chocolat, still warm from the oven and oozing with molten chocolate, make the ultimate weekend breakfast treat.

MAKES 8	1 HOUR	15–20 MINS	UP TO 4 WEEKS

Chilling time
5 hrs, plus overnight

Rising time
1 hr

Ingredients
1 quantity croissant dough,
  see pages 150–151, steps 1–10
200g (7oz) dark chocolate
1 egg, beaten

Method

1 Divide the dough into 4 equal pieces and roll each out into a rectangle, about 10 x 40cm (4 x 16in). Cut each piece in half, to give 8 rectangles approximately 10 x 20cm (4 x 8in).

2 Cut the chocolate into 16 even-sized strips. Two 100g bars can be easily divided into 8 strips each. Mark each piece of pastry along the long edge at one-third and two-thirds stages.

3 Put a piece of chocolate at the one-third mark, and fold the short end of the dough over it to the two-thirds mark. Now place a second piece of chocolate on top of the folded edge at the two-thirds mark, brush the dough next to it with beaten egg and fold the other side of the dough into the centre, making a triple-layered parcel with strips of chocolate tucked in on either side. Seal all the edges together to prevent the chocolate from oozing out while cooking.

4 Line a baking tray with parchment, place the pastries on it, cover and leave to rise in a warm place for 1 hour until puffed up and nearly doubled in size. Preheat the oven to 220°C (425°F/Gas 7). Brush the pastries with beaten egg and bake in the oven for 10 minutes, then reduce the oven temperature to 190°C (375°F/Gas 5). Bake for another 5–10 minutes, or until golden brown.

STORE The pastries will keep in an airtight container for 1 day.

Cheese and Chorizo Croissants

Spicy chorizo combined with tangy cheese is used here to great effect.

MAKES 8	1 HOUR	15–20 MINS	UP TO 4 WEEKS

Chilling time
5 hrs, plus overnight

Rising time
1 hr

Ingredients
1 quantity croissant dough,
  see pages 150–151, steps 1–10
8 slices chorizo, ham, or Parma ham
8 slices cheese, such as Emmental
  or Jarlsberg
1 egg, beaten

Method

1 Divide the dough into 4 equal pieces and roll each out into a rectangle, about 10 x 40cm (4 x 16in). Cut each piece in half, to give 8 rectangles approximately 10 x 20cm (4 x 8in).

2 Place a slice of chorizo or ham on the middle of each croissant and fold one side over it. Place a slice of cheese on the folded over piece, brush with beaten egg and fold the remaining side over it. Seal all the edges. Cover and leave in a warm place for 1 hour or until doubled in size. Preheat the oven to 220°C (425°F/Gas 7).

3 Brush the pastries with egg and bake for 10 minutes, then reduce the temperature to 190°C (375°F/Gas 5). Bake for a further 5–10 minutes or until golden brown.

STORE Keep in an airtight container for 1 day.

BAKER'S TIP
These pastries are endlessly adaptable and can be made with a variety of fillings. Ham and cheese are the most common, but try using a layer of smoked ham and a layer of overlapped chorizo, and sprinkling with smoked paprika, for a more piquant flavour.

Croissants aux amandes

These frangipane-stuffed pastries are light and delicious.

MAKES 12	1 HOUR	15–20 MINS	UP TO 4 WEEKS

Chilling time
5 hrs, plus overnight

Rising time
1 hr

Ingredients
25g (scant 1oz) unsalted butter, softened
75g (2½oz) caster sugar
75g (2½oz) ground almonds
2–3 tbsp milk, if needed
1 quantity croissant dough,
  see pages 150–151, steps 1–10
1 egg, beaten
50g (1¾oz) flaked almonds
icing sugar, to serve

Method

1 For the almond paste, cream the butter and sugar, and blend in the ground almonds. Add milk if the mixture is too thick.

2 Cut the dough into 2 and roll half out on a floured surface to a 12 x 36cm (5 x 14½in) rectangle. Cut into three 12cm (5in) squares, then cut diagonally to make 6 triangles. Repeat to make 6 more triangles.

3 Spread a spoonful of the paste onto each triangle, leaving a 2cm (¾in) border along the 2 longest sides. Brush the borders with egg. Roll the croissant up carefully from the longest side towards the opposite point.

4 Line 2 baking sheets with parchment and place the croissants on them. Cover and leave in a warm place for 1 hour till doubled. Preheat the oven to 220°C (425°F/Gas 7).

5 Brush the croissants with egg. Sprinkle with flaked almonds. Bake for 10 minutes, then reduce the temperature to 190°C (375°F/Gas 5). Bake for 5–10 minutes until golden. Cool. Dust with icing sugar to serve.

STORE Keep in an airtight container for 1 day.

CROISSANT VARIATIONS

Danish Pastries

Although these deliciously buttery pastries take time to prepare, the home-baked taste is incomparable.

MAKES 18   **30 MINS**   **15–20 MINS**   **UP TO 4 WEEKS**

Chilling time
1 hr

Rising time
30 mins

Ingredients
150ml (5fl oz) warm milk
2 tsp dried yeast
30g (1oz) caster sugar
2 eggs, plus 1 egg for glazing
475g (1lb 1oz) strong white bread
 flour, sifted, plus extra for dusting
½ tsp salt
vegetable oil, for greasing

250g (9 oz) chilled butter
200g (7oz) good-quality cherry,
 strawberry, or apricot jam,
 or compote

1 Mix the milk, yeast, and 1 tablespoon sugar. Cover for 20 minutes, then beat in the eggs.

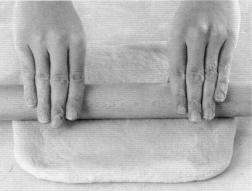

2 Place the flour, salt, and remaining sugar in a bowl. Make a well and pour in the yeast mix.

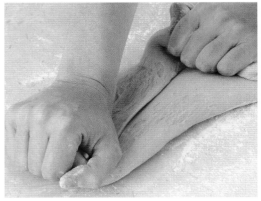

3 Mix the ingredients into a soft dough. Knead for 15 minutes on a floured surface until soft.

4 Place the dough in a lightly oiled bowl, cover with cling film and refrigerate for 15 minutes.

5 On a lightly floured surface, roll the dough out to a square, about 25 x 25cm (10 x 10in).

6 Cut the butter into 3–4 slices, each about 12 x 6 x 1cm (5 x 2½ x ½in).

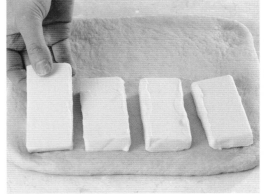

7 Lay the butter slices on one-half of the dough, leaving a border of 1–2cm (½–¾in).

8 Fold the other half of the dough over the top, pressing the edges with a rolling pin to seal.

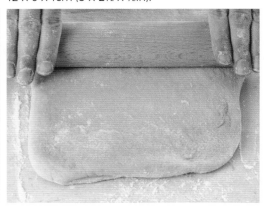

9 Generously flour and roll it into a rectangle 3 times as long as it is wide, and 1cm (½in) thick.

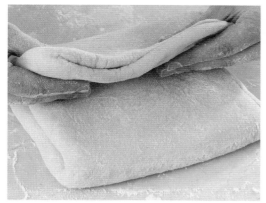

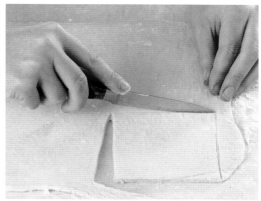

10 Fold the top third down into the middle, then the bottom third back over it.

11 Wrap, chill for 15 minutes. Repeat steps 9–10 twice, chilling for 15 minutes each time.

12 Roll onto a floured surface to 5mm–1cm (¼-½in) thick. Cut to 10 x 10cm (4 x 4in) squares.

13 With a sharp knife, make diagonal cuts from each corner to within 1cm (½in) of the centre.

14 Put 1 teaspoon of jam in the centre of each square and fold each corner into the centre.

15 Spoon more jam on the centre, transfer to a lined baking tray, and cover with a tea towel.

16 Leave in a warm place for 30 minutes until risen. Preheat the oven to 200°C (400°F/Gas 6).

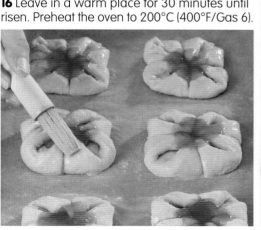

17 Brush with egg wash and bake at the top of the oven for 15–20 minutes until golden.

18 Leave to cool slighty then transfer to a wire rack. **STORE** These will keep in an airtight container for 2 days. **PREPARE AHEAD** Make up to end of step 11 and refrigerate overnight.

Danish Pastry variations

Almond Crescents

Butter, sugar, and ground almonds are combined here to make a delicious filling for these light and flaky, crescent-shaped Danish pastries. The pastry can be prepared the night before, ready for rolling.

MAKES 18	30 MINS	15–20 MINS	UP TO 4 WEEKS

Chilling time
1 hr

Rising time
30 mins

Ingredients
1 quantity danish pastry dough, see pages 154–155, steps 1–11
1 egg, beaten, for glazing
icing sugar, to serve

For almond paste
25g (scant 1oz) unsalted butter, softened
75g (2½oz) caster sugar
75g (2½oz) ground almonds

Method

1 Preheat the oven to 200°C (400°F/Gas 6). Roll half the dough out on a floured surface to a 30cm (12in) square. Trim the edges and cut out nine 10cm (4in) squares. Repeat with the remaining dough.

2 For the almond paste, cream together the butter and caster sugar, then beat in the ground almonds until smooth. Divide the paste into 18 small balls. Roll each one into a sausage shape a little shorter than the length of the dough squares. Place a roll of the paste at one edge of the square, leaving a gap of 2cm (¾in) between it and the edge. Press it down.

3 Brush the clear edge with egg and fold the pastry over the paste, pressing it down. Use a sharp knife to make 4 cuts into the folded edge to within 1½–2cm (½–¾in) of the sealed edge. Transfer to lined baking sheets, cover, and leave in a warm place for 30 minutes, or until puffed. Bend the edges in.

4 Brush with egg and bake in the top third of the oven for 15–20 minutes, until golden brown. Cool. Dust icing sugar over to serve.

STORE The pastries will keep in an airtight container for 2 days.

BAKER'S TIP
Danish pastry recipes often call for the butter to be rolled out between pieces of parchment or bashed with a rolling pin to render it pliable. This is a time-consuming business. Use sliced chilled butter instead, for a fuss-free result.

Cinnamon and Pecan Pinwheels

Try substituting hazelnuts or walnuts here if pecans are unavailable.

| MAKES 16 | 30 MINS | 15–20 MINS | UP TO 4 WEEKS |

Chilling time
1 hr

Rising time
30 mins

Ingredients
1 quantity danish pastry dough,
  see pages 154–155, steps 1–11
1 egg, beaten, for glazing
100g (3½oz) pecan nuts, chopped
100g (3½oz) soft light brown sugar
2 tbsp cinnamon
25g (scant 1oz) unsalted butter, melted

Method

1 To make the filling, mix the pecans, sugar, and cinnamon. Roll half the dough out on a floured work surface to a 20cm (8in) square. Trim the edges, brush the surface with half the butter and scatter half the pecan mixture over the top, leaving a 1cm (½in) border at the long side that is farthest from you. Brush the border with a little egg.

2 Press the pecan mixture with the palm of your hand to ensure it sticks to the dough. Roll the dough up, starting with the long side and working towards the border. Turn seam-side down. Repeat.

3 Trim the ends and cut each into 8 slices. Turn over and press them to allow the edges to stick. Secure the ends of the dough with a cocktail stick. Line 4 baking sheets with parchment paper. Place 4 pastries on each sheet. Cover and leave in a warm place for 30 minutes, until well puffed up.

4 Preheat the oven to 200°C (400°F/Gas 6). Brush with egg and bake in the top third of the oven for 15–20 minutes until golden.

STORE The pinwheels will keep in an airtight container for 2 days.

Apricot Pastries

The pastry can be prepared the night before, so that 30 minutes of rising in the morning and a quick bake will give you fresh pastries in time for coffee.

| MAKES 18 | 30 MINS | 15–20 MINS | UP TO 4 WEEKS |

Chilling time
1 hr

Rising time
30 mins

Ingredients
1 quantity danish pastry dough,
  see pages 154–155, steps 1–11
200g (7oz) apricot jam
2 x 400g cans apricot halves

Method.

1 Roll half the dough out on a well-floured work surface to a 30cm (12in) square. Trim the edges and cut out nine 10cm (4in) squares. Repeat with the remaining dough.

2 If the apricot jam has lumps, purée it until smooth. Take 1 tablespoon of jam and, using the back of the spoon, spread it all over a square, leaving a border of about 1cm (½in). Take 2 apricot halves and trim a little off their bottoms if too chunky. Place an apricot half in 2 opposite corners of the square.

3 Take the 2 corners without apricots and fold them into the middle. They should only partially cover the apricot halves. Repeat to fill all the pastries. Place on lined baking sheets, cover, and leave to rise in a warm place for 30 minutes until puffed up. Preheat the oven to 200°C (400°F/Gas 6).

4 Brush the pastries with egg and bake in the top third of the oven for 15–20 minutes until golden. Melt the remaining jam and brush over the pastries, to glaze. Cool for 5 minutes, then transfer to a wire rack.

STORE The pastries will keep in an airtight container for 2 days.

Cinnamon Rolls

If you prefer, leave the rolls to prove overnight in the fridge (after step 15) and bake in time for a breakfast treat.

MAKES 10–12 **40 MINS** **25–30 MINS** **UP TO 4 WEEKS**

Rising and proving time
3–4 hrs or overnight

Special equipment
30cm (12in) round springform cake tin

Ingredients
125ml (4fl oz) milk
100g (3½oz) unsalted butter, plus extra for greasing
2 tsp dried yeast
50g (1¾oz) caster sugar
550g (1¼lb) plain flour, sifted, plus extra for dusting
1 tsp salt

1 egg, plus 2 egg yolks
vegetable oil, for greasing

For the filling and glaze
3 tbsp cinnamon
100g (3½oz) soft light brown sugar
25g (scant 1oz) unsalted butter, melted
1 egg, lightly beaten
4 tbsp caster sugar

1 In a pan, heat 125ml (4fl oz) water, the milk, and butter until just melted. Let it cool.

2 When just warm, whisk in the yeast and a tablespoon of sugar. Cover for 10 minutes.

3 Place the flour, salt, and remaining sugar in a large bowl.

4 Make a well in centre of the dry ingredients and pour in the warm milk mixture.

5 Whisk the egg and egg yolks, and add to the mixture. Combine to form a rough dough.

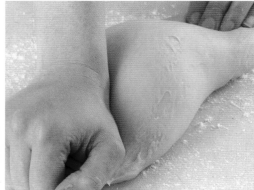

6 Place on a floured surface and knead for 10 minutes. Add extra flour if it's too sticky.

7 Put in an oiled bowl, cover with cling film and keep in a warm place for 2 hours until well risen.

8 Prepare the filling by mixing 2 tablespoons of cinnamon with the brown sugar.

9 When the dough has risen, turn it onto a floured work surface and gently knock it back.

10 Roll it out into a rectangle about 40 x 30cm (16 x 12in). Brush with the melted butter.

11 Scatter with the filling. Leave a 1cm (½in) border on one side and brush it with the egg.

12 Press the filling with the palm of your hand to ensure it sticks to the dough.

13 Roll the dough up, working towards the border. Do not roll too tightly.

14 Cut into 10–12 equal pieces with a serrated knife, taking care not to squash the rolls.

15 Grease and line the tin. Pack in the rolls. Cover and prove for 1–2 hours until well risen.

16 Preheat the oven to 180°C (350°F/Gas 4). Brush with egg and bake for 25–30 minutes.

17 Heat 3 tablespoons water and 2 of sugar until dissolved. Brush the glaze on the rolls.

18 Sprinkle over a mix of the remaining caster sugar and cinnamon, before turning out onto a wire rack to cool. **STORE** The rolls will keep in an airtight container for 2 days.

Sweet Roll variations

Chelsea Buns

These spicy, rolled currant buns were invented in the 18th century at The Bun House in Chelsea, London, where they proved a hit with royalty.

MAKES 9 | **30 MINS** | **30 MINS** | **UP TO 4 WEEKS**

Rising and proving time
2 hrs

Special equipment
23cm (9in) round cake tin

Ingredients
1 tsp dried yeast
100ml (3½fl oz) warm milk
280g (10oz) strong white bread flour, sifted, plus extra for dusting
½ tsp salt
2 tbsp caster sugar
45g (1½oz) butter, plus extra for greasing
1 egg, lightly beaten
115g (4oz) mixed dried fruit
60g (2oz) light muscovado sugar
1 tsp mixed spice
clear honey, for glazing

Method
1 Dissolve the yeast in the milk and leave for 5 minutes until frothy. Mix the flour, salt, and caster sugar in a bowl. Rub in 15g (½oz) of the butter. Pour in the egg, followed by the yeasted milk. Mix to form a soft dough. Knead for 5 minutes. Place in a bowl and cover with cling film. Leave in a warm place for 1 hour or until doubled in size.

2 Grease the tin. Tip the dough out onto a lightly floured surface and knead. Roll out to a 30 x 23cm (12 x 9in) rectangle. Melt the remaining butter in a pan over low heat, then brush onto the surface of the dough, leaving a border along the long edges.

3 Mix together the fruit, muscovado sugar, and spice, and scatter over the butter. Roll up the dough from the long edge like a Swiss roll, sealing the end with a little water. Cut the dough into 9 pieces. Place the pieces in the tin and cover with cling film. Leave to prove for up to 1 hour until doubled. Preheat the oven to 190°C (375°F/Gas 5). Bake for 30 minutes, then brush with honey and allow to cool before transferring to a wire rack.

STORE Keep in an airtight container for 2 days.

Spiced Fruit Buns

These sweet buns are simple to make as there is no rolling required.

MAKES 12 | **30 MINS** | **15 MINS** | **UP TO 4 WEEKS**

Rising and proving time
1½ hrs

Ingredients
240ml (8fl oz) milk
2 tsp dried yeast
500g (1lb 2oz) strong white bread flour, sifted, plus extra for dusting
1 tsp mixed spice
½ tsp nutmeg
1 tsp salt
6 tbsp caster sugar
60g (2oz) unsalted butter, diced, plus extra for greasing
vegetable oil, for greasing
150g (5½oz) mixed dried fruit
2 tbsp icing sugar
¼ tsp vanilla extract

Method
1 Warm the milk until tepid, stir in the yeast, cover, and leave for 10 minutes until frothy. Place the flour, spices, salt, and sugar in a bowl. Rub in the butter. Add the yeasted milk to form a soft dough. Knead well for 10 minutes. Shape into a ball, then place in a lightly oiled bowl and cover loosely. Leave in a warm place for 1 hour until risen.

2 Tip the dough onto a lightly floured work surface and gently knead in the dried fruit. Divide into 12 pieces, roll into balls, and place, well spaced, on greased baking sheets. Cover loosely and leave in a warm place for 30 minutes or until doubled. Preheat the oven to 200°C (400°F/Gas 6).

3 Bake for 15 minutes or until the buns sound hollow when tapped on the base. Transfer to a wire rack to cool. Meanwhile, combine the icing sugar, vanilla extract, and 1 tablespoon cold water, and brush over the top of the still-warm buns to glaze.

STORE The buns will keep in an airtight container for 2 days.

PATISSERIE

Hot Cross Buns

These delicious treats are too good to keep just for Easter.

MAKES 10–12	30 MINS	15–20 MINS	UP TO 4 WEEKS

Rising and proving time
2–4 hrs

Special equipment
piping bag with thin nozzle

Ingredients
200ml (7fl oz) milk
50g (1¾oz) unsalted butter
1 tsp vanilla extract
2 tsp dried yeast
100g (3½oz) caster sugar
500g (1lb 2oz) strong white bread flour,
    sifted, plus extra for dusting
1 tsp salt
2 tsp mixed spice
1 tsp cinnamon
150g (5½oz) mixed dried fruit (raisins,
    sultanas, and mixed peel)
1 egg, beaten, plus 1 extra for glazing
vegetable oil, for greasing

For the paste
3 tbsp plain flour
3 tbsp caster sugar

Method

1 Heat the milk, butter, and vanilla in a pan until the butter is just melted. Cool until tepid. Whisk in the yeast and 1 tablespoon of sugar. Cover for 10 minutes until it froths.

2 Put the remaining sugar, flour, salt, and spices into a bowl. Mix in the egg. Add the milk mixture and form a dough. Knead for 10 minutes on a floured surface. Press the dough out into a rectangle, scatter over the dried fruit, and knead briefly to combine.

3 Place in an oiled bowl, cover with cling film, and leave in a warm place for 1–2 hours until doubled. Turn out onto a floured surface, knock it back, divide into 10–12 pieces, and roll into balls. Place them on lined baking sheets. Cover with cling film and leave to prove for 1–2 hours.

4 Preheat the oven to 220°C (425°F/Gas 7). Brush the buns with the beaten egg. For the paste, mix the flour and sugar with water to make it spreadable. Put it into the piping bag and pipe crosses on the buns. Bake in the top of the oven for 15–20 minutes. Remove to a wire rack and allow to cool for 15 minutes.

STORE Will keep in an airtight container for 2 days.

BAKER'S TIP

These traditional Easter buns are very different and far superior to their bland shop-bought namesakes. They have a delicate, crispy exterior surface and a light, moist, fragrant crumb, with authentically assertive levels of fruit and spice. They are delicious still warm from the oven, spread with cold butter.

Profiteroles

These cream-filled choux pastry buns, drizzled with chocolate sauce, make a deliciously decadent dessert.

   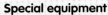

SERVES 4 · **30 MINS** · **22 MINS** · **12 WEEKS, UNFILLED**

Ingredients
60g (2oz) plain flour
50g (1¾oz) unsalted butter
2 eggs, beaten

For the filling and topping
400ml (14fl oz) double cream
200g (7oz) good-quality dark
  chocolate, broken into pieces
25g (scant 1oz) butter
2 tbsp golden syrup

Special equipment
2 piping bags with a 1cm (½in) plain
nozzle and 5mm (¼in) star nozzle

PATISSERIE

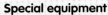

1 Preheat the oven to 220°C (425°F/Gas 7). Line 2 large baking trays with parchment.

2 Sift the flour into a large bowl, holding the sieve up high to aerate the flour.

3 Put the butter and 150ml (5fl oz) water into a small saucepan and heat gently until melted.

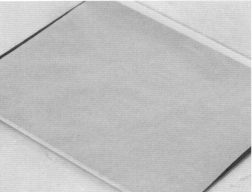

4 Bring to a boil, remove from the heat, and tip in the flour all at once.

5 Beat with a wooden spoon until smooth; the mixture should form a ball. Cool for 10 minutes.

6 Gradually add the eggs, beating very well after each addition to incorporate.

7 Continue adding the egg, little by little, to form a stiff, smooth, and shiny paste.

8 Spoon the mixture into a piping bag fitted with a 1cm (½in) plain nozzle.

9 Pipe walnut-sized rounds, set well apart. Bake for 20 minutes until risen and golden.

10 Remove from the oven and slit the side of each bun to allow the steam to escape.

11 Return to the oven for 2 minutes, to crisp, then transfer to a wire rack to cool completely.

12 Before serving, pour 100ml (3½fl oz) cream into a pan and whip the rest until just peaking.

13 Add the chocolate, butter, and syrup to the cream in the pan and heat gently until melted.

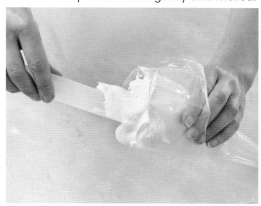

14 Pile the whipped cream into a piping bag fitted with a 5mm (¼in) star nozzle.

15 Pipe cream into each bun. Open the buns and fill them with the cream.

16 Arrange the buns on a serving plate or cake stand. Stir the sauce, pour it over, and serve immediately. **PREPARE AHEAD** The unfilled buns will keep in an airtight container for 2 days.

Choux Pastry variations

Chocolate Orange Profiteroles

A delicious twist on the original, heightened by sharp orange zest and liqueur. Try to use dark chocolate that is at least 60 per cent cocoa solids for a bitter chocolate orange taste.

SERVES 6 | **20 MINS** | **40 MINS** | **12 WEEKS, UNFILLED**

Special equipment
2 piping bags with a 1cm (½in) plain nozzle and 5mm (¼in) star nozzle

Ingredients

For the choux buns
60g (2oz) plain flour
50g (1¾oz) unsalted butter
2 eggs, beaten

For the filling
500ml (16fl oz) double cream or whipping cream
finely grated zest of 1 large orange
2 tbsp Grand Marnier

For the chocolate sauce
150g (5½oz) good-quality dark chocolate, broken into pieces
300ml (10fl oz) single cream
2 tbsp golden syrup
1 tbsp Grand Marnier

Method

1 Preheat the oven to 220°C (425°F/Gas 7). Line 2 large baking trays with parchment. Sift the flour into a large bowl, holding the sieve up high to aerate the flour.

2 Put the butter and 150ml (5fl oz) water into a small pan and heat gently until melted. Bring to a boil, remove from the heat, and tip in the flour. Beat with a wooden spoon until smooth; the mixture should form a ball. Cool for 10 minutes. Gradually add the eggs, beating well after each addition to incorporate. Continue adding the egg, little by little, to form a stiff and smooth paste.

3 Spoon the mixture into a piping bag fitted with a 1cm (½in) plain nozzle. Pipe walnut-sized rounds, set well apart. Bake for 20 minutes until risen and golden. Remove from the oven and slit the side of each bun to allow the steam to escape. Return to the oven for 2 minutes, to crisp, then transfer to a wire rack to cool completely.

4 To make the filling, whisk the cream, orange zest, and Grand Marnier in a bowl until just thicker than soft peaks. Fill the profiteroles with the cream using the piping bag with star nozzle.

5 To make the chocolate sauce, melt the chocolate, cream, syrup, and Grand Marnier together in a small pan, whisking until the sauce is smooth and glossy. Serve the profiteroles with the hot sauce spooned over.

PREPARE AHEAD The unfilled buns will keep in an airtight container for 2 days.

BAKER'S TIP
Immediately after removing choux pastries from the oven, it is vital to create a slit in each to allow the steam to escape. This will result in an open-textured, dry, and crisp pastry. If you do not slit the pastries, the steam will remain inside and the buns will be soggy.

Cheese Gougères with Smoked Salmon

These savoury choux pastry puffs are a traditional dish of the Burgundy region of France, where they are displayed in almost every bakery window. Stuffed with smoked salmon they make sophisticated canapés.

SERVES 8 | **40–45 MINS** | **30–35 MINS**

Ingredients
75g (2½oz) unsalted butter, plus extra for greasing
1¼ tsp salt
150g (5½oz) plain flour, sifted
6 eggs
125g (4½oz) Gruyère cheese, coarsely grated

For the smoked salmon filling
salt and pepper
1kg (2¼lb) fresh spinach, trimmed and washed
30g (1oz) unsalted butter
1 onion, finely chopped
4 garlic cloves, finely chopped
pinch of ground nutmeg
250g (9oz) cream cheese
175g (6oz) smoked salmon, sliced into strips
4 tbsp milk

Method

1 Preheat the oven to 190°C (375°F/Gas 5). Grease 2 baking sheets. Melt the butter in a pan with 250ml (8fl oz) water and ¾ teaspoon of salt. Bring to a boil. Remove from the heat and add the flour. Beat until smooth. Return the pan to the stove and beat over low heat for 30 seconds, to dry.

2 Remove from the heat. Add 4 eggs, 1 at a time, beating well. Beat the fifth egg; add gradually. Stir in half the cheese. Place eight 6cm (2½in) mounds of dough on the baking sheets. Beat the remaining egg and salt. Brush over each of the puffs. Sprinkle with the remaining cheese. Bake for 30–35 minutes until firm. Remove and transfer to a wire rack. Slice the tops and leave to cool.

3 Bring a pan of salted water to a boil. Add the spinach, and wilt for 1–2 minutes. Drain. When cool, squeeze to remove water, then chop. Melt the butter in a frying pan. Add the onion and cook until soft. Add the garlic, nutmeg, salt and pepper to taste, and the spinach. Cooking, stirring, until any liquid has evaporated. Add the cream cheese and stir until the mixture is thoroughly combined. Remove from the heat.

4 Add two-thirds of the smoked salmon, pour in the milk, and stir. Mound 2–3 tablespoons of filling into each cheese puff. Arrange the remaining smoked salmon on top. Rest the lid against the side of each filled puff and serve at once.

PATISSERIE

Chocolate Éclairs

These cousins of the profiterole can be easily adapted: try the chocolate orange topping and orange cream filling (see opposite), or filling with crème pâtissière (see page 166) or chocolate crème pâtissière (see page 296).

MAKES 30 | **30 MINS** | **25–30 MINS** | **12 WEEKS, UNFILLED**

Special equipment
piping bag with 1cm (½in) plain nozzle

Ingredients
75g (2½oz) unsalted butter
125g (4½oz) plain flour, sifted
3 eggs
500ml (16fl oz) double cream
  or whipping cream
150g (5½oz) good-quality dark chocolate,
  broken into pieces

Method
1 Preheat the oven to 200°C (400°F/Gas 6). Melt the butter in a pan with 200ml (7fl oz) cold water, then bring to the boil, remove from the heat, and stir in the flour. Beat with a wooden spoon until well combined.

2 Lightly beat the eggs and add to the flour and butter mixture a little at a time, whisking constantly. Continue whisking until the mixture is smooth and glossy and comes away easily from the sides of the pan. Transfer to the piping bag.

3 Pipe 10cm (4in) lengths of the mixture onto 2 baking trays lined with baking parchment, cutting the end of the length of pastry from the bag with a wet knife. You should have around 30 in all. Bake for 20–25 minutes or until golden brown, then remove from the oven and make a slit down the side of each.

Return to the oven for 5 minutes for the insides to cook through. Then remove and leave to cool.

4 Put the cream in a mixing bowl and beat with an electric hand whisk until soft peaks form. Spoon or pipe into each éclair. Place the chocolate pieces in a heatproof bowl. Sit the bowl over a pan of simmering water, making sure the bowl does not touch the water, and leave the chocolate to melt. Spoon over the éclairs and leave to dry before serving.

PREPARE AHEAD The unfilled éclairs will keep in an airtight container for 2 days.

Chestnut Millefeuilles

Sure to impress, this dessert is actually quite easy to make and can be prepared up to 6 hours ahead and chilled.

SERVES 8   **2 HOURS**   **20–25 MINUTES**

Chilling time
1 hr

Ingredients
375ml (13fl oz) milk
4 egg yolks
60g (2oz) granulated sugar
3 tbsp plain flour, sifted
2 tbsp dark rum

600g (1lb 5oz) puff pastry,
   shop-bought, or see pages
   174–175, steps 1–10
250ml (8fl oz) double cream
500g (1lb 2oz) marrons glacés,
   coarsely crumbled
45g (1½oz) icing sugar,
   plus extra if needed

PATISSERIE

1 Heat the milk in a pan over medium heat until it just comes to a boil. Take off heat.

2 Whisk the egg yolks and granulated sugar for 2–3 minutes until thick. Whisk in the flour.

3 Gradually whisk the milk into the egg mixture until smooth. Return to a clean pan.

4 Bring to a boil, whisking, until thickened. Reduce heat to low and whisk for 2 minutes.

5 If lumps form in the pastry cream, remove from the heat and whisk until smooth again.

6 Let cool, then stir in the rum. Transfer to a bowl, cover with cling film, and chill for 1 hour.

7 Preheat the oven to 200°C (400°F/Gas 6). Sprinkle a baking sheet evenly with cold water.

8 Roll out the pastry to a rectangle a little larger than the baking sheet, about 3mm (⅛in) thick.

9 Roll the dough around a rolling pin. Unroll it onto the baking sheet. Let the edges overhang.

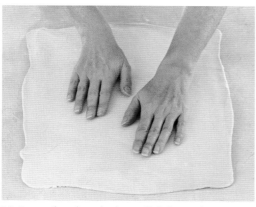

10 Press the dough down lightly on the baking sheet, then chill for about 15 minutes.

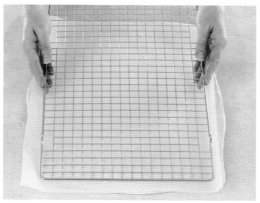

11 Prick the dough all over with a fork. Cover with parchment. Set a wire rack on top.

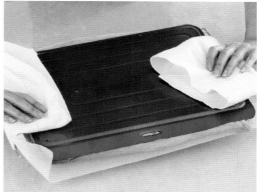

12 Bake for 15–20 minutes. Remove from the oven, grip the sheet and rack, invert the pastry.

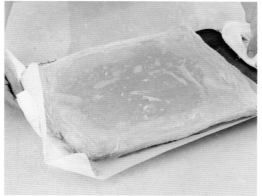

13 Slide the baking sheet back under the pastry and bake for a further 10 minutes.

14 Remove from the oven and carefully slide the pastry onto a chopping board.

15 While still warm, trim round the edges with a large, sharp knife to neaten.

16 Cut the trimmed sheet lengthways into 3 equal strips. Allow to cool.

17 Pour the cream into a bowl and whip until fairly firm.

18 Using a large metal spoon, fold the whipped cream into the chilled pastry cream.

19 With a palette knife, spread half the cream mixture evenly over one pastry strip.

20 Sprinkle with half the chestnuts. Repeat to make 2 layers and top with the last strip.

21 Sift over icing sugar and divide into portions with a serrated knife.

Millefeuilles variations

Chocolate Millefeuilles

Filled with dark chocolate cream and decorated with white chocolate drizzles, this version has wow factor in abundance.

SERVES 8   **2 HOURS**   **25–30 MINS**

Chilling time
1 hr

Ingredients
1 quantity pastry cream, see page 166, steps 1–5
2 tbsp brandy
600g (1lb 5oz) puff pastry, shop-bought,
  or see pages 174–175, steps 1–10
375ml (13fl oz) double cream
50g (1¾oz) dark chocolate, melted and cooled
30g (1oz) white chocolate, melted and cooled

Method

1 Stir brandy into the cream, cover with cling film, and chill for 1 hour. Preheat the oven to 200°C (400°F/Gas 6).

2 Sprinkle a baking sheet with cold water. Roll out the pastry to a rectangle larger than the baking sheet. Transfer to the sheet, letting the edges overhang. Press the dough down. Chill for 15 minutes. Prick all over with a fork. Cover with parchment, then set a wire rack on top. Bake for 15–20 minutes until it just begins to brown. Gripping the sheet and rack, invert the pastry, slide the baking sheet back under and continue baking for 10 minutes until both sides are browned. Remove from the oven and slide the pastry onto a chopping board. Trim the edges while still warm, then cut lengthways into 3 equal strips. Let cool.

3 Whip the double cream until stiff. Stir it into the pastry cream with two-thirds of the melted dark chocolate. Cover and chill. Spread the remaining melted chocolate over one of the pastry strips to cover it. Let it set.

4 Put another pastry strip on a plate, spread with half the cream, top with the remaining strip, and spread with the rest of the cream. Cover with the chocolate-coated strip.

5 Put the white chocolate into one corner of a plastic bag. Twist the bag to enclose the chocolate and snip off the tip of the corner. Pipe trails of chocolate over the millefeuilles.

PREPARE AHEAD The dish can be made ahead and chilled for up to 6 hours.

Vanilla Slices

Classic pastries sandwiched with thick custard and sweet, luscious jam.

MAKES 6   **2 HOURS**   **25–30 MINS**

Chilling time
1 hr

Special equipment
small piping bag with thin nozzle

Ingredients
250ml (13fl oz) double cream
1 quantity pastry cream, see page 166, steps 1–5
600g (1lb 5oz) puff pastry, shop-bought,
  or see pages 174–175, steps 1–10
100g (3½oz) icing sugar
1 tsp cocoa powder
½ jar smooth strawberry or raspberry jam

Method

1 Whip the double cream until stiff peaks form. Fold it into the pastry cream and chill. Preheat the oven to 200°C (400°F/Gas 6). Sprinkle a baking sheet with cold water. Roll out the pastry to a rectangle larger than the baking sheet and transfer to the sheet, letting the edges overhang. Press the dough down. Chill for 15 minutes.

2 Prick the dough with a fork. Cover with parchment, then set a wire rack on top. Bake for 15–20 minutes until it just begins to brown. Gripping the sheet and rack, invert the pastry. Slide the baking sheet back under and continue baking for 10 minutes until both sides are browned. Remove from the oven and slide the pastry on to a chopping board. While still warm, cut it into 5 x 10cm (2 x 4in) rectangles, in multiples of 3.

3 For the icing, mix the icing sugar with 1–1½ tablespoons cold water. Mix 2 tablespoons of the icing with the cocoa to make a small amount of chocolate icing. Place the chocolate icing in a piping bag with a thin nozzle. Take one-third of the pastry pieces and spread them with the white icing. While the icing is wet, pipe horizontal lines across it with the chocolate icing, then drag a skewer through the lines vertically to produce a striped effect. Allow to dry.

4 Spread the remaining pastry pieces with a thin layer of the jam. Spread a 1cm (½in) layer of pastry cream on top of the jam and tidy up the edges with a knife.

5 To assemble the vanilla slices, take a piece of pastry with jam and pastry cream, and place another gently on top. Press down lightly before topping with a third iced piece of pastry.

PREPARE AHEAD The dish can be made ahead and chilled for up to 6 hours.

Summer Fruit Millefeuilles

Beautiful and appetizing on a buffet table, or at a garden tea party. ▶

SERVES	2	25–30
8	HOURS	MINS

Chilling time
1 hr

Ingredients
1 quantity pastry cream, see page 166, steps 1–5
600g (1lb 5oz) puff pastry, shop-bought, or see pages 174–175, steps 1–10
250ml (8fl oz) double cream
400g (14oz) mixed summer fruits, such as strawberries, diced, and raspberries
icing sugar, for dusting

Method

1 Preheat the oven to 200°C (400°F/Gas 6). Sprinkle a baking sheet evenly with cold water. Roll out the pastry to a rectangle larger than the baking sheet, and about 3mm (⅛in) thick. Roll the dough around a rolling pin, then unroll it onto the baking sheet, letting the edges overhang. Press the dough down. Chill for about 15 minutes.

2 Prick the dough with a fork. Cover with parchment, then set a wire rack on top. Bake for 15–20 minutes until it just begins to brown. Gripping the sheet and rack, invert the pastry. Slide the baking sheet back under and continue baking for 10 minutes until both sides are browned.

Remove from the oven and slide the pastry onto a chopping board. While still warm, trim the edges, then cut lengthways into 3 equal strips. Allow to cool.

3 Whip the double cream until firm. Fold into the pastry cream. Spread half the pastry cream filling over 1 pastry strip. Sprinkle with half the fruit. Repeat with another pastry strip, to make 2 layers. Put the last pastry strip on top and press down gently. Sift the icing sugar thickly over the millefeuilles.

PREPARE AHEAD The dish can be made ahead and chilled for up to 6 hours.

BAKER'S TIP

Once you have mastered the art of assembling the pastry, millefeuilles can be made in endless variations: large, for an impressive buffet centrepiece, or in individual portions for an indulgent afternoon tea, sandwiched together with whatever filling you prefer.

Apple and Almond Galettes

These elegant and impressive desserts are deceptively simple to make. A sprinkling of sugar adds a caramelized flavour to the apples.

MAKES 8 · **25–30 MINS** · **20–30 MINS**

Ingredients

600g (1lb 5oz) puff pastry, shop-bought, or see pages 174–175, steps 1–10
plain flour, for dusting
215g (7½oz) marzipan
1 lemon
8 small, sharp dessert apples
50g (1¾oz) granulated sugar
icing sugar, for dusting

Method

1 Lightly flour a work surface. Roll out half the pastry to a 35cm (14in) square, about 3mm (⅛in) thick. Using a 15cm (6in) plate as a guide, cut out 4 rounds.

2 Sprinkle 2 baking sheets with water. Set the rounds on a baking sheet, and prick each with a fork, avoiding the edge. Repeat with the remaining dough. Chill for 15 minutes. Divide the marzipan into 8 portions, and roll each into a ball.

3 Spread a sheet of baking parchment on the work surface. Set a ball of marzipan on the parchment, and cover with another sheet of parchment. Roll out the marzipan to a 12.5cm (5in) round between the sheets. Set on top of a pastry round, leaving a border of 1cm (½in). Repeat with the remaining marzipan and pastry rounds. Chill, until ready to bake.

4 Cut the lemon in half, and squeeze the juice from one half into a small bowl. Peel, halve, and core the apples; then cut into thin slices. Drop the slices into the lemon juice, and toss (see Baker's Tip).

5 Preheat the oven to 220°C (425°F/Gas 7). Arrange the apple slices, overlapping them slightly, in an attractive spiral over the marzipan rounds. Leave a thin border of pastry dough around the edge.

6 Bake the galettes for 15–20 minutes until the pastry edges have risen around the marzipan and are light golden. Sprinkle the apples evenly with the sugar.

7 Return to the oven, and continue baking for 5–10 minutes or until the apples are golden brown, caramelized around the edges, and just tender when tested with the tip of a small knife. Transfer to warmed serving plates, dust with a little icing sugar, and serve at once.

PREPARE AHEAD Roll out the puff pastry rounds and top them with the marzipan up to 2 hours in advance. Galettes always taste best if baked just before serving.

BAKER'S TIP

When working with apples or pears, coating the slices with lemon juice will prevent discolouration. On contact with the air, both fruits will otherwise turn brown, which also makes the texture soften. If you are worried that the lemon juice will affect the flavour, it can be diluted with a little water.

APPLE AND ALMOND GALETTES

Apple Jalousie

In France, a *jalousie* is a louvred shutter. This pastry is slashed to look like a shutter, revealing the apple inside.

SERVES 6–8	1¼–1½ HOURS	30–40 MINS	UP TO 4 WEEKS

Chilling time
1¼ hrs

Ingredients

For the puff pastry
250g (9oz) unsalted butter, frozen for 30 minutes
250g (9oz) plain flour, sifted, plus extra for dusting
1 tsp salt
1 tsp lemon juice

For the filling
15g (½oz) unsalted butter
1kg (2¼lb) tart eating apples, peeled, cored, and diced
2.5cm (1in) fresh root ginger, finely chopped
100g (3½oz) caster sugar
1 egg white, beaten, for glazing

1 Coarsely grate the butter into a bowl. Sift over the flour and salt. Rub together until crumbly.

2 Pour in 90–100ml (3–3½fl oz) water and the lemon juice. Form a rough dough.

3 Turn the dough out onto a floured surface. Work into a ball, then flatten it slightly.

4 Place the dough into a plastic bag and chill in the refrigerator for 20 minutes.

5 On a floured surface, thinly roll it out to a long rectangle, short sides 25cm (10in).

6 Take one-third of the pastry and fold into the middle. Fold over the remaining third.

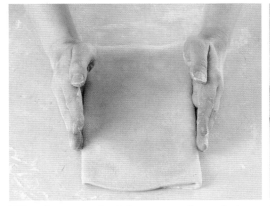

7 Turn it over so the joins are easily sealed when it is re-rolled. Give it a quarter turn.

8 Roll out again to a similar size as the original rectangle. Keep the short sides even in size.

9 Repeat the folding, turning, and rolling. Return it to the bag and chill for 20 minutes.

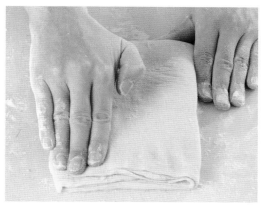

10 Roll, fold, and turn the pastry twice more, then chill for a final 20 minutes.

11 In a pan, melt the butter. Add the apples, ginger, and all but 2 tablespoons of the sugar.

12 Sauté and stir for 15–20 minutes until the apples are tender and caramelized. Let cool.

13 Roll out the pastry on a floured surface to 28 x 32cm (11 x 13in). Cut lengthways in half.

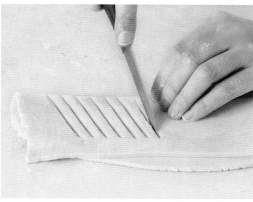

14 Fold one half lengthways and cut across the fold at 5mm (¼in) gaps, leaving a border.

15 Put the uncut dough on a non-stick baking sheet and spoon the apple along the centre.

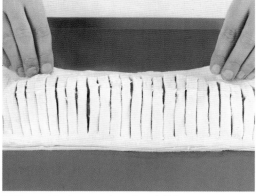

16 Top with the cut dough. Chill for 15 minutes. Preheat the oven to 220°C (425°F/Gas 7).

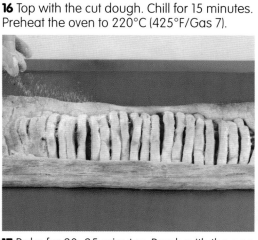

17 Bake for 20–25 minutes. Brush with the egg white and sprinkle over the remaining sugar.

18 Return to the oven and continue baking for 10–15 minutes. Serve the slices warm or at room temperature. **PREPARE AHEAD** The jalousie can be frozen at step 16.

APPLE JALOUSIE

Jalousie variations

Banana Shuttles

These miniature jalousies get their name from their resemblance to the shuttle tools traditionally used by weavers. Bananas and rum add a Caribbean spin.

MAKES 6 | **1¼–1½ HOURS** | **30–40 MINS** | **4 WEEKS, UNBAKED**

Chilling time
1 hr

Ingredients
50g (1¾oz) caster sugar, plus 2 tbsp for sprinkling
¼ tsp cloves
¼ tsp cinnamon
3 tbsp dark rum
3 bananas
600g (1lb 5oz) puff pastry, shop-bought, or see pages 174–175, steps 1–10
1 egg white, beaten, for glazing

Method

1 Mix the sugar, cloves, and cinnamon. Pour the rum into another dish. Peel the bananas and cut each in half. Dip in the rum and coat with the sugar mixture.

2 Sprinkle a baking sheet with water. Roll out the puff pastry dough and trim it to a 30–37cm (12–15in) rectangle. Cut the dough into twelve 7.5–12cm (3–5in) rectangles. Fold 6 of the rectangles in half lengthways, and make three 1cm (½in) cuts across the fold of each. Set the remaining rectangles on the baking sheet, pressing lightly.

3 Cut each banana half into thin slices; then set the slices in the centre of each puff pastry rectangle, leaving a 1cm (½in) border around the edge. Brush the borders with cold water.

4 Line up and unfold the slashed rectangles over the filled bases. Press the edges with to seal. Trim one end of each rectangle to a blunt point. Scallop the edges of the shuttles with the back of a small knife.

5 Chill the shuttles for 15 minutes. Preheat the oven to 220°C (425°F/Gas 7). Bake for 15–20 minutes. Brush with the egg white, and sprinkle over the remaining sugar. Return to the oven for 10–15 minutes until crisp and golden. Transfer to a wire rack and let cool. Serve warm or at room temperature.

PREPARE AHEAD The shuttles can be frozen at the chilling stage, step 5.

BAKER'S TIP
There is nothing wrong with buying ready-made puff pastry. However, do try to find pastry made only from butter, and not other fats. Some commercial pastries contain unhealthy trans fats. In any case, non-butter puff pastry will never taste as good, can have unwelcome trace flavours, and may be oily.

Chicken Jalousie

Jalousies also work well with savoury fillings.

| SERVES 4 | 25 MINS | 25 MINS | 4 WEEKS, UNBAKED |

Ingredients
25g (scant 1oz) unsalted butter
2 leeks, thinly sliced
1 tsp chopped thyme
1 tsp plain flour, plus extra for dusting
90ml (3fl oz) chicken stock
1 tsp lemon juice
600g (1lb 5oz) puff pastry, shop-bought, or see pages 174–175, steps 1–10
300g (10½oz) skinless, boneless, cooked chicken, chopped
salt and freshly ground black pepper
1 egg, beaten, for glazing

Method
1 Melt the butter in a pan. Add the leeks and cook over medium-low heat, stirring, for 5 minutes, or until fairly soft. Stir in the thyme, then sprinkle over the flour and stir in. Blend in the stock and bring to a boil, stirring until thickened. Remove from the heat, stir in the lemon juice, and leave to cool.

2 Preheat the oven to 220°C (425°F/Gas 7). Roll out just under half the pastry on a lightly floured work surface to a 25 x 15cm (10 x 6in) rectangle. Lay the pastry on a dampened baking tray. Roll out the remaining pastry to a 25 x 18cm (10 x 7in) rectangle, dust with flour, then fold in half lengthways. Make cuts 1cm (½in) apart along the folded edge to within 2.5cm (1in) of the outer edge.

3 Stir the chicken into the leek mixture and season. Spoon over the pastry base, leaving a 2.5cm (1in) border. Dampen the edges of the pastry with water. Place the second piece of pastry on top and press the edges together to seal; trim excess. Brush the top with egg and bake for 25 minutes or until golden brown and crisp. Leave to cool for a few minutes before serving.

PREPARE AHEAD The jalousie can be frozen after sealing and trimming excess.

Pear and Mincemeat Pie

Mincemeat is most often partnered with apple, but the more subtle flavours of pear can be even more appealing.

| SERVES 8–10 | 15 MINS | 40 MINS | 8 WEEKS, UNBAKED |

Ingredients
unsalted butter, for greasing
600g (1lb 5oz) puff pastry, shop-bought, or see pages 174–175, steps 1–10
plain flour, for dusting
400g (14oz) mincemeat
1 tbsp brandy
finely grated zest of 1 orange
25g (scant 1oz) ground almonds
1 ripe pear, peeled, cored, and thinly sliced
1 egg, beaten, for glazing

Method
1 Preheat the oven to 200°C (400°F/Gas 6). Grease a baking tray. On a floured surface, roll the pastry out on 2 sheets, each 28 x 20cm (11 x 8in).

2 Mix the mincemeat with the brandy and orange zest. Lay a sheet of pastry on the tray, then scatter over the almonds, leaving a 2cm (¾in) border around the edges.

3 Spoon the mincemeat mixture over the ground almonds, top with the pear, then brush the border with beaten egg.

4 Place the second sheet of pastry on top of the first. Press the edges, pinching the sides to decorate them. Make a few slashes on the top with a knife for the steam to escape.

5 Brush the pastry with beaten egg and bake for 30–40 minutes or until golden brown and cooked through.

PREPARE AHEAD The pie can be frozen at the end of the step 4.

Cinnamon Palmiers

Grating frozen butter is a great shortcut when making puff pastry – or use shop-bought puff if pressed for time.

MAKES 24 **45 MINS** **25–30 MINS** **UP TO 8 WEEKS**

Chilling time
1 hr 10 mins

Ingredients

For the puff pastry
250g (9oz) unsalted butter, frozen for 30 minutes
250g (9oz) plain flour, plus extra for dusting
1 tsp salt
1 egg, lightly beaten, for glazing

For the filling
100g (3½oz) unsalted butter, softened
100g (3½oz) soft light brown sugar
4–5 tsp cinnamon, to taste

1 Coarsely grate the butter into a bowl. Sift over the flour and salt. Rub together until crumbly.

2 Pour in 90–100ml (3–3½fl oz) water. Use a fork, then your hands to form a rough dough.

3 Place the dough into a plastic bag and chill in the refrigerator for 20 minutes.

4 On a floured surface, thinly roll it out to a long rectangle, short sides 25cm (10in).

5 Take one-third of the pastry and fold into the middle. Fold over the remaining third.

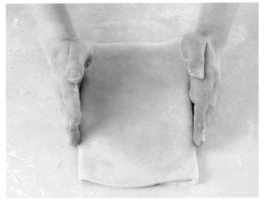

6 Turn it over so the joins are easily sealed when it is re-rolled. Give it a quarter turn.

7 Roll out again to a similar size as the original rectangle. Keep the short sides even in size.

8 Repeat the folding, turning, and rolling. Put back in the bag, and chill for 20 minutes.

9 Roll, fold, and turn the pastry twice more, then chill for a final 20 minutes.

10 Meanwhile, make the filling by beating together the butter, sugar, and cinnamon.

11 Preheat the oven to 200°C (400°F/Gas 6). Line 2 baking sheets with baking parchment.

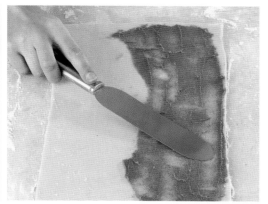

12 Roll the dough out once again. Trim the edges. Spread the filling thinly over the surface.

13 Loosely roll one of the long sides into the middle, and repeat with the other side.

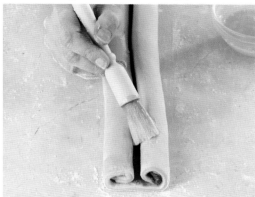

14 Brush with egg wash, press together, then turn over and chill for 10 minutes.

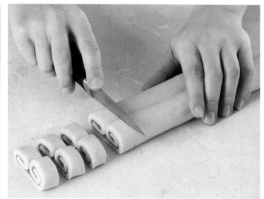

15 Carefully cut into 2cm (¾in) pieces and turn the palmiers face up.

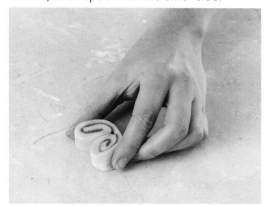

16 Squeeze them to form an oval, and press down lightly with your palm to flatten slightly.

17 Brush the palmiers with the beaten egg and bake for 25–30 minutes.

18 They are ready when golden brown, puffed up, and crisp in the centre. Remove to a wire rack to cool. **STORE** The palmiers will keep in an airtight container for 3 days.

CINNAMON PALMIERS

Palmiers variations

Chocolate Palmiers

Once the pastry is prepared, palmiers are quick and tasty snacks that are portable enough to take on a picnic.

MAKES 24   **45 MINS**   **25–30 MINS**   **UP TO 8 WEEKS**

Chilling time
1 hr 10 mins

Ingredients
1 quantity puff pastry, see page 178, steps 1–9
1 egg, beaten, for glazing

For the filling
150g (5½oz) dark chocolate, broken up

Method
1 Make the filling by melting the chocolate in a bowl set over a pan of simmering water. Set aside to cool. Preheat the oven to 200°C (400°F/Gas 6). Line 2 baking sheets with parchment.

2 Roll the dough to a rectangle 5mm (¼in) thick. Spread the filling over. Roll up one of the long sides of the pastry nearly into the middle, and repeat with the other side. Brush the sides with egg and roll them together. Turn over and chill for 10 minutes.

3 Trim the ends of the roll and cut it into 2cm (¾in) pieces. Turn the pastries face up, press them together to form an oval shape and press down to bring the roll together.

4 Transfer to the baking sheets, brush with a little beaten egg, and bake at the top of the oven for 25–30 minutes. They are ready when golden brown, puffed up, and crisp in the centre. Remove to a wire rack to cool.

STORE The palmiers will keep in an airtight container for 3 days.

ALSO TRY... Substitute Nutella or another chocolate and hazelnut spread, straight from the jar, for a quicker filling.

BAKER'S TIP
The secret to rolling a pinwheel shape with any type of dough or pastry is to make sure that it is rolled up evenly, but not too tightly. Over-tight rolls will result in the centre of the palmiers rising up as they cook, leaving an uneven finish to the pastries.

Tapenade Palmiers

Use a ready-made tapenade, if you like, for an even quicker filling.

MAKES 24   **55 MINS**   **25–30 MINS**   **UP TO 8 WEEKS**

Chilling time
1 hr 10 mins

Special equipment
food processor

Ingredients
1 quantity puff pastry, see page 178, steps 1–9
1 egg, beaten, for glazing

For the tapenade
140g (5oz) pitted black olives
2 garlic cloves, crushed
4 tbsp roughly chopped flat-leaf parsley
3–4 tbsp extra virgin olive oil, plus extra if needed
2 anchovy fillets (optional)
freshly ground black pepper

Method
1 Combine all the ingredients for the tapenade in a food processor and process to a coarse, spreadable paste, adding a little extra oil if necessary. Preheat the oven to 200°C (400°F/Gas 6). Line 2 baking sheets with parchment.

2 Roll the dough to a rectangle. Trim any irregular edges. Take the filling and spread it thinly over the surface of the pastry.

3 Roll the long sides of pastry nearly into the middle. Brush with beaten egg and roll them together to form the palmier. Turn the roll over and chill for 10 minutes.

4 Trim the ends of the roll and cut it into 2cm (¾in) pieces. Turn the pastries face up, press them together to form an oval shape, and press down to bring the roll together.

5 Transfer to the baking sheets, brush with egg, and bake at the top of the oven for 25–30 minutes until puffed up and crisp.

STORE The palmiers will keep in an airtight container for 3 days.

PATISSERIE

Parmesan Smoked Paprika Palmiers

A perfect snack to serve with pre-dinner drinks when entertaining.

| MAKES 24 | 45 MINS | 25–30 MINS | UP TO 8 WEEKS |

Chilling time
1 hr 10 mins

Ingredients
1 quantity puff pastry, see page 178, steps 1–9
1 egg, beaten, for glazing

For the filling
50g (1¾oz) Parmesan cheese, finely grated
1 tsp smoked paprika
50g (1¾oz) unsalted butter, softened

Method

1 Make the filling by tossing the Parmesan and the paprika together, then mixing with the butter until combined. Preheat the oven to 200°C (400°F/Gas 6). Line 2 baking sheets with parchment.

2 Roll the dough out to a rectangle. Trim any irregular edges. Spread the filling carefully over the surface of the pastry.

3 Roll up one of the long sides of the pastry nearly into the middle, and repeat with the other side. Brush the sides with egg and roll together. Turn the roll of pastry over and chill for 10 minutes to allow the sides to attach.

4 Trim the ends of the roll and cut it into 2cm (¾in) pieces. Turn the pastries face up, gently squeeze them together to form a more oval shape, and press down lightly to bring the roll together.

5 Transfer to the baking sheets, brush with a little beaten egg, and bake at the top of the oven for 25–30 minutes. They are ready when golden brown, puffed up, and crisp in the centre. Transfer to a wire rack to cool.

STORE The palmiers will keep in an airtight container for 3 days.

PALMIERS VARIATIONS

Jam Doughnuts

Doughnuts are surprisingly easy to make. These are light, airy, and taste far nicer than any shop-bought varieties.

MAKES 12 — **30 MINS** — **5–10 MINS**

Rising and proving time
3–4 hrs

Special equipment
oil thermometer
piping bag with thin nozzle

Ingredients
150ml (5fl oz) milk
75g (2½oz) unsalted butter
½ tsp vanilla extract
2 tsp dried yeast
75g (2½oz) caster sugar

2 eggs, beaten
425g (15oz) plain flour,
 preferably "00" grade,
 plus extra for dusting
½ tsp salt
1 litre (1¾ pints) sunflower oil,
 for deep-frying, plus extra
 for greasing

For coating and filling
caster sugar, for coating
250g (9oz) good-quality jam
 (raspberry, strawberry, or cherry),
 processed until smooth

1 Heat the milk, butter, and vanilla in a pan until the butter melts. Cool until tepid.

2 Whisk in yeast and a tablespoon of sugar. Cover, leave for 10 minutes. Mix in the eggs.

3 Sift the flour and salt into a large bowl. Stir in the remaining sugar.

 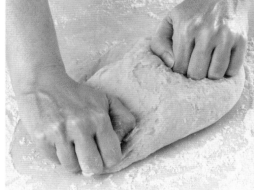 

4 Make a well in the flour and add the milk mixture. Bring together to form a rough dough.

5 Turn the dough onto a floured surface and knead for 10 minutes until soft and pliable.

6 Put in an oiled bowl and cover with cling film. Keep it warm for 2 hours until doubled.

7 On a floured surface, knock back the dough and divide into 12 equal pieces.

8 Roll them between your palms to form balls. Place on baking sheets, spaced well apart.

9 Cover with cling film and a tea towel. Leave in a warm place for 1–2 hours until doubled.

10 Heat a 10cm (4in) depth of oil to 170–180°C (340–350°F), keeping a lid nearby for safety.

11 Slide the doughnuts off the sheets. Do not worry if they are flatter on one side.

12 Carefully lower into the hot oil, rounded side down. Turn after about 1 minute.

13 Remove with a slotted spoon when golden brown on all sides. Switch off the heat.

14 Drain on kitchen paper, then, while still hot, toss them in caster sugar. Cool before filling.

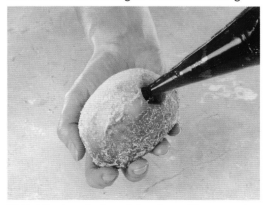

15 Put the jam in the piping bag. Pierce each doughnut on the side and insert the nozzle.

16 Gently squirt in about a tablespoon of jam, until it almost starts to spill out again. Dust the hole with a little more sugar, and serve. **STORE** These will keep in an airtight container for 1 day.

Doughnut variations

Ring Doughnuts

Doughnuts are simple to make and home-cooked ones taste delicious. Don't waste the cut-out middles, just fry them separately for a bonus bite-sized treat.

MAKES 12 **35 MINS** **5–10 MINS**

Rising and proving time
3–4 hrs

Special equipment
oil thermometer
4cm (1½in) round pastry cutter

Ingredients
1 quantity doughnut dough,
    see page 182, steps 1–6
1 litre (1¾ pints) sunflower oil, for deep-frying,
    plus extra for greasing
caster sugar, for coating

Method

1 Turn the dough out onto a lightly floured work surface. Gently knock it back, divide into 12, and roll into balls.

2 Place the balls on baking sheets, well apart to allow for them spreading. Cover with cling film and a tea towel, and leave in a warm place for about 1–2 hours until doubled in size.

3 Take a rolling pin and gently flatten the doughnuts to around 3cm (1¼in) in height. Oil the pastry cutter. Cut the centres out and set aside.

4 Pour the oil into a large pan to a depth of at least 10cm (4in) and heat it to 170–180°C (340–350°F). Keep the correct-sized saucepan lid near and do not leave the hot oil unattended. Keep the temperature even, or the doughnuts will burn.

5 Slide the doughnuts off the baking trays using a fish slice. Don't worry if they are flat on one side; they will puff up on cooking. Lower them, rounded-side down, into the hot oil and cook 3 at a time for about 1 minute, turning when the undersides are golden brown.

6 When golden brown all over, remove from the oil with a slotted spoon and drain them on kitchen paper. Turn off the heat when finished frying. The cut-out centres can be fried in a similar way; these are very popular with younger children. While still hot, toss them in caster sugar and leave to cool a little before eating.

STORE These will keep in an airtight container for 1 day.

Custard Doughnuts

Custard is my favourite filling for doughnuts. Use good-quality shop-bought custard here – one that is made with real eggs and plenty of cream.

MAKES 12 **30 MINS** **5–10 MINS**

Proving time
3–4 hrs

Special equipment
oil thermometer
piping bag with thin metal nozzle

Ingredients
1 quantity doughnut dough,
    see page 182, steps 1–6
1 litre (1¾ pints) sunflower oil, for deep-frying,
    plus extra for greasing
caster sugar, for coating
250ml (8fl oz) ready-made custard

Method

1 Turn the dough out onto a lightly floured work surface. Gently knock it back, divide into 12, and roll into balls.

2 Place the balls on baking sheets, well apart to allow for them spreading. Cover lightly with cling film and a tea towel, and leave in a warm place for 1–2 hours until almost doubled in size.

3 Pour the oil into a large, heavy saucepan to a depth of at least 10cm (4in) and heat it to 170–180°C (340–350°F). Keep the correct-sized saucepan lid nearby and never leave the hot oil unattended. Regulate the temperature, making sure it remains even, or the doughnuts will burn.

4 Slide the risen doughnuts off the baking trays using a fish slice. Do not worry if they are flatter on one side; they will puff up on cooking. Lower them, rounded-side down, into the hot oil and cook 3 at a time for about 1 minute, turning as soon as the undersides are golden brown. When golden brown on all sides, turn off the heat, remove the doughnuts from the oil with a slotted spoon and drain them on kitchen paper.

5 While hot, toss them in caster sugar and leave to cool. To fill the doughnuts, place the custard in the piping bag and pierce each doughnut on the side. Make sure the nozzle goes into the centre of the doughnut. Squirt a tablespoon of custard into the doughnut, until it almost starts to spill out. Dust the hole with sugar to disguise it.

STORE These will keep in an airtight container for 1 day.

Churros

These cinnamon- and sugar-sprinkled Spanish snacks take minutes to make and will be devoured just as quickly. Try them dipped in hot chocolate.

**SERVES
2–4**

**10
MINS**

**5–10
MINS**

Special equipment
oil thermometer
piping bag with 2cm (¾in) nozzle

Ingredients
25g (scant 1oz) unsalted butter
200g (7oz) plain flour
50g (1¾oz) caster sugar
1 tsp baking powder
1 litre (1¾ pints) sunflower oil, for deep-frying
1 tsp cinnamon

Method
1 Measure 200ml (7fl oz) boiling water into a jug. Add the butter and stir until it melts. Sift together the flour, half the sugar, and the baking powder into a bowl.

2 Make a well in the centre and slowly pour in the hot butter liquid, beating continuously, until you have a thick paste; you may not need all the liquid. Leave the mixture to cool and rest for 5 minutes.

3 Pour the oil into a large, heavy-based saucepan to a depth of at least 10cm (4in) and heat it to 170–180°C (340–350°F). Keep the correct-sized saucepan lid nearby and never leave the hot oil unattended. Regulate the temperature, making sure it remains even, or the churros will burn.

4 Place the cooled mixture into the piping bag. Pipe 7cm (scant 3in) lengths of the dough into the hot oil, using a pair of scissors to snip off the ends. Do not crowd the pan, or the temperature of the oil will go down. Cook the churros for 1–2 minutes on each side, turning them when they are golden brown.

5 When done, remove the churros from the oil with a slotted spoon and drain on kitchen paper. Switch off the heat.

6 Mix the remaining sugar and the cinnamon together on a plate and toss the churros in the mixture while still hot. Leave to cool for 5–10 minutes before serving while still warm.

STORE These will keep in an airtight container for 1 day.

BAKER'S TIP
Churros can be made in only a few minutes, making them an almost instant treat. The batter can be enriched with egg yolk, butter, or milk, but the basic quantities of liquid to dry ingredients should be maintained. The thinner the batter, the lighter the results, but frying with a liquid batter takes a little practice.

biscuits cookies & slices

Hazelnut and Raisin Oat Cookies

These biscuits are an ideal cookie jar staple – tasty enough to please the kids and healthy enough for the adults.

MAKES 18 · **20 MINS** · **10–15 MINS** · **UP TO 8 WEEKS**

Ingredients

100g (3½oz) hazelnuts
100g (3½oz) unsalted butter, softened
200g (7oz) soft light brown sugar
1 egg, beaten
1 tsp vanilla extract
1 tbsp runny honey

125g (4½oz) self-raising flour, sifted
125g (4½oz) jumbo porridge oats
pinch of salt
100g (3½oz) raisins
a little milk, if needed

1 Preheat the oven to 190°C (375°F/Gas 5). Toast the nuts on a baking sheet for 5 minutes.

2 Once toasted, rub with a clean tea towel to remove most of the skins.

3 Roughly chop the hazelnuts and then set aside.

4 In a bowl, cream together the butter and sugar with an electric whisk until smooth.

5 Add the egg, vanilla extract, and honey, and beat well until smooth once more.

6 Combine the flour, oats, and salt in a separate bowl, and stir to mix.

7 Stir the flour mixture into the creamed mixture and beat until very well combined.

8 Add the chopped nuts and raisins, and mix until evenly distributed throughout.

9 If the mixture is too stiff to work with easily, add a little milk until it becomes pliable.

10 Line 2 or 3 baking sheets with parchment. Roll the dough into walnut-sized balls.

11 Flatten each ball slightly, leaving plenty of space between them.

12 Bake in batches for 10–15 minutes until golden. Cool slightly, then move to a wire rack.

13 Leave to cool completely before serving. **STORE** The cookies will keep in an airtight container for 5 days, so if you make a batch on Sunday night they will last the school and working week.

Cookie variations

Pistachio and Cranberry Oat Cookies

The jewel colours of the pistachios and cranberries gleam out from these slightly more grown up versions of the classic fruit and nut cookies.

MAKES 24 | **20 MINS** | **10–15 MINS** | **UP TO 8 WEEKS**

Ingredients

100g (3½oz) unsalted butter, softened
200g (7oz) soft light brown sugar
1 egg
1 tsp vanilla extract
1 tbsp runny honey
125g (4½oz) self-raising flour, sifted
125g (4½oz) oats
pinch of salt
100g (3½oz) pistachio nuts, lightly toasted and roughly chopped.
100g (3½oz) dried cranberries, roughly chopped
a little milk, if needed

Method

1 Preheat the oven to 190°C (375°F/Gas 5). Put the butter and sugar in a bowl, and cream with an electric whisk until smooth. Add the egg, vanilla extract, and honey, and beat well until smooth.

2 Add the flour, oats, and salt, stirring with a wooden spoon to combine. Add the chopped nuts and cranberries and mix until thoroughly combined. If the mixture is too stiff, add a little milk until it becomes pliable.

3 Take walnut-sized pieces and roll them into a ball between your palms. Place on 2 or 3 baking sheets lined with parchment and flatten them slightly, leaving space for the biscuits to spread.

4 Bake for 10–15 minutes until golden brown (you may need to do this in batches). Leave on the tray to cool slightly before transferring to a wire rack.

STORE The cookies will keep in an airtight container for 5 days.

> **BAKER'S TIP**
> Once you have mastered the recipe for oatmeal cookies, try experimenting with different combinations of fresh or dried fruit and nuts, or adding seeds such as sunflower seeds and pumpkin seeds into the mix.

Apple and Cinnamon Oat Cookies

Adding grated apple to the dough makes these cookies soft and chewy.

MAKES 24 | **20 MINS** | **10–15 MINS** | **UP TO 8 WEEKS**

Ingredients

100g (3½oz) unsalted butter, softened
200g (7oz) soft light brown sugar
1 egg
1 tsp vanilla extract
1 tbsp runny honey
125g (4½oz) self-raising flour, sifted
125g (4½oz) oats
2 tsp cinnamon
pinch of salt
2 apples, peeled, cored, and finely grated
a little milk, if needed

Method

1 Preheat the oven to 190°C (375°F/Gas 5). Put the butter and sugar in a bowl and cream together with an electric whisk until smooth. Add the egg, vanilla extract, and honey, and beat well until smooth.

2 With a wooden spoon, stir the flour, oats, cinnamon, and salt into the creamed mixture to combine. Mix in the apple. If the mixture seems too stiff, add a little milk. Take walnut-sized pieces of dough and roll them into a ball between your palms.

3 Place on 2 or 3 baking sheets lined with parchment and flatten slightly, leaving space for the biscuits to spread.

4 Bake for 10–15 minutes until golden brown. Leave to cool slightly and then transfer to a wire rack to cool completely.

STORE The cookies will keep in an airtight container for 5 days.

White Chocolate and Macadamia Nut Cookies

Here classic chocolate cookies are given a sophisticated twist.

MAKES 24 | **25 MINS** | **10–15 MINS** | **UP TO 4 WEEKS**

Chilling time
30 mins

Ingredients
150g (5½oz) good-quality dark chocolate, broken into pieces
100g (3½oz) self-raising flour
25g (scant 1oz) cocoa powder
75g (2½oz) unsalted butter, softened
175g (6oz) soft light brown sugar
1 egg, beaten
1 tsp vanilla extract
50g (1¾oz) macadamia nuts, roughly chopped
50g (1¾oz) white chocolate chunks

Method

1 Preheat the oven to 180°C (350°F/Gas 4). Melt the chocolate in a heatproof bowl set over a pan of simmering water. The bowl should not touch the water. Set aside to cool. Sift the flour and cocoa together.

2 In a large bowl, cream together the butter and sugar with an electric whisk until light and fluffy. Beat in the egg and vanilla extract. Fold in the flour mixture. Add the chocolate and mix thoroughly to combine. Finally, fold in the macadamia nuts and white chocolate chunks. Cover the bowl and chill for 30 minutes.

3 Place tablespoons of the chilled cookie dough on 2 or 3 baking sheets lined with parchment, positioned at least 5cm (2in) apart, as they will spread.

4 Bake in the top third of the oven for 10–15 minutes until cooked through but still soft in the middle. Leave on the trays for a few minutes, then transfer to a wire rack to cool.

STORE The cookies will keep in an airtight container for 3 days.

Butter Biscuits

These thin, elegant biscuits are one of my favourite recipes. They are quick, simple, and decidedly moreish.

 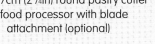

MAKES 30 | **15 MINS** | **10–15 MINS** | **UP TO 8 WEEKS**

Ingredients
100g (3½oz) caster sugar
225g (8oz) plain flour, sifted,
  plus extra for dusting
150g (5½oz) unsalted butter,
  softened and diced
1 egg yolk
1 tsp vanilla extract

Special equipment
7cm (2¾in) round pastry cutter
food processor with blade
  attachment (optional)

1 Preheat the oven to 180°C (350°F/Gas 4). Have several non-stick baking sheets to hand.

2 Put the sugar, flour, and butter into a large bowl, or into the bowl of a food processor.

3 Rub together, or pulse-blend, the ingredients until they look like fine breadcrumbs.

4 Add the egg yolk and vanilla extract, and bring the mixture together into a dough.

5 Turn the dough out onto a lightly floured work surface and knead it briefly until smooth.

6 Flour the dough and work surface well, and roll it out to a thickness of about 5mm (¼in).

7 Use a palette knife to move the dough around, to prevent sticking.

8 If the dough is too sticky to roll well, chill for 15 minutes, then try again.

9 With the pastry cutter, cut out round biscuits and transfer them to the baking sheets.

BISCUITS, COOKIES, AND SLICES

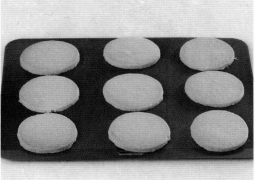

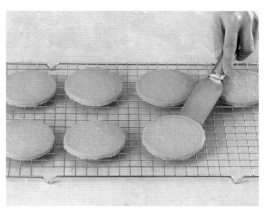

10 Re-roll the pastry offcuts to 5mm (¼in) thick. Cut out biscuits until all the dough is used.

11 Bake in batches for 10–15 minutes until golden brown at the edges.

12 Leave the biscuits to cool until firm enough to handle, then transfer to a wire rack.

13 Leave the butter biscuits to cool completely on the wire rack, before serving. **STORE** The biscuits will keep well in an airtight container for 5 days.

Butter Biscuit variations

Crystallized Ginger Biscuits

Here crystallized ginger adds warmth and depth of flavour.

MAKES 30 | **15 MINS** | **12–15 MINS** | **UP TO 8 WEEKS**

Special equipment
7cm (3in) round pastry cutter
food processor with blade attachment (optional)

Ingredients
100g (3½oz) caster sugar
225g (8oz) plain flour, sifted, plus extra for dusting
150g (5½oz) unsalted butter, softened and diced
1 tsp ground ginger
50g (1¾oz) crystallized ginger, finely chopped
1 egg yolk
1 tsp vanilla extract

Method
1 Preheat the oven to 180°C (350°F/Gas 4). Have 3 or 4 non-stick baking sheets to hand. Combine the sugar, flour, and butter in a bowl, or in the bowl of a food processor fitted with a blade, and rub or process together until the mixture forms crumbs. Stir in the ground and crystallized gingers.

2 Add the egg yolk and vanilla extract, and bring the mixture together into a dough. Turn out onto a lightly floured work surface and knead it briefly until smooth.

3 Flour the dough and work surface well, and roll it out to 5mm (¼in) thick. Cut out biscuit shapes with the pastry cutter and transfer them to the baking sheets.

4 Bake in the oven for 12–15 minutes until golden brown at the edges. Leave on the baking sheets for a few minutes, then transfer to a wire rack to cool completely.

STORE The biscuits will keep in an airtight container for 5 days.

Almond Butter Biscuits

The addition of almond extract makes these delicious biscuits quite grown up and not overly sweet.

MAKES 30 | **15 MINS** | **12–15 MINS** | **UP TO 8 WEEKS**

Special equipment
7cm (3in) round pastry cutter
food processor with blade attachment (optional)

Ingredients
100g (3½oz) caster sugar
225g (8oz) plain flour, sifted, plus extra for dusting
150g (5½oz) unsalted butter, softened and diced
40g (1½oz) flaked almonds, lightly toasted
1 egg yolk
1 tsp almond extract

Method
1 Preheat the oven to 180°C (350°F/Gas 4). Have 3 or 4 non-stick baking sheets to hand. Mix the sugar, flour, and butter in a bowl, or in the bowl of a food processor with a blade attachment. Rub or process together until it forms crumbs. Mix in the almonds.

2 Add the egg yolk and almond essence, and bring the mixture together into a dough. Knead briefly until smooth and roll out to 5mm (¼in) thick.

3 Cut out biscuit shapes with the cutter and transfer to the baking sheets. Bake in batches for 12–15 minutes until golden brown at the edges. Leave for a few minutes, then transfer to a wire rack to cool.

STORE The biscuits will keep in an airtight container for 5 days.

BAKER'S TIP
Always look for almond extract, as bottles labelled "essence" are made from synthetic flavourings. For excellent after-dinner biscuits to have with coffee, roll the biscuits out thinner and bake for 5–8 minutes.

Spritzgebäck Biscuits

These delicate, buttery biscuits are based on a classic German cookie traditionally served at Christmas. ▶

MAKES 45 | **45 MINS** | **15 MINS**

Special equipment
piping bag and star nozzle

Ingredients
380g (13oz) butter, softened
250g (9oz) caster sugar
few drops of vanilla extract
pinch of salt
500g (1lb 2oz) plain flour, sifted
125g (4½oz) ground almonds
2 egg yolks, if needed
100g (3½oz) dark or milk chocolate

Method
1 Preheat the oven to 180°C (350°F/Gas 4). Line 2–3 baking sheets with parchment. Place the butter in a bowl and beat until smooth. Stir in the sugar, vanilla, and salt until the mixture is thick, and the sugar has been absorbed. Gradually add two-thirds of the flour, stirring in a little at a time.

2 Add the rest of the flour and almonds, and knead the mixture to make a dough. Transfer the dough to the piping bag and squeeze 7.5cm (3in) lengths onto the baking sheets. Loosen the dough with 2 egg yolks, if necessary.

3 Bake for 12 minutes or until golden, and transfer to a wire rack. Melt the chocolate in a bowl over a pan of simmering water. Dip one end of the biscuits into the melted chocolate and return to the rack to set.

STORE The biscuits will keep in an airtight container for 2–3 days.

Gingerbread Men

All children love to make gingerbread men. This recipe is quick and the dough is easy for little bakers to handle.

MAKES 16 | **20 MINS** | **10–12 MINS** | **8 WEEKS, UNBAKED**

Special equipment
11cm (4½in) gingerbread man cutter
piping bag with thin nozzle (optional)

Ingredients
4 tbsp golden syrup
300g (10½oz) plain flour,
  plus extra for dusting
1 tsp bicarbonate of soda
1½ tsp ground ginger
1½ tsp mixed spice
100g (3½oz) unsalted butter,
  softened and diced
150g (5½oz) soft dark brown sugar

1 egg
raisins, to decorate
icing sugar, sifted (optional)

1 Preheat the oven to 190°C (375°F/Gas 5). Heat the golden syrup till it liquefies, then cool.

2 Sift the flour, bicarbonate of soda, and spices into a bowl. Add the butter.

3 Rub together with your fingertips until the mixture looks like fine breadcrumbs.

4 Add the sugar to the breadcrumbs mixture and mix well.

5 Beat the egg into the cooled syrup until well blended.

6 Make a well in the flour mixture. Pour in the syrup mix. Bring together to a rough dough.

7 On a lightly floured work surface, knead the dough briefly until smooth.

8 Flour the dough and the work surface well, and roll the dough out to 5mm (¼in) thick.

9 Using the cutter, cut out as many shapes as possible. Transfer to non-stick baking sheets.

10 Mix the offcuts of dough, re-roll, and cut out more shapes until all the dough is used.

11 Decorate the men with raisins, giving them eyes, a nose, and buttons down the front.

12 Bake for 10–12 minutes until golden. Transfer to a wire rack to cool completely.

13 If using, mix a little icing sugar in a bowl with enough water to form a thin icing.

14 Transfer the icing into the piping bag; placing the bag into a jug first will help.

15 Decorate the men with the piped icing to resemble clothes, hair, or whatever you prefer.

16 Leave the icing to set completely before serving or storing. **STORE** These gingerbread men will keep in an airtight container for 3 days.

Gingerbread variations

Swedish Spice Biscuits

A version of the traditional Swedish Christmas biscuits. Roll them as thin as you dare (and bake for less time) for a truly authentic result.

MAKES 60	**20 MINS**	**10 MINS**	**8 WEEKS, UNBAKED**

Chilling time
1 hr

Special equipment
7cm (3in) heart or star-shaped pastry cutters

Ingredients
125g (4½oz) unsalted butter, softened
150g (5½oz) caster sugar
1 egg
1 tbsp golden syrup
1 tbsp black treacle
250g (9oz) plain flour, plus extra for dusting
pinch of salt
1 tsp cinnamon
1 tsp ground ginger
1 tsp mixed spice

Method
1 With an electric whisk, cream the butter and sugar. Beat in the egg, golden syrup, and black treacle. Sift together the flour, salt, and spices in a separate bowl. Add the flour mixture to the biscuit batter, and bring it all together to form a rough dough.

2 Briefly knead until smooth, place in a plastic bag and chill for 1 hour.

3 Preheat the oven to 180°C (350°F/Gas 4). Roll the dough out to a thickness of 3mm (⅛in) and cut out shapes with pastry cutters.

4 Transfer the biscuits to several non-stick baking sheets and bake in the top third of the oven for 10 minutes until the edges darken slightly. Leave on the trays for a few minutes, then transfer onto a wire rack to cool completely.

STORE The biscuits will keep in an airtight container for 5 days.

> **BAKER'S TIP**
> These are based on a Swedish Christmas biscuit called *Pepparkakor*. To decorate a Christmas tree in traditional Swedish style, cut the biscuits into heart shapes and use a straw to cut a hole out of the top before cooking. Once baked, tie the biscuits onto the tree using red ribbon.

Gingernut Biscuits

The addition of chopped nuts makes these biscuits extra special.

MAKES 45	**30 MINS**	**8–10 MINS**	**8 WEEKS, UNBAKED**

Special equipment
7cm (3in) pastry cutters (any shape)

Ingredients
250g (9oz) plain flour, plus extra for dusting
2 tsp baking powder
175g (6oz) caster sugar
few drops of vanilla extract
½ tsp mixed spice
2 tsp ground ginger
100g (3½oz) clear honey
1 egg, separated
4 tsp milk
125g (4½oz) butter, softened and diced
125g (4½oz) ground almonds
chopped hazelnuts or almonds, to decorate

Method
1 Preheat the oven to 180°C (350°F/Gas 4). Line 2 baking trays with baking parchment.

2 Sift the flour and baking powder into a bowl. Add all the other ingredients except the chopped nuts. With a wooden spoon, bring the mixture together to form a soft dough. Use your hands to shape the dough into a ball.

3 Roll the dough out on a lightly floured surface to 5mm (¼in) thickness. Cut out the biscuits with cutters, and place on the baking trays, spaced apart to allow them to spread. Beat the egg white and brush over the biscuits, then sprinkle over the nuts. Bake for 8–10 minutes or until lightly golden brown.

4 Remove from the oven and allow to cool on the tray for a few minutes, then transfer to a wire rack to cool completely.

STORE These gingernut biscuits will keep in an airtight container for 3 days.

Cinnamon Stars

These classic German cookies make a great last-minute Christmas gift.

| MAKES 30 | 20 MINS | 12–15 MINS | 4 WEEKS, UNBAKED |

Chilling time
1 hr

Special equipment
7cm (3in) star-shaped pastry cutter

Ingredients
2 large egg whites
225g (8oz) icing sugar, plus extra for dusting
½ tsp lemon juice
1 tsp cinnamon
250g (9oz) ground almonds
vegetable oil, for greasing
a little milk, if needed

Method

1 Whisk the egg whites until they are quite stiff. Sift in the icing sugar, add the lemon juice and continue to whisk for another 5 minutes, until thick and glossy. Take out 2 tablespoons of the mixture, cover and set aside for topping the cookies later.

2 Gently fold the cinnamon and ground almonds into the remaining mixture. Cover and refrigerate for 1 hour or overnight. The mixture will resemble a thick paste.

3 Preheat the oven to 160°C (325°F/Gas 3). Dust a work surface with icing sugar and turn the paste out onto it. Bring together with a little icing sugar to form a soft dough. Dust a rolling pin with icing sugar and roll out the dough to 5mm (¼in) thick.

4 Oil the cutter and non-stick baking sheets. Cut star shapes out of the dough. Lay the cookies on the sheets. Brush a little of the meringue mix over the surface of each cookie, mixing it with a little milk, if too thick.

5 Bake in the top third of the oven for 12–15 minutes until the topping has set. Leave to cool for at least 10 minutes on the baking sheets, then transfer to a wire rack.

STORE The biscuits will keep in an airtight container for 5 days.

Canestrelli

These delightful Italian biscuits are as light as air and traditionally made with a flower-shaped cutter – a fitting shape for such a delicate biscuit.

MAKES 20–30 · **20 MINS** · **15–20 MINS** · **UP TO 4 WEEKS**

Chilling time
30 mins

Special equipment
flower-shaped pastry cutter,
or 2 different-sized round cutters

Ingredients

3 egg yolks, unbroken
150g (5½oz) unsalted butter, softened
150g (5½oz) icing sugar, sifted
finely grated zest of ½ lemon
150g (5½oz) potato flour
100g (3½oz) self-raising flour
  (or more potato flour if you are wheat
  intolerant), plus extra for dusting

Method

1 Gently slide the egg yolks into a pan of simmering water over low heat. Poach for 5 minutes, until completely hard, then take them out of the water and set aside to cool. When they are cool, push the egg yolks through a fine metal sieve with the back of a spoon. Scrape into a small bowl.

2 Cream together the butter and icing sugar with an electric whisk until light and fluffy. Add the egg yolks and lemon zest, and beat well to combine.

3 Sift the flours together and add to the biscuit batter, beating well to form a smooth, soft dough. Place the dough in a plastic bag and refrigerate for 30 minutes to firm up. Preheat the oven to 160°C (325°F/Gas 3) and have 3 or 4 non-stick baking sheets ready.

4 Roll out the chilled dough on a lightly floured work surface to 1cm (½in) thick. Cut out traditional flower-shaped cookies, or other shapes. If you do not have a flower-shaped cutter, use a larger and a smaller cutter to make ring shapes instead.

5 Place the cookies on the baking sheets and bake in the top third of the oven for 15–17 minutes until just turning golden. The canestrelli are very delicate when warm, so leave them to cool for at least 10 minutes on their baking sheets before removing to a wire rack to cool completely.

STORE The canestrelli will keep in an airtight container for 5 days.

BAKER'S TIP

These delicate biscuits originate from the Liguria region of Italy. Their light texture comes from the traditional use of potato flour in the recipe. If you cannot find any potato flour, an "00" grade flour (from larger supermarkets and Italian delicatessens), or even plain flour, will make a good substitute.

Macaroons

These almond meringue biscuits (not to be confused with French macarons) are crisp outside and chewy inside.

MAKES 24 **10 MINS** **12–15 MINS**

Special equipment
sheets of edible wafer paper (optional)

Ingredients
2 egg whites
225g (8oz) caster sugar
125g (4½oz) ground almonds
30g (1oz) rice flour
a few drops of almond extract
24 blanched almonds

1 Preheat the oven to 180°C (350°F/Gas 4). Use an electric whisk to stiffen the egg whites.

2 Gradually whisk in the sugar, a tablespoon at a time, to give a thick, glossy meringue.

3 Fold in the ground almonds, rice flour, and almond extract until well combined.

4 Divide the wafer paper, if using, between 2 baking sheets, or line them with parchment.

5 Use 2 teaspoons to scoop and shape the mixture, cleaning and drying between scoops.

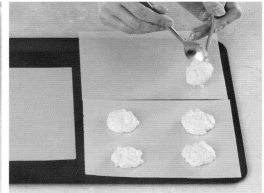

6 Place 4 teaspoons of mixture, spaced apart, on each piece of edible wafer paper.

7 Keep the mixture in rounds. Put a blanched almond in the centre of each biscuit.

8 Bake the macaroons in the centre of the oven for 12–15 minutes or until lightly golden.

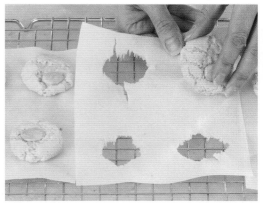

9 Transfer to a wire rack to cool completely, before tearing each biscuit from the paper.

Macaroons are prone to sticking, but by using edible wafer it doesn't matter if the paper tears off with the biscuit. **STORE** Macaroons are best eaten on the day they are made. They will keep for 2–3 days in an airtight container, but tend to dry out.

Macaroon variations

Coconut Macaroons

Coconut macaroons are simple to make and completely wheat-free. I've omitted chocolate from my version so that they remain a light treat.

MAKES 18–20 · **20 MINS** · **15–20 MINS**

Chilling time
2 hrs

Special equipment
sheets of edible wafer paper (optional)

Ingredients
1 egg white
50g (1¾oz) caster sugar
pinch of salt
½ tsp vanilla extract
100g (3½oz) desiccated,
  or sweetened shredded, coconut

Method

1 Preheat the oven to 160°C (325°F/Gas 3). In a large bowl, beat the egg whites with an electric whisk until stiff. Add the sugar a little at a time, whisking between each addition, until all the sugar is combined and the mixture is thick and glossy.

2 Add the salt and vanilla extract, and briefly whisk again to blend.

3 Gently fold in the coconut. Cover and refrigerate for 2 hours to firm up. This will also allow the desiccated coconut to hydrate and soften.

4 Line a baking sheet with parchment or wafer paper (if using). Place heaped teaspoons of the mixture onto the baking sheet; try to keep each portion of the mixture in a small heap.

5 Bake in the middle of the oven for 15–20 minutes until golden brown in places. Leave the macaroons to cool on the trays for at least 10 minutes to firm up, then transfer to a wire rack to cool completely.

STORE The macaroons will keep in an airtight container for 5 days.

Chocolate Macaroons

Add cocoa powder for a chocolate version of the basic macaroon.

MAKES 24 · **20 MINS** · **15 MINS** · **UP TO 4 WEEKS**

Chilling time
30 mins

Special equipment
sheets of edible wafer paper (optional)

Ingredients
2 egg whites
225g (8oz) caster sugar
100g (3½oz) ground almonds
30g (1oz) rice flour
25g (scant 1oz) cocoa powder, sifted
24 whole blanched almonds

Method

1 Preheat the oven to 180°C (350°F/Gas 4). In a large bowl, beat the egg whites with an electric whisk, until stiff. Add the sugar a little at a time, whisking between each addition, until all the sugar is combined and the mixture is thick and glossy.

2 Fold in the almonds, rice flour, and then the cocoa powder. Cover and refrigerate for 30 minutes to firm up. Line 2 baking sheets with parchment or wafer paper (if using).

3 Place heaped teaspoons of the mixture onto the prepared baking sheets, spacing them at least 4cm (1½in) apart as they will spread. Try to keep each portion of the mixture in a small heap. Place a blanched almond in the centre of each heap.

4 Bake the macaroons at the top of the oven for 12–15 minutes until the exterior is crisp and the edges firm to the touch. Leave the macaroons to cool on the sheets for at least 5 minutes, then transfer to a wire rack to cool completely.

STORE Best eaten on the day, these will keep in an airtight container for 2–3 days.

Coffee and Hazelnut Macaroons

These gorgeous little biscuits are easy to prepare, infused with flavour, and look very pretty served after dinner with coffee, especially if you make them on the smaller side.

| MAKES 20 | 30 MINS | 20 MINS | UP TO 4 WEEKS |

Chilling time
30 mins

Special equipment
food processor with blade attachment
sheets of edible wafer paper (optional)

Ingredients
150g (5½oz) hazelnuts, shelled, plus 20 extra
2 egg whites
225g (8oz) caster sugar
30g (1oz) rice flour
1 tsp strong instant coffee powder, dissolved
  in 1 tsp boiling water and cooled, or equivalent
  cooled espresso

Method

1 Preheat the oven to 180°C (350°F/Gas 4). Place the hazelnuts on a baking tray and toast for 5 minutes. Put them in a tea towel and rub to remove skin. Set aside to cool.

2 Whisk the egg whites until stiff. Add the sugar a little at a time, whisking, until all the sugar is combined and the mixture is thick.

3 In a food processor, blitz the hazelnuts to a powder. Fold them into the meringue mixture with the rice flour, and gently fold in a teaspoon of the coffee mixture. Cover and refrigerate for 30 minutes to firm up.

4 Place teaspoons of the mixture onto baking sheets lined with parchment or wafer paper, spacing them at least 4cm (1½in) apart. Keep each portion in a small heap and place a whole hazelnut in the centre.

5 Bake the macaroons at the top of the oven for 12–15 minutes, until crisp and colouring slightly; check after 10 minutes if making them small. Leave on the trays for 5 minutes and transfer to a wire rack to cool.

STORE Best eaten on the day, these will keep in an airtight container for 2–3 days.

BAKER'S TIP

Old-fashioned macaroons have been rather overshadowed of late by their prettier French cousins, macarons (see pages 246–251). However, macaroons are also wheat-free, easier to make, and just as pretty, in an understated kind of way.

Vanillekipferl

These crescent-shaped German biscuits are often served at the same time as Cinnamon Stars (see page 199), making a truly festive platter.

MAKES 30

35 MINS

15–17 MINS

UP TO 4 WEEKS

Chilling time
30 mins

Ingredients
200g (7oz) plain flour, plus extra for dusting
150g (5½oz) unsalted butter, softened and diced
75g (2½oz) icing sugar
75g (2½oz) ground almonds
1 tsp vanilla extract
1 egg, beaten
vanilla sugar or icing sugar, to serve

Method

1 Sift the flour into a large bowl. Rub in the softened butter until the mixture resembles fine crumbs. Sift in the icing sugar, and add the ground almonds.

2 Add the vanilla extract to the egg, then pour it into the flour mixture. Bring the mixture together to form a soft dough, adding a little more flour if the mixture is very sticky. Place the dough in a plastic bag and chill it for at least 30 minutes until firm.

3 Preheat the oven to 160°C (325°F/Gas 3). Divide the dough into 2 parts, and on a lightly floured work surface, roll each part into a sausage shape, approximately 3cm (1½in) in diameter. Use a sharp knife to cut 1cm (½in) pieces from the dough.

4 To form the cookies, take a piece of the dough and roll it between your palms to make a sausage shape of around 8 x 2cm (3½–¾in), tapering it slightly at each end.

Fold each end of the roll in slightly to form a crescent shape. Line 2 baking sheets with baking parchment, and place the formed cookies on them, leaving a little space between each.

5 Bake the vanillekipferl at the top of the oven for 15 minutes until they are very lightly coloured. They should not brown at all.

6 Leave the cookies to cool on their trays for 5 minutes, then either toss in vanilla sugar or liberally dust with icing sugar and transfer to a wire rack to cool completely.

STORE The vanillekipferl will keep in an airtight container for 5 days.

BAKER'S TIP
A German Christmas tradition, these crescent-shaped biscuits rely on the use of ground almonds for their delicate, crumbly texture. Many recipes recommend tossing the finished biscuits in vanilla sugar, but if that proves difficult to find, the vanilla extract in the biscuit dough will do just as well.

Florentines

These crisp Italian biscuits are packed full of fruit and nuts, and coated with luxurious dark chocolate – wonderful for a quick teatime treat.

MAKES 16–20 | 20 MINS | 15–20 MINS

Ingredients

60g (2oz) butter
60g (2oz) caster sugar
1 tbsp clear honey
60g (2oz) plain flour, sifted
45g (1½oz) chopped mixed peel
45g (1½oz) glacé cherries, finely chopped
45g (1½oz) blanched almonds, finely chopped
1 tsp lemon juice
1 tbsp double cream
175g (6oz) good-quality dark chocolate,
  broken into pieces

Method

1 Preheat the oven to 180°C (350°F/Gas 4) and line 2 baking sheets with parchment.

2 Put the butter, sugar, and honey into a small saucepan, and melt gently over low heat. Allow it to cool until it is just warm. Stir in all the other ingredients except the chocolate.

3 Using a teaspoon, drop spoonfuls of the mixture onto the baking sheets, leaving space between them for the biscuits to spread.

4 Bake for 10 minutes or until golden. Do not let them get too dark. Leave them on the baking sheets for a few minutes, before lifting them onto a wire rack to cool completely.

5 Put the chocolate pieces into a heatproof bowl set over a pan of gently simmering water. Make sure the bowl is not touching the water.

6 Once the chocolate has melted, use a palette knife to spread a thin layer of chocolate on the bottom of each biscuit. Place the biscuits chocolate-side up on a wire rack to set. Spread a second layer of chocolate over the biscuits, then just before it sets, make a wavy line in the chocolate with a fork.

STORE The Florentines will keep in an airtight container for 5 days.

BAKER'S TIP
You can make a beautiful display of three different colours of Florentines by topping one-third with milk chocolate, another third with white chocolate, and the remainder with dark chocolate. Or use different tones of chocolate both to top and to drizzle over in a zigzag fashion, for an impressive effect.

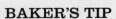

Biscotti

These crisp Italian biscuits make great presents, as they can be prettily packaged and will keep for days.

MAKES 25–30 **15 MINS** **40–45 MINS** **UP TO 8 WEEKS**

Ingredients

50g (1¾oz) unsalted butter
100g (3½oz) whole almonds,
  shelled and skinned
225g (8oz) self-raising flour,
  plus extra for dusting
100g (3½oz) caster sugar
2 eggs
1 tsp vanilla extract

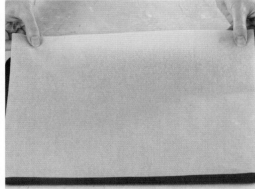

1 Melt the butter in small pan over low heat and then set aside to cool.

2 Preheat the oven to 180°C (350°F/Gas 4). Line a baking sheet with parchment.

3 Spread the almonds out on a non-stick baking sheet. Place in the centre of the oven.

4 Bake the almonds for 5–10 minutes until slightly coloured, tossing halfway.

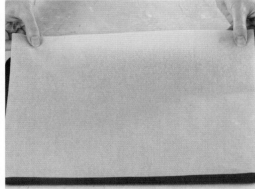

5 Allow the almonds to cool until they are comfortable to handle and roughly chop them.

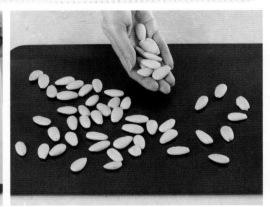

6 Sift the flour through a fine sieve held over a large bowl.

7 Add the sugar and chopped almonds to the bowl and stir until well combined.

8 In a separate bowl, whisk together the eggs, vanilla extract, and the melted butter.

9 Gradually pour the egg mixture into the flour, while stirring with a fork.

10 Using your hands, bring the ingredients together to form a dough.

11 If the mixture seems too wet to shape easily, work in a little flour until it is pliable.

12 Turn the dough out onto a lightly floured work surface.

13 With your hands, form the dough into 2 log shapes, each about 20cm (8in) long.

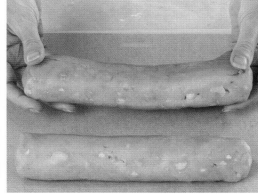

14 Place on the lined baking sheet and bake for 20 minutes in the middle of the oven.

15 Remove the logs from the oven. Cool slightly, then transfer to a chopping board.

16 With a serrated knife, cut the logs on a slant into 3–5cm (1½–2in) thick slices.

17 Put the biscotti on a baking sheet and return to the oven for 10 minutes to dry even more.

18 Turn the biscotti with a palette knife, and return to the oven for another 5 minutes.

19 Cool the biscotti on a wire rack to harden them and allow any moisture to escape.

TO FREEZE Place the cooled biscotti on baking sheets and freeze till solid.

Transfer to freezer bags. **STORE** Keep unfrozen in an airtight container for over 1 week.

BISCOTTI

Biscotti variations

Hazelnut and Chocolate Biscotti

Add chocolate chips to the biscotti dough for a child-friendly alternative.

MAKES 25–30 | **15 MINS** | **40–45 MINS** | **UP TO 8 WEEKS**

Ingredients
100g (3½oz) whole hazelnuts, shelled
225g (8oz) self-raising flour, sifted,
  plus extra for dusting
100g (3½oz) caster sugar
50g (1¾oz) dark chocolate chips
2 eggs
1 tsp vanilla extract
50g (1¾oz) unsalted butter, melted and cooled

Method

1 Preheat the oven to 180°C (350°F/Gas 4). Line a baking sheet with silicone paper. Spread the hazelnuts out on an unlined baking sheet and bake for 5–10 minutes, tossing halfway through, until slightly coloured. Allow to cool, rub in a tea towel to remove excess skin, then roughly chop.

2 In a bowl, mix together the flour, sugar, nuts, and chocolate chips. In a separate bowl, whisk together the eggs, vanilla extract, and butter. Combine the wet and dry ingredients, working them together to form a dough. If the mixture is too wet, knead in a little extra flour to shape easily.

3 Turn the dough out onto a floured surface and form into 2 logs, each 20cm (8in) long by 7cm (3in). Place on the lined baking sheet and bake for 20 minutes in the middle of the oven. Take the biscotti logs out of the oven, allow them to cool slightly. Cut them diagonally into 3–5cm (1¼–2in) thick slices with a serrated knife.

4 Return the sliced biscotti to the oven for another 15 minutes, turning them after 10 minutes. They are ready when golden at the edges and hard to the touch. Cool on a wire rack.

STORE These will keep in an airtight container for more than 1 week.

Chocolate and Brazil Nut Biscotti

These biscotti, darkened with cocoa powder, are ideal to serve after dinner with strong, black coffee.

MAKES 25–30 | **15 MINS** | **40–45 MINS** | **UP TO 8 WEEKS**

Ingredients
100g (3½oz) whole Brazil nuts, shelled
175g (6oz) self-raising flour, sifted,
  plus extra for dusting
50g (1¾oz) cocoa powder
100g (3½oz) caster sugar
2 eggs
1 tsp vanilla extract
50g (1¾oz) unsalted butter, melted and cooled

Method

1 Preheat the oven to 180°C (350°F/Gas 4). Line a baking sheet with silicone paper. Spread the nuts on an unlined baking sheet and bake for 5–10 minutes. Allow them to cool slightly, rub in a clean tea towel to remove excess skin, then roughly chop.

2 In a bowl, mix together the flour, cocoa powder, sugar, and nuts. In a separate bowl, whisk together the eggs, vanilla extract, and butter. Combine the wet and dry ingredients together to form a dough.

3 Turn the dough out onto a floured surface and form into 2 logs, each 20cm (8in) long by 7cm (3in). Place on the lined baking sheet and bake for 20 minutes. Cool slightly, then cut them diagonally into 3–5cm (1¼–2in) thick slices with a serrated knife.

4 Return to the oven for 15 minutes, turning after 10, until golden and hard to the touch.

STORE These will keep in an airtight container for more than 1 week.

> **BAKER'S TIP**
> The hard, crunchy texture and toasted taste of biscotti is obtained by double-baking. This technique also allows them to keep well for a relatively long time.

Pistachio and Orange Biscotti

These fragrant biscotti are delicious served either with coffee or dipped in a glass of sweet dessert wine. ▶

MAKES 25–30 | **15 MINS** | **40–45 MINS** | **UP TO 8 WEEKS**

Ingredients
100g (3½oz) whole pistachios, shelled
225g (8oz) self-raising flour,
  plus extra for dusting
100g (3½oz) caster sugar
finely grated zest of 1 orange
2 eggs
1 tsp vanilla extract
50g (1¾oz) unsalted butter, melted and cooled

Method

1 Preheat the oven to 180°C (350°F/Gas 4). Spread the pistachios on an unlined baking sheet. Bake for 5–10 minutes. Allow to cool, rub in a clean tea towel to remove excess skin, then roughly chop.

2 In a bowl, mix the flour, sugar, zest, and nuts. In a separate bowl, whisk together the eggs, vanilla extract, and butter. Mix the wet and dry ingredients to form a dough.

3 Turn the dough out onto a floured surface and form into 2 logs, each 20cm (8in) long by 7cm (3in). Place them on a baking sheet lined with silicone paper and bake for 20 minutes in the centre of the oven. Cool slightly, then cut diagonally into 3–5cm (1¼–2in) thick slices with a serrated knife.

4 Bake for another 15 minutes, turning after 10, until golden and hard to the touch.

STORE These will keep in an airtight container for more than 1 week.

Tuiles

Basic tuile batter is very simple to master. Shaping the tuiles is where the skill comes in, and here are several ideas.

MAKES 15 **15 MINS** **5–7 MINS**

Ingredients
50g (1¾oz) unsalted butter, softened
50g (1¾oz) icing sugar, sifted
1 egg, beaten
50g (1¾oz) plain flour
vegetable oil, for greasing

1 Preheat the oven to 200°C (400°F/Gas 6). Beat the butter and sugar with a whisk.

2 Add the egg and whisk to combine. Sift in the flour and fold in with a large metal spoon.

3 Baking 2–4 at a time, place tablespoons of batter well apart on non-stick baking sheets.

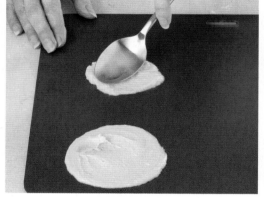

4 Using the back of a wet spoon, smooth them out to a thickness of 8cm (3¼in) in diameter.

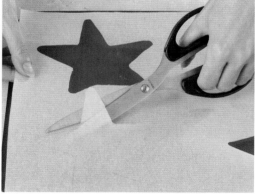

For alternative shapes, cut stencils out of silicone paper. Try stars or scalloped circles.

Place the stencils on a baking sheet and smooth a spoonful of batter evenly over each.

5 Bake at the top of the oven for 5–7 minutes until the edges start to colour to a pale gold.

6 Use a palette knife to lift them; you have only seconds to shape them before they harden.

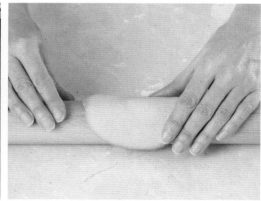

7 Drape over a greased rolling pin for a classic shape. If needed, re-bake for 1 minute to soften.

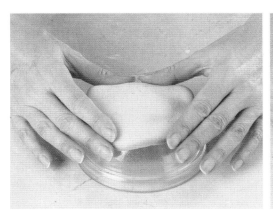

For a basket, press a tuile over the base of a small, greased, upturned circular bowl.

Use your hands or another bowl, to hold it in place for 1 minute until it starts to harden.

For a spiral, twist an oblong tuile around the lightly greased handle of a wooden spoon.

8 Leave the tuiles to cool for 2–3 minutes before gently sliding them off the rolling pin. Place on a wire rack to cool and dry completely. Tuiles are best eaten the day they are made.

Tuile variations

Brandy Snaps

So easy to make, brandy snaps deserve to be back in fashion. A basket will transform a simple chocolate mousse into an elegant dessert.

MAKES | **15** | **6–8**
16–20 | MINS | MINS

Special equipment
piping bag and medium nozzle (optional)

Ingredients
100g (3½oz) unsalted butter, diced
100g (3½oz) caster sugar
60g (2oz) golden syrup
100g (3½oz) plain flour, sifted
1 tsp ground ginger
finely grated zest of ½ lemon
1 tbsp brandy (optional)
vegetable oil, for greasing

For the filling (optional)
250ml (8fl oz) double cream, whipped
1 tbsp icing sugar
1 tsp brandy

Method
1 Preheat the oven to 180°C (350°F/Gas 4). Melt the butter and sugar in a pan over medium heat. Mix in the golden syrup well. Remove from the heat and beat in the flour, ginger, and zest. Stir in the brandy (if using).

2 Place heaped teaspoons of the mixture on 3 or 4 non-stick baking sheets, ensuring they are spaced well apart, as they will spread to about 8cm (3¼in) in diameter. Bake at the top of the oven for 6–8 minutes until golden brown and the edges are darkening slightly.

3 Leave on the baking sheets to cool for 3 minutes, until you are able to move them with a spatula, but they are still soft enough to shape. If they become difficult to work with, return them to the oven for 1–2 minutes to soften.

4 To make a classic shape, roll the biscuits around the greased handle of a wooden spoon and wait until they harden before sliding them off onto a wire rack. See page 217 for how to shape a basket.

5 To serve as a dessert, fold the filling ingredients together and pipe the mixture into the cooled, rolled brandy snaps. These are best eaten on the day they are made.

Parmesan Crisps

The simplest recipe imaginable – use these crisps as a garnish or canapé.

MAKES | **5** | **5–7**
24 | MINS | MINS

Special equipment
7cm (2¾in) pastry cutter

Ingredients

For the crisps
100g (3½oz) Parmesan cheese, finely grated

For the additional ingredients (optional)
1 tbsp poppy seeds, or 1 tbsp sesame seeds, or 1 tbsp chopped herbs, such as rosemary, thyme, or sage

Method
1 Preheat the oven to 200°C (400°F/Gas 6). Mix the cheese in a bowl with any one of the additional ingredients (if using).

2 Place the pastry cutter on a non-stick baking tray. Sprinkle a tablespoon of the grated cheese mixture inside the cutter, making sure to spread it out evenly. Gently remove the cutter. Repeat the process with the remaining cheese.

3 Bake them at the top of the oven for 5–7 minutes or until the cheese has melted and started to brown slightly at the edges.

4 Leave the crisps to harden on their trays for a couple of minutes, but transfer them to a wire rack before they cool completely, or they can be difficult to move. They are best eaten on the day they are made.

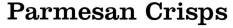

BISCUITS, COOKIES, AND SLICES

Almond Tuiles

These almond tuiles are so simple, yet they would enhance most desserts. Use them as a garnish for delicate fruit or vanilla-flavoured desserts.

MAKES 15	15 MINS	5–7 MINS

Ingredients

50g (1¾oz) unsalted butter, softened
50g (1¾oz) icing sugar, sifted
1 egg
50g (1¾oz) plain flour, sifted
25g (scant 1oz) flaked almonds
vegetable oil, for greasing

Method

1 Preheat the oven to 200°C (400°F/Gas 6). With an electric whisk, cream together the butter and icing sugar until pale and fluffy. Add the egg and mix well to combine. Gently fold in the flour.

2 Baking 2–4 at a time, place heaped tablespoons of the batter on a non-stick baking sheet. Using the back of a wet spoon, smooth them out in a circular motion to even circles, about 8cm (3¼in) in diameter. You can use stencils to shape the tuiles (see page 216), but ensure they are always of an even thickness.

3 Scatter a few flaked almonds over the tuiles and bake them at the top of the oven for 5–7 minutes. They are ready when the edges start to colour and they are pale gold in the middle.

4 Remove the tuiles from the oven; you have only a matter of seconds to shape them before they harden. If they start to become difficult to work with, return them to the oven for 1–2 minutes until they soften.

5 To make a classic tuile, drape the biscuits over a lightly greased rolling pin and leave them to cool for a couple of minutes before gently sliding them off (or shape differently, see page 217). Once the tuiles are set, put them on a wire rack to dry completely. They are best eaten on the day they are made.

BAKER'S TIP

Tuiles are deceptively simple to make, especially once you know that gently reheating them gives you more time to shape them. However, do not be tempted to shape these almond tuiles too tightly, as the almonds on the surface will not allow the biscuit to be bent too much without cracking.

Shortbread

A Scottish classic, shortbread should only colour very lightly in the oven, so remember to cover with foil if browning.

MAKES 8 WEDGES | **15 MINS** | **30–40 MINS**

Chilling time
1 hr

Special equipment
18cm (7in) loose-bottomed
  round cake tin

Ingredients
150g (5½oz) unsalted butter,
  softened, plus extra for greasing
75g (2½oz) caster sugar,
  plus extra for sprinkling

175g (6oz) plain flour
50g (1¾oz) cornflour

BISCUITS, COOKIES, AND SLICES

1 Preheat the oven to 160°C (325°F/Gas 3). Grease the tin and line with parchment.

2 Place the softened butter and sugar in a large bowl.

3 Cream together the butter and sugar with an electric whisk until light and fluffy.

4 Stir in the flour and cornflour very gently, stopping as soon as the flours are mixed in.

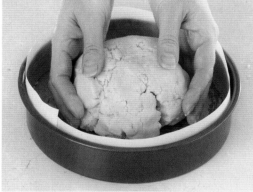

5 Bring together with your hands to form a very rough, crumbly dough. Transfer to the tin.

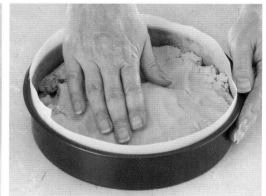

6 Firmly push the dough down with your hands to form a compact, even layer.

7 With a sharp knife, lightly score the circle of shortbread into 8 wedges.

8 Prick the shortbread all over with a fork to make a decorative pattern.

9 Cover the shortbread with cling film and chill in the refrigerator for 1 hour.

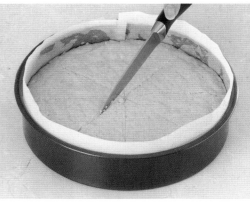

10 Bake in the centre of the oven for 30–40 minutes. Cover with foil if it browns quickly.

11 Take the shortbread out of the oven, and re-score the wedges with a sharp knife.

12 While it is still warm, sprinkle a thin layer of caster sugar evenly over the top.

13 When completely cool, turn the shortbread gently out of its tin and break or cut it into wedges along the scored lines.

STORE The shortbread will keep in an airtight container for up to 5 days.

Shortbread variations

Pecan Sandies

These addictive shortbread cookies are so-called because they are said to have the texture (though not the taste!) of fine sand.

MAKES 18–20 **15 MINS** **15 MINS**

Chilling time
30 mins (if needed)

Ingredients
100g (3½oz) unsalted butter, softened
50g (1¾oz) soft light brown sugar
50g (1¾oz) caster sugar
½ tsp vanilla extract
1 egg yolk
150g (5½oz) plain flour, sifted,
  plus extra for dusting
75g (2½oz) pecan nuts, chopped

Method
1 Preheat the oven to 180°C (350°F/Gas 4). In a large bowl, cream together the butter and sugars with an electric whisk, until light and fluffy. Add the vanilla extract and the egg yolk, and mix well to combine. Fold in the flour and then the pecans. Bring the ingredients together to form a rough dough.

2 Turn the dough out onto a lightly floured work surface and knead it to form a smooth dough. Roll into a log about 20cm (8in) long. If the dough seems too soft to cut, refrigerate it for 30 minutes to allow it to firm up.

3 Slice 1cm (½in) disks from the log, and place a little apart on 2 baking sheets lined with baking parchment. Bake in the top third of the oven for 15 minutes until golden brown at the edges. Leave on the sheets for a few minutes, then transfer them to a wire rack to cool completely.

STORE The sandies will keep in an airtight container for 5 days.

Chocolate Chip Shortbread Cookies

Chocolate chips make these shortbread cookies child-friendly.

MAKES 14–16 **15 MINS** **15–20 MINS**

Ingredients
100g (3½oz) unsalted butter, softened
75g (2½oz) caster sugar
100g (3½oz) plain flour, sifted,
  plus extra for dusting
25g (scant 1oz) cornflour, sifted
50g (1¾oz) dark chocolate chips

Method
1 Preheat the oven to 170°C (340°F/Gas 3½). In a large bowl, cream together the butter and sugar with an electric whisk, until light and fluffy. Stir in the flour, cornflour, and chocolate chips, and bring together to form a rough dough.

2 Turn the dough out onto a lightly floured work surface and gently knead it until it becomes smooth. Roll into a 6cm (2½in) diameter log, and slice at 5mm (¼in) intervals into biscuits. Place a little apart on 2 non-stick baking sheets.

3 Bake in the centre of the oven for about 15–20 minutes until lightly golden. They should not colour too much. Leave on the sheets for a few minutes before transferring to a wire rack to cool completely.

STORE The cookies will keep in an airtight container for 5 days.

Marbled Millionaire's Shortbread

A modern classic – extremely sweet and rich, just as it should be.

MAKES 16 SQUARES | **45 MINS** | **35–40 MINS**

Special equipment
20cm (8in) square cake tin

Ingredients
200g (7oz) plain flour
175g (6oz) unsalted butter, softened, plus extra for greasing
100g (3½oz) caster sugar

For the caramel filling
50g (1¾oz) unsalted butter
50g (1¾oz) light brown sugar
400g can condensed milk

For the chocolate topping
200g (7oz) milk chocolate
25g (scant 1oz) unsalted butter
50g (1¾oz) dark chocolate

Method

1 Preheat the oven to 160°C (325°F/Gas 3). Put the flour, butter, and sugar in a bowl and rub together to make crumbs. Grease the tin and line with parchment. Tip the mixture into the tin and press it down well with your hands until it is compact and even. Bake in the centre of the oven for 35–40 minutes until golden brown. Leave to cool in the tin.

2 For the caramel, melt the butter and sugar in a heavy saucepan over medium heat. Add the condensed milk and bring to a boil, stirring constantly. Reduce the heat and cook on a steady simmer, still stirring constantly, for 5 minutes until it thickens and darkens to a light caramel colour. Pour the caramel over the cooled shortbread and leave to cool.

3 To make the chocolate topping, place the milk chocolate and butter in a heatproof bowl over a pan of simmering water until just melted, stirring until smooth. Melt the dark chocolate without butter in a separate bowl set over simmering water.

4 Pour the milk chocolate over the set caramel and smooth out. Pour the dark chocolate over the surface in a zigzag pattern and drag a fine skewer through both the chocolates to create a marbled effect. Leave to cool and harden before cutting into squares.

STORE The shortbread will keep in an airtight container for 5 days.

BAKER'S TIP
The secret to a good millionaire's shortbread is to make a caramel that sets enough so that it does not squish out of the sides on cutting, and a chocolate topping that cuts easily. Adding butter to the chocolate softens it, and cooking the caramel until thickened will help achieve a perfect result.

Flapjacks

These chewy bars are great energy boosters and very simple to make, using only a few storecupboard ingredients.

MAKES 16–20 **15 MINS** **40 MINS**

Special equipment
25cm (10in) square cake tin

Ingredients
225g (8oz) butter,
 plus extra for greasing
225g (8oz) light soft brown sugar
2 tbsp golden syrup
350g (12oz) rolled oats

1 Preheat the oven to 150°C (300°F/Gas 2). Lightly grease the base and sides of the tin.

2 Put the butter, sugar, and syrup in a large saucepan and place over medium-low heat.

3 Stir constantly with a wooden spoon to prevent scorching. Remove from the heat.

4 Stir in the oats, making sure they are well coated, but do not over-work the mix.

5 Spoon the oat mixture from the saucepan into the prepared tin.

6 Press down firmly with the wooden spoon to make a roughly even layer.

7 To neaten the surface, dip a tablespoon in hot water and use the back to smooth the top.

8 Bake for 40 minutes or until evenly golden; you may need to turn the tin in the oven.

9 Leave to cool for 10 minutes, then cut into 16 squares, or 20 rectangles, with a sharp knife.

10 Leave in the tin to cool completely, then lever the flapjacks out of the tin; a fish slice is a useful tool for this.
STORE These will keep in an airtight container for 1 week.

Flapjack variations

Hazelnut and Raisin Flapjacks

Hazelnuts and raisins make these a chewy and wholesome treat.

MAKES 16–20 | **15 MINS** | **30 MINS** | **UP TO 4 WEEKS**

Special equipment
20 x 25cm (8 x 10in) brownie tin, or similar

Ingredients
225g (8oz) unsalted butter,
  plus extra for greasing
225g (8oz) soft light brown sugar
2 tbsp golden syrup
350g (12oz) rolled oats
75g (2½oz) chopped hazelnuts
50g (1¾oz) raisins

Method
1 Preheat the oven to 160°C (325°F/Gas 3). Grease the tin, and line the base and sides with baking parchment. Melt the butter, sugar, and syrup in a heavy saucepan over low heat until the butter has melted. Remove the pan from the heat and stir in the oats, hazelnuts, and raisins.

2 Transfer the mixture to the prepared tin and press it down firmly, until it is compact and even. Bake in the centre of the oven for 30 minutes until golden brown and darkening slightly at the edges.

3 Leave in the tin for 5 minutes, then cut the flapjacks into squares with a sharp knife. Leave in the tin until cold before turning out with a fish slice.

STORE The flapjacks can be kept in an airtight container for 1 week.

BAKER'S TIP
Nuts and raisins make these flapjacks healthier and, as in the recipes for Oat Cookies (see pages 188–190), you could also add a handful of pumpkin or sunflower seeds. Despite the health quotient of those ingredients, the butter content of flapjacks does make them a high-fat treat.

Cherry Flapjacks

Use dried cherries here for an unusual alternative to the more common dried fruits such as raisins and sultanas. ▶

MAKES 18 | **15 MINS** | **25 MINS**

Chilling time
10 mins

Special equipment
20cm (8in) square cake tin

Ingredients
150g (5½oz) unsalted butter,
  plus extra for greasing
75g (2½oz) light soft brown sugar
2 tbsp golden syrup
350g (12oz) rolled oats
125g (4½oz) glacé cherries, quartered, or
  75g (2½oz) dried cherries, roughly chopped
50g (1¾oz) raisins
100g (3½oz) white or milk chocolate,
  broken into small pieces, for drizzling

Method
1 Preheat the oven to 180°C (350°F/Gas 4). Lightly grease the cake tin. Place the butter, sugar, and syrup in a medium saucepan over low heat, and stir until melted. Remove from the heat, add the oats, cherries, and raisins, and stir until well mixed.

2 Transfer to the prepared tin and press down. Bake at the top of the oven for 25 minutes. Remove, cool slightly in the tin, then cut into 18 pieces with a knife.

3 When the flapjacks are cold, place the chocolate in a small heatproof bowl set over a saucepan of simmering water. Make sure the bowl does not touch the water, and leave the chocolate to melt. Drizzle the melted chocolate over the flapjacks using a teaspoon, then chill for 10 minutes or until the chocolate has set. Remove the flapjacks from the tin with a fish slice.

STORE The flapjacks can be kept in an airtight container for 1 week.

Sticky Date Flapjacks

The quantity of dates in this recipe gives these flapjacks a toffee-like flavour and wonderfully moist consistency.

MAKES 16 | **25 MINS** | **40 MINS**

Special equipment
20cm (8in) square cake tin
blender

Ingredients
200g (7oz) stoned dates, chopped
½ tsp bicarbonate of soda
200g (7oz) unsalted butter
200g (7oz) light soft brown sugar
2 tbsp golden syrup
300g (10½oz) rolled oats

Method
1 Preheat the oven to 160°C (325°F/Gas 3). Line the tin with baking parchment. Place the dates and bicarbonate of soda in a pan with enough water to cover, simmer for 5 minutes, then drain, reserving the liquid. Whizz to a purée in a blender with 3 tablespoons of cooking liquid. Set aside.

2 Melt the butter, sugar, and syrup in a large pan, stirring to mix. Stir in the oats, then press half the mixture into the tin.

3 Spread the date purée over the top of the oats, then spoon the remaining oat mixture over the top. Bake for 40 minutes or until golden brown. Leave to cool in the tin for 10 minutes, then cut into 16 squares with a knife. Leave to cool completely in the tin before turning out with a fish slice.

STORE The flapjacks can be kept in an airtight container for 1 week.

Chocolate and Hazelnut Brownies

A classic American recipe, these brownies are moist and squidgy in the centre and crisp on top.

MAKES 24 **25 MINS** **12–15 MINS**

Special equipment
23 x 30cm (9 x 12in) brownie tin, or similar

Ingredients
100g (3½oz) hazelnuts
175g (6oz) unsalted butter, diced
300g (10½oz) good-quality dark chocolate, broken into pieces
300g (10½oz) caster sugar
4 large eggs, beaten
200g (7oz) plain flour
25g (scant 1oz) cocoa powder, plus extra for dusting

BISCUITS, COOKIES, AND SLICES

1 Preheat the oven to 200°C (400°F/Gas 6). Scatter the hazelnuts over a baking sheet.

2 Toast the nuts in the oven for 5 minutes until browned, being careful not to burn them.

3 Remove from the oven and rub the hazelnuts in a tea towel to remove the skins.

4 Chop the hazelnuts roughly – some big chunks and some small. Set aside.

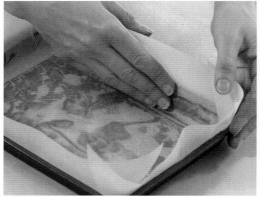

5 Line the base and sides of the tin with parchment. Some should hang over the sides.

6 Place the butter and chocolate in a heatproof bowl over a pan of simmering water.

7 Melt the butter and chocolate, stirring until smooth. Remove and leave to cool.

8 Once the mixture has cooled, mix in the sugar until very well blended.

9 Now add the eggs, a little at a time, being careful to mix well between additions.

10 Sift in the flour and cocoa powder, lifting the sieve up above the bowl to aerate.

11 Fold in the flour and cocoa until the batter is smooth and no patches of flour can be seen.

12 Stir in the chopped nuts to distribute them evenly in the batter; the batter should be thick.

13 Pour into the prepared tin and spread so the mixture fills the corners. Smooth the top.

14 Bake for 12–15 minutes or until just firm to the touch on top and still soft underneath.

15 A skewer inserted should come out coated with a little batter. Remove from the oven.

16 Leave the brownie to cool completely in the tin to maintain the soft centre.

17 Lift the brownie from the tin using the edges of the parchment to get a good grip.

18 Using a long, sharp, or serrated knife, score the surface of the brownie into 24 even pieces.

19 Boil a kettle, and pour the boiling water into a shallow dish. Keep the dish close at hand.

20 Cut the brownie into 24, wiping the knife between cuts and dipping it in the hot water.

21 Sift cocoa powder over the brownies.
STORE Keep in an airtight container for 3 days.

Brownie variations

Sour Cherry and Chocolate Brownies

The sharp flavour and chewy texture of the dried sour cherries contrast wonderfully here with the rich, dark chocolate.

MAKES 16   **15 MINS**   **20–25 MINS**

Special equipment
20 x 25cm (8 x 10in) brownie tin, or similar

Ingredients
150g (5½oz) unsalted butter, diced, plus extra for greasing
150g (5½oz) good-quality dark chocolate, broken into pieces
250g (9oz) soft light brown muscovado sugar
150g (5½oz) self-raising flour, sifted
3 eggs
1 tsp vanilla extract
100g (3½oz) dried sour cherries
100g (3½oz) dark chocolate chunks

Method
1 Preheat the oven to 180°C (350°F/Gas 4). Grease the brownie tin and line with baking parchment. Melt the butter and chocolate in a heatproof bowl over a small amount of simmering water. Remove from the heat, add the sugar, and stir well to combine thoroughly. Cool slightly.

2 Mix the eggs and vanilla extract into the chocolate mixture. Pour the wet mix into the sifted flour and fold together, being careful not to over-mix. Fold in the sour cherries and chocolate chunks.

3 Pour the brownie mixture into the tin and bake in the centre of the oven for 20–25 minutes. They are ready when the edges are firm, but the middle is soft to the touch.

4 Leave the brownie to cool in the tin for 5 minutes. Turn out and cut into squares. Put the brownies onto a wire rack to cool.

STORE The brownies will keep in an airtight container for 3 days.

BAKER'S TIP
The texture of a brownie is very much a matter of personal taste. Some people like them so squishy that they fall apart, while others prefer a firmer cake. If you like squidgy brownies, reduce the cooking time slightly.

Walnut and White Chocolate Brownies

Slightly soft in the centre, these make a tempting teatime treat.

MAKES 16   **10 MINS**   **1 HOUR 15 MINS**

Special equipment
20cm (8in) deep square tin

Ingredients
25g (scant 1oz) unsalted butter, diced, plus extra for greasing
50g (1¾oz) good-quality dark chocolate, broken into pieces
3 eggs
1 tbsp clear honey
225g (8oz) soft light brown sugar
75g (2½oz) self-raising flour
175g (6oz) walnut pieces
25g (scant 1oz) white chocolate, chopped

Method
1 Preheat the oven to 160°C (325°F/Gas 3). Lightly grease the tin, or line the base and sides with baking parchment.

2 Put the dark chocolate and butter into a small heatproof bowl over a saucepan of simmering water until melted, stirring occasionally. Do not let the bowl touch the water. Remove the bowl from the pan and set aside to cool slightly.

3 Beat together the eggs, honey, and brown sugar, then gradually beat in the melted chocolate mixture. Sift the flour over, add the walnut pieces and white chocolate, and gently fold the ingredients together. Pour the mixture into the prepared tin.

4 Put the tin in the oven and bake for 30 minutes. Cover loosely with foil and bake for another 45 minutes. The centre should be a little soft. Leave to cool completely in the tin on a wire rack. When cold, turn out onto a board and cut into squares.

STORE The brownies will keep in an airtight container for 5 days.

White Chocolate Macadamia Blondies

A white chocolate version of the ever-popular brownie.

MAKES 24   **15 MINS**   **20 MINS**

Special equipment
20 x 25cm (8 x 10in) brownie tin, or similar

Ingredients
300g (10oz) white chocolate, broken into pieces
175g (6oz) unsalted butter, diced
300g (10oz) caster sugar
4 large eggs
225g (8oz) plain flour
100g (3½oz) macadamia nuts, roughly chopped

Method

1 Preheat the oven to 200°C (400°F/Gas 6). Line the base and sides of the tin with baking parchment. In a bowl set over a pan of simmering water, melt the chocolate and butter, stirring occasionally until smooth. Do not let the bowl touch the water. Remove and leave to cool for 20 minutes.

2 Once the chocolate has melted, mix in the sugar (the mixture may well become thick and grainy, but the eggs will loosen the mixture). Using a balloon whisk, beat in the eggs one at a time, making sure each is well mixed in before you add the next. Sift in the flour, gently fold it in, then stir in the nuts.

3 Pour the mixture into the tin and gently spread it out into the corners. Bake for 20 minutes or until just firm to the touch on top, but still soft underneath. Leave to cool completely in the tin, then cut into 24 squares, or fewer rectangles for bigger blondies.

STORE The blondies will keep in an airtight container for 5 days.

Stilton and Walnut Biscuits

These savoury biscuits are an ideal way to use up the leftover Stilton and nuts you usually have after Christmas.

MAKES 24 | **10 MINS** | **20 MINS** | **12 WEEKS, UNBAKED**

Chilling time
1 hr

Special equipment
5cm (2in) round pastry cutter

Ingredients
120g (4¼oz) Stilton cheese,
  or other blue cheese
50g (1¾oz) unsalted butter, softened
125g (4½oz) plain flour, sifted,
  plus extra for dusting

60g (2oz) walnuts, chopped
freshly ground black pepper
1 egg yolk

1 Mix together the cheese and butter in a bowl with an electric whisk until soft and creamy.

2 Add the flour to the cheese mixture and rub in with your fingertips to form breadcrumbs.

3 Add the walnuts and black pepper, and stir to mix through.

4 Finally add the egg yolk and bring the mixture together to form a stiff dough.

5 Knead the dough briefly on a lightly floured work surface to help blend in the walnuts.

6 Wrap the dough in cling film. Chill for 1 hour. Preheat the oven to 180°C (350°F/Gas 4).

7 Turn the dough out onto a floured work surface and knead briefly to soften slightly.

8 Roll it out to a thickness of 5mm (¼in) and cut out the biscuits with the pastry cutter.

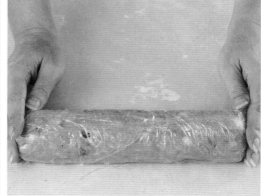

9 Alternatively, the dough can be chilled as an even 5cm (2in) diameter log.

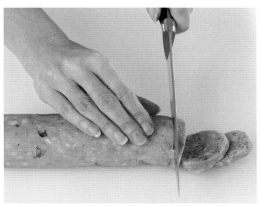

10 Slice the dough log carefully into 5mm (¼in) rounds with a sharp knife.

11 Put the rounds on non-stick baking sheets and bake at the top of the oven for 15 minutes.

12 Turn them over and bake for another 5 minutes until golden brown on both sides.

13 Remove from the oven, allow to cool a little on their trays, then transfer to a wire rack to cool completely.
STORE The biscuits will keep in an airtight container for 5 days.

Cheese Biscuit variations

Parmesan and Rosemary Thins

These savoury biscuits are light and elegant, and are equally good served as an appetizer before a meal or after dinner with cheese.

MAKES 15–20 | **10 MINS** | **15 MINS** | **12 WEEKS, UNBAKED**

Chilling time
1 hr

Special equipment
6cm (2½in) round pastry cutter
food processor with blade attachment (optional)

Ingredients
60g (2oz) unsalted butter, softened and diced
75g (2½oz) plain flour, plus extra for dusting
60g (2oz) Parmesan cheese, finely grated
freshly grated black pepper
1 tbsp chopped rosemary, or thyme, or basil

Method

1 Place the butter and flour in a bowl, or in the bowl of a food processor. Rub together with your fingertips, or pulse-blend, until the mixture resembles crumbs. Add the Parmesan, black pepper, and chopped herbs and mix in thoroughly. Bring the mixture together to form a dough.

2 Turn the dough out onto a floured surface and briefly knead to help it amalgamate. Wrap in cling film and chill for 1 hour.

3 Preheat the oven to 180°C (350°F/Gas 3). Turn the dough out onto a lightly floured surface and knead again to soften slightly.

4 Roll the dough out to 2mm (½in) thick and cut out biscuits with the pastry cutter. Place on several non-stick baking sheets and bake at the top of the oven for 10 minutes. Then turn them over and continue to bake for another 5 minutes until lightly browned.

5 Remove the biscuits from the oven and leave on the trays for 5 minutes, before transferring to a wire rack to cool completely.

STORE The thins will keep in an airtight container for 3 days.

Cheese Thins

These spicy biscuits can be made in bulk for an easy party snack.

MAKES 30 | **10 MINS** | **15 MINS** | **8 WEEKS, UNBAKED**

Chilling time
1 hr

Special equipment
6cm (2½in) round pastry cutter
food processor with blade attachment (optional)

Ingredients
50g (1¾oz) unsalted butter, softened and diced
100g (3½oz) plain flour, plus extra for dusting
150g (5½oz) strong Cheddar cheese, finely grated
½ tsp smoked paprika or cayenne pepper
1 egg yolk

Method

1 Place the butter and flour in a bowl, or in the bowl of a food processor. Rub together with your fingertips, or pulse-blend, until the mixture resembles crumbs. Add the Cheddar and the paprika, and mix thoroughly. Add the egg yolk and bring the mixture together to form a dough.

2 Turn the dough out onto a floured surface and briefly knead to help it amalgamate. Wrap in cling film and chill for 1 hour. When ready to bake, preheat the oven to 180°C (350°F/Gas 4). Turn the dough out onto a lightly floured work surface and knead briefly again to soften slightly.

3 Roll the dough out to a thickness of 2mm (½in) and cut out the biscuits with the pastry cutter. Place the biscuits on several non-stick baking sheets and bake at the top of the oven for 10 minutes. Then turn them over, pressing them down gently with a spatula. Continue to bake for another 5 minutes until golden brown on both sides.

4 Remove the biscuits from the oven and leave them on the sheets for 5 minutes, before transferring to a wire rack to cool.

STORE The thins will keep in an airtight container for 3 days.

Cheese Straws

A great way of using up any leftover bits of hard cheese.

| MAKES 15–20 | 10 MINS | 15 MINS | 12 WEEKS, UNBAKED |

Chilling time
1 hr

Special equipment
food processor with blade attachment (optional)

Ingredients
75g (2½oz) plain flour, sifted,
  plus extra for dusting
pinch of salt
50g (1¾oz) unsalted butter, softened and diced
30g (1oz) strong Cheddar cheese, finely grated
1 egg yolk, plus 1 egg, beaten, for glazing
1 tsp Dijon mustard

Method

1 Place the flour, salt, and butter in a bowl, or the bowl of a food processor. Rub together with your fingertips, or pulse-blend, until the mixture resembles crumbs. Add the Cheddar and mix in. Whisk the egg yolk with 1 tablespoon cold water and the mustard until combined. Add to the crumbs and bring it together to form a dough.

2 Turn the dough out onto a lightly floured work surface and knead briefly. Wrap it in cling film and chill for 1 hour. Preheat the oven to 200°C (400°F/Gas 6). When ready to cook, briefly knead the dough again.

3 Roll the dough out to a 30 x 15cm (12 x 6in) rectangle; it should be 5mm (¼in) thick. With a sharp knife, cut 1cm (½in) wide strips along the shorter side. Brush the strips of pastry with a little beaten egg. Holding the top of each strip, twist the bottom a few times to form spirals.

4 Place the straws on non-stick baking sheets, pressing down the ends if the spirals appear to be unwinding. Bake at the top of the oven for 15 minutes. Cool on the trays for 5 minutes. Transfer to a wire rack to cool.

STORE The straws will keep in an airtight container for 3 days.

Oatcakes

These Scottish oatcakes are perfect with cheese and chutney. Made with just oatmeal (see Baker's Tip) they become a good wheat-free option.

MAKES 16 · 20 MINS · 15 MINS · UP TO 4 WEEKS

Special equipment
6cm (2½in) round pastry cutter

Ingredients
100g (3½oz) medium oatmeal,
  plus extra for dusting

100g (3½oz) wholemeal flour,
  plus extra for dusting
¾ tsp salt
freshly ground black pepper
½ tsp bicarbonate of soda
2 tbsp olive oil

Method

1 Preheat the oven to 180°C (350°F/Gas 4). Mix the dry ingredients together in a bowl. Whisk together the oil with 4 tablespoons of freshly boiled water. Make a well in the centre of the flour mixture and pour in the liquid. Mix together with a spoon to form a thick paste.

2 Lightly flour a work surface with a mixture of flour and medium oatmeal and turn the paste out onto it. Knead together briefly until it forms a dough. Gently roll the dough out to a thickness of 5mm (¼in); if you are making the dough with 100 per cent oatmeal (see Baker's Tip) it will be even more delicate and likely to crack.

3 Cut out as many oatcakes as possible, as it is difficult to bring the pastry together again after the first rolling. If the dough has difficulty coming together after the first cutting, put it back in the bowl and add a drop or two of water to help it amalgamate again, then re-roll and cut more oatcakes.

4 Place the oatcakes on several non-stick baking sheets and bake at the top of the oven for 10 minutes, then turn them over and continue to bake for another 5 minutes until golden brown on both sides. Remove the biscuits from the oven and leave on the trays for 5 minutes, before transferring to a wire rack to cool completely.

STORE The oatcakes will keep in an airtight container for 3 days.

BAKER'S TIP
These traditional Scottish biscuits can be made using just oatmeal, or with a mixture of both oatmeal and wholemeal flour. Made using only oatmeal, they are ideal for those who want to avoid wheat, but this will produce a more delicate, crumbly biscuit, and will need gentle handling when cutting.

meringues & soufflés

Raspberry Cream Meringues

These mini meringues are filled with fresh raspberries and whipped cream, perfect for a summer buffet.

MAKES 6–8 **10 MINS** **1 HOUR**

Special equipment
metal mixing bowl
piping bag with plain nozzle
(optional)

Ingredients
4 egg whites, at room temperature
  (each medium egg white will
  weigh about 30g/1oz)
about 240g (8¾oz) caster sugar,
  see step 3

For the filling
100g (3½oz) raspberries
300ml (10fl oz) double cream
1 tbsp icing sugar, sifted

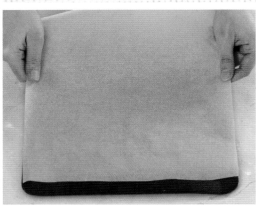

1 Preheat the oven to around 120°C (250°F/Gas ¼). Line a baking sheet with parchment.

2 Ensure the bowl is clean and dry; use a lemon to remove traces of grease, if need be.

3 Weigh the egg whites. You will need exactly double the weight of sugar to egg whites.

4 Whisk the egg whites in the metal bowl until they are stiff and form strong peaks.

5 Gradually add half the sugar, a couple of tablespoons at a time, whisking in between.

6 Gently fold the remaining sugar into the egg whites, trying to lose as little air as possible.

7 Put tablespoons of the mixture onto the baking tray leaving 5cm (2in) gaps between.

8 Alternatively, pipe with a plain nozzle. Bake in the centre of the oven for 1 hour.

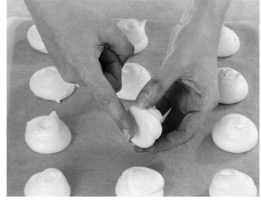

9 They are ready when they lift easily from the parchment and sound hollow when tapped.

10 Turn off the oven and leave the meringues to cool inside. Remove to a wire rack until cold.

11 Put the raspberries in a bowl and crush them with the back of a fork, so they break up.

12 In a separate bowl whisk up the double cream until firm but not stiff.

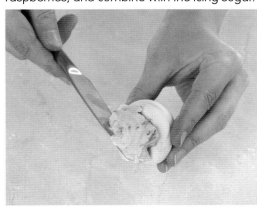

13 Gently fold together the cream and crushed raspberries, and combine with the icing sugar.

14 Spread a little of the raspberry mixture onto half the meringues.

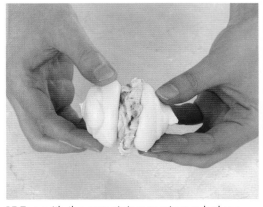

15 Top with the remaining meringue halves and gently press together to form sandwiches.

For sweet canapés, pipe smaller meringues and reduce the cooking time to 45 minutes; makes about 20 sandwiches. **PREPARE AHEAD** Keep unfilled in an airtight container for 5 days.

RASPBERRY CREAM MERINGUES

Meringue variations

Giant Pistachio Meringues

Too large to sandwich with cream, these beautiful creations are eaten like oversized biscuits.

MAKES 8   **15 MINS**   **1½ HOURS**

Special equipment
food processor with blade attachment
large metal mixing bowl

Ingredients
100g (3½oz) unsalted, shelled pistachio nuts
4 egg whites, at room temperature
about 240g (8¾oz) caster sugar,
  see page 242, step 3

Method
1 Preheat the oven to the lowest setting, around 120°C (250°F/Gas ¼). Spread the pistachio nuts on a baking sheet and bake for 5 minutes, then turn them out into a tea towel and rub to remove excess skin. Cool. Finely grind just less than half the nuts in a food processor, and roughly chop the rest.

2 Put the egg whites into the metal bowl and whisk with an electric whisk until stiff peaks form. Add the sugar 2 tablespoons at a time, whisking between each addition, until you have added at least half. Fold in the remaining sugar, and the ground pistachios, trying to lose as little air as possible.

3 Line a baking sheet with parchment. Put large heaped tablespoons of the meringue mixture on to the sheet, leaving at least 5cm (2in) gaps between them. Scatter the tops with the chopped pistachios.

4 Bake in the centre of the oven for 1½ hours. Turn off the oven and leave the meringues to cool inside, to help stop them cracking. Remove the meringues from the oven to a wire rack to cool completely. Serve the meringues piled on top of each other, for maximum impact.

STORE The meringues will keep in an airtight container for 3 days.

Lemon and Praline Meringues

Similar to Monts Blancs (see right), these have added crunch.

SERVES 6   **35 MINS**   **1½ HOURS**

Special equipment
piping bag with star nozzle

Ingredients
3 egg whites, at room temperature
about 180g (6oz) caster sugar,
  see page 242, step 3
vegetable oil, for greasing
60g (2oz) granulated sugar
60g (2oz) whole blanched almonds
pinch of cream of tartar
85g (3oz) dark chocolate, broken up
150ml (5fl oz) double cream
3 tbsp lemon curd

Method
1 Preheat the oven to 120°C (250°F/Gas ¼) and line a baking sheet with parchment. Whisk the egg whites until stiff. Add 2 tablespoons caster sugar, and whisk until smooth and shiny. Add sugar, 1 tablespoon at a time, whisking well after each addition. Spoon into the piping bag, and pipe six 10cm (4in) circles onto the baking sheet. Bake for 1½ hours or until crisp.

2 Meanwhile, make the praline. Oil a baking sheet and put the granulated sugar, almonds, and cream of tartar into a small, heavy saucepan. Set the pan over a gentle heat and stir until the sugar dissolves. Boil until the syrup turns golden, then pour out onto the greased baking sheet. Leave until completely cold, then coarsely chop.

3 Melt the chocolate in a bowl set over simmering water. Whip the cream until just holding a trail, and fold in the lemon curd. Spread each meringue with chocolate. Allow to set, then pile the lemon curd cream on top, sprinkle with praline, and serve.

PREPARE AHEAD The meringue bases will keep in an airtight container for 5 days.

Monts Blancs

If using sweetened chestnut purée, omit the caster sugar in the filling.

MAKES 8 | **20 MINS** | **45–60 MINS**

Special equipment
large metal mixing bowl
10cm (4in) pastry cutter

Ingredients
4 egg whites, at room temperature
about 240g (8¾oz) caster sugar,
  see page 242, step 3
sunflower oil, for greasing

For the filling
435g can sweetened or unsweetened
  chestnut purée
100g (3½oz) caster sugar (optional)
1 tsp vanilla extract
500ml (16fl oz) double cream
icing sugar, for dusting

Method

1 Preheat the oven to the lowest setting, around 120°C (250°F/Gas ¼). Put the egg whites into a large, clean metal bowl and whisk them until they are stiff, and leave peaks when the whisk is removed from the egg whites. Gradually add the sugar 2 tablespoons at a time, whisking well between each addition, until you have added at least half. Gently fold the remaining sugar into the egg whites, trying to lose as little air as possible.

2 Lightly grease the pastry cutter. Line 2 baking sheets with silicone paper. Place the pastry cutter on the sheets, and spoon the meringue mixture into the ring, to a depth of 3cm (1¼in). Smooth over the top and gently remove the ring. Repeat until there are 4 meringue bases on each baking sheet.

3 Bake the meringues in the centre of the oven for 45 minutes if you like them chewy, otherwise bake for 1 hour. Turn off the oven and leave the meringues to cool inside, to stop them cracking. Remove to a wire rack to cool completely.

4 Put the chestnut purée in a bowl with the caster sugar (if using), vanilla extract, and

4 tablespoons of double cream, and beat together until smooth. Push through a fine sieve to make a light, fluffy filling. In a separate bowl, whisk up the remaining double cream until firm.

5 Gently smooth 1 tablespoon chestnut filling over the top of the meringues, using a palette knife to smooth the surface level. Top each meringue with a spoonful of whipped cream, smoothed round with a palette knife to give the appearance of soft peaks. Dust with icing sugar and serve.

PREPARE AHEAD The meringue bases can be prepared 5 days ahead and stored in an airtight container.

BAKER'S TIP
Make sure that the bowl you are using to whisk the egg whites in is completely clean and dry. For absolute accuracy, it is best to weigh the egg whites. You will need precisely double the weight of sugar to egg whites. An electronic scale is best.

Strawberries and Cream Macarons

The art of macaron making can seem complex, but here I have tried to devise a recipe that will suit the home cook.

MAKES 20 **30 MINS** **18–20 MINS**

Special equipment
food processor with
   blade attachment
piping bag with small,
   plain nozzle

Ingredients
100g (3½oz) icing sugar
75g (2½oz) ground almonds
2 large egg whites,
   at room temperature
75g (2½oz) granulated sugar

For the filling
200ml (7fl oz) double cream
5–10 very large strawberries,
   preferably the same diameter
   as the macarons

MERINGUES AND SOUFFLÉS

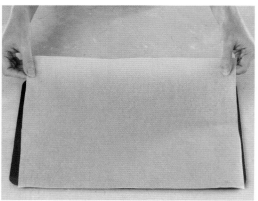

1 Preheat the oven to 150°C (300°F/Gas 2). Line 2 baking sheets with silicone paper.

2 Trace 20 x 3cm (1¼in) circles, leaving 3cm (1¼in) between circles. Invert the paper.

3 In a food processor, whizz together the almonds and icing sugar to a very fine meal.

4 In a large bowl, whisk the egg whites to stiff peaks using an electric whisk.

5 Whisking, add the granulated sugar a little at a time, whisking well between additions.

6 The meringue mixture should be very stiff at this point, more than for a Swiss meringue.

7 Gently fold in the almond mixture a spoonful at a time, until just incorporated.

8 Transfer the macaron mix to the piping bag, placing the bag into a bowl to help.

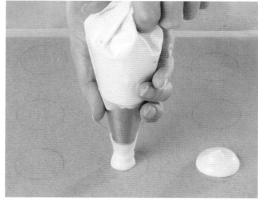

9 Using the guidelines, pipe the mix into the centre of each circle, holding the bag vertically.

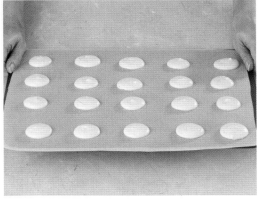

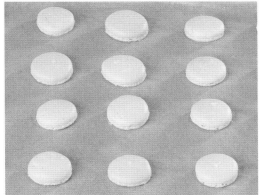

10 Try to keep the disks even in size and volume; the mix will spread only very slightly.

11 Bang the baking sheets down a few times if there are any peaks left in the centre.

12 Bake in the middle of the oven for 18–20 minutes until the surface is set firm.

13 Test one shell: a firm prod with a finger should crack the top of the macaron.

14 Leave for 15–20 minutes, then transfer to a wire rack to cool completely.

15 Whisk the cream until thick; a soft whip would ooze out the sides and soften the shells.

16 Transfer the cream into the (cleaned) piping bag used earlier, with the same nozzle.

17 Pipe a blob of the whipped cream onto the flat side of half the macarons.

18 Slice the strawberries widthways into thin slices, the same diameter as the macarons.

19 Put a slice of strawberry on top of the cream filling of each macaron.

20 Add the remaining macaron shells and sandwich gently. The fillings should peek out.

21 Serve immediately. **PREPARE AHEAD** Unfilled macaron shells can be stored for 3 days.

Macaron variations

Tangerine Macarons

Sharp, zesty tangerines are used here, rather than the more usual oranges, to counter-balance the sweetness of the meringues.

MAKES 20 · 30 MINS · 18–20 MINS

Special equipment
food processor with blade attachment

Ingredients
100g (3½oz) icing sugar
75g (2½oz) ground almonds
1 scant tsp finely grated tangerine zest
2 large egg whites, at room temperature
75g (2½oz) granulated sugar
3–4 drops orange food colouring

For the filling
100g (3½oz) icing sugar
50g (1¾oz) unsalted butter, softened
1 tbsp tangerine juice
1 scant tsp finely grated tangerine zest

Method

1 Preheat the oven to 150°C (300°F/Gas 2). Line 2 baking sheets with silicone paper. Draw on 3cm (1¼in) circles with a pencil, leaving 3cm (1¼in) gap between each one. Whizz the icing sugar and ground almonds in a food processor, until finely mixed. Add the tangerine zest and whizz briefly.

2 In a bowl, whisk the egg whites to form stiff peaks. Add the granulated sugar a little at a time, whisking well with each addition. Whisk in the food colouring.

3 Fold in the almond mixture, a spoonful at a time. Transfer to the piping bag. Holding the bag vertically, pipe meringue into the centre of each circle.

4 Bake in the middle of the oven for 18–20 minutes until the surface is set firm. Leave the macarons to cool on the baking sheets for 15–20 minutes and then transfer to a wire rack to cool completely.

5 For the filling, cream together the icing sugar, butter, tangerine zest, and juice until smooth. Transfer into the (cleaned) piping bag, using the same nozzle. Pipe a blob of icing onto the flat side of half the macarons, and sandwich with the rest. Serve the same day, or the macarons will start to go soft.

PREPARE AHEAD The unfilled shells can be stored for 3 days in an airtight container.

Chocolate Macarons

These delicious macarons are filled with a rich, dark chocolate buttercream.

MAKES 20 · 30 MINS · 18–20 MINS

Special equipment
food processor with blade attachment

Ingredients
50g (1¾oz) ground almonds
25g (scant 1oz) cocoa powder
100g (3½oz) icing sugar
2 large egg whites, at room temperature
75g (2½oz) granulated sugar

For the filling
50g (1¾oz) cocoa powder
150g (5½oz) icing sugar
50g (1¾oz) unsalted butter, melted
3 tbsp milk, plus a little extra if needed

Method

1 Preheat the oven to 150°C (300°F/Gas 2). Line 2 baking sheets with silicone paper. Draw on 3cm (1¼in) circles with a pencil, leaving 3cm (1¼in) gap between each. In a food processor, whizz the ground almonds, cocoa, and icing sugar until mixed.

2 Whisk the egg whites until stiff. Add the granulated sugar, whisking. The mixture should be stiff. Fold in the almond mixture a spoonful at a time. Transfer to the piping bag. Holding the bag vertically, pipe meringue into the centre of each circle.

3 Bake in the middle of the oven for 18–20 minutes. Leave to cool on the sheets 15–20 minutes, before transferring to a wire rack.

4 For the filling, sift the cocoa and icing sugar into a bowl. Add the butter and milk, and whisk. Add a little milk if is too thick. Transfer into the piping bag and pipe icing onto the flat side of half the macarons, and sandwich together with the rest. Serve the same day, or the macarons will go soft.

PREPARE AHEAD The unfilled shells can be stored for 3 days in an airtight container.

Raspberry Macarons

Pretty as a picture, these macarons look almost too good to eat.

MAKES 20   **30 MINS**   **18–20 MINS**

Special equipment
food processor with blade attachment

Ingredients
100g (3½oz) icing sugar
75g (2½oz) ground almonds
2 large egg whites, at room temperature
75g (2½oz) granulated sugar
3–4 drops of pink food colouring

For the filling
150g (5½oz) mascarpone
50g (1¾oz) seedless raspberry conserve

Method

1 Preheat the oven to 150°C (300°F/Gas 2). Line 2 baking sheets with silicone paper. Draw on 3cm (1¼in) circles with a pencil, leaving 3cm (1¼in) gap between each. In a food processor, whizz together the icing sugar and ground almonds until very finely mixed and smooth.

2 In a bowl, whisk the egg whites until they form stiff peaks. Add the granulated sugar, a little at a time, whisking well between each addition. Whisk in the food colouring.

3 Fold in the almond mixture a spoonful at a time, until just mixed. Transfer the mix to the piping bag. Holding the bag vertically, pipe meringue into the centre of each circle.

4 Bake in the middle of the oven for 18–20 minutes until the surface is firm. Leave to cool on the sheets for 15–20 minutes, before transferring to a wire rack to cool.

5 For the filling, beat the mascarpone and raspberry conserve until smooth and transfer to the (cleaned) piping bag used earlier, with the same nozzle. Pipe a blob of the filling onto the flat side of half the macarons, and sandwich together with the rest of the halves. Serve the same day, or the macarons will go soft.

PREPARE AHEAD The unfilled shells can be stored for 3 days in an airtight container.

BAKER'S TIP
The skill in making macarons comes in the technique, not in the proportions of the ingredients. Gentle folding, a heavy, flat baking sheet, and piping the mix completely vertically downwards should all help to produce the perfect macaron.

Strawberry Pavlova

Freeze your leftover egg whites, one at a time if necessary, until you have enough to make this well-loved dessert.

SERVES	15	1¼
8	MINS	HOURS

Ingredients

6 egg whites, at room temperature
pinch of salt
about 360g (12¼oz) caster sugar,
  see page 242, step 3
2 tsp cornflour
1 tsp vinegar
300ml (10fl oz) double cream
strawberries, to decorate

MERINGUES AND SOUFFLÉS

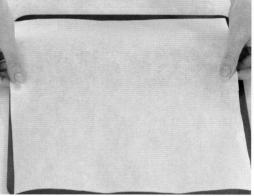

1 Preheat the oven to 180°C (350°F/Gas 4). Line a baking tray with baking parchment.

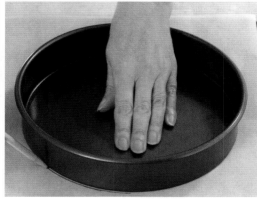

2 Draw a 20cm (8in) diameter circle on the parchment using a pencil.

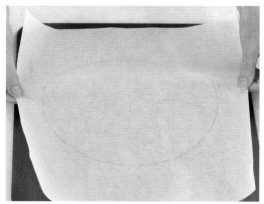

3 Reverse the parchment, so the pencil mark is below and won't transfer to the meringue.

4 Put the egg whites in a large, clean, grease-free bowl with the salt.

5 Using an electric whisk, beat the egg whites until stiff peaks form.

6 Start whisking in the sugar 1 tablespoon at a time, whisking well after each addition.

7 Continue whisking until the whites are stiff and glossy. Whisk in the cornflour and vinegar.

8 Spoon it into a mound inside the circle on the parchment. Spread it to the edges of the circle.

9 Form neat swirls, using a palette knife, as you spread out the meringue.

10 Bake for 5 minutes, then reduce the heat to 120°C (250°F/Gas ¼) and cook for 75 minutes.

11 Leave to cool completely in the oven. Whip the cream until it holds its shape.

12 Spoon the cream onto the meringue base and decorate with the strawberries.

13 Serve in wedges, with extra berries, or a fruit coulis. **PREPARE AHEAD** The meringue base will keep in a dry, airtight container for 1 week. Add the cream and berries just before serving.

Pavlova variations

Rhubarb Ginger Meringue Cake

A classic combination makes a tasty filling for this unusual cake

SERVES 6–8 | **30 MINS** | **1 HOUR 5 MINS**

Ingredients

For the meringues
4 egg whites, at room temperature
pinch of salt
about 240g (8³⁄₄oz) caster sugar, see page 242, step 3

For the filling
600g (1lb 5oz) rhubarb, chopped
85g (3oz) caster sugar
4 pieces of stem ginger, chopped
½ tsp ground ginger
250ml (8fl oz) double cream
icing sugar, for dusting

Method

1 Preheat the oven to 180°C (350°F/Gas 4). Line 2 baking trays with parchment. Whisk the egg whites, salt, and 115g (4oz) of the sugar until stiff, glossy peaks form. Fold in the rest of the sugar a spoonful at a time.

2 Divide the meringue between the baking trays and spread into 18cm (7in) circles. Bake for 5 minutes, then reduce the oven temperature to 130°C (250°F/Gas ½) and bake for 1 hour. Open the oven door and leave the meringue to cool completely.

3 Meanwhile, put the rhubarb, caster sugar, stem ginger, ground ginger, and a splash of water in a large saucepan and cook, covered over a low heat for 20 minutes or until tender. Allow to cool. If too wet, drain to get rid of some of the liquid, and chill until required.

4 Whip the cream and fold in the rhubarb. Place 1 meringue on a serving plate, spread it with the filling, and top with the remaining meringue. Dust with icing sugar and serve.

PREPARE AHEAD The meringue bases will keep in a dry, airtight container for 1 week.

Mini Pavlovas

A fantastic way to feed a crowd, the bases here can be prepared in advance and filled at the last moment with the best of the season's fruit.

MAKES 8 | **15 MINS** | **45–60 MINS**

Ingredients

1 quantity meringue mix, see page 252, steps 4–7
300ml (10fl oz) double cream
400g (14oz) mixed summer berries

Method

1 Preheat the oven to 120°C (250°F/Gas ¼). Line 2 baking sheets with baking parchment. Spoon large tablespoons of the meringue mix evenly onto the baking sheets, and smooth them out with the back of a spoon to 10cm (4in) in diameter and 3cm (1¼in) high.

2 Bake for 45–60 minutes, or until crisp. Leave to cool completely before transferring to a serving plate.

3 For the filling, whip the cream until it holds its shape. Top each Pavlova with 1 tablespoon of the cream and top the cream with summer berries.

PREPARE AHEAD The meringue bases will keep in a dry, airtight container for 1 week. Fill just before serving.

Mocha Coffee Pavlova

With its coffee-infused meringue and drizzled chocolate, this is an impressive and sophisticated Pavlova to serve at a dinner party.

MAKES 8 | **15 MINS** | **1 HOUR 20 MINS**

Ingredients

6 egg whites, at room temperature
pinch of salt
about 360g (12¼oz) caster sugar, see page 242, step 3
2 tsp cornflour
1 tsp vinegar
3 tbsp strong coffee powder mixed with 3 tbsp boiling water, cooled, or 3 tbsp cooled espresso
60g (2oz) good-quality dark chocolate, broken into pieces, plus extra to decorate
white chocolate, to decorate
300ml (10fl oz) double cream

Method

1 Preheat the oven to 180°C (350°F/Gas 4). Line a baking sheet with parchment. Using an electric whisk, beat the egg whites with the salt until stiff peaks form. Whisk in the sugar 1 tablespoon at a time, until stiff and glossy, then whisk in the cornflour and vinegar. Gently fold in the coffee.

2 Draw a 20cm (8in) diameter circle on the parchment with a pencil and reverse the paper. Spoon tablespoons of the meringue inside the circle, and smooth out.

3 Bake for 5 minutes, then reduce to 120°C (250°F/Gas ¼) and cook for 1 hour 15 minutes or until crisp. Turn off the oven and leave the meringue inside to cool.

4 Melt the dark chocolate pieces in a heatproof bowl set over a pan of simmering water, and cool. Make white and dark chocolate shavings using a vegetable peeler. Before serving, whip the cream until it holds its shape. Top the Pavlova with the cream. Drizzle over the melted chocolate and sprinkle with chocolate shavings.

PREPARE AHEAD The meringue base will keep in a dry, airtight container for 1 week. Fill just before serving.

Tropical Fruit Pavlova

The contrast between tangy passion fruit, cool whipped cream, and sweet meringue in this Pavlova is really hard to beat. A refreshing dessert for a summer's day.

| MAKES 8 | 15 MINS | 65–80 MINS |

Ingredients

1 quantity meringue mix,
  see page 252, steps 4–7
300ml (10fl oz) double cream
400g (14oz) mango and papaya,
  peeled and chopped
2 passion fruits

Method

1 Preheat the oven to 180°C (350°F/Gas 4). Line a baking sheet with baking parchment.

2 Draw a 20cm (8in) diameter circle on the parchment using a pencil. Reverse so the pencil is on the underside. Spoon large tablespoons of the meringue inside the circle, and smooth out with a palette knife.

3 Bake for 5 minutes, then reduce the temperature to 120°C (250°F/Gas ¼) and cook for a further 1 hour 15 minutes or until crisp and easy to remove from the baking parchment. Turn off the oven and leave the meringue inside to cool completely before transferring to a serving plate.

4 Just before serving, whip the cream until it holds its shape. Top the Pavlova with the cream, then the chopped tropical fruits. Halve the passion fruits, squeeze out the juice and pips, and pour over the Pavlova just before serving.

PREPARE AHEAD The meringue bases will keep in a dry, airtight container for 1 week. Fill just before serving.

BAKER'S TIP

Pavlovas do not keep very well, as the meringue base tends to go soggy after a few hours. However, to revitalise a leftover Pavlova, try making a quick Eton mess by breaking it up into bite-sized chunks and folding with freshly whipped double cream and extra fruit.

Lemon Meringue Pie

With the sharpness of lemon combined with a smooth vanilla meringue topping, it is no wonder this pie is an American family favourite.

SERVES 8 **30 MINS** **40–50 MINS**

Special equipment
23cm (9in) loose-bottomed tart tin
baking beans

Ingredients
45g (1½oz) butter, diced, plus extra for greasing
400g (14oz) sweet shortcrust pastry,
  shop-bought, or see page 286, steps 1–5

3 tbsp plain flour, plus extra for dusting
6 eggs, at room temperature, separated
3 tbsp cornflour
400g (14oz) caster sugar
juice of 3 lemons
1 tbsp finely grated lemon zest
½ tsp cream of tartar
½ tsp vanilla extract

Method

1 Preheat the oven to 200°C (400°F/Gas 6). Lightly grease the flan tin with butter. Roll out the pastry on a lightly floured surface and use it to line the tin.

2 Line the pastry case with parchment, then fill with baking beans. Place on a baking tray and bake for 10–15 minutes or until the pastry looks pale golden. Lift off the paper and beans, return to the oven, and bake for 3–5 minutes until golden. Reduce the oven temperature to 180°C (350°F/Gas 4). Leave to cool slightly in the tin.

3 Place the egg yolks in a bowl and lightly beat. Combine the cornflour, flour, and 225g (8oz) of the sugar in a saucepan. Slowly add 360ml (12fl oz) water and heat gently, stirring, until the sugar dissolves and there are no lumps. Increase the heat slightly and cook, stirring, for 3–5 minutes or until the mixture starts to thicken.

4 Beat several spoonfuls of the hot mixture into the egg yolks. Pour this mixture back into the pan and slowly bring to a boil, stirring constantly. Boil for 3 minutes, then stir in the lemon juice, zest, and butter.

Continue boiling for another 2 minutes or until the mixture is thick and glossy, stirring constantly and scraping down the sides of the pan as necessary. Remove the pan from the heat; cover to keep warm.

5 Whisk the egg whites in a large clean bowl until foamy. Sprinkle over the cream of tartar and whisk. Continue whisking, adding the remaining sugar, 1 tablespoon at a time. Add the vanilla with the last tablespoon of the sugar, whisking until the meringue is thick and glossy.

6 Place the pastry case on a baking tray, pour in the lemon filling, then top with the meringue, spreading it so it completely covers the filling right up to the pastry edge (see Baker's Tip). Take care not to spill it over the pastry, or the tart will be difficult to remove from the tin after baking.

7 Place in the oven, and bake for 12–15 minutes or until the meringue is lightly golden. Transfer to a wire rack and leave to cool completely, before turning out of the tin and serving.

PREPARE AHEAD The unfilled pastry case can be made 3 days in advance and stored in an airtight container.

BAKER'S TIP
The meringue topping of this pie has a tendency to slide around on top of the lemon filling, if you are not careful. Make sure that the meringue is touching the sides of the pastry case around the entire pie before baking, as this will help to stop it from dislodging.

Baked Alaska

The secret to this recipe is the cake base, which insulates the ice cream from the oven's heat when assembled and sealed properly.

SERVES 8–10 | **45–50 MINS** | **30–40 MINS**

Special equipment
20cm (8in) round cake tin
sugar thermometer (optional)
food processor with blade attachment

Ingredients
60g (2oz) unsalted butter, plus extra for greasing
125g (4½oz) plain flour, plus extra for dusting

pinch of salt
4 eggs
135g (5oz) caster sugar
1 tsp vanilla extract

For the filling
300g (10½oz) strawberries, hulled
2–3 tbsp icing sugar, to taste
7–8 scoops of vanilla ice cream

For the meringue
300g (10½oz) caster sugar, plus extra for sprinkling
6 egg whites, at room temperature

Method

1 Preheat the oven to 180°C (350°F/Gas 4). Grease the tin. Line the base with greased parchment. Sprinkle in 2 tablespoons of flour, and tilt to coat the bottom and sides. Turn it upside down to remove excess flour.

2 Sift the flour with the salt. Melt the butter in a pan and let it cool. Whisk the eggs with an electric whisk for a few seconds. Add the sugar and whisk for about 5 minutes until pale and thick. Whisk in the vanilla extract.

3 Gently fold in the flour in stages, sifted over the egg mixture. Fold in the cooled, melted butter. Pour the cake mix into the tin. Bake in the oven for 30–40 minutes. Run a knife around the edge and turn it out onto a wire rack. Peel off the paper and cool.

4 Purée the strawberries in a food processor, then pour into a bowl. Stir in icing sugar. For the meringue, heat the sugar with 250ml (9fl oz) water in a pan, until dissolved. Boil until it reaches the hard ball stage. To test, remove the pan from the heat, take a teaspoon of syrup and let it cool for a few seconds, then take the syrup between finger and thumb: it should form

a ball. Alternatively, check if it registers 120°C (248°F) on a sugar thermometer.

5 Whisk the egg whites until stiff. Pour in the hot syrup, beating constantly for 5 minutes until the meringue is cool and stiff.

6 Butter a heatproof serving plate. Remove the ice cream from the freezer and leave until soft enough to scoop. When the cake is cooled, use a serrated knife to cut the cake horizontally in 2 layers. Use one layer for the base and the other layer to make cake crumbs by blitzing it in a food processor.

7 Transfer the crumbs to bowl and add 250ml (9fl oz) of the coulis to the crumbs, and blend to mix. Spread the remaining coulis over the cake.

8 Scoop the ice cream into balls and place them in a layer on the cake. Scoop and arrange a second layer of ice-cream balls. Smooth the ice cream layers. Cover the top of the ice cream layer with the prepared strawberry cake crumbs. Using a metal spoon, spoon the meringue on top. Work quickly, as the ice cream must stay as firm as possible at this point before baking.

9 Spread the meringue over the top and sides to cover completely, and seal it to the serving plate to insulate the ice cream. Keep in the freezer for up to 2 hours. When ready to bake, preheat the oven to 220°C (425°F/Gas 7). Take the dessert from the freezer, sprinkle with sugar and let stand for 1 minute. Bake for just 3–5 minutes until lightly browned. Serve at once.

BAKER'S TIP
Baking a dessert filled with ice cream may seem like a foolish idea, but there are a few things you can do to ensure success. Make sure your cake base is thick enough, and that the ice cream is completely sealed in by the meringue, as these things will help to insulate the ice cream from the oven's heat.

Lemon Meringue Roulade

The traditional Lemon Meringue Pie filling is given a new twist in this impressive dinner party dessert.

SERVES 8	**30 MINS**	**15 MINS**	**UP TO 8 WEEKS**

Special equipment
25 x 35cm (10 x 14in) Swiss roll tin

Ingredients
5 egg whites, at room temperature
225g (8oz) caster sugar
½ tsp white wine vinegar
1 tsp cornflour
½ tsp vanilla extract
250ml (8fl oz) double cream
4 tbsp good-quality lemon curd
icing sugar, for dusting

1 Preheat the oven to 180°C (350°F/Gas 4) and line the tin with baking parchment.

2 Whisk the egg whites with an electric whisk on high speed, until stiff peaks form.

3 Reduce the speed and whisk in the sugar, a little at a time, until thick and glossy.

4 Fold in the vinegar, cornflour, and vanilla extract, trying to keep the mixture well aerated.

5 Spread the mixture into the tin and bake in the centre of the oven for 15 minutes.

6 Remove the meringue from the oven and allow to cool to room temperature.

7 Meanwhile, whisk the cream until thick but not stiff; it should remain unctuous.

8 Fold in the lemon curd until just well blended; a few ripples will enhance the roulade.

9 Sprinkle icing sugar over a fresh sheet of baking parchment.

10 Carefully turn the cooled roulade out of the tin onto the sugared parchment.

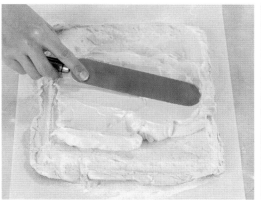

11 Spread the lemon cream over the unbaked side of the roulade with a palette knife.

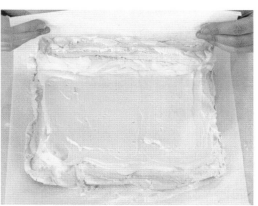

12 Use the parchment to roll up the meringue firmly but without squeezing out the cream.

13 Place the meringue seam-side down on a serving plate, cover, and chill. Sift over icing sugar to serve. **PREPARE AHEAD** The meringue can be made up to 3 days in advance and stored, unfilled, in a dry, airtight container.

Meringue Roulade variations

Apricot Meringue Roulade

An impressive dessert that uses storecupboard ingredients.

SERVES 8 | 30 MINS | 15 MINS | UP TO 8 WEEKS

Special equipment
23 x 32.5cm (9 x 13in) Swiss roll tin

Ingredients
5 egg whites, at room temperature
225g (8oz) caster sugar
½ tsp white wine vinegar
1 tsp cornflour
½ tsp vanilla extract
25g (scant 1oz) flaked almonds
icing sugar, for dusting
250ml (8fl oz) double cream
400g can apricot halves, drained and diced
2 passion fruit, seeds and pulp reserved

Method
1 Preheat the oven to 180°C (350°F/Gas 4). Line the tin with baking parchment. Put the egg whites and salt in a bowl, and beat with an electric whisk until soft peaks form. Whisk in the sugar, 1 tablespoon at a time, until the mixture is stiff and shiny.

2 Spoon the mixture into the tin and smooth into the corners. Scatter the flaked almonds over the top and bake for 15 minutes. Remove from the oven and allow to cool to room temperature. Meanwhile, put the cream in a bowl and beat with an electric whisk until soft peaks form.

3 Dust icing sugar over a fresh sheet of parchment and turn the cooled roulade out of the tin onto the parchment, topside down. Spread the cream over the underside of the meringue, then scatter over the apricots and passion fruit seeds. Roll the meringue up, starting from one short end and using the parchment to help you. Place seam-side down on a serving plate, cover, and chill. Sift over icing sugar to serve.

PREPARE AHEAD The meringue can be made 3 days ahead and stored, unfilled.

Summer Fruit Meringue Roulade

Stuffed with seasonal fruits, this delicious roulade makes an ideal dessert for a summer buffet.

SERVES 8 | 25 MINS | 15 MINS | UP TO 8 WEEKS

Special equipment
25 x 35cm (10 x 14in) Swiss roll tin

Ingredients
1 quantity meringue for roulade, see page 260, steps 1–6
250ml (8fl oz) double cream
icing sugar, for dusting
250g (9oz) mixed berry fruit, such as strawberries, raspberries, cherries, and blueberries, any large fruit chopped (see Baker's Tip)

Method
1 Whisk the cream until thick but not stiff. Place the cooled roulade on a piece of parchment dusted with icing sugar.

2 Spread the cream over the underside of the roulade with a palette knife. Sprinkle the fruits over it. Roll the meringue up around the cream filling. Place seam-side down on a serving plate, cover, and chill. Sift over icing sugar to serve.

PREPARE AHEAD Make 3 days ahead and store, unfilled, in an airtight container.

BAKER'S TIP
Any soft fruits can be used to fill this summery dessert. Cut them all to a uniform size, which should be no more than 1.5cm (½–¾in). This will help stop the roulade appearing lumpy when it is rolled up, with large chunks of fruit bulging through the meringue base.

Chocolate and Pear Meringue Roulade

If you are tired of Christmas pudding every year, try this rich, chocolatey roulade as an alternative Christmas dessert. ►

SERVES 8 | 25 MINS | 15 MINS | UP TO 8 WEEKS

Special equipment
25 x 35cm (10 x 14in) Swiss roll tin

Ingredients
5 egg whites, at room temperature
225g (8oz) caster sugar
½ tsp white wine vinegar
1 tsp cornflour
½ tsp vanilla extract
30g (1oz) cocoa powder, sifted
250ml (8fl oz) double cream
icing sugar, for dusting
410g can pears, drained and diced

Method
1 Preheat the oven to 180°C (350°F/Gas 4) and line the tin with parchment. Beat the egg whites with an electric whisk until stiff peaks form. Continue whisking at a slower speed and gradually add the caster sugar, a little at a time. Gently fold in the vinegar, cornflour, vanilla extract, and cocoa powder. Pour the mixture into the tin, smooth the surface, and bake in the centre of the oven for 15 minutes.

2 Remove the meringue from the oven and let it cool to room temperature. Meanwhile, whisk the cream until thick but not stiff. Carefully turn the cooled roulade out of the tin onto another piece of baking parchment dusted with icing sugar.

3 Spread the cream over the underside of the roulade with a palette knife. Sprinkle the pears over it. Roll the meringue up around the cream filling. Place seam-side down on a serving plate, cover, and chill. Sift over icing sugar to serve.

PREPARE AHEAD Make the meringue 3 days ahead and store, unfilled, in an airtight container.

Orange Soufflés

Soufflés are not difficult to make, but they do need a little care. This one is flavoured with orange zest.

   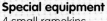

SERVES 4   **20 MINS**   **12–15 MINS**   **4 WEEKS, UNBAKED**

Special equipment
4 small ramekins

Ingredients

50g (1¾oz) unsalted butter, melted, plus extra for greasing
60g (2oz) caster sugar, plus extra for dusting
45g (1½oz) plain flour
300ml (10fl oz) milk

finely grated zest of 2 oranges
2 tbsp orange juice
3 eggs, separated, plus 1 egg white, at room temperature
icing sugar, for dusting

MERINGUES AND SOUFFLÉS

1 Place a baking tray in the oven and preheat to 200°C (400°F/Gas 6). Grease the ramekins.

2 Dust the insides of the buttered ramekins with sugar, making sure there are no gaps.

3 Add the flour to the butter and cook over low heat for 1 minute. Remove from the heat.

4 Add the milk, whisking to achieve a smooth sauce. Heat and stir, slowly bringing to a boil.

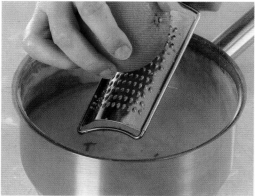

5 Simmer for 1–2 minutes, then remove from the heat and add the orange zest and juice.

6 Put in all but 1 teaspoon of the sugar, and stir until all the sugar has dissolved.

7 When the mixture has cooled slightly, add the egg yolks to the sauce, beating in well.

8 Whisk the egg whites to medium peaks and beat in the remaining teaspoon of sugar.

9 Thoroughly mix 1 tablespoon of the egg whites into the sauce to loosen the mix.

10 Now gently fold in the rest of the egg whites until all the ingredients are well mixed.

11 Pour the mixture into the ramekins so that it sits just above the rim of each ramekin.

12 Run a finger around the top edge of the mix, for a "top hat" to help them rise straight.

13 Place on the hot baking tray and bake for 12–15 minutes or until the puddings are golden and risen, but still a little runny in the centre. Dust with a little icing sugar and serve immediately.

Soufflé variations

Coffee Soufflés

Perfect served with coffee at the end of a special meal, the cardamom cream adds a Moorish flavour to the dish.

SERVES 6 • **30–35 MINS** • **10–12 MINS**

Special equipment
6 small ramekins

Ingredients
375ml (13fl oz) single cream
2 cardamom pods, lightly crushed
30g (1oz) coarsely ground coffee
375ml (13fl oz) milk
4 egg yolks, at room temperature
150g (5½oz) caster sugar
45g (1½oz) plain flour
75ml (2½fl oz) Tia Maria or other coffee liqueur
unsalted butter, melted, for greasing
6 egg whites, at room temperature
cocoa powder, to serve

Method
1 Put the cream and cardamom in a pan, and bring to a boil. Remove from the heat and infuse for 10–15 minutes, then strain, cover, and chill. At the same time, add the coffee to the milk, cover, and set aside to infuse for 10–15 minutes.

2 Bring the milk to a boil. Whisk the egg yolks with three-quarters of the caster sugar for 2–3 minutes. Whisk in the flour, then strain in the hot milk through a sieve until the mixture is smooth. Pour it back into the pan and bring it to a boil over medium heat, whisking constantly. Reduce the heat to low and cook for 2 minutes, whisking. Remove from the heat and stir in the Tia Maria.

3 Preheat the oven to 200°C (400°F/Gas 6) and place a baking sheet to heat up. Brush butter into the ramekins to grease. Whisk the egg whites until stiff. Sprinkle in the remaining caster sugar, and whisk for 20 seconds to form a glossy meringue. Gently fold meringue and coffee base together.

4 Divide the mix between the ramekins and run a finger around the top edge of the mix. Place the ramekins on the hot baking sheet. Bake for 10–12 minutes until risen.

5 Sift cocoa powder over the top of the soufflé, and serve at once, with the spiced cardamom cream.

Cheese Soufflé

Any hard cheese can be used for this dish; pick one with a strong flavour.

SERVES 4 • **20 MINS** • **30–35 MINS**

Special equipment
1.2-litre (2-pint) soufflé dish

Ingredients
45g (1½oz) unsalted butter
45g (1½oz) plain flour
225ml (8fl oz) milk
salt and freshly ground black pepper
125g (4½oz) mature Cheddar cheese, grated
½ tsp French mustard
5 large eggs, at room temperature, separated
1 tbsp grated Parmesan cheese

Method
1 Melt the butter in a small pan, stir in the flour until smooth, and cook over medium heat for 1 minute. Whisk in the milk until blended, then bring it to a boil, stirring, until thickened. Remove from the heat, season to taste, and stir in the cheese and mustard. Gradually stir in 4 of the egg yolks (save the remaining egg yolk for another recipe).

2 Preheat the oven to 190°C (375°F/Gas 5), and place a baking sheet to heat up. Whisk all the egg whites, until stiff peaks form. Stir 1 tablespoon of the egg whites into the cheese mixture to loosen it. Gently fold in the rest.

3 Pour the mixture into the dish, run a finger around the top edge of the mix, and sprinkle the Parmesan over it. Place the dish on the baking sheet, and bake for 25–30 minutes, or until puffed and golden. Serve at once.

> **BAKER'S TIP**
> For perfect soufflés always butter and sprinkle the sides of the ramekins with a sweet or savoury dusting, to give the mix "grip" as it rises. Run your finger around the top edge of the mix so that it rises straight and high, like a "top hat". In addition, always bake on a preheated baking sheet.

Raspberry Soufflés

Use only the sweetest, juiciest raspberries for this spectacular dish.

| SERVES 6 | 20–25 MINS | 10–12 MINS |

Special equipment
food processor with blade attachment
6 small ramekins

Ingredients
unsalted butter, for greasing
100g (3½oz) caster sugar, plus extra for sprinkling
500g (1lb 2oz) raspberries
5 egg whites, at room temperature
icing sugar, for dusting

For the Kirsch custard
375ml (12fl oz) milk
50g (1¾oz) caster sugar
5 egg yolks, at room temperature
1 tbsp cornflour
2–3 tbsp Kirsch

Method

1 For the custard, pour the milk into a pan and bring to a boil over medium heat. Set aside one-quarter. Add the sugar to the remaining milk and stir until dissolved.

2 Put the yolks with the cornflour into a bowl and whisk until smooth. Add the sweetened milk, whisking. Cook over medium heat, stirring, until thick. Remove from the heat. Stir in the reserved milk, strain it into a cold bowl and let it cool. If a skin forms on it, whisk it. Stir in the Kirsch. Cover and refrigerate.

3 Brush ramekins with butter and sprinkle with caster sugar. Preheat the oven to 190°C (375°F/Gas 5). Purée the raspberries with half the caster sugar. Work this through a sieve. Whisk the egg whites until stiff. Add the remaining sugar and whisk until glossy. Add one-quarter of the meringue to the purée, and stir to combine. Add to the remaining meringue and fold in gently.

4 Spoon the mixture into the ramekins and run a finger around the top edge of the mix. Bake for 10–12 minutes until puffed and lightly browned on top. Sift icing sugar over the soufflés and serve with the custard.

cheesecakes

Blueberry Ripple Cheesecake

The marbled effect on this cheesecake is simple to achieve and always looks impressive.

SERVES 8 **20 MINS** **40 MINS**

Special equipment
20cm (8in) deep springform cake tin
food processor with blade
attachment

Ingredients
50g (1¾oz) unsalted butter,
 plus extra for greasing
125g (4½oz) digestive biscuits
150g (5½oz) blueberries
150g (5½oz) caster sugar,
 plus 3 tbsp extra
400g (14oz) cream cheese
250g (9oz) mascarpone
2 large eggs, plus 1 large egg yolk

½ tsp vanilla extract
2 tbsp plain flour, sifted

For the compote
100g (3½oz) blueberries
1 tbsp caster sugar
squeeze of lemon juice

1 Preheat the oven to 180°C (350°F/Gas 4). Grease the base and sides of the cake tin.

2 Put the biscuits in a food bag and crush with a rolling pin until they turn into fine crumbs.

3 Melt the butter in a saucepan set over low heat; it should not begin to turn brown.

4 Add the crumbs to the pan and stir until they are coated in butter. Remove from the heat.

5 Press the crumbs into the base of the tin, pushing them down with the back of a spoon.

6 Put the blueberries and 3 tablespoons of sugar in a processor, and whizz until smooth.

7 Push the mixture through a nylon sieve (metal will taint it) into a small pan.

8 Boil and then simmer for 3–5 minutes or until thickened and jammy. Set aside.

9 Place the remaining sugar and next 5 ingredients for the cheese mix in the processor.

10 Whizz the cream cheese mixture until smooth and very well combined.

11 Pour the mixture onto the biscuit base and smooth the top with a palette knife.

12 Drizzle over the berry jam and make swirls by drawing a metal skewer through the mix.

13 Boil a kettle of water. Put the cake in a deep roasting tray and wrap the sides with tin foil.

14 Pour hot water into the tray, to come halfway up the cake tin; this prevents cracking.

15 Bake for 40 minutes till set but a bit wobbly. Turn off the oven and wedge open the door.

16 After 1 hour, remove the cake and place on a wire rack. Remove the sides of the tin.

17 Slide 1 or 2 fish slices between the biscuit base and the base of the tin.

18 Transfer the cheesecake to a serving plate or cake stand, and leave to cool completely.

19 Meanwhile, put all the ingredients for the compote in a small pan.

20 Heat the compote gently, stirring occasionally, until all the sugar dissolves.

21 Transfer to a jug to serve. **PREPARE AHEAD** Can be made 3 days in advance and chilled.

Baked Cheesecake variations

Chocolate Marble Cheesecake

This all-American favourite is dense, rich, and spectacular, making it an ideal dessert for entertaining.

SERVES 8–10   **35–40 MINS**   **50–60 MINS**

Chilling time
4½–5 hrs

Special equipment
20cm (8in) round springform cake tin

Ingredients
75g (2½oz) unsalted butter, melted, plus extra for greasing
150g (5½oz) digestive biscuits, crushed
150g (5½oz) good-quality dark chocolate, broken into pieces
500g (1lb 2oz) cream cheese, softened
150g (5½oz) caster sugar
1 tsp vanilla extract
2 eggs

Method

1 Grease the tin with butter and chill. Add the butter to the biscuit crumbs. Stir well and press the mixture onto the bottom and sides of the tin. Chill for 30–60 minutes until firm.

2 Preheat the oven to 180°C (350°F/Gas 4). Place the chocolate in a heatproof bowl and melt over a saucepan of simmering water. Allow to cool. Whisk the cream cheese until smooth. Add the sugar and vanilla, and beat well. Add the eggs, one at a time, beating well after each addition. Pour half the filling into the biscuit base.

3 Mix the chocolate into the remaining filling. Spoon a ring of the chocolate filling over the plain filling. Using a metal skewer, swirl the fillings to make a marbled pattern. Bake for 50–60 minutes; the centre should remain soft. Turn off the oven and leave the cheesecake inside until cool. Refrigerate for at least 4 hours. Run a knife round the side of the cheesecake to loosen it, remove the tin and transfer to a serving plate.

PREPARE AHEAD The cheesecake can be made 3 days ahead and kept refrigerated; the flavour will mellow.

Vanilla Cheesecake

This rich yet light cheesecake is guaranteed to be a crowd pleaser.

SERVES 10–12   **20 MINS**   **50 MINS**

Chilling time
6 hrs

Special equipment
23cm (9in) round springform cake tin

Ingredients
60g (2oz) unsalted butter, plus extra for greasing
225g (8oz) digestive biscuits, finely crushed
1 tbsp demerara sugar
675g (1½lb) cream cheese, at room temperature
4 eggs, separated
200g (7oz) caster sugar
1 tsp vanilla extract
500ml (16fl oz) soured cream
kiwi fruit slices, to garnish

Method

1 Preheat the oven to 180°C (350°F/Gas 4). Grease and line the tin with parchment. Melt the butter in a pan over medium heat. Add the biscuit crumbs and demerara sugar, and stir until blended. Press the crumbs over the base of the tin.

2 Beat the cream cheese, egg yolks, 150g (5½oz) caster sugar, and vanilla in a bowl until blended. In a separate bowl, beat the egg whites until stiff. Fold the egg whites into the cream cheese mixture. Pour into the tin and smooth the top.

3 Place the tin in the oven and bake for 45 minutes until set. Remove the tin from the oven and leave it to stand for 10 minutes. Combine the soured cream and remaining sugar in a bowl, and beat well. Pour over the cheesecake and smooth.

4 Increase the temperature to 240°C (475°F/Gas 9), and bake the cheesecake for 5 minutes. Leave to cool on a wire rack, then chill for at least 6 hours. When ready to serve, garnish with slices of kiwi fruit.

PREPARE AHEAD The cheesecake can be made 3 days ahead and kept refrigerated.

Ginger Cheesecake

Chopped stem ginger adds warmth to the zesty, smooth filling.

SERVES 8–10 | **40–45 MINS** | **50–60 MINS**

Chilling time
4 hrs

Special equipment
20cm (8in) round springform cake tin

Ingredients
1 biscuit base, see Chocolate Marble
  Cheesecake, opposite, step 1
500g (1lb 2oz) cream cheese
125g (4½oz) stem ginger in syrup, chopped,
  plus 3 tbsp syrup
finely grated zest of 1 lemon, plus 2 tsp juice
250ml (8fl oz) soured cream
150g (5½oz) granulated sugar
1 tsp vanilla extract
4 eggs
150ml (5fl oz) double cream, to top (optional)

Method
1 Preheat the oven to 180°C (350°F/Gas 4). Beat the cream cheese in a bowl. Add all but 2 tablespoons of the ginger, ginger syrup, zest and juice, soured cream, sugar, and vanilla. Beat until smooth. Add the eggs, one at a time, beating after each addition.

2 Pour the filling onto the base, and shake to level the surface. Place the tin on a baking sheet. Bake for 50–60 minutes. Turn off the oven but leave the cheesecake in there for 1½ hours. Chill for 4 hours.

3 Whip the cream (if using) to soft peaks. Run a knife round the cheesecake, then remove the tin. Swirl the cream on top. Scatter the reserved stem ginger before serving.

PREPARE AHEAD The cheesecake can be made 3 days ahead and kept refrigerated.

BAKER'S TIP
When baking cheesecakes, there is always a danger that the surface will crack. To avoid this, allow the cheesecake to cool completely in the oven, so it deflates slowly, creating less chance of cracking.

German Cheesecake

The use of quark here is typical of German cookery. If you cannot find any, substitute it with low-fat cottage cheese puréed until smooth.

SERVES 8–12 **30 MINS** **85–95 MINS**

Chilling time
30 mins

Special equipment
22cm (9in) round springform cake tin,
 ideally 4cm (1½in) deep
food processor with blade attachment
baking beans

Ingredients
250g (9oz) plain flour
50g (1¾oz) caster sugar
150g (5½oz) unsalted butter, diced
1 egg yolk

For the filling
750g (1lb 10oz) quark or fat-free cottage cheese,
 processed until smooth
125g (4½oz) caster sugar
4 eggs, separated
finely grated zest and juice of 1 lemon
2 tsp vanilla extract

Method

1 Line the base of the tin with parchment. For the pastry, pulse the flour, sugar, and butter in a food processor until they form fine breadcrumbs. Add the egg yolk and 2 tablespoons water, bringing the mixture together to form a dough. If it is a little dry, add extra water, a tablespoon at a time. Roll it into a smooth ball, wrap in cling film and refrigerate for 30 minutes.

2 Preheat the oven to 180°C (350°F/Gas 4). Once the dough has rested, roll it out to a thickness of about 5mm (¼in) and use to line the tin. The pastry should be large enough to hang over the edge. Place a disk of parchment inside the pastry and weigh it down with baking beans. Bake for 20 minutes, then remove the beans and paper, and bake for another 5 minutes.

3 Meanwhile, blend together the quark or processed cottage cheese, sugar, egg yolks, lemon zest and juice, and vanilla until smooth. In a separate bowl, whisk the egg whites to soft peaks. Fold the egg whites gently into the cream cheese mixture until thoroughly blended. Pour the filling into the baked pastry case.

4 Bake for another 60–70 minutes. The cheesecake is ready when golden brown and puffed up. Turn the oven off and, wedging the door open, let the cheesecake cool in the oven for at least 30 minutes before allowing it to cool fully at room temperature for 1 hour (see Baker's Tip). Use a knife to trim any excess pieces of pastry for an even finish. Serve at room temperature or slightly chilled.

PREPARE AHEAD The pastry case can be blind baked the day before and stored in an airtight container. The cheesecake can be stored in the refrigerator for 2 days, although the pastry will soften.

BAKER'S TIP
The whisked egg whites make the filling puff up during baking. It always collapses slightly as it cools, which is normal, and you should expect the surface of the cheesecake to crack. Leaving the cheesecake to cool in the oven will help to minimize the damage.

Lemon Cheesecake

This cold-set cheesecake needs no baking, and thus produces a lighter, more delicate result.

SERVES 8

30 MINS

Chilling time
4 hrs or overnight

Special equipment
22cm (9in) round springform cake tin

Ingredients
250g (9oz) digestive biscuits
100g (3½oz) unsalted butter, diced
4 sheets gelatine, roughly cut up
finely grated zest and juice
 of 2 lemons
350g (12oz) cream cheese
200g (7oz) caster sugar
300ml (10fl oz) double cream

1 Line the tin with parchment. Put the biscuits in a bag and crush with a rolling pin to crumbs.

2 Melt the butter and pour over the crushed biscuits, mixing well to combine.

3 Press the biscuit mixture firmly into the base of the tin using a wooden spoon.

4 In a small heatproof bowl, soak the gelatine in the lemon juice for 5 minutes to soften.

5 Place the bowl over a pan of hot water and stir until the gelatine melts. Set aside to cool.

6 Beat together the cream cheese, caster sugar, and lemon zest until smooth.

7 In a separate bowl, whisk the double cream to soft peaks. Make sure it is not stiff.

8 Beat the gelatine mixture into the cream cheese mixture, stirring well to combine.

9 Gently fold the whisked cream into the cheese mixture. Be careful not to lose volume.

CHEESECAKES

10 Tip the cheese mixture onto the chilled biscuit base and spread evenly.

11 Smooth the top with a damp palette knife or the back of a damp spoon.

12 Chill for at least 4 hours or overnight. Run a sharp, thin knife around the inside of the tin.

13 Gently turn the cheesecake out onto a plate, making sure you remove the baking parchment before cutting into slices.

PREPARE AHEAD The cheesecake can be made 2 days ahead and stored in the refrigerator.

Cold-set Cheesecake variations

Strawberry Cheesecake

This no-cook cheesecake takes very little time to make and is given a delicious twist with the use of mascarpone cheese.

SERVES 8–10   **15 MINS**   **5 MINS**

Chilling time
at least 1 hr

Special equipment
20cm (8in) loose-bottomed tart tin

Ingredients
50g (1¾oz) unsalted butter
100g (3½oz) good-quality dark chocolate, broken into pieces
150g (5½oz) digestive biscuits, crushed
400g (14oz) mascarpone cheese
finely grated zest and juice of 2 limes
2–3 tbsp icing sugar, plus extra for dusting
225g (8oz) strawberries, hulled and halved

Method

1 Melt the butter and chocolate in a bowl set over a saucepan of gently simmering water, stirring now and again. Once melted, stir in the biscuit crumbs. Transfer the mixture to the tin and press it down firmly and evenly using a wooden spoon.

2 Beat the mascarpone in a bowl with the lime zest and juice, reserving some zest to decorate. Stir in the icing sugar, to taste. Spread the cheese mixture over the biscuit base and refrigerate for at least 1 hour.

3 To serve, arrange the strawberries around the edge of the cheesecake and sprinkle the reserved lime zest in the centre. Dust with icing sugar and cut into slices.

PREPARE AHEAD The cheesecake can be made 1 day ahead and kept refrigerated.

BAKER'S TIP

Try using different biscuit bases to complement your choice of filling. I used ginger biscuits for the marmalade and ginger cheesecake (see right), but Oreo cookies or other chocolate biscuits work well with a chocolate filling, and crushed shortbread biscuits would complement the strawberries well here.

Marmalade and Ginger Cheesecake

Spicy preserved ginger and zesty marmalade revive this old favourite.

SERVES 8–10   **30 MINS**   **5 MINS**

Chilling time
at least 4 hrs or overnight

Special equipment
22cm (9in) round springform cake tin

Ingredients
100g (3½oz) unsalted butter, diced
250g (9oz) ginger biscuits, crushed
4 sheets gelatine, cut into small pieces
finely grated zest and juice of 2 small oranges
300ml (10fl oz) double cream
350g (12oz) cream cheese
200g (7oz) caster sugar
2 heaped tbsp fine-cut marmalade
1 piece of preserved stem ginger in syrup, drained and finely chopped

Method

1 Line the tin with baking parchment. Melt the butter and combine it with the crushed biscuits. Press the biscuit base firmly and evenly into the cake tin with a wooden spoon. Cover and chill.

2 In a pan, soak the gelatine in the orange juice for 5 minutes to soften. Gently heat the juice and gelatine, stirring until the gelatine is dissolved; do not boil. Set aside to cool.

3 Whisk the double cream to soft peaks. In a separate bowl, beat together the remaining ingredients, then beat in the gelatine, and fold in the cream. Pour over the base and smooth with a damp palette knife or back of a spoon. Chill for 4 hours or overnight.

4 To serve, run a sharp knife around the inside of the tin. Turn it out gently onto a plate, making sure to remove the paper before cutting.

PREPARE AHEAD The cheesecake can be made 2 days ahead and kept refrigerated.

Cherry Cheesecake

Luscious and deceptively light, this is a great dessert for any time of year.

SERVES 6 **30 MINS** **5 MINS**

Chilling time
at least 2 hrs

Special equipment
20cm (8in) round springform cake tin

Ingredients
75g (2½oz) unsalted butter,
  plus extra for greasing
200g (7oz) digestive biscuits, crushed
2 x 250g tubs ricotta cheese
75g (2½oz) golden caster sugar
finely grated zest and juice of 4 lemons
140ml (4½fl oz) double cream
6 sheets gelatine, cut into small pieces
400g can black cherries, or morello cherries in
  juice, drained and juice reserved

Method

1 Grease and line the tin. Melt the butter in a pan, add the biscuits, and stir until coated. Transfer the mixture to the tin, pressing it down firmly with the back of a spoon.

2 Mix together the ricotta, sugar, and zest. In a separate bowl, whisk the cream to soft peaks. Add to the ricotta mixture and beat with a wooden spoon until well combined.

3 In a pan, soak the gelatine in the lemon juice for 5 minutes to soften. gently heat, but do not boil, stirring to dissolve. Set aside. Add to the ricotta mixture and stir well. Pour the mixture on top of the biscuits, spreading it out evenly. Place in the refrigerator for at least 2 hours or until set and firm.

4 In a pan, bring the cherry juice to a boil, then simmer until reduced by about three-quarters. Leave to cool, then arrange the cherries on top of the cheesecake, spoon over the sauce, and serve.

PREPARE AHEAD The cheesecake can be made 2 days ahead and kept refrigerated.

Crostata di ricotta

Ricotta is mixed with candied peel and almonds, and baked in a sweet lemon pastry crust in this Italian classic. The fresher the cheese, the better.

| SERVES 8–10 | 35–40 MINS | 1–1¼ HOURS |

Chilling time
45–60 mins

Special equipment
23–25cm (9–10in) round springform cake tin

Ingredients
175g (6oz) unsalted butter, plus extra for greasing
250g (9oz) plain flour, plus extra for dusting
finely grated zest of 1 lemon
50g (1¾oz) caster sugar
4 egg yolks
pinch of salt
1 egg, beaten, for glazing

For the filling
1.25kg (2¾lb) ricotta cheese
100g (3½oz) caster sugar
1 tbsp plain flour
pinch of salt
finely grated zest of 1 orange
2 tbsp chopped candied orange peel
1 tsp vanilla extract
45g (1½oz) sultanas
30g (1oz) flaked almonds
4 egg yolks

Method

1 Pound the butter between 2 sheets of parchment with a rolling pin to soften it. Sift the flour onto a work surface and make a well in the centre. Put the lemon zest, sugar, butter, egg yolks, and salt into the well. With your fingertips, work all the ingredients together until they are mixed. Draw in the flour and press the dough into a ball.

2 On a floured work surface, knead the dough for 1–2 minutes until very smooth. Shape it into a ball, wrap in cling film, and chill for 30 minutes. Grease the tin. Flour the work surface and roll out three-quarters of the dough to make a 35–37cm (14–15in) round. Roll up the dough around the rolling pin, then drape it over the tin. Press it into the bottom of the tin and up the sides. Trim the excess dough. Chill the shell, with the dough and trimmings, for 15 minutes.

3 Place the ricotta in a bowl and beat in the sugar, flour, and salt. Add the orange zest, candied peel, vanilla, sultanas, almonds, and egg yolks. Beat the mixture to combine. Spoon the filling into the pastry shell. Tap the tin on the work surface to remove air pockets. Smooth the top of the filling, using the back of a wooden spoon.

4 Press the trimmings into the remaining dough, and roll it out to a 25cm (10in) round on a floured surface. Cut it into strips, about 1cm (½in) wide, and place them on the top in a criss-cross fashion. Trim off the hanging ends, so that the strips are even with the edge of the pastry shell.

5 Moisten the ends of the strips with the egg glaze, then seal them to the edge. Brush the lattice with the glaze and chill the cake for 15–30 minutes until firm. Preheat the oven to 180°C (350°F/Gas 4), and place a baking sheet near the bottom of the oven.

6 Bake the cake on the baking sheet for 1–1¼ hours until the top is firm and golden brown. Let it cool in its tin until just warm. Remove the sides of the tin and let it cool completely. Then transfer to a plate, cut into wedges, and serve at room temperature.

PREPARE AHEAD The crostata can be made 1 day ahead and kept refrigerated, though the texture will not be as light.

BAKER'S TIP

This traditional Italian version of the cheesecake uses ricotta for a light texture and taste. The ricotta must be fresh and of the very best quality for perfect results, so buy it from an Italian delicatessen.

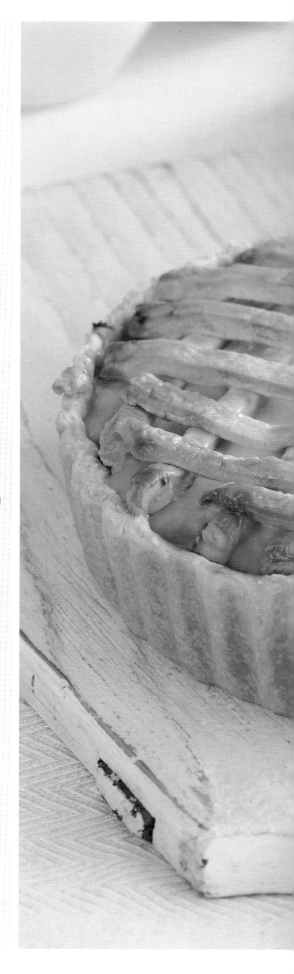

sweet
tarts
& pies

Normandy Pear Tart

This frangipane-filled fruit tart is a signature dish of Normandy, France, where they grow wonderful pears.

SERVES 6–8 **40–45 MINS** **37–45 MINS**

Chilling time
45 mins

Special equipment
23–25cm (9–10in) tart tin
food processor with
    blade attachment

Ingredients
175g (6oz) plain flour,
    plus extra for dusting
3 egg yolks
60g (2oz) sugar

pinch of salt
75g (2½oz) unsalted butter,
    plus extra for greasing
½ tsp vanilla extract
3–4 ripe pears
juice of 1 lemon

For the frangipane
125g (4½oz) whole
    blanched almonds

125g (4½oz) unsalted butter, softened
100g (3½oz) caster sugar
1 egg, plus 1 egg yolk
1 tbsp Kirsch
2 tbsp plain flour, sifted

For the glaze
150g (5½oz) apricot jam
2–3 tbsp Kirsch or water

1 To make the pastry, sift the flour onto a work surface and make a well in the centre.

2 Add the egg yolks, sugar, and salt to the well. Using a rolling pin, pound the butter.

3 Add the butter and vanilla to the well. Mix the ingredients using your fingertips.

4 Work the flour into the other ingredients until crumbs form. If dry, add a little water.

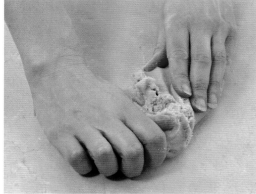

5 Flour a work surface and knead the dough for 1–2 minutes. Wrap and chill for 30 minutes.

6 Grease the tin. On a floured surface, roll the dough to a round, 5cm (2in) larger than the tin.

7 Roll the dough around the rolling pin, then unroll it over the greased tin and line it.

8 Prick the pastry base with a fork. Chill for at least 15 minutes until firm.

9 Preheat the oven to 200°C (400°F/Gas 6). Grind the almonds to a "flour" in the processor.

SWEET TARTS AND PIES

10 With an electric whisk, beat the butter and sugar for 2–3 minutes until fluffy.

11 Gradually add the eggs, beating well after each addition.

12 Add the Kirsch, then gently stir in the almonds and flour until well blended.

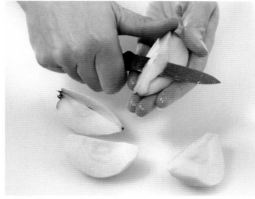

13 Peel and core the pears, cut into wedges, and toss with the lemon juice.

14 Spoon the frangipane into the pastry shell and spread it with a palette knife.

15 Place the pears in a spiral pattern. Set the tin on a baking sheet. Bake for 12–15 minutes.

16 Reduce the heat to 180°C (350°F/Gas 4). Bake for 25–30 minutes, till the frangipane sets.

17 Make a glaze by melting the jam with the Kirsch, and working it through a sieve.

18 Cool and unmould the tart, then brush with the glaze. Serve at room temperature.
STORE It is best eaten the same day but can be kept up to 2 days in an airtight container.

Frangipane Tart variations

Normandy Peach Tart

When pears are not in season, use the very ripest of the summer's peaches in this version for a wonderfully indulgent dessert.

SERVES 6–8 | **40–45 MINS** | **37–45 MINS**

Chilling time
45 mins

Special equipment
23–25cm (9–10in) loose-bottomed tart tin
food processor with blade attachment

Ingredients
1 sweet pastry case, see page 286, steps 1–8
125g (4½oz) whole blanched almonds
125g (4½oz) unsalted butter,
  at room temperature
100g (3½oz) caster sugar
1 egg, plus 1 egg yolk
1 tbsp Kirsch, plus 2–3 tbsp more for glazing
2 tbsp plain flour, sifted
1kg (2¼lb) ripe peaches
150g (5½oz) apricot jam

Method

1 Make the pastry case. Preheat the oven to 200°C (400°F/Gas 6). Heat a baking sheet at the bottom of the oven. For the frangipane, grind the almonds to a "flour" in the food processor. Whisk the butter and sugar until fluffy. Add the egg and egg yolk, beating well. Add the Kirsch, then stir in the almonds and flour. Spoon into the pastry case.

2 Immerse the peaches in a pan of boiling water, leave for 10 seconds, then transfer to a bowl of cold water. Cut each peach in half, remove the stone, and peel off the skin. Cut each half into thin slices and arrange on the frangipane.

3 Set the tin on the preheated baking sheet and bake for 12–15 minutes. Reduce the oven heat to 180°C (350°F/Gas 4) and bake for another 25–30 minutes until the frangipane is puffed up and set. Cool.

4 Make a glaze by melting the jam with the Kirsch, and work through a sieve. Unmould the tart, then brush with the glaze.

STORE Best eaten the same day but can be kept for 2 days in an airtight container.

> **BAKER'S TIP**
> Frangipane makes a delicious filling, and its almond flavour pairs well with certain fruits. Stone fruits such as peaches, nectarines, cherries, and plums make the best flavour pairings with almonds, but experiment by adding apples, raspberries, or gooseberries.

Prune and Almond Tart

Prunes and brandy are a classic combination in French cuisine and work especially well with the almond flavours of a frangipane filling.

MAKES 8 SLICES | **20 MINS** | **45 MINS**

Chilling time
30 mins

Special equipment
23cm (9in) loose-bottomed tart tin
food processor with blade attachment
baking beans

Ingredients
175g (6oz) plain flour, plus extra for dusting
1 tbsp caster sugar
85g (3oz) unsalted butter, chilled
1 small egg

For the filling
200g (7oz) pitted prunes
2 tbsp brandy
100g (3½oz) flaked almonds, toasted
85g (3oz) caster sugar
2 eggs, plus 1 egg yolk
1 tbsp finely grated orange zest
few drops of almond extract
30g (1oz) unsalted butter, softened
120ml (4fl oz) double cream

Method

1 Using your fingertips or a food processor, mix together the flour, sugar, and butter until it forms crumbs. Add the egg and bring together to form a dough. Roll the dough out on a floured surface and use it to line the tart tin, trimming off any excess. Chill for at least 30 minutes.

2 Preheat the oven to 190°C (375°F/Gas 5). Line the pastry case with parchment and baking beans. Bake for 10 minutes, then remove the paper and beans, and bake for a further 5 minutes. Cool on a wire rack.

3 Reduce the temperature of the oven to 180°C (350°F/Gas 4). Place the prunes in a saucepan, cover with water, and add the brandy. Simmer for 5 minutes, then turn off the heat and set aside. Place half the flaked almonds with the sugar in a food processor, and pulse until finely ground. Add the eggs, egg yolk, orange zest, almond extract, butter, and cream, and process until smooth.

4 Drain the prunes and cut any large ones in half. Pour the almond cream into the tart, spread to cover evenly, then arrange the prunes on top. Scatter over the remaining flaked almonds, and bake for 30 minutes, or until just set.

STORE Best eaten the same day but can be kept for 2 days in an airtight container.

Almond and Peach Tart

This easy frangipane tart is even quicker with shop-bought pastry.

| SERVES 8 | 20 MINS | 30 MINS | UP TO 8 WEEKS |

Special equipment
12 x 36cm (5 x 14½in) loose-bottomed tart tin

Ingredients
300g (10½oz) sweet shortcrust pastry,
  shop-bought, or see page 290, step 1
100g (3½oz) unsalted butter, softened
100g (3½oz) caster sugar
2 large eggs
25g (scant 1oz) plain flour, sifted,
  plus extra for dusting
100g (3½oz) ground almonds
4 peaches, halved and stoned
icing sugar, for dusting

Method
1 Preheat the oven to 200°C (400°F/Gas 6) and put a baking tray in to heat up. On a lightly floured surface, roll the pastry out to a thickness of about 5mm (¼in), then use it to line the tin. Trim off the excess pastry.

2 In a bowl, whisk the butter and sugar until light and fluffy, then beat in the eggs. Mix in the flour and ground almonds until well combined, then smooth into the pastry case. Press the peach halves, cut-side down, into the mixture.

3 Put the tin on the baking tray and bake for 30 minutes, or until the mixture is golden brown and cooked through.

4 Leave to cool slightly in the tin, then turn out and transfer to a wire rack, or serve warm, dusted with icing sugar.

STORE Best eaten the same day but can be kept for 2 days in an airtight container.

Bakewell Tart

With its frangipane topping and buttery pastry case, this version of the English tea-time classic can even be served warm with cream as a dessert.

| SERVES 6–8 | 30 MINS | 60–65 MINS | 12 WEEKS, TART CASE |

Chilling time
1 hr

Special equipment
22cm (9in) loose-bottomed tart tin
food processor with blade attachment (optional)
baking beans

Ingredients
150g (5½oz) plain flour, sifted, plus extra
  for dusting
100g (3½oz) unsalted butter, chilled and diced

50g (1¾oz) caster sugar
finely grated zest of ½ lemon
1 egg yolk
½ tsp vanilla extract

For the filling
125g (4½oz) unsalted butter, softened
125g (4½oz) caster sugar
3 large eggs
½ tsp almond extract
125g (4½oz) ground almonds
150g (5½oz) good-quality raspberry jam
25g (scant 1oz) flaked almonds
icing sugar, to serve

Method

1 Rub together the flour and butter with your fingers, or pulse-blend in a food processor, to form fine crumbs. Stir in the sugar and lemon zest. Beat the egg yolk with the vanilla extract and mix into the crumbs, bringing the mixture together to form a soft dough; add a little water to bring it together, if needed. Wrap the dough in cling film and chill for 1 hour.

2 Preheat the oven to 180°C (350°F/Gas 4). Roll the dough out on a floured surface to a thickness of about 3mm (⅛in). It will be quite fragile, so if it begins to crumble, bring it together with your hands and give it a gentle knead to get rid of any joins. Use it to line the tin, leaving an overlapping edge of at least 2cm (¾in). Prick the base all over with a fork. Line the pastry case with parchment and top with the baking beans.

3 Place the case on a baking sheet and blind bake it for 20 minutes. Remove the beans and the paper, and return it to the oven for another 5 minutes, if the centre still looks a little uncooked.

4 To make the filling, cream together the butter and sugar until pale and fluffy. Beat in the eggs and almond extract until well combined. Fold in the ground almonds to form a thick paste.

5 Spread the jam over the base of the cooked tart case. Tip the frangipane over the jam layer and use a palette knife to spread it out evenly. Scatter the flaked almonds over the top.

6 Bake in the centre of the oven for 40 minutes until golden brown. Remove from the oven and allow it to cool for 5 minutes. Then take a small, sharp knife and use it to trim the excess pastry from the edges of the tart (see Baker's Tip). Allow the tart to cool before dusting with icing sugar to serve.

STORE The baked tart will keep in an airtight container for 2 days.

PREPARE AHEAD The unfilled pastry case can be prepared ahead and stored in an airtight container for up to 3 days or frozen for 12 weeks.

BAKER'S TIP
Leaving an overlapping edge to the pastry allows you to trim after baking for a neat, professional finish. When trimming, take care to cut down and away from the tart, so that no crumbs fall on the surface.

Strawberry Tart

Master the basics of this fresh fruit tart and you can adapt it by replacing the strawberries with other soft fruit.

SERVES 6–8

40 MINS

25 MINS

12 WEEKS, TART CASE

Chilling time
1 hr

Special equipment
22cm (9in) loose-bottomed tart tin
baking beans

Ingredients
150g (5½oz) plain flour,
  plus extra for dusting
100g (3½oz) unsalted butter,
  chilled and diced

50g (1¾oz) caster sugar
1 egg yolk
½ tsp vanilla extract
6 tbsp redcurrant jelly, for glazing
300g (10½oz) strawberries,
  washed and thickly sliced

For the crème pâtissière
100g (3½oz) caster sugar
50g (1¾oz) cornflour
2 eggs
1 tsp vanilla extract
400ml (14fl oz) whole milk

1 In a bowl, rub the flour and butter together to form fine crumbs. Stir in the sugar.

2 Beat together the egg yolk and vanilla extract, and add them to the flour mixture.

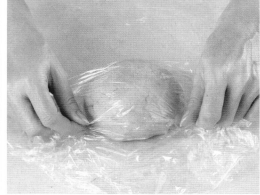

3 Bring together to form a dough; add a little water if dry. Wrap in cling film. Chill for 1 hour.

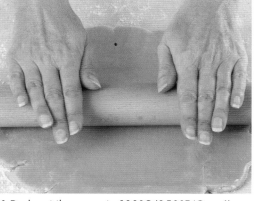

4 Preheat the oven to 180°C (350°F/Gas 4). Roll out the pastry to a thickness of 3mm (⅛in).

5 If the pastry starts to crumble, bring it together with your hands and gently knead.

6 Use the rolled-out pastry to line the tin, leaving an overlapping edge of 2cm (¾in).

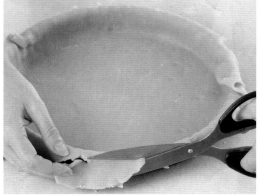

7 Use a pair of scissors to trim any excess pastry that hangs down further than this.

8 Prick the pastry base all over with a fork, to prevent air bubbles forming as it bakes.

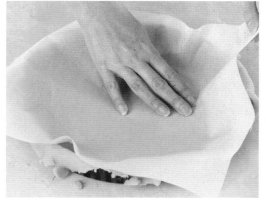

9 Carefully line the pastry case with a piece of baking parchment.

SWEET TARTS AND PIES

10 Scatter baking beans over the paper. Place on a baking sheet and bake for 20 minutes.

11 Remove the beans and paper, and bake for 5 minutes more. Trim any excess pastry.

12 Melt the jelly with 1 tablespoon water and brush a little over the pastry case. Cool.

13 For the crème pâtissière, beat the sugar, cornflour, eggs, and vanilla extract in a bowl.

14 In a heavy saucepan, bring the milk to a boil and take it off the heat just as it bubbles.

15 Pour the hot milk onto the egg mixture, whisking all the time.

16 Return the crème to a pan and bring to a boil over medium heat, whisking constantly.

17 When the crème thickens, reduce the heat to low, and continue to cook for 2–3 minutes.

18 Transfer to a bowl, cover with cling film and leave it to cool completely.

19 Beat the crème pâtissière and spread it over the pastry case. Top with the strawberries.

20 Heat the jelly glaze again and brush over the strawberries, then leave to set.

21 Remove from the tin to serve. **STORE** Best eaten on the day but will keep chilled overnight.

Crème Pâtissière Tart variations

Raspberry Tart with Chocolate Cream

A fruit tart with a twist, here chocolate is baked into and brushed over the pastry case, and the crème pâtissière is enriched with melted dark chocolate – a perfect partner for fresh raspberries.

SERVES 6–8 | **40 MINS** | **20–25 MINS** | **12 WEEKS, TART CASE**

Chilling time
1 hr

Special equipment
22cm (9in) loose-bottomed tart tin
baking beans

Ingredients
130g (4½oz) plain flour, plus extra for dusting
20g (¾oz) cocoa powder
100g (3½oz) unsalted butter, chilled and diced
150g (5½oz) caster sugar
1 egg yolk, plus 2 eggs
1½ tsp vanilla extract
50g (1¾oz) cornflour, sifted
450ml (15fl oz) whole milk
175g (6oz) good-quality dark chocolate, broken into pieces
400g (14oz) raspberries
icing sugar, for dusting

Method

1 Rub together the flour, cocoa, and butter, until they resemble fine crumbs. Stir in 50g (1¾oz) sugar. Beat the egg yolk with ½ teaspoon vanilla and add to the flour mixture, bringing it together to form a soft dough. Add a little cold water if it seems too stiff. Wrap in cling film and chill for 1 hour.

2 Preheat the oven to 180°C (350°F/Gas 4). Roll the pastry out to a thickness of 3mm (⅛in). Use it to line the tin, leaving an overlapping edge of 2cm (¾in); trim excess with scissors. Prick the base with a fork.

3 Line the case with parchment, and weigh down with baking beans. Place on a baking sheet and bake for 20 minutes. Remove the beans and paper, and return it to the oven for another 5 minutes. Trim excess pastry.

4 For the crème pâtissière, beat together 100g (3½oz) sugar, cornflour, eggs, and 1 teaspoon vanilla extract. In a pan, bring the milk and 100g (3½oz) of the chocolate to a boil, whisking all the time. Take it off the heat just as it starts to bubble up. Pour the milk onto the egg mixture, whisking all the time.

5 Return to the cleaned-out pan and bring to a boil over medium heat, whisking. When it thickens, reduce the heat to its lowest and cook for 2–3 minutes, whisking. Turn into a bowl, cover the surface with cling film to prevent a skin forming, and leave to cool.

6 Melt the remaining chocolate in a bowl set over a pan of simmering water, and brush around the inside of the tart case. Leave to set. Beat the cold crème pâtissière with a wooden spoon, and transfer into the case. Arrange the raspberries over, remove from the tin, and serve dusted with icing sugar.

STORE Best eaten the same day it is made, this will store in the refrigerator overnight.

Fruit Tartlets

Any mix of fruits will look attractive; choose whatever is in season.

SERVES 8	40–45 MINS	11–13 MINS	12 WEEKS, CASES

Chilling time
1 hr

Special equipment
8 x 10cm (4in) tartlet tins

Ingredients
175g (6oz) plain flour, plus extra for dusting
4 egg yolks
90g (3oz) caster sugar
½ tsp salt
½ tsp vanilla extract
90g (3oz) unsalted butter, diced,
   plus extra for greasing

For the filling
375ml (13fl oz) milk
1 vanilla pod, split, or 2 tsp vanilla extract
5 egg yolks
60g (2oz) caster sugar
30g (1oz) plain flour
500g (1lb 2oz) mixed fresh fruit,
   such as kiwi fruit, raspberries, grapes, peaches
175g (6oz) apricot jam or redcurrant jelly,
   for glazing

Method

1 Sift the flour onto a work surface and make a well in the centre. Add the egg yolks, sugar, salt, vanilla, and butter. Work the ingredients with your fingertips until well mixed, then draw in the flour until coarse crumbs form. Press the dough into a ball, and knead for 1–2 minutes until smooth. Wrap it in cling film and chill for 30 minutes.

2 For the filling, bring the milk to a boil in a pan with the vanilla pod or extract. Remove the pan from the heat, cover, and let it stand for 10–15 minutes. In a bowl, whisk together the egg yolks, sugar, and flour. Beat in the hot milk. Return the mixture to the cleaned-out pan and cook over low heat, whisking constantly, until the flour has cooked and the cream has thickened. Simmer over low heat for 2 minutes.

3 Transfer the pastry cream to another bowl and remove the vanilla pod (if using) or stir in the vanilla extract. Press cling film over the surface to prevent a skin from forming, and leave to cool.

4 Grease the tartlet tins. Lightly flour a work surface and roll the dough out to a thickness of 3mm (⅛in). Group the tins together, with their edges nearly touching. Roll the dough loosely around the rolling pin and drape it over the tins so all are covered. Roll the rolling pin over the tops of the tins to remove excess dough, then press the dough into each tin. Set the tartlet tins on a baking sheet and prick the dough all over with a fork. Chill for 30 minutes.

5 Preheat the oven to 200°C (400°F/Gas 6). Line each tartlet case with a piece of foil, pressing it down well. Bake for 6–8 minutes, then remove the foil and continue baking for another 5 minutes more. Transfer to a wire rack to cool, then turn out.

6 Peel and slice the fruits. Melt the jam or jelly with 2–3 tablespoons water in a small saucepan, and work it through a sieve. Brush the inside of each tartlet case with the melted jam glaze. Half fill each shell with the cooled pastry cream, smoothing the top with the back of a spoon. Arrange the fruit on top, and brush with the jam glaze.

STORE These will keep in an airtight container in the refrigerator for 2 days.

BAKER'S TIP
Crème pâtissière is one of the most useful sweet recipes to master, and once you have got the hang of it, impressive to serve. For a lighter finish to the pastry cream, fold about 100ml (3½fl oz) whipped double cream into the cooled crème pâtissière.

Tarte aux pommes

This French classic uses two types of apples: cooking apples that will reduce down to a purée, and dessert apples that keep their shape.

MAKES 8 SLICES | **20 MINS** | **50–55 MINS** | **12 WEEKS, TART CASE**

Chilling time
30 mins

Special equipment
22cm (9in) loose-bottomed tart tin
baking beans

Ingredients
375g sweet pastry, shop-bought,
  or see page 300, step 1
plain flour, for dusting
50g (1¾oz) unsalted butter
750g (1lb 10oz) cooking apples,
  peeled, cored, and chopped
125g (4½oz) caster sugar
finely grated zest and juice of ½ lemon
2 tbsp Calvados or brandy
2 dessert apples
2 tbsp apricot jam, sieved, for glazing

Method

1 Roll the pastry out on a floured surface to a thickness of about 3mm (⅛in) and use it to line the tin, leaving an overlapping edge of at least 2cm (¾in). Prick the pastry base with a fork. Chill for at least 30 minutes.

2 Preheat the oven to 200°C (400°F/Gas 6). Line the pastry case with parchment and fill with baking beans. Bake for 15 minutes. Remove the paper and beans, then return to the oven for another 5 minutes or until the pastry is a light golden colour.

3 Meanwhile, melt the butter in a saucepan and add the cooking apples. Cover and cook over low heat, stirring occasionally, for 15 minutes or until soft and mushy.

4 Push the cooked apple through a sieve to produce a smooth purée, then return it to the saucepan. Reserve a tablespoon of caster sugar and add the rest to the apple purée. Stir in the lemon zest and Calvados or brandy. Return the pan to the heat and simmer, stirring continuously until it thickens.

5 Spoon the purée into the pastry case. Peel, core, and thinly slice the dessert apples and arrange on top of the purée. Brush with the lemon juice and sprinkle with the reserved caster sugar.

6 Bake for 30–35 minutes, or until the apple slices have softened and are starting to turn pale golden. Use a small, sharp knife to trim the excess pastry for a neat edge (see Baker's Tip, page 290).

7 Warm the apricot jam and brush it over the top. Cut into slices and serve.

STORE The baked tart will keep in an airtight container for 2 days.

PREPARE AHEAD The unfilled pastry case can be prepared ahead and stored in an airtight container for up to 3 days, or frozen for 12 weeks.

BAKER'S TIP
A glaze will make any home-made fruit tart look as appetizing as those in a patisserie. Apricot jam works well for apples and pears; for a red fruit tart, use warmed redcurrant jelly brushed over the fruits. Press the jam through a sieve before using as a glaze, to remove any lumps of fruit.

Pumpkin Pie

This version of the classic American dessert produces a delicate result, gently set and fragrant with warm tones of cinnamon and mixed spice.

SERVES 6–8 | **30 MINS** | **65–75 MINS** | **12 WEEKS, PIE CASE**

Chilling time
1 hr

Special equipment
22cm (9in) loose-bottomed tart tin
food processor with blade attachment (optional)
baking beans

Ingredients
150g (5½oz) plain flour, plus extra for dusting
100g (3½oz) unsalted butter, chilled and diced

50g (1¾oz) caster sugar
1 egg yolk
½ tsp vanilla extract

For the filling
3 eggs
100g (3½oz) soft light brown sugar
1 tsp cinnamon
1 tsp mixed spice
200ml (7fl oz) double cream
425g can processed pumpkin,
  or 400g (14oz) roasted and puréed pumpkin
thick cream or vanilla ice cream,
  to serve (optional)

Method

1 To make the pastry, rub together the flour and butter, or pulse-blend in a processor, to form fine crumbs. Stir in the sugar. Beat together the egg yolk and the vanilla, and mix into the dry ingredients, bringing the mixture together to form a soft dough; add a little water to bring it together, if needed. Wrap in cling film and chill for 1 hour.

2 Preheat the oven to 180°C (350°F/Gas 4). Roll out the pastry on a floured surface to a thickness of 3mm (⅛in). It will be fragile, so should it begin to crumble, bring it together with your hands and knead it gently to get rid of any joins. Use it to line the tin, leaving an overlapping edge of at least 2cm (¾in). Prick the base all over with a fork. Line the pastry case with parchment and weigh it down with baking beans.

3 Place the case on a baking sheet and blind bake it for 20 minutes. Remove the beans and the paper, and return it to the oven for 5 minutes if the centre is uncooked.

4 In a large bowl, whisk together the eggs, sugar, spices, and cream. When they are well blended, beat in the canned or puréed pumpkin to make a smooth filling. Partially pull out an oven rack from the centre of the oven, and place the pastry case on it. Pour the filling into the case and slide the rack back into the oven.

5 Bake for 45–50 minutes until the filling is quite set, but before it begins to bubble up at the edges. Trim the pastry edge with a small, sharp knife while still warm (see Baker's Tip, page 290), then leave the pie to cool in its tin for at least 15 minutes before turning out. Serve warm with thick cream or vanilla ice cream.

STORE The pie can be kept in an airtight container in the refrigerator for 2 days.

PREPARE AHEAD The unfilled pastry case can be prepared ahead and stored in an airtight container for 3 days, or frozen for 12 weeks.

BAKER'S TIP

Tins of ready prepared pumpkin are a short cut to producing this delicate pie, full of autumn flavours. However, fresh pumpkin, or even butternut squash, can be roasted until tender and puréed for a home-made version. It will be denser than the tinned pumpkin, so less is needed to set the filling.

Almond and Raspberry Lattice Tart

This is the Viennese speciality "Linzertorte" made with almond lattice pastry.

SERVES 6–8 **30–35 MINS** **40–45 MINS**

Chilling time
1¼–2¼ hrs

Special equipment
23cm (9in) loose-bottomed tart tin
food processor with
  blade attachment
fluted pastry wheel (optional)

Ingredients
125g (4½oz) plain flour,
  plus extra for dusting
pinch of cloves

½ tsp cinnamon
175g (6oz) ground almonds
125g (4½oz) unsalted butter,
  softened and diced,
  plus extra for greasing
1 egg yolk
100g (3½oz) caster sugar
¼ tsp salt
finely grated zest of 1 lemon
  and juice of ½

For the filling
125g (4½oz) caster sugar
375g (13oz) raspberries
1–2 tbsp icing sugar, for dusting

1 Sift the flour into a bowl. Mix in the cloves, cinnamon, and almonds, and make a well.

2 Using your fingers, mix the butter, yolk, sugar, salt, zest, and juice. Place in the well.

3 Draw in the flour and work it until coarse crumbs form. Mix the dough into a ball.

4 Knead the dough for 1–2 minutes until smooth. Wrap in cling film. Chill for 1–2 hours.

5 Cook the caster sugar and raspberries in a pan for 10–12 minutes until thick. Cool.

6 With the back of a wooden spoon, press half of the fruit pulp through a sieve.

7 Stir in the remaining pulp. Grease the tin and preheat the oven to 190°C (375°F/Gas 5).

8 Flour the work surface. Roll out two-thirds of the dough into a 28cm (11in) round.

9 Use the dough to line the tin, and cut off any excess overhanging the sides.

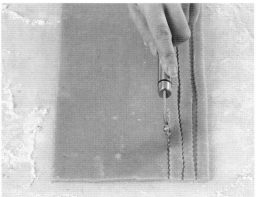

10 Spread the filling in the case. Roll the rest of the dough to a 15 x 30cm (6 x 12in) rectangle.

11 Using a fluted wheel, for a decorative edge, cut the dough into 12 x 1cm (5 x ½in) strips.

12 Arrange half the strips from left to right over the tart, 2cm (¼in) apart. Turn the tart 45°.

13 Put the other strips diagonally over. Trim overhang, roll out trimmings, and cut 4 strips.

14 Brush the edge with water and fix the edge strips. Chill for 15 minutes.

15 Bake for 15 minutes. Reduce to 180°C (350°F, Gas 4) and bake for 25–30 minutes more.

16 Leave to cool, then remove from the tin and, about 30 minutes before serving, lightly dust with icing sugar.
STORE The tart can be stored in an airtight container for up to 2 days; the flavour will mellow.

Lattice Tart and Pie variations

Cherry Pie

The most famous of all American pies. The juice from the fruit is thickened with flour to help bring the filling together and make it easier to cut.

SERVES 8	40–45 MINS	40–45 MINS

Chilling time
45 mins

Special equipment
23cm (9in) pie dish

Ingredients
250g (9oz) plain flour, plus extra for dusting
½ tsp salt
125g (4½oz) lard or white vegetable fat, chilled
75g (2½oz) unsalted butter, chilled

For the filling and glaze
500g (1lb 2oz) cherries, stoned
200g (7oz) caster sugar
45g (1½oz) plain flour
¼ tsp almond extract (optional)
1 egg
½ tsp salt

Method
1 Sift the flour and salt into a bowl. Dice the lard and butter, and rub into the flour with your fingers until crumbs form. Sprinkle with 3 tablespoons water, and blend until the dough turns into a ball. Wrap in cling film and chill for 30 minutes. Preheat the oven to 200°C (400°F/Gas 6), and put in a baking sheet. On a floured surface, roll out two-thirds of the dough, and use to line the dish with some overhang. Press the dough into the dish and chill for 15 minutes.

2 Put the cherries in a bowl and add the sugar, flour, and almond extract (if using). Stir until well mixed, then spoon into the tin.

3 Roll out the remaining dough into a rectangle. Cut out 8 strips, each 1cm (½in) wide, and arrange them in a lattice-like pattern on top of the pie; trim the pastry. Beat the egg and salt, and use this to glaze the lattice and secure the strips to the edge of the pie. Bake for 40–45 minutes until the pastry is golden brown. Serve at room temperature or chilled.

STORE The pie can be kept in an airtight container for 2 days, but is really best eaten on the day it is baked.

Crostata di marmellata

This Italian tart is quickly made with a few storecupboard essentials.

SERVES 6–8	30 MINS	50 MINS	12 WEEKS, TART CASE

Chilling time
1 hr

Special equipment
22cm (9in) loose-bottomed tart tin
baking beans

Ingredients
175g (6oz) plain flour, plus extra for dusting
100g (3½oz) unsalted butter, chilled and diced
50g (1¾oz) caster sugar
1 egg yolk, plus 1 egg, beaten, for glazing
2 tbsp milk, plus extra if needed
½ tsp vanilla extract
450g (1lb) good-quality raspberry, cherry, or apricot jam

Method
1 With your fingers, rub the flour and butter together in a bowl until fine crumbs form. Stir in the sugar. Beat the egg yolk with the milk and vanilla extract, and add it to the dry ingredients, bringing the mixture together to form a soft dough. Use an extra tablespoon of milk if the mixture seems a little dry. Wrap in cling film and chill for 1 hour.

2 Preheat the oven to 180°C (350°F/Gas 4). Roll out the pastry on a well-floured surface to a thickness of 3mm (⅛in). It will be quite fragile, so if it begins to crumble, just bring it together again with your hands and gently knead to get rid of any joins. Line the tin with the pastry, leaving an overlapping edge of 2cm (¾in). Use a pair of scissors to trim any excess pastry. Prick the base all over with a fork. Roll up the excess pastry and chill for later use.

3 Line the pastry case with a piece of baking parchment and weigh it down with the baking beans. Place the case on a baking sheet and blind bake for 20 minutes. Remove the beans and

paper, and return it to the oven for another 5 minutes, if the centre still looks uncooked.

4 Increase the oven temperature to 200°C (400°F/Gas 6). Spread the jam in a 1–2cm (½–¾in) layer over the pastry case. Roll out the remaining pastry into a square just larger than the tart and 3mm (⅛in) thick. Cut the pastry into at least 12 strips, each 1cm (½in) wide, and use these to top the tart in a lattice-like pattern.

5 Use beaten egg to secure the strips to the sides of the tart and to gently brush the lattice. Return the tart to the oven for 20–25 minutes until the pastry lattice is cooked through and golden brown on top. Cool for 10 minutes before eating. Serve while still warm or at room temperature.

STORE The tart will keep in an airtight container for 2 days.

Peach Pie

Less famous than its cherry cousin but no less tasty, this American classic is a splendid summer dessert. Choose perfectly ripe peaches full of juice. ▲

SERVES	40–45	40–45
8	MINS	MINS

Chilling time
45 mins

Special equipment
23cm (9in) pie tin

Ingredients
1 pastry case, see Cherry Pie, opposite, step 1
4–5 ripe peaches
30g (1oz) plain flour
150g (5½oz) granulated sugar
pinch of salt
1–2 tbsp lemon juice, to taste

For the glaze
1 egg
½ tsp salt

Method
1 Immerse the peaches in boiling water for 10 seconds, then transfer to a bowl of cold water. Halve the peaches, remove the stones, and peel off the skins. Cut into 1cm (½in) slices and put in a large bowl.

2 Sprinkle the peaches with the flour, sugar, salt, and lemon juice, to taste. Carefully stir the peaches, then transfer them to the pastry case, in the pie tin, with their juices.

3 Lightly beat together the egg and salt, and use this to glaze the pie.

4 Bake for 40–45 minutes until the pastry is golden brown, and the peaches are soft and bubbling. Serve warm.

STORE The pie can be kept in an airtight container for 2 days, but is really best eaten on the day it is baked.

Pecan Pie

This sweet, crunchy pie originated in the southern United States, where pecan nuts are widely grown.

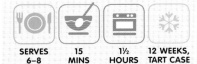

SERVES 6–8 | **15 MINS** | **1½ HOURS** | **12 WEEKS, TART CASE**

Chilling time
30 mins

Special equipment
22cm (9in) loose-bottomed tart tin
food processor with blade attachment (optional)
baking beans

Ingredients
150g (5½oz) plain flour, plus extra for dusting
100g (3½oz) unsalted butter, chilled and diced
50g (1¾oz) caster sugar

1 egg yolk
½ tsp vanilla extract
crème fraîche or whipped cream,
   to serve (optional)

For the filling
150ml (5fl oz) maple syrup
60g (2oz) butter
175g (6oz) light soft brown sugar
few drops of vanilla extract
pinch of salt
3 eggs
200g (7oz) pecan nuts

Method

1 Using your fingertips, rub together the flour and butter, or pulse-blend in a food processor until they form fine crumbs. Stir in the sugar. Beat the egg yolk with the vanilla and mix them into the dry ingredients, bringing the mixture together to form a soft dough; a little water to bring the dough together, if needed. Wrap in cling film and chill for 1 hour. Preheat the oven to 180°C (350°F/Gas 4).

2 Roll out the pastry on a well-floured surface to 3mm (⅛in) thick. It will be fragile, so if it begins to crumble, bring it together again with your hands and gently knead to get rid of any joins. Use it to line the tin, leaving an overlapping edge of at least 2cm (¾in). Prick the base all over with a fork.

3 Line the pastry case with parchment and weigh it down with baking beans. Place the case on a baking sheet and blind bake it for 20 minutes. Remove the beans and paper, and bake for a further 5 minutes if the centre still looks a little uncooked.

4 Pour the maple syrup into a pan, and add the butter, sugar, vanilla extract, and salt. Place the pan over low heat, and stir constantly until the butter has melted and the sugar dissolved. Remove the pan from the heat and leave the mixture to cool until it feels just tepid, then beat in the eggs, one at a time. Stir in the pecan nuts, then pour the mixture into the pastry case.

5 Bake for 40–50 minutes or until just set. Cover with a sheet of foil if it is browning too quickly. Remove the pie from the oven, transfer it to a wire rack and leave to cool for 15–20 minutes. Remove from the tin and either serve it warm or leave it on the wire rack to cool completely. Serve with crème fraîche or whipped cream.

STORE The pie will keep in an airtight container for 2 days.

PREPARE AHEAD The unfilled pastry case can be prepared ahead and stored in an airtight container for up to 3 days, or frozen for 12 weeks.

BAKER'S TIP

Try to buy nuts fresh, each time you want to bake with them. Remember to buy them in small batches and never store them for very long. Nuts turn rancid quickly, due to the large amount of oil they contain, and a single rancid nut can taint and ruin this tart.

Treacle Tart

A classic English tart that remains a favourite with young and old alike. Try making this more sophisticated version, rich with cream and eggs.

SERVES 6–8

30 MINS

50–55 MINS

12 WEEKS, TART CASE

Chilling time
1 hr

Special equipment
22cm (9in) loose-bottomed tart tin
food processor with blade attachment (optional)
baking beans
hand-held blender (optional)

Ingredients
150g (5½oz) plain flour, plus extra for dusting
100g (3½oz) unsalted butter, chilled and diced
50g (1¾oz) caster sugar
1 egg yolk
½ tsp vanilla extract

For the filling
200ml (7fl oz) golden syrup
200ml (7fl oz) double cream
2 eggs
finely grated zest of 1 orange
100g (3½oz) brioche or croissant crumbs
thick cream or ice cream, to serve

Method

1 Using your fingertips, rub together the flour and butter, or pulse-blend in a food processor, to form fine crumbs. Stir in the sugar. Beat together the egg yolk and vanilla extract, and mix them into the dry ingredients. Bring the mixture together to form a soft dough, adding a little water if it seems dry. Wrap the dough in cling film and chill for 1 hour. Preheat the oven to 180°C (350°F/Gas 4).

2 Roll out the dough on a well-floured surface to a thickness of 3mm (⅛in). It will be quite fragile, so should it begin to crumble, just bring it together with your hands and gently knead it to get rid of any joins. Line the tin with the rolled-out dough, leaving an overlapping edge of at least 2cm (¾in). Prick the base all over with a fork.

3 Line the pastry case with parchment and weigh it down with the baking beans. Place the pastry case on a baking sheet, and blind bake it for 20 minutes. Remove the beans and paper, and return it to the oven for another 5 minutes if the centre still looks uncooked. Reduce the temperature of the oven to 170°C (340°F/Gas 3½).

4 Measure out the golden syrup into a large measuring jug. Measure the cream on top of it (the density of the syrup will keep the two separate, making measuring easy). Add the eggs and orange zest, and whizz together with a hand-held blender until well combined. Alternatively, transfer to a bowl and whisk. Gently fold in the brioche crumbs.

5 Place the tart case on a baking tray, pull out an oven rack from the centre of the oven and put the baking tray on it. Pour the filling into the case and carefully slide the rack back into the oven.

6 Bake the tart for 30 minutes until just set, but before the filling starts to bubble up. Trim the pastry edge with a small, sharp knife while still warm (see Baker's Tip, page 290), then leave to cool in its tin for at least 15 minutes before turning out. Serve warm with thick cream or ice cream.

STORE The tart will keep in an airtight container for 2 days.

PREPARE AHEAD The unfilled pastry case can be prepared ahead and stored in an airtight container for up to 3 days, or frozen for 12 weeks.

BAKER'S TIP

Traditional treacle tarts are made from little more than pastry, syrup, and breadcrumbs. For a delicious, more luxurious tart, I've used cream and eggs here to lighten the filling. They lend a smoothness and incorporate air, to give a more mousse-like result than the sometimes solid, classic recipe.

Tarte Tatin

Named after two French sisters who earned a living by baking their father's favourite apple tart.

SERVES 8 **45–50 MINS** **35–50 MINS**

Chilling time
30 mins

Special equipment
23–25cm (9–10in) ovenproof pan or Tatin dish

Ingredients
175g (6oz) plain flour, plus extra for dusting
2 egg yolks
1½ tbsp caster sugar

pinch of salt
75g (2½oz) unsalted butter, softened

For the filling
14–16 apples, total weight about 2.4kg (5½lb)
1 lemon
125g (4½oz) unsalted butter
200g (7oz) caster sugar
crème fraîche, to serve (optional)

1 For the pastry, sift the flour into a large bowl and make a well in the centre.

2 Put the egg yolks, sugar, and salt in the well. Add the butter and 1 tablespoon of water.

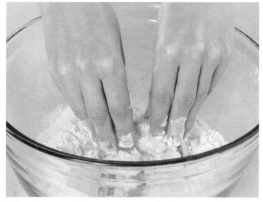

3 Using your fingertips, work the ingredients in the well until thoroughly mixed.

4 Work the flour into the mixture until coarse crumbs form. Press the dough into a ball.

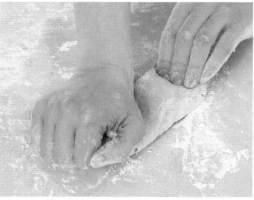

5 Flour the work surface and knead the dough for 2 minutes until smooth.

6 Shape the dough into a ball, wrap in cling film, and chill for about 30 minutes until firm.

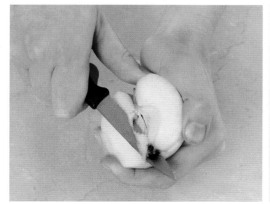

7 For the filling, carefully peel the apples, then halve and core them.

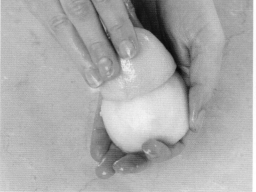

8 Cut the lemon in half, and rub the apples all over with it, to prevent discolouration.

9 Melt the butter in the frying pan. Add the sugar and stir it together.

10 Cook over medium heat, stirring now and again, till caramelized to deep golden brown.

11 Remove from the heat. Let it cool to tepid. Put the apple in concentric circles to fill the pan.

12 Cook the apples over high heat for 15–25 minutes until caramelized. Turn once.

13 Remove from the heat. Cool for 15 minutes. Preheat the oven to 190°C (375°F/Gas 5).

14 Roll out the pastry to a round, 2.5cm (1in) larger than the pan. Drape it over the pan.

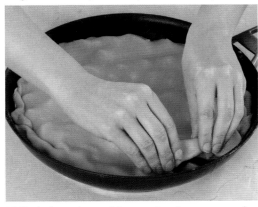

15 Tuck the edges of the pastry down around the apples. Bake for 20–25 minutes till golden.

16 Cool to tepid, then set a plate on top, hold firmly together, and invert. Spoon some caramel over the apples. Serve with crème fraîche.

Tarte Tatin variations

Pear Tarte Tatin

Pears are an easy substitute for apples, but will take longer to cook. Use pears that are ripe but still holding their shape – Comice pears are a good choice.

SERVES 8 **30 MINS** **40–55 MINS**

Chilling time
40–45 mins

Special equipment
23–25cm (9–10in) ovenproof pan or Tatin dish

Ingredients

For the pastry
175g (6oz) plain flour,
   plus extra for dusting
2 egg yolks
1½ tbsp caster sugar
pinch of salt
75g (2½oz) unsalted butter, softened

For the filling
125g (4½oz) unsalted butter
200g (7oz) caster sugar
12–14 pears, total weight 2.4kg (5½lb), peeled,
   halved, cored, and rubbed with lemon halves
crème fraîche, to serve (optional)

Method

1 For the pastry, sift the flour into a large bowl and make a well in the centre. Put the egg yolks, sugar, and salt in the well. Add the butter and 1 tablespoon of water. Using your fingertips, work the ingredients in the well until thoroughly mixed. Work the flour into the mixture until coarse crumbs form.

2 Press the dough into a ball. Flour the work surface and knead the dough for 2 minutes, until smooth. Wrap in cling film and chill for about 30 minutes, until firm.

3 For the filling, melt the butter in the frying pan. Add the sugar and stir together. Cook over medium heat for 3–5 minutes, stirring, until caramelized to a deep golden brown. Remove from the heat, and let cool.

4 Arrange the pear halves on their sides in the pan with the tapered ends towards the centre of the pan. Cook the pears over high heat for 20–30 minutes until caramelized. Turn once to caramelize on both sides. The pears should be tender but still retain their shape, and very little juice should remain.

5 Take the pan from the heat and cool for 10–15 minutes. Preheat the oven to 190°C (375°F/Gas 5). Roll out the pastry to a round 2.5cm (1in) larger than the pan. Drape it over the pan and tuck the edges around the pears. Bake for 20–25 minutes.

6 Cool to tepid, then set a plate on top, hold together, and invert. Spoon some caramel over the pears. Serve with crème fraîche.

PREPARE AHEAD The tart can be baked 6–8 hours ahead and warmed briefly on the hob before unmoulding.

> **BAKER'S TIP**
> Pears may produce more liquid than apples and so take longer cook in the caramel until the liquid has evaporated. Make sure very little liquid remains or the Tatin may be soggy.

Caramel Banana Tart

Not one for purists, but this tropical take on a tarte Tatin is so delicious and easy to prepare, no one will mind – and the flavours are particularly appealing to kids.

SERVES 6 **15 MINS** **30–35 MINS**

Special equipment
20cm (8in) tart dish or tin (not loose-bottomed)

Ingredients
75g (2½oz) butter
150g (5½oz) golden syrup
4 medium bananas, peeled and sliced
   1cm (½in) thick
200g (7oz) puff pastry, shop-bought,
   or see page 178, steps 1–9
plain flour, to dust
vanilla ice cream or crème fraîche,
   to serve (optional)

Method

1 Preheat the oven to 200°C (400°F/Gas 6). Heat the butter and syrup in a small pan until the butter has melted and the mixture is smooth, then allow to boil for 1 minute.

2 Pour into the tart dish or tin. Arrange the banana slices on top of the syrup mixture; this will be the top of the tart when turned out. Place the dish or tin on a baking tray and bake for 10 minutes.

3 Meanwhile, on a lightly floured surface, roll out the pastry into a round, about 23cm (9in) in diameter. It should be about 5mm (¼in) thick. Trim off any excess, if necessary.

Carefully remove the tart dish or tin from the oven and place the pastry circle on top of the caramelized bananas. Use the handle of a knife to tuck the edge down into the tin, being careful of the hot caramel.

4 Return the tart to the oven and bake for 20–25 minutes or until the pastry is golden brown. Leave to stand for 5–10 minutes. Place a serving plate on top and turn it upside-down. Serve immediately with vanilla ice cream or crème fraîche.

Peach Tarte Tatin

This more unusual tarte Tatin is a good choice for a late summer dessert. Choose firm peaches to ensure the fruit holds its shape as it cooks. Mango slices would also work well here.

SERVES 6   **40–45 MINS**   **20–25 MINS**

Chilling time
45 mins

Special equipment
25cm (10in) round baking dish

Ingredients
3 egg yolks
½ tsp vanilla extract
215g (7½oz) plain flour, plus extra for dusting
60g (2oz) caster sugar
¼ tsp salt
90g (3oz) unsalted butter, diced

For the filling
200g (7oz) caster sugar
1kg (2¼lb) peaches

Method

1 In a small bowl, mix the egg yolks with the vanilla. Mix together the flour, sugar, and salt in a large bowl. Add the butter and, with your fingertips, mix to form crumbs. Add the egg mix and bring together to form a dough. Knead until smooth and chill for 30 minutes.

2 For the filling, place the sugar in a saucepan and heat gently until dissolved, stirring occasionally. Boil, without stirring, until the mixture starts to turn golden around the edge. Do not stir, or it may crystallize. Lower the heat and continue cooking, swirling the saucepan once or twice so the syrup colours evenly, until the caramel is golden. Cook the caramel only until medium gold; if it gets too dark, it will become bitter in the oven.

3 Remove the saucepan from the heat and immediately plunge the base of the saucepan into a bowl of cold water, until cooking stops. Stand back in case of splashes; there are few things hotter than caramel. Pour the caramel into the bottom of the baking dish. Working quickly, tilt the dish so the bottom is coated with a thin, even layer. Let it cool.

4 Immerse the peaches in a pan of boiling water for 10 seconds, then transfer to a bowl of cold water. Cut them in half, remove the stones, and peel off the skin. Cut the peach halves lengthways into two. Tightly pack the peach wedges on top of the caramel, rounded-side down, in concentric circles.

5 On a lightly floured work surface, roll out the dough to a 28cm (11in) round. Wrap it around the rolling pin and drape over the dish. Tuck the edge of the dough down around the peaches. Chill for 15 minutes. Preheat the oven to 200°C (400°F/Gas 6).

6 Bake for 30–35 minutes. Let the tart cool to tepid. To unmould, set a platter on top of the baking dish. Hold dish and platter firmly together and invert them, then remove the baking dish. Serve at once, cut into wedges.

Custard Tart

A filling of gently set egg custard, delicately spiced with nutmeg, makes a simple yet elegant tart.

SERVES 8	20 MINS	45–50 MINS	12 WEEKS, TART CASE

Chilling time
1 hr

Special equipment
22cm (9in) loose-bottomed tart tin
baking beans

Ingredients
170g (6oz) plain flour,
 plus extra for dusting
100g (3½oz) unsalted butter,
 chilled and diced
50g (1¾oz) caster sugar
2 egg yolks
½ tsp vanilla extract

For the filling
225ml (7½fl oz) milk
150ml (5fl oz) double cream
2 eggs
30g (1oz) caster sugar
½ tsp vanilla extract
¼ tsp freshly grated nutmeg

SWEET TARTS AND PIES

1 In a bowl, mix the flour and butter together until they form fine crumbs. Stir in the sugar.

2 Beat the egg yolks with the vanilla extract and add them to the dry ingredients.

3 Bring the mixture together to form a soft dough. Wrap in cling film and chill for 1 hour.

4 Preheat the oven to 180°C (350°F/Gas 4). Roll it out on a floured surface to 3mm (⅛in) thick.

5 It will be quite fragile, so if it crumbles, bring it together with your hands and knead gently.

6 Use it to line the tin, leaving an overlapping edge of at least 2cm (¾in).

7 Prick the pastry all over with a fork, to prevent air bubbles forming during baking.

8 Line with parchment and weigh it down with beans. Bake for 20 minutes on a baking sheet.

9 Remove the beans and paper and bake for 5 minutes. Trim the overhanging pastry.

10 Reduce the temperature to 170°C (340°F/ Gas 3½). Heat the milk and the cream in a pan.

11 Meanwhile whisk together the eggs, sugar, vanilla extract, and nutmeg.

12 Once the milk and cream have come to a boil, pour them over the egg mixture, whisking.

13 Place the tart case on a baking sheet; this will make it easier to transfer to the oven.

14 Transfer the filling to a jug and pour into the case. Place in the top third of the oven.

15 Bake for 20–25 minutes or until just set but still with a slight wobble in the centre.

16 Remove the tart from the oven and leave to cool, then remove from the tin.
STORE The tart will keep in an airtight container in the refrigerator for 1 day.

Custard Tart variations

Gooseberry Tart

The sharp gooseberries quiver in smooth, just-set custard, all held together in a light sweet pastry crust for a sublime seasonal treat.

SERVES 6–8 | **30 MINS** | **1 HOUR** | **12 WEEKS, TART CASE**

Chilling time
30 mins

Special equipment
24cm (10in) loose-bottomed tart tin
baking beans

Ingredients
170g (6oz) plain flour
75g (2½oz) butter
25g (scant 1oz) caster sugar
2 egg yolks

For the filling
250ml (8fl oz) double cream
2 eggs
50g (1¾oz) caster sugar
400g (14oz) gooseberries, topped and tailed
thick cream, to serve (optional)

Method

1 In a large bowl, mix together the flour and butter with your fingertips until it resembles fine crumbs. Stir in the sugar, add the egg yolks, then bring together to form a dough. Wrap in cling film and chill for 30 minutes.

2 Preheat the oven to 180°C (350°F/Gas 4). To make the custard, whisk together the double cream, eggs, and sugar in a bowl. Put the custard in the refrigerator.

3 Roll out the pastry into a circle, a little larger than the tin. Line the tart tin with the pastry. Line the pastry case with baking parchment and baking beans, and blind bake for 20 minutes. Remove the beans and paper, and bake for another 5 minutes until cooked through but still pale.

4 Remove from the oven and put a single layer of gooseberries in the pastry case. Pour the custard over and bake for another 35 minutes until set and golden. Trim any excess pastry from the edge of the tart case with a sharp knife. Cool slightly before removing from the tin and serve with thick cream. Best eaten the same day.

Flan nature

A classic French dessert, this custard tart is best served chilled.

SERVES 6–8 | **20 MINS** | **75–85 MINS** | **12 WEEKS, TART CASE**

Chilling time
1 hr

Special equipment
18cm (7in) loose-bottomed cake tin
baking beans

Ingredients
1 sweet pastry case, see page 314, steps 1–9
125g (4½oz) plain flour
125g (4½oz) caster sugar
3 eggs
50g (1¾oz) unsalted butter, melted and cooled
½ tsp vanilla extract
500ml (16fl oz) milk

Method

1 Make the pastry case. Preheat the oven to 150°C (300°F/Gas 2). In a bowl, whisk the flour, sugar, eggs, butter, and vanilla extract to a thick, smooth paste. Whisk in the milk and transfer the mixture to a jug.

2 Rest the baking tray that holds the pastry case on the edge of the oven's middle shelf and, holding it with one hand, carefully pour the filling into the tart case with the other. When it is as full as possible without spilling, gently push the tart case onto the shelf and close the door.

3 Bake for 50–60 minutes until just set, but not at all puffed up. The surface should be golden brown. Trim the excess pastry from the sides of the tin with a sharp knife. Leave to cool completely in the tin before serving.

STORE This will keep in an airtight container in the refrigerator for 2 days.

Tarta di nata

These bite-sized custard pastries are a Portuguese favourite.

MAKES 16 | **30 MINS** | **20–25 MINS**

Special equipment
16-hole muffin tin

Ingredients
30g (1oz) plain flour,
  plus extra for dusting
500g (1lb 2oz) puff pastry, shop-bought,
  or see page 178, steps 1–9
500ml (16fl oz) milk
1 cinnamon stick
1 large piece lemon zest
4 egg yolks
100g (3½oz) caster sugar
1 tbsp cornflour

Method

1 Preheat the oven to 220°C (425°F/Gas 7). On a floured work surface, roll out the puff pastry to a 40 x 30cm (16 x 12in) rectangle. Roll up the pastry from the long end nearest you to make a log. Trim the ends. Cut the pastry into 16 equal-sized slices.

2 Take a piece of rolled pastry and tuck the loose end underneath it. Lay it down and lightly roll into a thin circle, about 10cm (4in) in diameter, turning it over only once to ensure a natural curve to the finished pastry. You should be left with a shallow bowl type piece of pastry. Use your thumbs to press it into a muffin tin, ensuring it is well-shaped to the tin. Take a fork and lightly prick the bottom. Repeat the process with the rest of the pastries. Leave in the refrigerator, while you make the filling.

3 Heat the milk, cinnamon stick, and lemon zest in a heavy saucepan. When the milk starts to boil, take it off the heat.

4 In a bowl, whisk together the egg yolks, sugar, flour, and cornflour until it forms a thick paste. Remove the cinnamon stick and the lemon zest from the hot milk, and pour the milk gradually over the egg yolk mixture, whisking constantly. Return the custard to the cleaned-out pan and place

over medium heat, whisking constantly, until it thickens. When it does, take it immediately off the heat.

5 Fill each pastry case, two-thirds full, with the custard and bake at the top of the oven for 20–25 minutes until the custards are puffed and blackened in places on the surface. Remove from the oven and allow to cool. The custards will deflate slightly, but this is quite normal. Leave for at least 10–15 minutes before eating warm or cold.

STORE The finished tarts will keep in an airtight container for 1 day.

PREPARE AHEAD Both the custard and the pastry cases can be prepared ahead and stored separately in the refrigerator overnight before using.

Tarte au citron

This French classic is both rich and refreshing, with melt-in-the-mouth pastry and a creamy filling cut through by tangy lemon.

| SERVES 6–8 | 35 MINS | 45 MINS | 12 WEEKS, TART CASE |

Chilling time
1½ hrs

Special equipment
food processor with blade attachment (optional)
24cm (9½in) loose-bottomed tart tin
baking beans

Ingredients
175g (6oz) plain flour, plus extra for dusting
85g (3oz) butter, chilled
45g (1½oz) caster sugar
1 egg

For the filling
5 eggs
200g (7oz) caster sugar
finely grated zest and juice of 4 lemons
250ml (8fl oz) double cream
icing sugar, to serve
lemon zest, to serve

Method

1 To make the pastry, mix together the flour and butter with your fingertips, or blitz in a food processor, until it resembles fine crumbs. Add the egg and draw together to form a ball of pastry dough. On a lightly floured surface, roll out the pastry into a large circle, and use it to line the tart tin. Chill for at least 30 minutes.

2 Beat together the eggs and sugar until combined. Whisk in the lemon zest and juice, and then the cream. Chill for 1 hour.

3 Preheat the oven to 190°C (375°F/Gas 5). Line the pastry case with baking parchment, fill with the baking beans, and bake blind for 10 minutes. Remove the paper and beans, and bake for 5 minutes or until the pastry base is crisp.

4 Reduce the temperature of the oven to 140°C (275°F/Gas 1). Place the tart tin on a baking tray. Pour in the lemon filling, being careful not to allow the filling to spill over the edges. Bake for 30 minutes or until just set.

5 Remove from the oven and leave to cool. Turn out and serve, dusted with icing sugar and sprinkled with lemon zest.

STORE The tart will keep in an airtight container for 2 days.

PREPARE AHEAD The unfilled pastry case can be prepared ahead and stored in an airtight container for up to 3 days, or frozen for 12 weeks.

BAKER'S TIP

When baking with lemons, try to choose unwaxed fruits, especially if a recipe calls for lemon zest. If unwaxed lemons are unavailable, scrub the fruits to remove the wax. Pick lemons which are heavy for their size, indicating that they have lots of juice.

Key Lime Pie

This pie takes its name from the small limes that grow in the Florida Keys, where the recipe originated.

8 SLICES   **20–30 MINS**   **15–20 MINS**

Special equipment
23cm (9in) loose-bottomed tart tin
zester (optional)

Ingredients
100g (3½oz) unsalted butter
225g (8oz) digestive biscuits, crushed
5 limes
3 large egg yolks
400g can condensed milk
pouring cream, to serve (optional)

Method

1 Preheat the oven to 180°C (350°F/Gas 4). Melt the butter in a saucepan over low heat. Add the biscuit crumbs and stir until well combined. Remove from the heat and tip the mixture into the flan tin, then use a spoon to press it evenly and firmly all over the base and sides of the tin. Place on a baking tray and bake for 5–10 minutes.

2 Meanwhile, finely grate the zest of 3 of the limes into a bowl and, if you like, use a zester to pare long strands of zest from a fourth lime to decorate. Juice all 5 limes and set aside.

3 Place the egg yolks into the bowl with the lime zest, and whisk with an electric whisk until the egg has thickened. Pour in the condensed milk and continue whisking for another 5 minutes. Add the lime juice and whisk again until it is incorporated. Pour the mixture into the tin and bake for 15–20 minutes or until set but still with a wobble in the centre.

4 Remove the pie from the oven and leave it to cool completely. Serve the pie decorated with the fine strands of lime zest, if using, and accompanied by pouring cream.

STORE The pie will keep in an airtight container in the refrigerator for 2 days.

BAKER'S TIP
A common baking mistake with deep-filled sweet tarts is to overcook them. Remove them from the oven when they still have a slight wobble to them at the centre. They will cool and set to an unctuous, creamy texture. Overcooking will result in a tart with an unpleasantly "rubbery" texture.

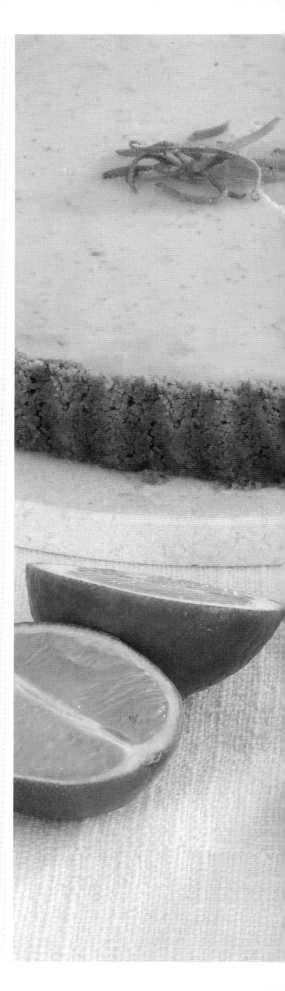

Chocolate Tart

This rich, dark chocolate tart is best served just set, while still warm, and with plenty of thick, cold cream.

SERVES 8–10	30 MINS	35–40 MINS	12 WEEKS, TART CASE

Chilling time
1 hr

Special equipment
22cm (9in) loose-bottomed tart tin
baking beans

Ingredients
150g (5½oz) plain flour
100g (3½oz) unsalted butter,
  chilled and diced

50g (1¾oz) caster sugar
1 egg yolk
½ tsp vanilla extract

For the filling
150g (5½oz) unsalted butter, diced
200g (7oz) good-quality dark
  chocolate, broken into pieces

3 eggs
30g (1oz) caster sugar
100ml (3½fl oz) double cream

1 In a bowl, rub the flour and butter together until fine crumbs form.

2 Add the sugar to the crumb mixture and stir to combine.

3 Beat the egg yolk with the vanilla, then add them to the dry ingredients.

4 Bring together to form a dough; add a little water if dry. Wrap in cling film. Chill for 1 hour.

5 Preheat the oven to 180°C (350°F/Gas 4). Roll out the pastry to a thickness of 3mm (⅛in).

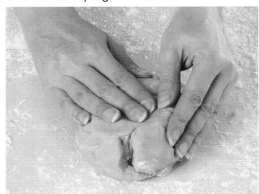

6 If the pastry begins to crumble, bring it together with your hands and knead gently.

7 Use it to line a 22cm (9in) tart tin, leaving an overlapping edge of 2cm (¾in).

8 With a pair of scissors, trim any excess pastry that hangs down further than this.

9 Prick the pastry base all over with a fork to prevent air bubbles forming during baking.

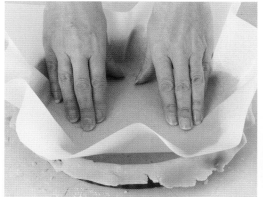

10 Carefully line the pastry case with a piece of baking parchment.

11 Scatter baking beans over the paper, place on a baking sheet and bake for 20 minutes.

12 Remove the beans and paper and bake for 5 minutes more. Trim any excess pastry.

13 Melt the butter and chocolate in a bowl set over a pan of simmering water, stirring.

14 When just melted, remove from the heat and set aside to cool.

15 Whisk together the eggs and caster sugar until well blended.

16 Pour in the the cooled chocolate mixture and whisk gently but thoroughly to combine.

17 Finally, mix in the double cream. Pour the chocolate mixture into a jug.

18 Place the pastry case on a baking sheet so that it is easy to carry to the oven.

19 Pour the filling into the pastry case and transfer to the top of the preheated oven.

20 Bake for 10–15 minutes until just set. Leave to cool for 5 minutes; it will continue to harden.

21 Transfer to a serving plate. **STORE** Keep refrigerated in an airtight container for 2 days.

Chocolate Tart variations

Double Chocolate Raspberry Tart

This impressive dessert is even quicker with a shop-bought case.

SERVES 6-8 | **40 MINS** | **25 MINS** | **12 WEEKS TART CASE**

Chilling time
1 hr

Special equipment
22cm (9in) loose-bottomed tart tin
baking beans

Ingredients
1 chocolate pastry case, shop-bought, or see pages 322–323, steps 1–12, reducing the quantity of plain flour to 130g (4¾oz) and adding 20g (¾oz) cocoa instead

For the filling
100g (3½oz) good-quality white chocolate, broken into pieces
75g (2½oz) good-quality dark chocolate, broken into pieces
250ml (8fl oz) double cream
400g (14oz) raspberries
icing sugar, for dusting

Method

1 Melt the white chocolate in a heatproof bowl, set over a pan of barely simmering water. Leave to cool.

2 Melt the dark chocolate in the same way, and use a pastry brush to paint the inside of the tart case with a layer of chocolate. This will stop the pastry case going soggy once it is filled with the filling. Leave until it sets.

3 Whip the cream stiffly. Fold the cooled white chocolate into the whipped cream. Crush half the raspberries and fold them through the cream mixture. Pile the filling into the case evenly. Decorate with the remaining raspberries, dust with icing sugar, and serve.

STORE The tart will keep in an airtight container in the refrigerator for 2 days.

PREPARE AHEAD The unfilled, cooked pastry case can be kept in an airtight container for 3 days, or frozen for 12 weeks.

Chocolate Walnut Truffle Tart

The Italian sweet pastry *pasta frolla* acts as a container for a rich filling. Cocoa powder sifted over the tart echoes the coating for chocolate truffles.

SERVES 6-8 | **45–50 MINS** | **35–40 MINS**

Chilling time
45 mins

Special equipment
23cm (9in) springform cake tin
food processor with blade attachment

Ingredients
150g (5½oz) plain flour, plus extra for dusting
75g (2½oz) unsalted butter, plus extra for greasing
50g (1¾oz) caster sugar
¼ tsp salt
1 egg

For the filling
150g (5½oz) walnuts
100g (3½oz) caster sugar
60g (2oz) good-quality dark chocolate, finely chopped
150g (5½oz) unsalted butter
2 tsp plain flour
2 egg yolks, plus 1 whole egg
1 tsp vanilla extract

For the chocolate glaze
175g (6oz) good-quality dark chocolate, broken into pieces
75g (2½oz) unsalted butter
2 tsp Grand Marnier
cocoa powder, for dusting

Method

1 Sift the flour onto a work surface and make a well in the centre. Pound the butter with a rolling pin to soften. Put the butter, sugar, salt, and egg into the well and mix. Draw in the flour and rub until coarse crumbs form. Press the dough into a ball. Knead for 1–2 minutes, wrap in cling film, and chill for 30 minutes.

2 Grease the tin. Flour a surface, and roll the dough out into a 28cm (11in) round. Wrap it around the rolling pin and press into the tin, sealing any cracks. Prick the bottom of the shell with a fork. Chill for 15 minutes until firm.

3 Preheat the oven to 180°C (350°F/Gas 4). Spread out the nuts on a baking sheet, and toast for 5–10 minutes until they are lightly browned. Let cool. Return the baking sheet to the oven. Reserve 8 walnut halves. Grind the remaining nuts with the sugar in a food processor.

4 Beat the butter until creamy. Add the flour and hazelnut mixture. Beat for 2–3 minutes until fluffy. Add the yolks and egg, one at a time, beating after each addition. Mix in the chocolate and vanilla.

5 Spread the filling over the pastry and smooth the top. Bake on the baking sheet for 35–40 minutes. Let cool on a wire rack.

6 Put the chocolate for the glaze in a bowl, set over a pan of simmering water. Stir until melted. Dip the reserved walnuts in the chocolate to coat, then set aside. Cut the butter into pieces and stir it into the chocolate. Add the Grand Marnier. Let cool.

7 Remove the tart from the tin. Pour the glaze on the tart and spread it on top. Leave to cool and set. Before serving, sift cocoa powder over and place the walnuts. Serve at room temperature.

STORE The tart can be baked and stored for up to 2 days in an airtight container, and the flavours will mellow. Add the glaze not more than 4 hours before serving.

PREPARE AHEAD The dough can be made up to 2 days ahead and kept, tightly wrapped, in the refrigerator.

BAKER'S TIP
Toasting nuts intensifies their flavour and adds crunch to their texture. You can tell that they are toasted when the skins start to pop and the nuts smell fragrant. Though the walnut skins are not removed in this recipe, toasting also makes it easier to remove thin skins from nuts.

Banoffee Pie

This version of the modern classic is incredibly rich and sweet, just as it should be. Great for a party, as a little goes a long way.

SERVES 6–8   **20 MINS**   **8 WEEKS**

Chilling time
1 hr

Special equipment
22cm (9in) round springform cake tin or loose-bottomed tart tin

Ingredients
250g (9oz) digestive biscuits
100g (3½oz) unsalted butter, melted and cooled

For the caramel
50g (1¾oz) unsalted butter
50g (1¾oz) soft light brown sugar
400g can condensed milk

For the topping
2 large, ripe bananas
250ml (8fl oz) double cream, whipped
a little dark chocolate, for grating

Method

1 Line the tin with baking parchment. Put the biscuits in a sturdy plastic bag, and use a rolling pin to crush them finely. Mix the biscuits with the melted butter, and tip them into the prepared tin. Press them down firmly to create a compressed, even layer. Cover and refrigerate.

2 To make the caramel, melt the butter and sugar in a small, heavy saucepan over medium heat. Add the condensed milk and bring to a boil. Reduce the heat and simmer for 2–3 minutes, stirring constantly. It will thicken and take on a light caramel colour. Pour the caramel over the biscuit base and leave to set.

3 Once set, remove the biscuit and caramel base from the tin and transfer to a serving plate. Slice the bananas thinly into 5mm (¼in) disks, cut slightly on a diagonal, and use them to cover the surface of the caramel.

4 Whip the cream smooth it over the bananas using a spatula. Decorate the cream with finely grated chocolate and larger chocolate curls made by grating the chocolate with a vegetable peeler.

STORE The pie will keep in an airtight container in the refrigerator for 2 days.

BAKER'S TIP
This no-cook dessert is a favourite with children and adults alike. The base and caramel layers need to be chilled to firm up, but take the pie out of the refrigerator for 30 minutes before topping it with bananas and cream to serve. This will allow the biscuit and caramel base to be cut more easily.

Apple Pie

Perhaps the ultimate in home-baked comfort food, this autumn pie is best served warm with vanilla ice cream.

SERVES 6–8 | **30–35 MINS** | **50–55 MINS**

Chilling time
45 mins

Special equipment
23cm (9in) shallow pie dish

Ingredients
330g (12oz) plain flour,
  plus extra for dusting
½ tsp salt
150g (5½oz) lard or white vegetable
  fat, plus extra for greasing
2 tbsp caster sugar,
  plus extra for sprinkling
1 tbsp milk, for glazing

For the filling
1kg (2¼lb) tart apples
juice of 1 lemon
2 tbsp plain flour
½ tsp ground cinnamon, or to taste
¼ tsp grated nutmeg, or to taste
100g (3½oz) caster sugar, or to taste

1 Sift the flour and salt into a bowl. Add the fat, cutting it in with 2 round-bladed knives.

2 With your fingertips, rub the fat into the flour until crumbs form. Lift the mixture to aerate it.

3 Add the sugar. Sprinkle with 6–7 tablespoons cold water. Mix with a fork.

4 Press the crumbs into a ball, wrap, and chill for 30 minutes. Meanwhile, grease the dish.

5 Flour a surface. Roll two-thirds of the dough out to a round, 5cm (2in) larger than the dish.

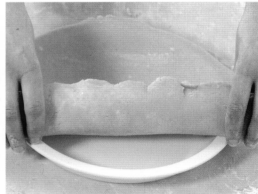

6 Using the rolling pin, drape the pastry over the dish, then gently push it into the contours.

7 Trim any excess pastry, then chill for 15 minutes until firm.

8 Peel the apples, cut into quarters, and cut out the cores of each quarter.

9 Set each quarter, cut-side down, on a chopping board and cut into medium slices.

SWEET TARTS AND PIES

10 Put the apple slices in a bowl and pour on the lemon juice. Toss to coat.

11 Sprinkle the flour, cinnamon, nutmeg, and sugar, over the apples. Toss to coat.

12 Put the apple in the pie dish and arrange so that it is slightly mounded in the centre.

13 Brush the edge of the pastry with water. Roll the rest of the dough to a 28cm (11in) round.

14 Wrap it around the rolling pin and drape it over the filling. Trim the top crust.

15 Press the edges together to seal, crimping with the back of a knife as you go.

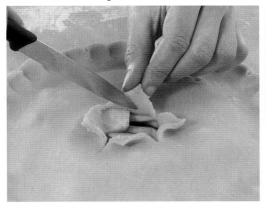

16 Cut an "x" in the top crust. Gently pull back the point of each triangle to reveal the filling.

17 Roll out the trimmings, cut into strips, and moisten. Lay on the pie in a criss-cross pattern.

18 Using a pastry brush, glaze the pie with the milk so that it bakes to a golden colour.

19 Sprinkle over sugar. Chill for 30 minutes. Preheat the oven to 220°C (425°F/Gas 7).

20 Bake for 20 minutes. Reduce to 180°C (350°F/Gas 4) and bake for 30–35 minutes.

21 Insert a skewer through the steam vent to check the apples are tender. Serve warm.

Fruit Pie variations

Rhubarb and Strawberry Pie

This is a great pie to cook in early summer, when the rhubarb and strawberry seasons happily coincide.

SERVES 6–8 | **30–35 MINS** | **50–55 MINS**

Chilling time
45 mins

Special equipment
23cm (9in) shallow pie dish

Ingredients
1 uncooked pie case and pastry for lid,
  see page 330, steps 1–7

For the filling
1kg (2¼lb) rhubarb, sliced
finely grated zest of 1 orange
250g (9oz) caster sugar, plus 1 tbsp to glaze
¼ tsp salt
30g (1oz) plain flour
375g (13oz) strawberries, hulled, and halved
  or quartered
15g (½oz) unsalted butter
1 tbsp milk, for glazing

Method

1 In a bowl, combine the rhubarb, orange zest, sugar, salt, and flour, and stir to mix. Add the strawberries and toss. Spoon the fruit mixture into into the pie dish already lined with pastry, doming the mixture slightly. Cut the butter into small pieces and dot the pieces all over the filling.

2 Brush the edge of the pastry shell with cold water. Roll out the remaining dough into a 28cm (11in) round. Drape the pastry over the filling, trim it even with the bottom crust, and press the edges to seal.

3 Cut a steam vent in the centre of the pie. Brush with milk, and sprinkle with the sugar. Chill for 15 minutes. Preheat the oven to 220°C (425°F/Gas 7). Put a baking sheet in the centre of the oven to heat up.

4 Bake on the baking sheet for 20 minutes. Reduce the temperature to 180°C (350°F/Gas 4) and bake for another 30–35 minutes until the crust is browned. Test the fruit with a skewer and if it needs longer but the top could burn, loosely cover with foil. Transfer to a wire rack, and let cool.

PREPARE AHEAD The pastry can be made 2 days ahead and kept in the refrigerator.

Cherry Pie

This pie makes good use of sweet, ripe cherries when at their best.

SERVES 4–6 | **30 MINS** | **45–50 MINS**

Chilling time
1 hr

Special equipment
20cm (8in) metal pie dish with a lip

Ingredients
200g (7oz) plain flour, plus extra for dusting
125g (4½oz) unsalted butter, chilled and diced
50g (1¾oz) caster sugar
2 tbsp milk

For the filling
50g (1¾oz) caster sugar
500g (1lb 2oz) fresh cherries, pitted
juice of 1 small or ½ large lemon
1 tbsp cornflour
1 egg, beaten

Method

1 To make the pastry, rub the flour and butter with fingertips until they form crumbs. Stir in the sugar. Add the milk and mix to form a dough. Wrap in cling film and chill for 1 hour. Preheat the oven to 180°C (350°F/Gas 4).

2 For the filling, melt the sugar and 3½ tablespoons water in a pan. Once the sugar has dissolved, add the cherries and lemon juice. Bring to a boil, cover, and simmer for 5 minutes. Mix the cornflour with 1 tablespoon water to make a paste. Add it to the cherries. Continue to cook over a low heat until the mixture thickens. Leave the cherries to cool.

3 On a floured surface, roll out the pastry to 3–5mm (⅛–¼in) thick. Lift it over the pie dish and line the bottom and the sides of the dish. Use scissors to trim off the excess pastry, leaving an overhang of 2cm (¾in). Brush the edge with beaten egg.

4 Bring the excess pastry together into a ball and roll it out again to make a circle just bigger than the dish. Fill the pastry case with the cherries, then place the remaining pastry carefully on top, pressing it firmly down around the edges to create a seal.

Trim off the overhanging pastry with a sharp knife, and brush with beaten egg. Cut 2 small slits in the top of the pie to allow the steam to escape.

5 Bake the pie in the top third of the oven for 45–50 minutes until the top is golden brown. Leave to cool for 10–15 minutes but serve when still warm.

STORE The pie will keep in an airtight container for 1 day.

PREPARE AHEAD The filling can be made 3 days ahead and refrigerated. The pastry can be made 1 day ahead and refrigerated.

Blackberry and Apple Pie

Traditionally cooking apples are used, but I prefer sweet Granny Smiths. ▶

SERVES 4–6 | **35–40 MINS** | **50–60 MINS**

Chilling time
45 mins

Special equipment
1 litre (1¾ pint) pie dish
pie funnel

Ingredients
215g (7½oz) plain flour, plus extra for dusting
1½ tbsp caster sugar
¼ tsp salt
45g (1½oz) lard or white vegetable fat, chilled and diced
60g (2oz) unsalted butter, chilled and diced

For the filling
875g (1lb 15oz) Granny Smith apples, peeled, cored, and diced
juice of 1 lemon
150g (5½oz) caster sugar, or to taste
500g (1lb 2oz) blackberries

Method
1 Sift the flour, sugar, and salt into a bowl. Add the lard and butter, and rub together with your fingertips until crumbs form. Sprinkle water over the mix, 1 tablespoon at a time, stopping as soon as clumps form;

too much water toughens the pastry. Press the dough lightly into a ball, wrap in cling film, and chill for 30 minutes.

2 Put the apples in a bowl, add the lemon juice and all but 2 tablespoons of sugar and toss. Add the blackberries and toss again.

3 Roll out the dough to a shape 7.5cm (3in) larger than the top of the dish. Invert the dish onto the pastry. Cut a 2cm (¾in) strip the dough, leaving a shape 4cm (1½in) larger than the dish. Place a pie funnel in the centre. Spoon the fruit around.

4 Moisten the edge of the dish with water and transfer the strip of pastry, pressing firmly. Brush the strip with cold water and transfer the pastry top, pressing down to seal. Cut a hole over the pie funnel and trim the edges. Chill for 15 minutes. Preheat the oven to 190°C (375°F/Gas 5). Bake for 50–60 minutes until lightly browned and crisp. Sprinkle with sugar and serve hot or warm.

PREPARE AHEAD The pastry can be made 2 days ahead and kept in the refrigerator, wrapped in cling film.

Mince Pies

The mincemeat in this recipe is quick to prepare and needs no time to mature, making these an easy festive treat to bake.

| MAKES 18 | 20 MINS | 10–12 MINS | UP TO 8 WEEKS |

Chilling time
10 mins

Special equipment
7.5cm (3in) round pastry cutter and 6cm (2½in) round or shaped cutter
fairy cake tin

Ingredients
1 small cooking apple
30g (1oz) butter, melted
85g (3oz) sultanas
85g (3oz) raisins
55g (1¾oz) currants
45g (1½oz) mixed peel, chopped
45g (1½oz) chopped almonds or hazelnuts
finely grated zest of 1 lemon
1 tsp mixed spice
1 tbsp brandy or whisky
30g (1oz) dark brown muscovado sugar
1 small banana, finely diced
500g (1lb 2oz) shortcrust pastry, shop-bought, or see page 330, steps 1–4
plain flour, for dusting
icing sugar, for dusting

Method

1 Preheat the oven to 190°C (375°F/Gas 5). To make the mincemeat, grate the apple (including the skin) into a large bowl. Add the melted butter, sultanas, raisins, currants, mixed peel, nuts, lemon zest, mixed spice, brandy or whisky, and sugar. Mix until well combined. Add the banana and mix again.

2 Roll out the pastry on a lightly floured work surface to a thickness of 2mm (scant ⅛in) and cut out 18 circles using the larger biscuit cutter. Re-roll the pastry, and cut 18 smaller circles or festive shapes, such as stars.

3 Line fairy cake tins with the larger pastry circles, and place a heaped teaspoon of mincemeat in each case. Top with the smaller circles or shapes.

4 Chill for 10 minutes, then bake for 10–12 minutes or until the pastry is golden. Carefully remove from the tins and cool on a wire rack. Dust with icing sugar to serve.

STORE The pies will keep for 3 days in an airtight container.

PREPARE AHEAD The pastry can be made 2 days ahead and kept in the refrigerator, wrapped in cling film.

BAKER'S TIP

Home-made mincemeat will always taste far superior to any shop-bought version. The diced banana used in this mincemeat recipe might not be an orthodox ingredient, but it does lend a rich, velvety texture to the mincemeat.

Galette des rois

Traditionally, rum or brandy is used to flavour the frangipane in this classic French pie, but milk can easily be substituted for a child-friendly version.

SERVES 6–8 **25 MINS** **30 MINS** **UP TO 8 WEEKS**

1 tsp almond extract
1 tbsp brandy, rum, or milk
plain flour, for dusting
500g (1lb 2oz) puff pastry, shop-bought,
  or see page 178, steps 1–9

Ingredients

100g (3½oz) caster sugar
100g (3½oz) unsalted butter, softened
1 egg, plus 1 extra, beaten, for glazing
100g (3½oz) ground almonds

Method

1 Preheat the oven to 200°C (400°F/Gas 6). In a bowl, cream together the sugar and butter with an electric whisk. Beat in the egg and blend well.

2 Mix in the ground almonds, almond extract, and rum, brandy, or milk, to make a thick paste.

3 On a well-floured work surface, roll out the pastry to a 50 x 25cm (20 x 10in) rectangle. The measurements do not have to be exact, but the pastry should be 3–5mm (⅛–¼in) thick.

4 Fold the pastry in half and use a 25cm (10in) dinner plate, or similar, to cut out 2 disks. Lay 1 disk out on a non-stick baking tray. Use a little beaten egg to brush around the edge of the disk. Spoon the frangipane filling on the pastry disk, spreading it out smoothly to within 1cm (½in) of the edge.

5 Put the other pastry disk on top of the filling, and use your fingers or the back of a fork to press down and seal the 2 disks together. Use a small, sharp knife to score a series of thin slivers on the top of the pastry, in a spiral design, being careful not to allow them to meet in the centre or the pastry will pull apart when cooking. If you are feeling very artistic, you could also try cutting the edges of the pastry into a scalloped edge before cooking.

6 Brush the top of the pastry with beaten egg, and bake the gallette at the top of the oven for 30 minutes, until golden brown and puffed up. Allow the galette to cool for 5 minutes on its tray before removing to a wire rack. Serve either warm or cold.

STORE The galette will keep in an airtight container for 3 days.

PREPARE AHEAD The frangipane can be prepared 3 days ahead and stored in the refrigerator.

BAKER'S TIP
In France, this frangipane-filled puff pastry is eaten on 6 January to celebrate Epiphany. However, it is so simple and delicious that it should definitely be eaten more than once a year, and makes a great picnic dish.

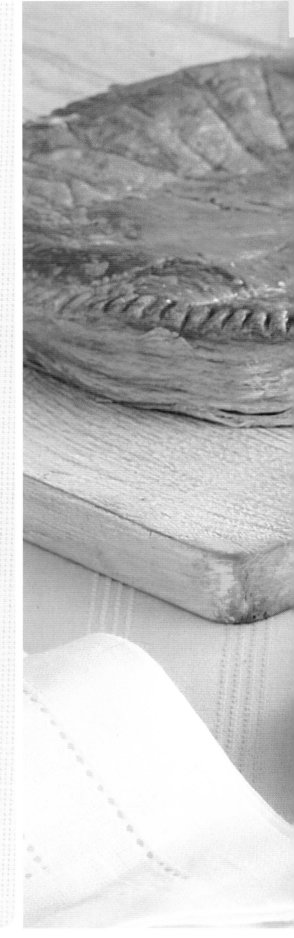

SWEET TARTS AND PIES

Cherry Strudel

Don't be intimidated by the making of this ultra-thin pastry; the trick is to knead it well so the dough is elastic.

SERVES 6–8 | 45–50 MINS | 30–40 MINS | UP TO 4 WEEKS

Ingredients
250g (9oz) plain flour, plus extra for dusting
1 egg
½ tsp lemon juice
pinch of salt
125g (4½oz) unsalted butter, plus extra for greasing

For the filling
500g (1lb 2oz) cherries
1 lemon
75g (2½oz) walnuts
100g (3½oz) light soft brown sugar
1 tsp ground cinnamon
icing sugar, for sprinkling
crème fraîche, to serve (optional)

1 Sift the flour onto a work surface and make a well in the centre.

2 In a bowl, beat the egg with 125ml (4fl oz) water, lemon juice, and salt. Pour into the well.

3 With your fingertips, work the ingredients in the well, gradually drawing in the flour.

4 Knead in just enough flour so the dough forms a ball; it should be quite soft.

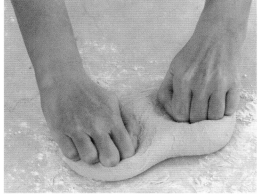

5 On a floured work surface, knead for 10 minutes until shiny and smooth.

6 Shape the dough into a ball, cover with a bowl, and let it rest for 30 minutes.

7 Stone the cherries. Grate the zest from the lemon onto a plate to retain the essential oils.

8 Coarsely chop the walnuts until even in size but with some larger chunks. Set aside.

9 Cover a work table with an old, clean bed sheet. Lightly and evenly flour it.

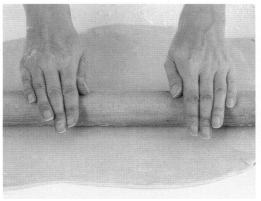

10 Roll out the dough to a very large square. Cover with damp tea towels for 15 minutes.

11 Preheat the oven to 190°C (375°F/Gas 5). Grease a baking sheet and melt the butter.

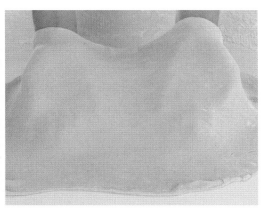

12 Flour your hands and stretch the dough, starting at the centre and working outwards.

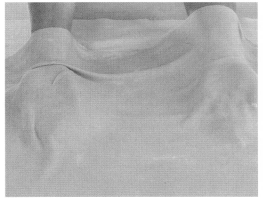

13 Continue to work outwards until the dough is as thin as possible; it should be translucent.

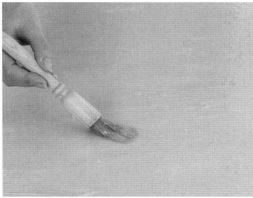

14 Immediately brush the dough evenly with about three-quarters of the melted butter.

15 Sprinkle the buttered dough with the cherries, walnuts, sugar, zest, and cinnamon.

16 Trim off the thicker edges, pulling them out and pinching them off with your fingers.

17 Roll up the strudel using the sheet, working gently but firmly and ensuring even pressure.

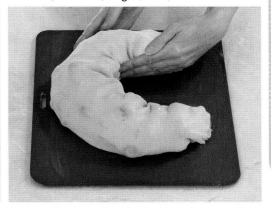

18 Transfer the roll to the baking sheet and shape it into a crescent, or a loose circle.

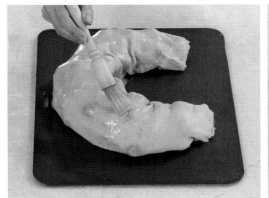

19 Brush with the remaining melted butter and bake for 30–40 minutes until crisp.

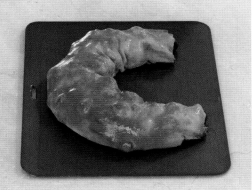

20 Leave for a few minutes before moving to a wire rack, using a fish slice.

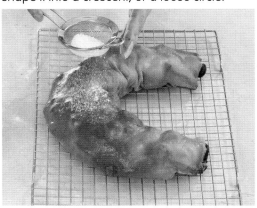

21 Sprinkle with icing sugar and serve warm, with crème fraîche.

Strudel variations

Dried Fruit Strudel

Ideal for the colder months, when many fresh fruits are out of season, this strudel would make an impressive alternative Christmas dessert.

| SERVES 6–8 | 45–50 MINS | 30–40 MINS | UP TO 4 WEEKS |

Ingredients
500g (1lb 2oz) mixed dried fruit (apricots, prunes, dates, raisins, figs)
125ml (4½fl oz) dark rum
125g (4½oz) unsalted butter, melted, plus extra for greasing
1 quantity strudel pastry, see pages 340–341, steps 1–6 and 9–14, or 4 sheets filo pastry, about 25 x 45cm (10 x 18in)
75g (2½oz) walnuts, coarsely chopped
100g (3½oz) light soft brown sugar
1 tsp ground cinnamon
icing sugar, for sprinkling

Method
1 Put the dried fruit into a pan with the rum and 125ml (4½fl oz) water. Place over low heat for 5 minutes, stirring. Remove from the heat and leave until cool. The fruit will plump up. Grease a baking sheet and preheat the oven to 190°C (375°F/Gas 5).

2 If using filo, place a sheet on a clean work surface and brush with melted butter. Lay another sheet on top and brush with butter. Repeat with the remaining pastry sheets.

3 Drain the dried fruit and sprinkle over the strudel or filo pastry, leaving a 2cm (¾in) border around the edge. Sprinkle over the walnuts, brown sugar, and cinnamon.

4 Roll the pastry, starting from one of the longer sides, and press the ends together tightly. Transfer the strudel to the baking tray and brush with a little more melted butter.

5 Bake for 30–40 minutes until crisp and golden brown. Let it cool before transferring to a wire rack, using a fish slice. Sprinkle with icing sugar and serve warm.

PREPARE AHEAD The uncooked strudel can be stored in the refrigerator a few hours before baking. The cooked strudel can be warmed in the oven 1 day later.

Squash and Goat's Cheese Strudel

This makes a good vegetarian alternative at a festive gathering.

| MAKES 4 STRUDELS | 15 MINS | 20–25 MINS | UP TO 4 WEEKS |

Ingredients
2 tbsp olive oil
3 red onions, finely sliced
2 tbsp balsamic vinegar
pinch of sugar
sea salt and freshly ground black pepper
plain flour, for dusting
1 quantity strudel pastry, see pages 340–341, steps 1–6 and 9–14, or 12 sheets filo pastry, about 25 x 25cm (10 x 10in)
50g (1¾oz) unsalted butter, melted
500g (1lb 2oz) butternut squash, peeled, deseeded, and coarsely grated
2 tbsp finely chopped, sage leaves
250g (9oz) soft goat's cheese, roughly diced

Method
1 Preheat the oven to 200°C (400°F/Gas 6). Heat the olive oil in a frying pan over medium heat. Add the onions and cook for around 5 minutes until soft. Add the balsamic vinegar, sugar, and a generous amount of salt and pepper, and cook over low heat for a further 5 minutes.

2 If using filo, on a well-floured work surface, lay out 4 sheets of pastry, one for each strudel. Brush the sheets with melted butter, cover with a second layer, and brush again. Repeat with the remaining pastry sheets. Brush the top layer with butter, being careful to brush around the edges first (this will help to seal the strudels later).

3 Now scatter the butternut squash evenly over the strudel bases, leaving a clean border of at least 2cm (¾in) around all the edges except those nearest to you. Scatter the onions on top, then the sage. Finally, add the goat's cheese, and season with black pepper and a little salt.

4 Fold in the 2 sides of each strudel that are free of filling, then roll up, starting with the side nearest you. Take care to tuck the sides in as you roll, and finish with the joins tucked underneath. Transfer the strudels to a non-stick baking sheet and brush the tops with any remaining butter.

5 Bake at the top of a hot oven for 20–25 minutes until golden brown and crispy. If serving hot, leave the strudels to cool for at least 10 minutes; they are also good cold.

PREPARE AHEAD The uncooked strudel can be stored in the refrigerator, covered, a few hours before baking. The cooked strudel can be warmed in the oven 1 day later.

BAKER'S TIP
This vegetarian strudel takes only minutes to make with the help of shop-bought filo pastry. Grating the squash adds a lovely texture, and, if you have a food processor with a grater attachment, the preparation is even quicker.

Apple Strudel

A Viennese speciality, this is delicious served warm or cold. ▶

| SERVES 10–12 | 50 MINS | 40 MINS | UP TO 4 WEEKS |

Ingredients

60g (2oz) unsalted butter, melted,
  plus extra for greasing
1kg (2¼lb) crisp dessert apples, such as Cox
  or Braeburn, peeled, cored, and diced
finely grated zest of ½ lemon
3 tbsp rum
60g (2oz) raisins
100g (3½oz) caster sugar
few drops of vanilla extract
60g (2oz) blanched almonds, chopped
1 quantity strudel pastry, see pages 340–341,
  steps 1–6 and 9–14, or 4 sheets filo pastry,
  about 25 x 45cm (10 x 18in)
60–85g (2–3oz) fresh breadcrumbs
icing sugar, for dusting

Method

1 Preheat the oven to 180°C (350°F/Gas 4). Grease a large baking sheet. Place the apples in a bowl, and mix with the lemon zest, rum, raisins, caster sugar, vanilla extract, and almonds. If using filo, place a sheet on a work surface and brush it with the melted butter. Lay another sheet on top and brush with more butter. Repeat with the remaining pastry sheets.

2 Sprinkle the breadcrumbs over the pastry, leaving a 2cm (¾in) border. Gently spoon the filling over the breadcrumbs. Then fold the edges of the short sides, which have been left uncovered, over the filling. Roll the pastry carefully, starting from one of the longer sides, and press the ends together tightly. Transfer to a baking tray, and brush with more butter.

3 Bake for 30–40 minutes, brushing with the remaining butter after 20 minutes. Cool on a baking tray, dust with icing sugar and serve warm or cold.

PREPARE AHEAD The uncooked strudel can be stored in the refrigerator a few hours before baking. The cooked strudel can be warmed in the oven 1 day later.

Baklava

This crispy Middle Eastern confection, filled with chopped nuts and spices and drenched with honey syrup, has long been a favourite.

MAKES 36 | **50–55 MINS** | **1¼–1½ HOURS**

Special equipment

30 x 40cm (12 x 16in) baking tray
with deep sides
sugar thermometer (optional)

Ingredients

250g (9oz) shelled unsalted pistachio nuts,
  coarsely chopped
250g (9oz) walnut pieces, coarsely chopped
250g (9oz) caster sugar
2 tsp ground cinnamon
large pinch of ground cloves
500g pack of filo pastry
250g (9oz) unsalted butter
250ml (8fl oz) honey
juice of 1 lemon
3 tbsp orange flower water

Method

1 Set aside 3–4 tablespoons of the chopped pistachios for decoration. Put the remainder in a bowl with the walnuts, 50g (1¾oz) of the sugar, cinnamon, and cloves. Stir to mix.

2 Preheat the oven to 180°C (350°F/Gas 4). Lay a damp tea towel on a work surface, unroll the filo sheets on it, and cover with a second dampened towel. Melt the butter in a small saucepan. Brush the baking tin with a little butter. Take a sheet of filo and line the tin with it, folding over one end to fit.

3 Brush the filo with butter, and gently press it into the corners and sides of the tin. Lay another sheet on top, brush it with butter, and press it into the tin as before. Continue layering the filo, buttering each sheet, until one-third has been used. Scatter half the nut filling over the top sheet.

4 Layer another third of the filo sheets as before, then sprinkle the remaining nut filling over it. Layer the remaining sheets in the same manner. Trim off excess with a knife. Brush with butter, and pour any remaining butter on top. With a small

knife, cut diagonal lines, 1cm (½in) deep, in the filo to mark out 4cm (1½in) diamond shapes. Do not press down when cutting.

5 Bake on a low shelf for 1¼–1½ hours until golden. A skewer inserted in the centre for 30 seconds should come out clean.

6 For the syrup, put the remaining sugar and 250ml (8fl oz) water in a pan and heat until dissolved, stirring occasionally. Pour in the honey and stir to mix. Boil for about 25 minutes without stirring, until the syrup reaches the soft ball stage, 115°C (239°F) on a sugar thermometer. To test the syrup without a thermometer, take the pan from the heat and dip a teaspoon in the hot syrup. Let the syrup cool a few seconds, then take a little between your finger and thumb; a soft ball should form.

7 Remove the syrup from the heat and let it cool to lukewarm. Add the lemon juice and orange flower water. Remove the tin from the oven and immediately pour the syrup over the pastries. With a sharp knife, cut along the marked lines, almost to the bottom (see Baker's Tip), then let the pastries cool.

8 Cut through the marked lines completely. Carefully lift out the pastries with a palette knife and arrange them on each dessert plate. Sprinkle the top of each pastry with the reserved chopped pistachio nuts.

PREPARE AHEAD The pastries can be made 5 days before serving. Store in an airtight container; the flavour will mellow.

BAKER'S TIP

Filo pastry is very delicate and can crumble slightly when cut. The syrup used in this recipe will help minimize this, but not stop it completely. Make sure you use a sharp, slim blade to cut the baklava, and be sure to score it first, as instructed in the recipe, for the neatest finish.

Blueberry Cobbler

A classic American summer-fruit pudding, easy to make and great for a hungry family.

SERVES 6–8 | **15 MINS** | **30 MINS**

Special equipment
shallow ovenproof dish

Ingredients

For the filling
450g (1lb) blueberries
2 dessert apples or
  2 large peaches, sliced
2 tbsp caster sugar
finely grated zest of ½ lemon

For the cobbler
225g (8oz) self-raising flour
2 tsp baking powder
75g (2½oz) caster sugar, plus
  1 tbsp for sprinkling
pinch of salt
75g (2½oz) unsalted butter,
  chilled and diced
100ml (3½fl oz) buttermilk
1 egg
handful of flaked almonds
custard, or double cream,
  to serve (optional)

1 Preheat the oven to 190°C (375°F/Gas 5). Put the fruit in the dish and add sugar and zest.

2 For the cobbler top, sift the flour, baking powder, caster sugar, and salt into a bowl.

3 Add the butter and mix with your fingers until the mixture resembles breadcrumbs.

4 Beat together the buttermilk and egg, add to the dry ingredients and mix to form a dough.

5 Place walnut-sized spoonfuls over the fruit, leaving space for the mix to spread.

6 Lightly press down on the balls of mixture to help them combine with the fruit.

7 Evenly sprinkle over the flaked almonds and the remaining 1 tablespoon sugar.

8 Bake for 30 minutes until golden and bubbling. If it browns quickly, cover with foil.

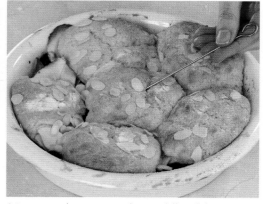

9 Insert a skewer into the middle of the centre "cobble". It should emerge clean.

10 If the skewer has uncooked mixture on it, return the cobbler to the oven for another 5 minutes, then take out and test again. Leave the cobbler to cool briefly before serving straight from the dish, with plenty of custard or double cream. Best eaten the same day.

Cobbler variations

Peach Cobbler

Gently poaching the peaches for a few minutes first helps them to break down to a lovely, sticky mass after baking. Really ripe peaches will need no poaching.

SERVES 6-8 | **20 MINS** | **30-35 MINS**

Special equipment
shallow ovenproof dish

Ingredients

For the filling
50g (1¾oz) caster sugar
8 ripe peaches, peeled, stoned, and quartered
1 tsp cornflour
juice of ½ lemon

For the cobbler
225g (8oz) self-raising flour
2 tsp baking powder
75g (2½oz) caster sugar
pinch of salt
½–¾ tsp ground cinnamon, to taste
75g (2½oz) unsalted butter
1 egg
100ml (3fl oz) buttermilk
1 tbsp soft light brown sugar
ice cream, custard, or cream, to serve (optional)

Method

1 Preheat the oven to 190°C (375°F/Gas 5). Heat the sugar and 3–4 tablespoon water in a large, heavy saucepan. Once the sugar has dissolved, add the peaches and cook over medium heat, covered, for 2–3 minutes.

2 Mix the cornflour with the lemon juice to make a paste, then add it to the peaches. Continue to cook, uncovered, over low heat until the liquid thickens around the peaches. Transfer the peaches and syrup to the dish.

3 To make the cobbler, sift the flour, baking powder, caster sugar, salt, and cinnamon into a bowl. Rub in the butter until the mixture resembles fine crumbs. Whisk together the egg and the buttermilk. Add the liquid to the dry ingredients, and bring it together to form a soft, sticky dough.

4 Drop heaped tablespoonfuls of the dough over the surface of the fruit, leaving a little space between them. Sprinkle with the brown sugar. Bake at the top of the oven for 25–30 minutes or until golden and bubbling. It is ready when a skewer inserted into the centre of the topping comes out clean. Leave to cool for 5 minutes before serving with ice cream, custard, or cream.

BAKER'S TIP
Once you have mastered the art of making a cobbler topping, you can use it as a quick and easy finishing touch to any fresh fruit. Harder fruits may need to be gently poached first, but most can be tossed in a little sugar and a few spices before topping with the cobbler mix.

Apple and Blackberry Cobbler

The classic autumnal fruit pairing of blackberry and apple is given a twist here with a cobbler topping, rather than the more usual pie casing or crumble top.

SERVES 6-8 | **20 MINS** | **30 MINS**

Special equipment
shallow ovenproof dish

Ingredients

For the filling
1kg (2¼lb) apples, peeled, cored and roughly chopped
250g (9oz) blackberries
juice of ½ lemon
2 tbsp caster sugar
2 tbsp soft light brown sugar
25g (scant 1oz) unsalted butter, chilled and diced

For the cobbler
225g (8oz) self-raising flour
2 tsp baking powder
75g (2½oz) caster sugar
pinch of salt
½–¾ tsp ground cinnamon, to taste
75g (2½oz) unsalted butter
1 egg
100ml (3fl oz) buttermilk
1 tbsp soft light brown sugar
ice cream, custard, or cream, to serve (optional)

Method

1 Preheat the oven to 190°C (375°F/Gas 5). Toss the apples and blackberries in the lemon juice, then mix them together with the 2 types of sugar. Put them in the dish and dot with the butter.

2 To make the cobbler, sift the flour, baking powder, caster sugar, salt, and cinnamon into a bowl. Rub in the butter until the mixture resembles fine crumbs. Whisk together the egg and the buttermilk. Add the liquid to the dry ingredients, and bring it together to form a soft, sticky dough.

3 Drop heaped tablespoonfuls of the dough over the surface of the fruit, leaving a little space between them. Sprinkle with the soft light brown sugar.

4 Bake in the centre of the oven for 30 minutes or until golden and bubbling. The cobbler is ready when a skewer inserted into the centre of the topping comes out clean. Leave to cool for at least 5 minutes before serving with ice cream, custard, or cream.

Cinnamon and Plum Cobbler

Use brown sugar and cinnamon to add a sweet, dark, spicy flavour to really ripe plums. Cobblers are quick to make, but to speed things up even more use a food processor to make the crumbs for the cobbler dough.

SERVES **20** **30**
6–8 **MINS** **MINS**

Special equipment
shallow ovenproof dish

Ingredients

For the filling
1kg (2¼lb) plums, stoned and halved
50g (1¾oz) soft light brown sugar
1 tsp cinnamon
25g (scant 1oz) unsalted butter, chilled and diced

For the cobbler
225g (8oz) self-raising flour
2 tsp baking powder
75g (2½oz) caster sugar
pinch of salt
½–¾ tsp ground cinnamon, to taste
75g (2½oz) unsalted butter

1 egg
100ml (3fl oz) buttermilk
1 tbsp soft light brown sugar
ice cream, custard, or cream, to serve (optional)

Method

1 Preheat the oven to 190°C (375°F/Gas 5). Toss the plum halves with the sugar and cinnamon. Put them in the dish and dot with the butter.

2 To make the cobbler, sift the flour, baking powder, caster sugar, salt, and cinnamon into a bowl. Rub in the butter until the mixture resembles fine crumbs. Whisk together the egg and the buttermilk. Add the liquid to the dry ingredients, and bring it together to form a soft, sticky dough.

3 Drop heaped tablespoonfuls of the dough over the surface of the fruit, leaving a little space between them. Sprinkle with the soft light brown sugar.

4 Bake in the centre of the preheated oven for 30 minutes or until golden and bubbling. The cobbler is ready when a skewer inserted into the centre of the topping comes out clean. Leave to cool for at least 5 minutes before serving with ice cream, custard, or cream.

Plum Crumble

This popular dessert is quick and easy to make, and suitable for any occasion.

| SERVES 4 | 10 MINS | 30–40 MINS | 4 WEEKS, TOPPING |

Ingredients

For the crumble topping
150g (5½oz) plain flour
100g (3½oz) unsalted butter, chilled, and cubed
75g (2½oz) light soft brown sugar
60g (2oz) rolled oats

For the filling
600g (1lb 5oz) plums, stoned and halved
maple syrup or honey, to drizzle

Method

1 Preheat the oven to 200°C (400°F/Gas 6). To make the crumble topping, place the flour in a large mixing bowl. Rub in the butter with your fingertips until the mixture resembles breadcrumbs. Do not make it too fine or your crumble will have a stodgy top. Stir in the sugar and the oats.

2 Place the plums in a medium ovenproof dish, drizzle over with the maple syrup or honey, and top with the crumble.

3 Bake for 30–40 minutes or until the top is golden brown and the plum juices are bubbling.

PREPARE AHEAD The crumble mix can be made up to 1 month in advance and kept frozen until ready to use.

BAKER'S TIP
Though a homely dessert, there are few more welcome sights on the dinner table than a crumble. Use a recipe when making a crumble topping: it may seem like child's play, but it is easy to include too much fat, creating a topping that "melts" when baked, or too little, resulting in a dry crumble.

Apple Brown Betty

A "betty" is a baked fruit pudding topped with buttered breadcrumbs. This dessert was made popular in the US during the colonial era.

SERVES 4
15 MINS
35–45 MINS

Special equipment
1.2-litre (2-pint) baking dish

Ingredients
85g (3oz) unsalted butter
175g (6oz) fresh breadcrumbs
900g (2lb) apples, such as Bramley,
  Granny Smith, or Golden Delicious
85g (3oz) soft brown sugar
1 tsp cinnamon
½ tsp mixed spice
finely grated zest of 1 lemon
2 tbsp lemon juice
1 tsp vanilla extract

Method

1 Preheat the oven to 180°C (350°F/Gas 4). Melt the butter in a saucepan, add the breadcrumbs, and mix well.

2 Peel, quarter, and core the apples. Cut each quarter into slices and place in a bowl. Add the sugar, cinnamon, mixed spice, lemon zest and juice, and vanilla extract, and mix well.

3 Put half the apple mixture into the baking dish. Cover with half the breadcrumbs, then put in the rest of the apples and top with the remaining breadcrumbs.

4 Bake for 35–45 minutes, checking after 35 minutes. If it is getting too brown, reduce the temperature to 160°C (325°F/Gas 3) and cover with baking parchment. It is cooked when the crumbs are golden brown and the apples are soft. Serve immediately.

BAKER'S TIP

A betty is simplicity itself to make. The recipe lends itself well to all sorts of different fruits, though orchard fruits are best. Try changing the spices to suit your palate. Be creative: try lemon thyme with pears, or star anise or cardamom with plums.

savoury tarts & pies

Swiss Chard and Gruyère Tart

If chard proves difficult to find, you can substitute spinach; add to the pan in step 14 but cook for slightly less time.

SERVES 6–8 | **20 MINS** | **55–70 MINS** | **UP TO 8 WEEKS**

Chilling time
1 hr

Special equipment
22cm (9in) loose-bottomed tart tin
baking beans

Ingredients

For the pastry
150g (5½oz) plain flour,
 plus extra for dusting

75g (2½oz) unsalted butter,
 chilled and diced
1 egg yolk

For the filling
1 tbsp olive oil
1 onion, finely chopped
sea salt
2 garlic cloves, finely chopped

few sprigs of fresh rosemary,
 leaves picked and finely chopped
250g (9oz) Swiss chard,
 stalks trimmed
125g (4½oz) Gruyère cheese, grated
125g (4½oz) feta cheese, cubed
freshly ground black pepper
2 eggs, lightly beaten
200ml (7fl oz) double cream
 or whipping cream

1 For the pastry, rub the flour and butter together until the mixture forms fine crumbs.

2 Lightly beat the egg yolk with 1 tablespoon of cold water.

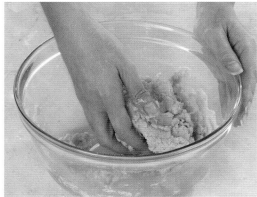

3 Add to the crumbs and bring together to form a soft dough. Add extra water if too dry.

4 Wrap in cling film and chill for 1 hour. Preheat the oven to 180°C (350°F/Gas 4).

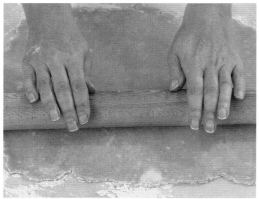

5 On a floured work surface, roll the pastry out to a large circle, about 3mm (⅛in) thick.

6 Lift the pastry carefully, using the rolling pin to help you, and place it into the tart tin.

7 Push it in with your fingers. The pastry should overlap the sides by at least 2cm (¾oz).

8 Prick the bottom all over with a fork, and line with baking parchment.

9 Weigh the parchment down with baking beans. Place the pastry case on a baking sheet.

10 Bake in the centre of the oven for 20–25 minutes. Remove the beans and paper.

11 Bake for 5 more minutes to crisp the bottom. Leave to cool and trim the edges with a knife.

PREPARE AHEAD The pastry can be made 2 days ahead, wrapped in cling film, and chilled.

12 Meanwhile, heat the oil in a pan over a low heat. Add the onion and a pinch of salt.

13 Sweat the onion until soft. Add the garlic and rosemary, and cook for a few seconds.

14 Roughly chop the Swiss chard and add to the pan. Stir for about 5 minutes until it wilts.

15 Set the pastry case on a baking sheet and spoon in the onion and chard mixture.

16 Sprinkle over the Gruyère cheese, and scatter with the feta. Season well.

17 With a fork, mix together the cream and the 2 eggs until well combined.

18 Carefully pour the cream and egg mix over the tart filling.

19 Bake for 30–40 minutes until golden. Leave to cool before releasing from the tin.

20 Serve warm or at room temperature. Best eaten the same day. Can be chilled overnight.

SWISS CHARD AND GRUYÈRE TART

Savoury Tart variations

Onion Tart

A deep-filled onion tart is one of my favourite dishes – it is amazing how a simple filling of onions, cream, and eggs can produce such delicious results.

| SERVES 6–8 | 25 MINS | 80–85 MINS | UP TO 8 WEEKS |

Chilling time
1 hr

Special equipment
22cm (9in) loose-bottomed tart tin

Ingredients
1 pastry case, see pages 358–359, steps 1–11

For the filling
2 tbsp olive oil
25g (scant 1oz) butter
500g (1lb 2oz) finely sliced onions
sea salt and freshly ground black pepper
200ml (7fl oz) double cream
1 large egg, plus 1 egg yolk

Method

1 Heat the olive oil and butter in a pan and add the onions. Season well and, when sizzling, reduce the heat and cook on a low heat, covered, for 20 minutes, stirring occasionally. The onions should soften, but not brown. Take the lid off, increase the heat and cook the onions for 5–10 minutes to allow any water to dry.

2 Place the onions in the pastry case, and spread them out. Whisk together the double cream, egg, egg yolk and seasoning. Place the tart back on a baking tray and pour the cream mixture over the onions. Use a fork to help distribute the cream evenly, by pushing the onions from side to side a little.

3 Bake in the centre of the oven for 30 minutes until just set, lightly golden and puffy on top. Remove from the oven, trim the edges of the pastry, and allow it to cool for 10 minutes before eating warm or cold.

STORE This is best eaten the day it is made but the tart can be chilled overnight and gently reheated in a medium oven.

PREPARE AHEAD The pastry case can be prepared 2 days in advance, and wrapped in cling film until needed.

Smoked Trout Tartlets

These tartlets are perfect for taking on a picnic lunch or as part of a buffet, and work equally well as a first course or for a light supper.

| MAKES 6 | 30 MINS | 25–30 MINS | UP TO 4 WEEKS |

Chilling time
30 mins

Special equipment
6 x 10cm (4in) tartlet tins
baking beans

Ingredients
125g (4½oz) plain flour, plus extra for dusting
75g (1½oz) unsalted butter, chilled and diced
pinch of salt
1 small egg

For the filling
115ml (4fl oz) crème fraîche
1 tsp creamed horseradish
½ tsp lemon juice
finely grated zest of ½ lemon
1 tsp capers, rinsed and chopped
sea salt and freshly ground black pepper, to taste
4 egg yolks, beaten

200g (7oz) smoked trout
bunch of dill, chopped

Method

1 To make the pastry, place the flour, butter, and salt in a bowl and mix together with your fingertips until fine crumbs form. Add the egg and bring together to form a dough.

2 Roll the dough out on a well-floured surface, and line the tartlet tins. Line the pastry cases with baking parchment, fill with baking beans, and chill for 30 minutes.

3 Preheat the oven to 200°C (400°F/Gas 6). Bake blind the pastry cases for 10 minutes, then remove the beans and parchment, and bake for a further 5 minutes.

4 Mix the crème fraîche, horseradish, lemon juice and zest, and capers in a bowl, and season to taste with salt and pepper. Stir in the egg yolks, fish, and herbs.

5 Divide the mixture among the tart cases and return to the oven for 10–15 minutes, or until set. Allow to cool for 5 minutes before removing from the tins and serving.

STORE These are best eaten the day they are made but can be chilled overnight and gently reheated in a medium oven.

PREPARE AHEAD The pastry cases can be prepared 2 days in advance, and wrapped in cling film until needed.

BAKER'S TIP
A good quiche or savoury tart is a simple combination of short, buttery pastry, cream, and eggs, plus filling, of course. I always blind bake the cases for these type of tarts before filling them, as this helps the pastry to remain crisp on the base even after contact with the creamy filling.

Quiche Lorraine

A French classic, this egg and bacon flan is the original quiche.

SERVES 4–6 | **35 MINS** | **47–52 MINS**

Chilling time
30 mins

Special equipment
23 x 4cm (9 x 1½in) deep tart tin
baking beans

Ingredients
225g (8oz) plain flour, plus extra for dusting
115g (4oz) unsalted butter, cubed
1 egg yolk

For the filling
200g (7oz) bacon lardons
1 onion, finely chopped
75g (2½oz) Gruyère cheese, grated
4 large eggs, lightly beaten
150ml (5fl oz) double cream
150ml (5fl oz) milk
freshly ground black pepper

Method

1 To make the pastry, put the flour and butter in a large bowl and rub with your fingertips, until the mixture resembles fine crumbs. Then add the egg yolk and 3–4 tablespoons chilled water, and mix to make a smooth dough. Turn the dough out on a floured surface and knead briefly. Wrap in cling film and chill for 30 minutes. Preheat the oven to 190°C (375°F/Gas 5).

2 On a lightly floured surface, roll out the pastry and line the tin with it, pressing it to the sides. Prick the base of the pastry with a fork, and line with baking parchment and baking beans. Blind bake for 12 minutes, then remove the paper and beans, and bake for a further 10 minutes or until it is light golden in colour.

3 Meanwhile, heat a large frying pan and dry-fry the bacon lardons for 3–4 minutes, which will start to release their fat. Add the onion, fry for a further 2–3 minutes, then spread the onions and bacon over the pastry case. Add the cheese.

4 Whisk together the eggs, cream, milk, and black pepper, and pour into the pastry case. Place the tin on a baking tray and bake for 25–30 minutes or until golden and just set. Allow to set, then slice and serve while still hot.

PREPARE AHEAD Cook up to 48 hours in advance, let cool, then refrigerate. Reheat gently in a medium oven.

Savoury Tart variations

Crab and Prawn Saffron Tart

A tart to impress with, the delicate flavours of crab and prawns balance wonderfully with the assertive pungency and musky taste of saffron, balanced by the fresh zest of the herbs.

| SERVES 2–4 | 20 MINS | 50–65 MINS | UP TO 8 WEEKS |

Chilling time
1 hr

Special equipment
15cm (6in) loose-bottomed tart tin
baking beans

Ingredients
100g (3½oz) plain flour, plus extra for dusting
50g (1¾oz) unsalted butter, chilled and diced
1 egg yolk

For the filling
pinch of saffron
125g (4½oz) white crab meat
100g (3½oz) small cold water prawns
200ml (7fl oz) double cream
1 egg
1 tbsp finely chopped tarragon or chervil
sea salt and freshly ground black pepper

Method

1 Rub together the flour and butter until the mixture forms fine crumbs. Add the egg yolk and 1 tablespoon cold water and bring the mixture together to form a soft dough. Add a little extra water if the mixture is too dry to form a dough easily. Wrap in cling film and chill for 1 hour.

2 Preheat the oven to 180°C (350°F/Gas 4). On a well floured work surface, roll the pastry out to a large circle about 3mm (⅛in) thick. Carefully lift the pastry using the rolling pin to help you, and place it into the tart tin, making sure it overlaps the sides. Take a pair of scissors and trim off all but 2cm (¾in) of the overhanging pastry. Use your fingers to push the pastry down into the tin. Prick the bottom all over with a fork, line with baking parchment, weigh it down with baking beans and place it on a baking tray.

3 Blind bake the case in the centre of the oven for 20–25 minutes until cooked. Remove the beans and paper and return the case to the oven for 5 minutes to crisp up the bottom, if necessary. Allow to cool.

4 Boil the kettle and splash 1 tablespoon of hot water over the saffron in a small bowl to allow the colour to develop. Put the crab meat and prawns into a sieve and press down well over a sink to remove any excess water, as this will make the tart soggy. Use your fingers to mix the crab and prawns together, then scatter them over the surface of the tart.

5 Whisk together the double cream and the egg in a jug. Add the herbs, the saffron and its soaking water, and seasoning, and mix well. Place the pastry case back onto a baking sheet and, with the oven door open, rest it half on, half off the middle oven shelf. Hold the sheet with one hand and with the other carefully pour as much of the cream and egg mixture as possible into the tart, then carefully slide it into the oven.

6 Bake for 30–35 minutes until golden in places and puffed up. Remove from the oven and leave to cool for 10 minutes. Trim off the overhanging pastry and remove the tart from the tin. Serve warm or cold.

PREPARE AHEAD The pastry case can be prepared 2 days in advance, wrapped in cling film, and chilled until needed.

BAKER'S TIP

Tarts containing crab are very rich, and you may find that a little goes a long way. For a more pronounced crab flavour, replace the total weight of white crab meat and prawns with a mixture of white and brown crab meat, which will also usually be more economical.

SAVOURY TARTS AND PIES

Spinach and Goat's Cheese Tart

Fast becoming a modern classic, vegetarians can omit the pancetta.

SERVES 6–8	**20 MINS**	**55–65 MINS**	**UP TO 8 WEEKS**

Chilling time
1 hr

Special equipment
22cm (9in) loose-bottomed tart tin
baking beans

Ingredients
1 pastry case, see pages 358–359, steps 1–11

For the filling
150g (5½oz) pancetta, diced
1 tbsp olive oil
150g (5½oz) baby spinach, washed
100g (3½oz) goat's cheese
sea salt and freshly ground black pepper
300ml (10fl oz) double cream
2 eggs

Method

1 In a frying pan, cook the pancetta in the olive oil for 5 minutes until golden brown. Add the spinach and cook it for a few minutes until it wilts. Drain off any water before using the filling. Leave to cool.

2 Spread the spinach and pancetta mixture over the base of the pastry case. Cube or crumble the goat's cheese and spread it over the spinach. Season with a little salt (the pancetta is salty) and black pepper.

3 Whisk together the cream and eggs in a jug. Place the pastry case onto a baking sheet and, with the oven door open, rest it half on, half off the middle oven shelf. Hold the sheet with one hand and with the other pour the cream and egg mixture into the tart, then slide it in to the oven.

4 Bake for 30–35 minutes until puffed up and golden. Remove from the oven and leave to cool for 10 minutes. Trim off the overhanging pastry and remove the tart from the tin. The tart is best eaten warm from the oven but can be served cold.

STORE The tart can be chilled overnight and gently reheated in a medium oven.

PREPARE AHEAD The pastry case can be prepared 2 days in advance, wrapped in cling film, and chilled until needed.

Flamiche

This classic leek pie originates from the Picardy region of northern France. Although not traditional, the inclusion of blue cheese adds piquancy.

| SERVES 4–6 | 20 MINS | 40–45 MINS |

Special equipment
18cm (7in) loose-bottomed cake tin

Ingredients
50g (1¾oz) unsalted butter
2 tbsp olive oil, plus extra for greasing
500g (1lb 2oz) leeks, washed, trimmed, and finely shredded
sea salt and freshly ground black pepper
whole nutmeg, for grating
2 tbsp plain flour, plus extra for dusting
250ml (8fl oz) milk
100g (3½oz) blue cheese, such as Stilton (optional)
500g (1lb 2oz) puff pastry, shop-bought, or 1 quantity puff pastry, see page 178, steps 1–9
1 egg, beaten, for glazing

Method

1 Preheat the oven to 200°C (400°F/Gas 6). In a large saucepan, melt the butter and olive oil. Add the leeks and cook over a low heat for 10 minutes, stirring occasionally, until well softened but not browned. Season well with salt, pepper, and a little grated nutmeg. Scatter the flour over the surface of the leeks and stir it in well.

2 Pour the milk onto the leeks, a little at a time, stirring constantly. The mixture will thicken to begin with, then gradually loosen as all the milk is added. Bring to a boil, reduce the heat, and cook for 3–5 minutes until well thickened. Remove from the heat and stir in the cheese (if using).

3 Roll out the puff pastry on a well-floured work surface into a 20 x 40cm (8 x 16in) rectangle. It should be 3–5mm (⅛–¼in) thick. Place the tin onto one short edge of the pastry and cut a circle around it to make the lid; the remaining pastry should be large enough to line the bottom of the tin.

4 Oil the tin, trim the remaining pastry and use it to line the tin, allowing the sides to overhang slightly. Brush the interior with a little beaten egg and set aside for 5 minutes; this may seem unusual, but the dried egg wash creates a sort of lacquer that prevents the pastry from going soggy.

5 Fill the pastry case with the leek mixture and brush a little beaten egg around the edges of the pastry. Top with the disk of pastry and press around the edges to seal together. Brush the top of the flamiche with beaten egg, then cut 2 small slits in the top to allow the steam to escape.

6 Bake in the top third of the oven for 25–30 minutes until puffed up and golden brown. Remove the flamiche from the oven, trim the excess pastry, and cool for at least 10 minutes before serving warm or cold.

PREPARE AHEAD The flamiche will keep overnight, covered, and chilled in the refrigerator. Gently reheat, or bring back to room temperature, before eating.

BAKER'S TIP

A flamiche is traditionally decorated by scoring a criss-cross pattern of lines over the top of the uncooked pastry. In my experience, however, such overlapping lines can cause the pastry to split. Simply use a very sharp knife to draw lines coming out of the centre, like the spokes of a wheel.

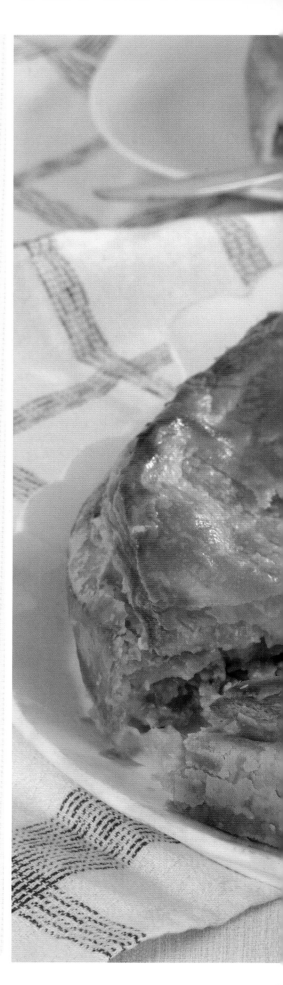

Zweibelkuchen

The combination of sour cream and caraway seeds contrast well with the sweet, melting onions used to top this traditional German tart.

SERVES 8 | **30 MINS** | **60–65 MINS**

Rising and proving time
1½–2½ hrs

Special equipment
26 x 32cm (10 x 13in) baking tray with raised edges

Ingredients
4 tsp dried yeast
3 tbsp olive oil, plus extra for greasing
400g (14oz) strong white bread flour, plus extra for dusting
1 tsp salt

For the filling
50g (1¾oz) unsalted butter
2 tbsp olive oil
600g (1lb 5oz) onions, finely sliced
½ tsp caraway seeds
sea salt and freshly ground black pepper
150ml (5fl oz) soured cream
150ml (5fl oz) crème fraîche
3 eggs
1 tbsp plain flour
75g (2½oz) smoked streaky bacon, chopped

Method

1 To make the crust, dissolve the yeast in 225ml (7½fl oz) warm water. Add the olive oil and set aside. Sift the flour and salt into a large bowl. Make a well in the middle of the flour mixture and pour in the liquid ingredients, stirring all the time. Use your hands to bring the mixture together to form a soft dough. Turn it out onto a well-floured work surface and knead for 10 minutes until soft, smooth, and elastic.

2 Place the dough in a large, lightly oiled bowl, cover with cling film and leave to rise in a warm place for 1–2 hours until doubled in size.

3 To make the filling, heat the butter and olive oil in a large, heavy saucepan. Put in the onions and caraway seeds, and season well with salt and pepper. Cook gently for about 20 minutes, covered, until they are soft but not brown. Remove the lid and cook for another 5 minutes until any excess water evaporates.

4 In a separate bowl, whisk together the soured cream, crème fraîche, eggs, and plain flour, and season well. Mix in the cooked onions and set aside to cool.

5 When the dough has risen, turn it out onto a floured work surface and push it down gently with your knuckles to knock it back. Lightly oil the baking tray. Roll the dough out to roughly the size of the tray and line the tray with it, making sure the pie has an upturned edge. Use your fingers to ease the dough into position, if necessary. Cover with lightly oiled cling film and leave to rise in a warm place for another 30 minutes until puffy in places.

6 Preheat the oven to 200°C (400°F/Gas 6). Gently push down the dough if it has risen too much around the edges of the tray. Spread the filling out over the pie base, and sprinkle the chopped bacon on top.

7 Place the baking tray in the top shelf of the oven and bake for 35–40 minutes until golden brown. Remove from the oven and leave to cool for at least 5 minutes before serving. Serve warm or cold.

STORE Cover and chill overnight.

BAKER'S TIP
This delicious onion and sour cream tart looks like a cross between a pizza and a quiche, and is indeed made with a traditional pizza dough base. It is not much known outside its native Germany, but is well worth making. It was traditionally served during grape harvesting time.

Steak and Wild Mushroom Pie

A quick puff pastry recipe is incredibly useful in your repertoire, but use bought puff pastry if you're short of time.

SERVES 4–6 | **50–55 MINS** | **2½–3 HOURS**

Chilling time
1 hr

Special equipment
2-litre (3½-pint) pie dish

Ingredients

500g (1lb 2oz) mixed wild mushrooms, fresh, or 75g (2½oz) dried wild mushrooms, soaked for 30 minutes and drained
35g (1oz) plain flour
salt and freshly ground black pepper
1kg (2¼lb) braising steak, cut into 2.5cm (1in) cubes

4 shallots, finely chopped
6 parsley sprigs, leaves finely chopped
900ml (1½ pints) beef stock or water, plus extra if needed

For the quick puff pastry

250g (9oz) plain flour, plus extra for dusting
½ tsp fine salt
175g (6oz) unsalted butter, diced
1 egg, beaten, for glazing

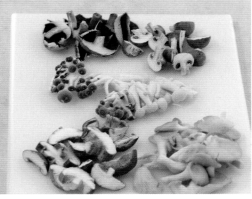

1 Preheat the oven to 180°C (350°F/Gas 4) and slice the mushrooms.

2 Make the filling by seasoning the flour with salt and pepper. Toss the steak in it to coat.

3 Put the meat, mushrooms, and shallots in a casserole. Add the stock and heat, stirring well.

4 Bring to a boil, stirring constantly. Cover and cook in the oven for 2–2¼ hours until tender.

5 To make the pastry, sift the flour and salt into a bowl. Rub in one-third of the butter.

6 Add 100ml (3½fl oz) water and bring it to together to form a dough. Chill for 15 minutes.

7 On a lightly floured surface, roll the dough out to a 15 x 38cm (6 x 15in) rectangle.

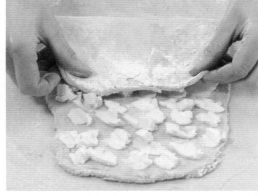

8 Dot the rest of the butter over two-thirds. Fold the unbuttered side over half the buttered side.

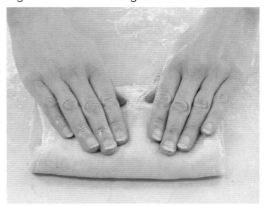

9 Fold the dough again so the butter is completely enclosed in layers of dough.

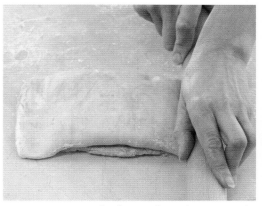

10 Turn it over and roll over the edges to seal. Wrap in cling film and chill for 15 minutes.

11 Roll to 15 x 45cm (6 x 18in), fold in thirds, make a quarter turn. Seal. Chill for 15 minutes.

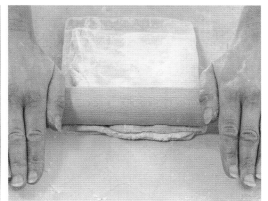

12 Repeat step 11 three more times, chilling the dough for 15 minutes between each turn.

13 Add the parsley to the meat and season to taste. Spoon it into the dish.

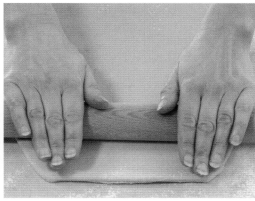

14 Increase the heat to 220°C (425°F/Gas 7). Flour a work surface and roll out the dough.

15 Cut a strip from the edge. Moisten the rim of the pie dish, and press the strip onto it.

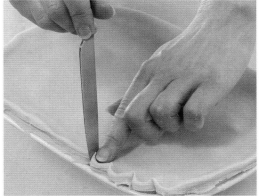

16 Place the rolled-out dough over the pie. Press firmly to seal it to the rim of the dish.

17 Brush with the beaten egg. Make a hole in the centre of the lid to allow steam to escape.

18 Chill the pie for 15 minutes, then bake for 25–35 minutes until golden brown. If browning too quickly, cover with foil. **PREPARE AHEAD** The pie filling can be made 2–3 days ahead.

Savoury Pie variations

Fish Pie

Try to use small, cold-water prawns in this dish, which are not only tastier but also less likely to have been farmed, making them more sustainable.

SERVES 4 · **20 MINS** · **20–25 MINS**

Special equipment
18cm (7in) pie dish

Ingredients
300g (10½oz) skinless salmon fillet, bones picked
200g (7oz) skinless smoked haddock fillet, bones picked
50g (1¾oz) unsalted butter
5 tbsp plain flour, plus extra for dusting
350ml (12fl oz) milk
sea salt and freshly ground black pepper
pinch of freshly grated nutmeg
200g (7oz) prawns
100g (3½oz) baby spinach, washed
250g (9oz) puff pastry, shop-bought, or see pages 370–371, steps 5–12, reducing by one-third
1 egg, beaten, for glazing

Method
1 Preheat the oven to 200°C (400°F/Gas 6). Poach the salmon and haddock in lightly simmering water for 5 minutes until just cooked. Drain and cool. Melt the butter in a pan. Remove from the heat and whisk in the flour until a thick paste is formed. Add the milk a little at a time, whisking to avoid any lumps. Season and add nutmeg. Bring the sauce to a boil, stirring. Reduce the heat and cook for 5 minutes, stirring.

2 Flake the fish into a bowl. Add the prawns. Spread the uncooked spinach over the top and pour the hot sauce over it. Season to taste. When the spinach is wilted, mix the filling together and transfer to the pie dish.

3 On a floured surface, roll out the pastry to a circle bigger than the pie dish, 3–5mm (⅛–¼in) thick. Cut a circle to fit the pie. Roll some of the trimmings out into long strips. Brush the rim of the dish with egg and press the pastry strips around the rim.

4 Brush the edging with egg and top with the pastry lid. Press down to seal the lid, and trim off any overhang. Brush the top with egg and cut 2 slits in it. Bake in the top of the oven for 20–25 minutes until golden, and allow to rest for 5 minutes before serving.

PREPARE AHEAD Best eaten the same day, the pie can be chilled overnight and reheated.

Chicken Pie

Shop-bought pastry makes this an easy option for a weekday supper.

SERVES 4 · **20 MINS** · **20–25 MINS**

Special equipment
18cm (7in) pie dish

Ingredients
1 onion, finely chopped
3 tbsp olive oil
50g (1¾oz) diced pancetta
2 leeks, about 200g (7oz), cut in 1cm (½in) slices
150g (5½oz) button mushrooms, wiped, halved or quartered if necessary
2 large chicken breasts, about 400g (14oz), cut in 2.5cm (1in) chunks
1 heaped tbsp chopped thyme
1 heaped tbsp chopped flat-leaf parsley
1 tbsp plain flour, plus extra for dusting
300ml (10fl oz) single cream
1 tbsp Dijon mustard
sea salt and freshly ground black pepper
250g (9oz) puff pastry, shop-bought, or see pages 370–371, steps 5–12, reducing by one-third
1 egg, beaten, for glazing

Method
1 Preheat the oven to 200°C (400°F/Gas 6). In a pan, fry the onion in 2 tablespoons of the olive oil for 5 minutes until softened, but not brown. Add the pancetta and cook for 2 minutes. Add the leeks and button mushrooms and cook for 3–5 minutes until the pancetta is crispy.

2 Add the remaining olive oil to the pan and add the chicken and herbs. Fry over a high heat for 3–4 minutes until coloured on all sides. Sprinkle the flour over the pie filling and stir it in well. Pour over the cream, add the mustard and seasoning and bring to a boil, stirring. The mixture should thicken as it heats. Continue to cook for 5 minutes over low heat until the liquid has reduced. Turn the filling out into the pie dish.

3 Roll out the pastry, cover the pie, and bake as directed for Fish Pie, see left, steps 3–4.

Steak and Kidney Double Crust Pie

Old-fashioned suet crust gives this pastry a light, crumbly finish.

| SERVES 4 | 30 MINS | 2¾–3¼ HOURS | 8 WEEKS, UNBAKED |

Special equipment
18cm (7in) pie dish

Ingredients

For the filling
4 tbsp olive oil, plus extra for greasing
2 onions, finely chopped
100g (3½oz) button mushrooms, wiped, halved or quartered, if necessary
600g (1lb 5oz) stewing steak, such as chuck, cut in 3cm (1¼in) chunks
sea salt and freshly ground black pepper
4 tbsp plain flour
600ml (1 pint) beef stock
large sprig of thyme
30g (1oz) unsalted butter, softened
4 fresh lamb's kidneys, about 200g (7oz)

For the suet crust pastry
300g (10½oz) self-raising flour
150g (5½oz) beef or vegetable suet
½ tsp salt
1 egg, beaten, for glazing

Method

1 In a pan, heat 2 tablespoons of oil and fry the onion for 5 minutes until softened but not browned. Add the mushrooms and fry for 3–4 minutes until they begin to colour in places. Remove the vegetables from the pan with a slotted spoon and set aside.

2 Toss the diced steak in 2 tablespoons of seasoned flour. Heat the remaining oil in the pan, on high heat, and fry off the meat, until browned. Take care not to overcrowd the pan or the meat will begin to steam rather than brown. Remove the meat as it cooks and add it to the vegetables.

3 Once the meat is seared, return it and the vegetables to the pan. Cover with the beef stock. Season, add the thyme, and bring to a boil. When boiled, reduce the heat to low, cover, and cook for 2–2½ hours until tender.

4 For the pastry, rub together the flour and suet until it resembles crumbs. Add the salt and enough cold water to bring the mixture together to a soft dough. Wrap in cling film. Rest the dough for at least 1 hour.

5 Make a paste out of 2 tablespoons of plain flour mashed into the butter. Uncover the stew and increase the heat. When it begins to boil, add the flour mixture a little at a time, stirring. Reduce the heat and cook over low heat for 30 minutes, until the sauce thickens.

6 Preheat the oven to 180°C (350°F/Gas 4). Trim the kidneys of any skin, cut out the central core, and cut into chunks. Add them to the stew. Roll out the pastry on a floured surface into a 20cm x 40cm (8 x 16in) rectangle. It should be 3–5mm (⅛-¼in) thick. Place the pie dish onto a short edge of the pastry and cut a circle around it for the lid.

7 Oil the tin, trim the remaining pastry and use it to line the pie dish, allowing the sides to overhang. Fill the case with the pie filling and brush egg around the edges of the pastry. Top with the disk of pastry and press down around the edges to seal.

8 Brush the pie with egg, then cut 2 small slits in the top to allow the steam to escape. Bake in the middle of a preheated oven for 40–45 minutes until golden brown. Remove the pie from the oven and allow it to cool for at least 5 minutes before serving.

PREPARE AHEAD The filling can be made 2 days ahead and chilled until needed. Do not add the uncooked kidneys until you are ready to bake the pie. This pie is best eaten the day it is made, but can be chilled overnight. Reheat well before eating.

Beef and Ale Cobbler

Great for feeding a crowd, the filling can be prepared days ahead and the whole dish needs no additional attention once it has gone into the oven.

| SERVES 4 | 40 MINS | 2½–3¼ HOURS | 8 WEEKS, STEW |

Special equipment
5cm (2in) pastry cutter

Ingredients

For the filling
4 tbsp olive oil
2 onions, finely chopped
1 celery stick, finely diced
1 leek, trimmed and finely sliced
150g (5½oz) button mushrooms, wiped, halved or quartered, if needed
600g (1lb 5oz) stewing steak, such as chuck, in 3cm (1¼in) chunks
2 tbsp plain flour

sea salt and freshly ground black pepper
500ml (16fl oz) dark ale, such as stout or porter
1 beef stock cube
1 bouquet garni
1 tbsp sugar
2 large carrots, in 2cm (¾in) chunks

For the cobbler
300g (10½oz) self-raising flour, plus extra for dusting
1 tsp baking powder
½ tsp salt
125g (4½oz) unsalted butter, chilled and diced
1 tbsp finely chopped parsley
3 tbsp horseradish sauce or horseradish cream
2–4 tbsp milk
1 egg, beaten, for glazing

Method

1 In a large ovenproof casserole, heat 2 tablespoons olive oil and fry the onion, celery, and leek for about 5 minutes until soft but not brown. Add the mushrooms and fry for 3–4 minutes until they begin to colour in places. Remove the vegetables with a slotted spoon and set aside.

2 Toss the steak in 2 tablespoons seasoned flour. Heat the remaining oil in the casserole and fry the meat, a few pieces at a time, until well browned on all sides. Take care not to overcrowd the pan, or the meat will begin to steam rather than brown. Remove the meat as it cooks, and add it to the vegetables.

3 Return the meat to the casserole with the vegetables, and cover with the ale. Crumble over the stock cube, 300ml (10fl oz) boiling water, bouquet garni, sugar, and carrots. Check for seasoning, and bring to a boil. Reduce the heat to its lowest setting, cover,

and cook for 2–2½ hours, until the meat is tender. Check it from time to time, and add a little water if it is drying out.

4 Preheat the oven to 200°C (400°F/Gas 6). Sift together the flour, baking powder, and salt. Using your fingertips, rub in the butter until the mixture resembles fine crumbs. Add the parsley. Whisk the horseradish sauce and milk, and use the liquid to bind the dry ingredients to form a soft dough.

5 On a floured surface, roll out the dough to a thickness of 2cm (¾in). Using the pastry cutter cut out circles. Re-roll the offcuts and re-cut until the dough is used up. When the stew is cooked, remove the bouquet garni and top it with the disks of cobbler dough. Overlap them slightly so that there are very few gaps where the filling can be seen.

6 Brush the tops with beaten egg, and bake the cobbler in the middle of the oven for 30–40 minutes until it is puffed up and golden brown. Remove it from the oven and let it rest for 5 minutes before serving.

PREPARE AHEAD Prepare the filling 2 days ahead and chill, before topping with the cobbler and baking. The cooked cobbler can be chilled overnight; reheat before eating.

BAKER'S TIP
A cobbler topping is easier to make than dumplings or pastry, and can turn a simple stew into a hearty, one-pot meal. Any kind of meat or vegetable stew can be transformed with the addition of these savoury scones; try adding mustard, horseradish, herbs, or spices to the mix to complement the filling.

Chicken Pot Pies with Herb Crust

A delicious and deeply comforting recipe with a tasty scone topping. Serve simply with some steamed green vegetables alongside.

SERVES 6 | **25–35 MINS** | **22–25 MINS**

Special equipment
8.5cm (3½in) pastry cutter
6 large ramekins

Ingredients
1 litre (1¾ pints) chicken stock
3 carrots, sliced
750g (1lb 10oz) large potatoes, diced
3 celery sticks, thinly sliced
175g (6oz) peas
500g (1lb 2oz) cooked skinless, boneless chicken
60g (2oz) unsalted butter

1 onion, chopped
30g (1oz) plain flour
175ml (6fl oz) double cream
whole nutmeg, for grating
sea salt and freshly ground black pepper
leaves from 1 small bunch of parsley, chopped
1 egg

For the topping
250g (9oz) plain flour, plus extra for dusting
1 tbsp baking powder
1 tsp salt
60g (2oz) unsalted butter, diced
leaves from 1 small bunch of parsley, chopped
150ml (5fl oz) milk, plus extra if needed

Method

1 Boil the stock in a large saucepan. Add the carrots, potatoes, and celery, and simmer for 3 minutes. Add the peas and simmer for another 5 minutes until all the vegetables are tender. Drain, reserving the stock. Cut the chicken into slivers and put in a bowl. Add the vegetables.

2 Melt the butter in a small saucepan over moderate heat. Add the onion and cook for 3–5 minutes, until softened but not browned. Sprinkle the flour over the onions and cook for 1–2 minutes, stirring. Add 500ml (16fl oz) stock and heat, whisking, until the sauce comes to a boil and thickens. Simmer for 2 minutes, add the cream and a grating of nutmeg, and season. Pour the sauce over the chicken and vegetables, add the parsley and mix gently.

3 Sift the flour into a large bowl with the baking powder and salt. Make a well in the centre and add the butter. Rub with your fingertips to form crumbs. Add the parsley, make a well again and pour in the milk, cutting in quickly with a knife to form coarse crumbs. Add a little more milk if it is dry. Bring the dough together with your fingers.

4 Knead the dough lightly on a well-floured surface until smooth. Pat the dough out to a thickness of 1cm (½in). Cut out rounds with the pastry cutter. Pat the trimmings and cut out additional rounds to make 6 in total.

5 Preheat the oven to 220°C (425°F/Gas 7). Divide the chicken filling evenly among the 6 dishes. Place a scone round on each pie (it's nice if the scone is positioned slightly off-centre, so you can see some of the creamy filling). Lightly beat the egg with a pinch of salt and use to glaze the rounds.

6 Bake for 15 minutes. Reduce the heat to 180°C (350°F/Gas 4) and bake until the crust is golden brown and the filling is bubbling. It should take another 7–10 minutes. If the scone topping threatens to scorch, cover the pies loosely with a sheet of foil.

PREPARE AHEAD The filling can be prepared 1 day ahead, covered, and chilled. Bring it to room temperature before baking.

BAKER'S TIP
Though this scone topping is very easy to make, you can also make the pies with a puff pastry (see pages 370–371, steps 5–12) or shortcrust (see page 358, steps 1–5) topping instead. Try experimenting with the filling too, adding different herbs; tarragon is a particularly good choice here.

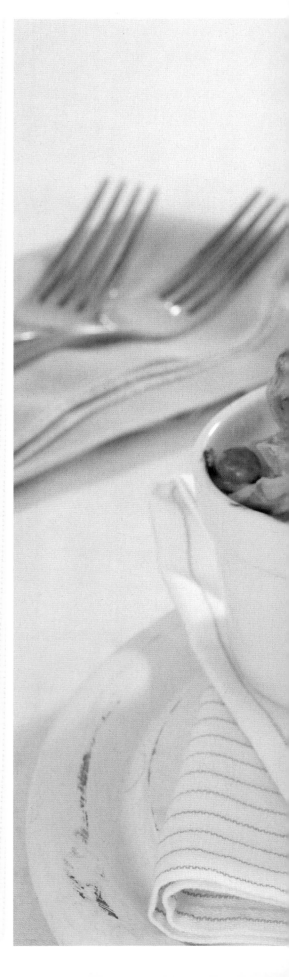

Chicken and Ham Raised Pie

This is wonderful to take on a picnic, served with chutney and a crisp green salad.

SERVES 8–10 | **50–60 MINS** | **1½ HOURS**

Special equipment
20–23cm (8–9in) springform cake tin
mincer or food processor with blade attachment

Ingredients

For the pastry
500g (1lb 2oz) plain flour, plus extra for dusting
2 tsp salt
75g (2½oz) butter, chilled and diced, plus extra for greasing
75g (2½oz) lard, chilled and diced

For the filling
9 eggs
4 skinless, boneless chicken breasts, total weight 750g (1lb 10oz)
375g (13oz) lean boneless pork
finely grated zest of ½ lemon
1 tsp dried thyme
1 tsp dried sage
large pinch of ground nutmeg
sea salt and freshly ground black pepper
375g (13oz) cooked lean ham

1 Sift the flour and salt into a large bowl. Rub in the butter and lard until fine crumbs form.

2 Make a well, add 150ml (5fl oz) water and cut in with a knife to form coarse crumbs.

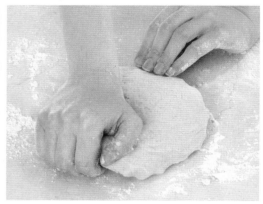

3 Form a dough and knead until smooth. Wrap in cling film and chill for 30 minutes.

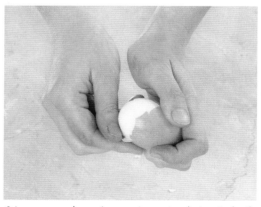

4 In a pan, place 6 eggs in water, bring to boil, simmering for 7 minutes. Drain, cool, and peel.

5 Cut 2 of the chicken breasts and pork into chunks. Mince or process, but not too finely.

6 Put the minced meats in a bowl. Add lemon zest, thyme, sage, nutmeg, salt, and pepper.

7 Whisk 2 eggs and add to the minced meats. Beat the filling until it pulls away from the sides.

8 Cut the reserved chicken breasts and ham into 2cm (¾in) cubes, and stir into the filling.

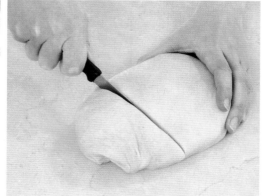

9 Grease the tin. Shape about three-quarters of the dough into a ball; keep the rest covered.

10 On a floured surface, roll the dough out to the size of the tin, with a 2cm (1in) overhang.

11 Preheat the oven to 200°C (400°F/Gas 6). Spread half the filling and put the eggs on top.

12 Gently push in the eggs and cover with the remaining mix. Fold over the dough overhang.

13 Beat the remaining egg with a pinch of salt, and brush the edges with the egg glaze.

14 Roll out the remaining dough 5mm (¼in) thick. Lay on top, press to seal, and trim.

15 Poke a hole in the lid. Insert a roll of foil to form a chimney. Decorate with the trimmings.

16 Cut out strips, 2.5cm (1in) wide, and cut them into leaf shapes. Mark veins with a knife.

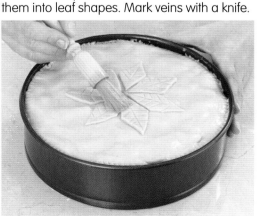

17 Arrange the leaves, glaze, and bake for 1 hour. Reduce the heat to 180°C (350°F/Gas 4).

18 Bake for another 30 minutes. Discard the foil chimney and chill before unmoulding. Serve at room temperature. **STORE** The pie will keep in the refrigerator for 3 days.

Raised Pie variations

Game Pie

This traditional raised pie makes an impressive centrepiece for a summer buffet and keeps well for days in the fridge.

SERVES 8   **30 MINS**   **1¾ HOUR**

Chilling time
overnight

Special equipment
900g (2lb) loaf tin
small funnel

Ingredients

For the hot water pastry
400g (14oz) plain flour, plus extra for dusting
½ tsp fine salt
150g (5½ oz) lard or beef dripping, cubed
1 egg, beaten, for glazing

For the filling
150g (5½oz) pork shoulder, cut in 1cm (½in) chunks
150g (5½oz) pork belly, trimmed, cut in 1cm (½in) chunks
250g (9oz) venison, cut in 1cm (½in) chunks
2 pheasant breasts, cut in 1cm (½in) slices
sea salt and freshly ground black pepper

For the jelly
4 sheets of leaf gelatine, cut into pieces
350ml (12fl oz) chicken stock

Method

1 Preheat the oven to 200°C (400°F/Gas 6). To make the hot water crust, place the flour and salt in a bowl and make a well. Boil a kettle, then measure out 150ml (5fl oz) boiling water into a jug. Add the lard or dripping to the water, and stir until the fat has melted. This reduces the temperature of the water and makes it easy to work with.

2 Pour the liquid into the centre of the flour and mix together with a wooden spoon. At the end, you will need to use your hands to bring it all together into a soft dough. Be careful, as it will be hot. Cut off one-quarter of the pastry, wrap it in a clean tea towel and put it somewhere warm for later.

3 Working quickly, as the pastry will harden as it cools, turn the dough out on to a well-floured work surface and roll it out to a thickness of 5mm (¼in). Use the rolling pin to carefully lift the pastry into the loaf tin. Press it firmly all around the bottom and the sides of the tin. Trim off any excess pastry, allowing an overhang of 2cm (¾in).

4 Pack the pastry case with layers of the pork, venison, and pheasant, seasoning liberally between each layer. Brush the edges of the pastry with a little beaten egg. Now roll out the set-aside pastry and use it to top the pie. Press down firmly all around the edges of the tin with your fingers to seal, and trim off any excess. Decorate the pie, if desired, with pastry leaves made from the offcuts, and brush the top with a little beaten egg. Use a chopstick or other implement to make a hole in the top of the pie, so you can fill with jelly after it has cooked.

5 Bake the pie in the centre of the oven for 30 minutes, then reduce the heat to 160°C (325°F/Gas 3) and cook for a further 1¼ hours until golden brown. Remove the pie from the oven and leave it to cool in the tin.

6 Soak the gelatine in a little cold water for 5 minutes until softened. Heat the chicken stock and add the softened gelatine, stirring constantly until it dissolves. Leave it to cool. Once the liquid starts to thicken, but not solidify, pour it using a small funnel into the top of the pie, a little at a time. You may need to re-open the hole in the top of the pie if it has closed up when cooking. Refrigerate to set the jelly overnight before eating.

STORE The pie will keep for 3 days in an airtight container in the refrigerator.

BAKER'S TIP
Hot water pastry has a reputation for being difficult to handle. It does need to be used quickly, before it starts to cool and harden, but is remarkably pliable and can be squashed and shaped to fit the tin far more easily than other types of pastry. It is also extremely resilient, and will remain crisp for days.

Individual Pork Pies

Try making these bite-sized pork pies for a special picnic treat.

MAKES 12   **40 MINS**   **1 HOUR**

Chilling time
overnight

Special equipment
food processor with blade attachment (optional)
12-hole muffin tray
small funnel (optional)

Ingredients

For the filling
200g (7oz) pork belly, trimmed of fat and skin, and cubed
200g (7oz) pork shoulder, trimmed and cubed
50g (1¾oz) unsmoked back or streaky bacon, trimmed and diced
10 sage leaves, finely chopped
sea salt and freshly ground black pepper
¼ tsp nutmeg
¼ tsp allspice

For the hot water pastry
400g (14oz) plain flour, plus extra for dusting
½ tsp fine salt
150g (5½ oz) lard or beef dripping, cubed
1 egg, beaten, for glazing

For the jelly (optional)
2 sheets of leaf gelatine, cut into pieces
250ml (8fl oz) chicken stock

Method

1 Preheat the oven to 200°C (400°F/Gas 6). Put the pork belly, pork shoulder, bacon, herbs, seasoning, and spices into a food processor and whizz until the meat is chopped, but not mushy. If you do not have a processor, cut the meat by hand into 5mm (¼in) dice, then mix in the other ingredients.

2 To make the hot water crust, place the flour and salt in a bowl and make a well. Boil a kettle, then measure out 150ml (5fl oz) boiling water into a jug. Add the lard or dripping to the water, and stir until the fat has melted. This will also reduce the temperature of the water and make it easier to work with.

3 Pour the liquid into the centre of the flour and mix together with a wooden spoon. At the end, you will need to use your hands to bring it all together into a soft dough. Be careful, as it will be hot. Cut off one-quarter of the pastry, wrap it in a clean tea towel and put it somewhere warm for later.

4 You will need to work quickly as the pastry will begin to harden as it cools. Turn the dough out onto a well-floured work surface and roll it out to 5mm (¼in) thick. Cut circles big enough to line the muffin tray, allowing the pastry to overlap the edges slightly. Make 12 pastry cases. Pack the pork filling into each of the lined muffin cases, and brush a little beaten egg around the edges of each.

5 Roll out the set-aside pastry. Cut out 12 lids to fit the muffin cases. Top the filling with the lids, and press down the sides to seal. Brush the tops with egg. Use a chopstick or other implement to make a hole in each pie if you wish to fill it with jelly later, or cut 2 slits to allow the steam to escape if you don't.

6 Bake the pies in the centre of the oven for 30 minutes, then reduce the heat to 160°C (325°F/Gas 3) and cook for a further 30 minutes until golden brown. Remove from the oven and leave to cool in the tray for 10 minutes before turning out. At this stage they can be eaten hot, allowed to cool, or cooled and filled with jelly.

7 To make the jelly (if using), soak the gelatine in a little cold water for 5 minutes until softened. Heat the chicken stock and add the softened gelatine, stirring constantly until it dissolves. Cool. Once the liquid starts to thicken, but not solidify, use a small funnel to pour it into each cooled pie, a little at a time. You may need to re-open the holes in the tops of the pies if they have closed up a little when cooking. Each pie will need only 2–3 tablespoons of liquid. Refrigerate to set the jelly overnight before eating.

STORE The pies will keep for 3 days in an airtight container in the refrigerator.

Boeuf en croûte

Also known as Beef Wellington, this rich and luxurious dish is simple to finish off and serve, perfect for entertaining.

SERVES 6 | 45 MINS | 42–60 MINS

Ingredients

1kg (2¼lb) fillet of beef, cut from the thick end, trimmed of fat
sea salt and freshly ground black pepper
2 tbsp sunflower oil
45g (1½oz) unsalted butter
2 shallots, finely chopped
1 garlic clove, crushed

250g (9oz) mixed wild mushrooms, finely chopped
1 tbsp brandy or Madeira
500g (1lb 2oz) puff pastry, shop-bought, or see pages 370–371, steps 5–12
beaten egg, for glazing

SAVOURY TARTS AND PIES

1 Preheat the oven to 220°C (425°F/Gas 7). Season the meat with salt and pepper.

2 Heat the oil in a large frying pan and fry the beef until browned all over.

3 Place the beef in a roasting tin and roast for 10 minutes. Remove and leave it to cool.

4 Melt the butter in a pan. Fry the shallots and garlic for 2–3 minutes, stirring, until softened.

5 Add the mushrooms, and cook, stirring, or 4–5 minutes until the juices evaporate.

6 Add the brandy. Let it bubble for 30 seconds. Remove from the heat and leave to cool.

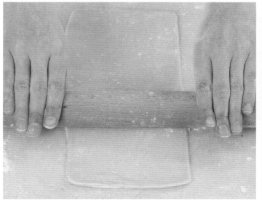

7 Roll out one-third of the pastry to a rectangle, about 5cm (2in) larger than the beef.

8 Place on a baking sheet and prick with a fork. Bake for 12–15 minutes until crisp. Cool.

9 Spread one-third of the mushroom mixture on the centre of the cooked pastry.

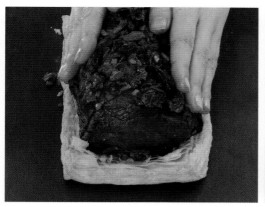

10 Place the beef on top and spread the remaining mushroom mixture over the meat.

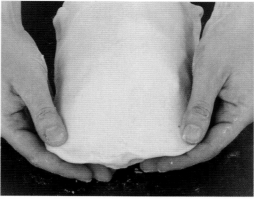

11 Roll out the remaining pastry and place it over the beef, tucking in the edges.

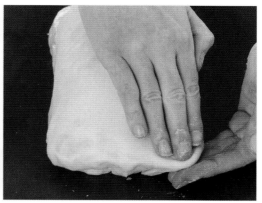

12 Brush the beaten egg around the edges, and press down the raw pastry to seal.

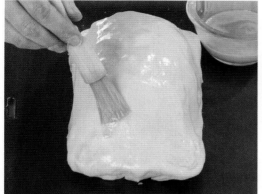

13 Brush the egg all over the uncooked pastry case to glaze.

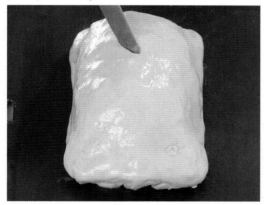

14 Slit the top for steam to escape. Bake 30 minutes for rare, and 45 minutes for well done.

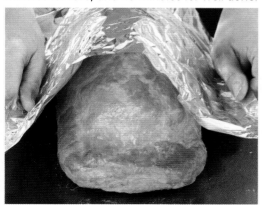

15 If the pastry starts to become too brown, cover loosely with a sheet of foil.

16 Remove from the oven and let it stand for 10 minutes before serving. Slice the dish using a very sharp knife.

En Croûte variations

Sausage Rolls

Classic finger food for picnics and parties, sausage rolls are so easy to make from scratch you will never go back to shop-bought.

MAKES 24	30 MINS	10–12 MINS	12 WEEKS, UNCOOKED

Chilling time
30 mins

Ingredients
250g (9oz) puff pastry, shop-bought, or see pages 370–371, steps 5–12, reducing by one-third
675g (1½lb) sausage meat
1 small onion, finely chopped
1 tbsp thyme leaves
1 tbsp finely grated lemon zest
1 tsp Dijon mustard
1 egg yolk
sea salt and freshly ground black pepper
plain flour, for dusting
1 egg, beaten, for glazing

Method
1 Preheat the oven to 200°C (400°F/Gas 6). Line a baking tray with parchment and chill. Cut the pastry in half lengthways. Roll each piece out to form a 30 x 15cm (12 x 6in) rectangle. Cover with cling film and chill for 30 minutes. Combine the sausage meat with the onion, thyme, lemon zest, mustard, and egg yolk. Season with salt and pepper.

2 Lay the pastry on a floured surface. Form the sausage mixture into 2 thinly rolled tubes and place in the centre of each piece of pastry. Brush the inside of the pastry with the beaten egg, then roll the pastry over and press to seal. Cut each roll into 12 pieces.

3 Place the rolls on the chilled tray, make 2 snips at the top of each with scissors, then brush with the beaten egg. Bake for 10–12 minutes or until the pastry is golden and flaky. Serve warm, or transfer to a wire rack to cool completely.

STORE These can be stored in an airtight container in the fridge for 2 days.

Venison Wellingtons

Perfect for a special occasion meal or dinner party.

SERVES 4	40 MINS	20–25 MINS

Ingredients
10g (¼oz) dried wild mushrooms (optional)
2 tbsp olive oil
4 venison loin steaks, each 120–150g (4–5½oz)
sea salt and freshly ground black pepper
30g (1oz) unsalted butter
2 shallots, finely chopped
1 garlic clove, finely chopped
200g (7oz) mixed mushrooms, including wild mushrooms if possible
1 tbsp thyme leaves
1 tbsp brandy or Madeira
500g (1lb 2oz) puff pastry, shop-bought, or see pages 370–371, steps 5–12
1 egg, beaten, for glazing

Method
1 Preheat the oven to 200°C (400°F/Gas 6). If fresh wild mushrooms are not available, put the dried wild mushrooms in a bowl and cover with boiling water. Leave for at least 15 minutes.

2 Heat the olive oil in a frying pan. Season the venison steaks on all sides with salt and pepper and fry them, two at a time, for 2 minutes each side, until they are browned all over. Take them out of the pan and set aside to cool completely.

3 Melt the butter in the same pan. Add the shallot and cook it for 5 minutes over medium heat until softened, but not brown. Add the garlic and cook for 1–2 minutes.

4 Roughly chop the mushrooms and add them to the pan with the thyme. Season and cook for 5 minutes until they are well softened and any juices have evaporated. Add the brandy and cook over high heat for 1 minute until that has evaporated too. Remove from the heat and let cool. If using dried mushrooms, drain them, chop them roughly, and add to the mushroom mixture.

5 Divide the pastry into 4 equal pieces and roll out rectangles about 5mm (¼in) thick and large enough to wrap around each steak. Pat each steak dry with kitchen paper.

6 Place one-quarter of the mushroom filling in a rectangle roughly the same shape as the venison steak to one side of the pastry, leaving a clean edge of at least 2cm (¾in). Flatten the mushrooms down and place a steak on top. Brush the edges of the pastry with beaten egg and fold the pastry over the meat. Press the edges down firmly to seal in the meat. Crimp them in to give an attractive finish. Repeat with the remaining steaks and pastry. Cut small slits in the top of the wellingtons to allow the steam to escape, and brush the tops with more beaten egg.

7 Place the pastries on a heavy baking tray with a rim and bake in the top third of the oven for 20–25 minutes or until puffed up and golden. The longer the wellington is cooked, the more well done the meat will be. Remove from the oven and allow to cool for 5 minutes before serving.

Salmon En Croûte

Baking salmon in puff pastry keeps it moist and succulent. ▶

SERVES 4 | **25 MINS** | **30 MINS**

Ingredients
85g (3oz) watercress, coarse stems removed
115g (4oz) cream cheese
sea salt and freshly ground black pepper
600g (1lb 5oz) skinless salmon fillet
250g (9oz) puff pastry, shop-bought, or see pages 370–371, steps 5–12, reducing by one-third
plain flour, for dusting
unsalted butter, for greasing
1 egg, beaten, or milk, for glazing

Method
1 Preheat the oven to 200°C (400°F/Gas 6). Chop the watercress very finely, place in a bowl, add the cream cheese, season with salt and pepper, and mix well.

2 Cut the salmon fillet into 2 pieces. Roll out the pastry on a lightly floured surface

to a thickness of 3mm (⅛in). It should be roughly 7.5cm (3in) longer than the salmon pieces and just over twice as wide. Trim the edges straight. Transfer to a lightly greased baking tray.

3 Place 1 piece of salmon in the middle of the pastry. Spread the top with the watercress cream and place the other piece of salmon on top. Lightly brush the pastry edges with water, then fold both ends over the salmon. Fold in the sides so they overlap slightly and press together to seal. Re-roll the trimmings and use to decorate the top of the pastry, if liked. Brush with the beaten egg, and make 2 or 3 holes with a skewer to allow steam to escape.

4 Bake for 30 minutes or until the pastry is well risen and golden brown. Test if the

salmon is cooked by pushing a skewer halfway through the thickest part and leaving it for 4–5 seconds; when removed, it should feel hot.

5 Remove from the oven and allow to stand for a few minutes, then slice and serve.

PREPARE AHEAD The whole dish can be made up to 12 hours before baking. Cover with cling film and chill until ready to cook.

Feta Filo Pie

Crisp pastry encases a delicious blend of spinach, feta, and pine nuts in this classic Middle Eastern dish.

SERVES 6 **30 MINS** **35–40 MINS**

Special equipment
20cm (8in) springform cake tin

Ingredients
900g (2lb) fresh spinach leaves
100g (3½oz) unsalted butter,
  plus extra for greasing
1 tsp ground cumin
1 tsp ground coriander
1 tsp ground cinnamon
2 red onions, finely chopped
60g (2oz) dried apricots, chopped

60g (2oz) pine nuts, toasted
6 sheets filo pastry, 40 x 30cm
  (16 x 12in), thawed if frozen
sea salt and freshly ground
  black pepper
300g (10½oz) feta cheese, crumbled

1 Rinse the spinach leaves, shake off excess water, and stuff into a large saucepan.

2 Cover and cook over medium heat for 8–10 minutes, turning occasionally, until just wilted.

3 Drain through a colander, pressing against the sides to extract as much water as possible.

4 Leave to cool slightly. When cool enough, squeeze out more water with your hands.

5 Meanwhile, melt 25g (1oz) of the butter in a small frying pan until it begins to bubble.

6 Gently fry the spices with the onions over low heat, stirring occasionally.

7 Fry for 7–8 minutes until the onions are softened but not browned.

8 Stir in the apricots and pine nuts, then set aside to cool slightly.

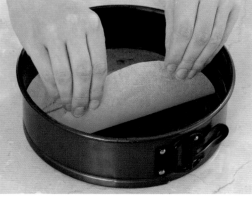

9 Preheat the oven to 200°C (400°F/Gas 6). Grease the tin and line it with parchment.

10 To assemble the pie, melt the remaining butter, and use a little to brush around the tin.

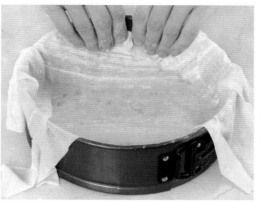

11 Cover the base with a sheet of filo pastry, leaving the edges overhanging.

12 Brush melted butter over the pastry sheet, including the overhang.

13 Layer 5 more sheets, brushing each with butter and leaving the edges overhanging.

14 Blot the cooled spinach with kitchen paper to absorb moisture completely. Chop it finely.

15 Stir the spinach into the cooked onion mixture and season with salt and pepper.

16 Pile half the spinach mixture into the pastry case and spread evenly.

17 Sprinkle the feta cheese over the top and cover with the remaining spinach mixture.

18 Fold the overhanging pastry over the spinach, piece by piece, brushing with butter.

19 Brush the top with any remaining butter and place the tin on a baking tray.

20 Bake for 35–40 minutes until crisp and golden. Leave to cool for 10 minutes.

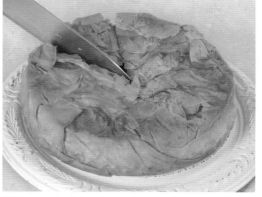

21 Turn out of the tin and serve hot or warm, cut into wedges.

Filo Pie variations

Filo Pie with Spicy Kale and Sausage

In their native Greece, filo pies are made with a mixture of wild bitter greens, but any greens work well, provided they have a pronounced, slightly bitter flavour. Try substituting the kale for spring greens or spinach.

SERVES 6	35–40 MINS	45–55 MINS	8 WEEKS, UNBAKED

Special equipment
28cm (11in) springform cake tin

Ingredients
200g (7oz) unsalted butter
250g (9oz) sausage meat
3 onions, finely chopped
500g pack of filo pastry
750g (1lb 10oz) kale, washed, trimmed, and shredded
½ tsp ground allspice
sea salt and freshly ground black pepper
2 eggs, beaten

Method

1 Heat 30g (1oz) of the butter in a sauté pan, add the sausage meat, and cook, stirring, until it is crumbly and brown. Transfer to a bowl with a slotted spoon, leaving the fat behind. Add the onions to the pan and cook, stirring, until soft. Add the kale, cover, and cook very gently until the kale is wilted. Remove the lid and cook for 5 minutes, stirring constantly, until the moisture has evaporated.

2 Return the sausage meat to the pan with the allspice and stir into the kale mixture. Season to taste. Remove from the heat and let cool completely. Stir in the eggs.

3 Preheat the oven to 180°C (350°F/Gas 4). Melt the remaining butter in a saucepan; brush the tin with a little butter.

4 Lay a folded damp tea towel on the work surface. Unroll the filo sheets onto the towel. Using the tin as a guide, cut through the pastry sheets to leave a 7.5cm (3in) border around the tin where possible. Cover the sheets with a second folded damp towel.

5 Put 1 filo sheet on top of a third damp towel and brush with butter. Transfer to the flan tin, pressing it well into the side. Butter another filo sheet and put it in the tin at a right angle to the first. Continue buttering and layering until half the filo is used, arranging alternate layers at right angles.

6 Spoon the kale and sausage meat filling into the case. Butter another sheet of filo and cover the filling with it. Top with the remaining sheets of filo, brushing each, including the top one, with melted butter. Fold the overhanging dough over the top and drizzle with the remaining butter.

7 Bake the pie in the heated oven for 45–55 minutes until golden brown. Let cool slightly, then cut into wedges and serve hot or at room temperature.

PREPARE AHEAD The pie can be prepared ahead up to the point of baking, wrapped in cling film, and refrigerated for 2 days.

Potato and Blue Cheese Filo Pie

This is an excellent dish to prepare ahead for a midweek meal.

SERVES 6 | **35–40 MINS** | **45–55 MINS**

Special equipment
28cm (11in) springform cake tin

Ingredients
190g (6½oz) unsalted butter
125g (4½oz) bacon, cut into strips
500g pack of filo pastry
1kg (2¼lb) potatoes, very thinly sliced
125g (4½oz) blue cheese, crumbled
4 shallots, finely chopped
4–5 sprigs each parsley, tarragon,
  and chervil, leaves finely chopped
sea salt and freshly ground black pepper
3–4 tbsp soured cream

Method

1 Preheat the oven to 180°C (350°F/Gas 4). Melt 15g (½oz) butter in a frying pan and cook the bacon for about 5 minutes until brown. Drain on paper towels. Melt the rest of the butter in a saucepan. Brush the tin with a little butter. Lay a damp tea towel on a work surface, and unroll the filo pastry sheets onto the towel.

2 Using the tin as a guide, cut through the pastry to leave a 7.5cm (3in) border around the tin. Cover with a second damp towel.

3 Put 1 filo sheet on a third damp towel and brush with butter, then press into the tin. Repeat with another sheet, putting it in the tin at a right angle to the first. Continue until half the filo is used.

4 Arrange half the potatoes in the tin. Sprinkle with half the cheese, shallots, herbs, salt, and pepper. Repeat with the remaining filling ingredients. Cover the pie with the remaining filo, buttering and layering. Cut a 7.5cm (3in) hole from the centre, so the filling shows. Bake for 45–55 minutes, until golden brown. While still hot, spoon the soured cream into the centre of the pie and serve in wedges.

PREPARE AHEAD The pie can be prepared ahead up to the point of baking, wrapped in cling film, and refrigerated for 2 days.

Cornish Pasties

Although not traditional, I find a splash of Worcestershire sauce adds a depth of flavour to the pasty filling.

MAKES 4 **20 MINS** **40–45 MINS**

Chilling time
1 hr

Ingredients
100g (3½oz) lard, chilled and diced
50g (1¾oz) unsalted butter,
  chilled and diced
300g (10½oz) plain flour,
  plus extra for dusting
½ tsp salt
1 egg, beaten, for glazing

For the filling
250g (9oz) beef skirt, trimmed,
  cut into 1cm (½in) cubes
80g (2¾oz) swede, peeled,
  cut into 5mm (¼in) cubes
100g (3½oz) waxy potatoes,
  peeled, cut into 5mm (¼in) cubes
1 large onion, finely chopped

splash of Worcestershire sauce
1 tsp plain flour
sea salt and freshly ground
  black pepper

1 Rub the lard and butter into the flour until the mixture resembles fine crumbs.

2 Add the salt and enough cold water to bring the mixture together into a soft dough.

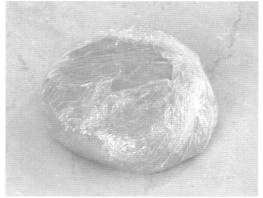

3 Knead the dough briefly on a lightly floured surface. Wrap in cling film and chill for 1 hour.

4 Preheat the oven to 190°C (375°F/Gas 5). Mix all the filling ingredients and season well.

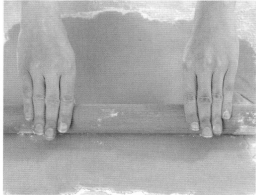

5 On a well-floured work surface, roll the pastry out to a thickness of 5mm (¼in).

6 Using a side plate, or saucer, cut 4 circles from the dough. Re-roll the offcuts.

7 Fold the circles in half, then flatten them out again, leaving a slight mark down the centre.

8 Pile one-quarter of the filling into each circle, leaving a 2cm (¾in) border all around.

9 Brush the border of the pastry with a little beaten egg.

SAVOURY TARTS AND PIES

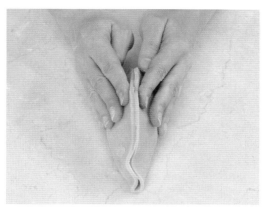

10 Pull both edges up over the filling and press together to seal.

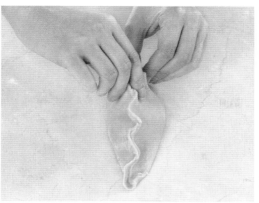

11 Crimp the sealed edge with your fingers to form a decorative ridge along the top.

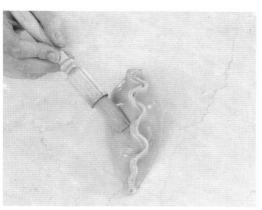

12 Brush a little beaten egg all over the finished pasties.

13 Bake in the centre of the oven for 40–45 minutes until golden brown. Remove the pasties from the oven and allow to cool for at least 15 minutes before eating warm or cold. **STORE** These will keep in the refrigerator for 2 days.

Pasty variations

Chicken Pasties

A complete and filling lunch in a pastry packet, these chicken pasties, a lighter alternative to the traditional beef pasties, go down particularly well with children.

SERVES 4 | **30 MINS** | **35 MINS**

Chilling time
20 mins

Ingredients
1 quantity pasty dough, see page 392, steps 1–3
1 egg, beaten, for glazing

For the filling
115g (4oz) cream cheese
6 spring onions, sliced
2 tbsp chopped parsley
sea salt and freshly ground black pepper
2–3 chicken breasts, about 350g (12oz),
    cut into 2cm (¾in) chunks
150g (5½oz) potatoes, cut into 1cm (½in) cubes
150g (5½oz) sweet potatoes, cut into 1cm (½in)
    cubes

Method
1 Mix the cream cheese, onions, and parsley in a bowl, and season to taste with salt and pepper. Stir in the chicken, potato, and sweet potato.

2 Preheat the oven to 200°C (400°F/Gas 6). Divide the pastry into 4 pieces. Roll out each piece on a lightly floured surface and, using a small plate as a guide, cut into a 20cm (8in) round. Spoon one-quarter of the filling into the centre of each round. Brush the edges with water and bring together to seal, then crimp for a decorative finish.

3 Place the pasties on a baking tray and brush with beaten egg. Make a slit in the tops and bake for 10 minutes, then reduce the heat to 180°C (350°F/Gas 4) and cook for 25–30 minutes or until a thin knife comes out clean when inserted into the centre. Remove from the oven and serve the pasties hot or cold.

STORE The pasties will keep in the refrigerator for 2 days.

Empanadas

These bite-sized savoury pastries originated from Spain and Portugal, the name translating as "wrapped in bread". Perfect for a buffet or picnic, they can also be served as starters or canapés.

MAKES 24 | **45 MINS** | **40–50 MINS**

Chilling time
30 mins

Special equipment
9cm (3½in) round pastry cutter

Ingredients
450g (1lb) plain flour, plus extra for dusting
sea salt
85g (3oz) unsalted butter, diced
2 eggs, beaten, plus extra for glazing

For the filling
1 tbsp olive oil, plus extra for greasing
1 onion, finely chopped
120g can tomatoes, drained
2 tsp tomato purée
140g can tuna, drained
2 tbsp finely chopped parsley
freshly ground black pepper

Method
1 To make the pastry, sift the flour into a large mixing bowl with ½ teaspoon salt. Add the butter and rub in with your fingertips until it resembles fine crumbs. Add the beaten eggs with 4–6 tablespoons water and combine to form a dough. Wrap in cling film and chill for 30 minutes.

2 Meanwhile, heat the oil in a frying pan, add the onion, and fry over medium heat, stirring often, for 5–8 minutes or until translucent. Add the tomatoes, tomato purée, tuna, and parsley, and season to taste with salt and pepper. Reduce the heat and simmer for 10–12 minutes, stirring occasionally. Allow to cool completely.

3 Preheat the oven to 190°C (375°F/Gas 5). Roll out the pastry to a thickness of 3mm (⅛in). Cut out 24 rounds with the pastry cutter. Put 1 teaspoon of the filling on each, then brush the edges with water, fold over, and pinch together.

4 Place the empanadas on an oiled baking tray and brush with egg. Bake for 25–30 minutes or until golden brown. Serve warm.

STORE The empanadas will keep in the refrigerator for 2 days.

Forfar Bridie

These simple savoury pastries are a classic Scottish dish.

| MAKES 4 | 15 MINS | 20–25 MINS |

Chilling time
1 hr

Ingredients

150g (5½oz) lard, chilled and diced
200g (7oz) self-raising flour,
  plus extra for dusting
100g (3½oz) plain flour
½ tsp salt

For the filling

300g (10½oz) finely chopped beef skirt,
  or beef steak
1 onion, finely chopped
splash of Worcestershire sauce
sea salt and freshly ground black pepper
1 egg, beaten, for glazing

Method

1 For the pastry, rub the lard into the 2 types of flour until the mixture resembles crumbs. Add the salt and enough cold water to form a soft dough. Bring the dough together, wrap it in cling film, and chill for 1 hour. Preheat the oven to 200°C (400°F/Gas 6).

2 Mix the beef, onion, Worcestershire sauce, and seasoning together, then set aside. On a floured work surface, roll the pastry out to 5mm (¼in) thick. Using a side plate or saucer, cut 4 circles out of the pastry. You may need to re-roll the off cuts to get all 4. If the pastry cracks on rolling, gather it together and start again; the re-rolling will make it more robust. Fold the circles in half, trim the sides so that they are more rectangular in shape, then flatten them out again.

3 Pile one-quarter of the filling onto one-half of each pastry circle. Leave a 2cm (¾in) border. Brush the border with a little beaten egg. Now fold the pastry over and crimp the edges together. Brush the finished bridies with a little beaten egg, and cut a slit in the top of each one to allow the steam to escape.

4 Bake in the centre of the oven for 20–25 minutes until golden brown. Remove the bridies from the oven and allow them to cool for at least 10 minutes before eating.

STORE The bridies will keep in the refrigerator for 2 days.

BAKER'S TIP

This traditional Scottish pie is a close relation to the Cornish pasty, despite being from opposite ends of Britain. Here, a simple filling of chopped or minced steak and onions is cooked in a crumbly suet pastry. As there are very few ingredients, it is worth using the best meat possible; I prefer finely chopped beef skirt.

classic & artisan breads

Wholemeal Cottage Loaf

Stone-ground wholemeal flour can vary in its absorbency, and you may need more or less flour and water.

MAKES 2 LOAVES | 35–40 MINS | 40–45 MINS | UP TO 8 WEEKS

Rising and proving time
1¾–2¼ hrs

Ingredients
60g (2oz) unsalted butter, plus extra for greasing
3 tbsp honey
3 tsp dried yeast

1 tbsp salt
625g (1lb 6oz) stone-ground strong wholemeal bread flour
125g (4½oz) strong white bread flour, plus extra for dusting

1 Melt the butter. Mix 1 tablespoon of honey and 4 tablespoons lukewarm water in a bowl.

2 Sprinkle the yeast over the honey mixture. Leave it for 5 minutes to dissolve, stirring once.

3 Mix the butter, yeast, salt, remaining honey, and 400ml (14fl oz) lukewarm water.

4 Stir in half the wholemeal flour with the white flour, and mix it with your hands.

5 Add the remaining wholemeal flour, 125g (4½oz) at a time, mixing after each addition.

6 The dough should be soft and slightly sticky, and pull away from the sides of the bowl.

7 Turn the dough out onto a floured work surface, and sprinkle it with white flour.

8 Knead for 10 minutes until it is very smooth, elastic, and forms a ball.

9 Grease a large bowl with butter. Put in the dough and flip it to butter the surface lightly.

10 Cover with a damp tea towel. Leave it in a warm place for 1–1½ hours until doubled.

11 Grease a baking sheet. Place the dough on a floured work surface and knock out the air.

12 Cover and let it rest for 5 minutes. Cut it into 3 equal pieces, then cut 1 piece in half.

13 Cover 1 large and 1 small piece of dough with a tea towel, and shape the rest.

14 Shape 1 large piece into a loose ball. Fold in the sides, turn, and pinch to make a tight ball.

15 Flip the ball, seam side down, onto the prepared baking sheet.

16 Similarly, shape 1 small piece into a ball. Set it, seam side down, on top of the first ball.

17 Using your forefinger, press through the centre of the balls down to the baking sheet.

18 Repeat with the remaining 2 dough balls, to shape a second loaf.

19 Cover both loaves with tea towels. Leave in a warm place for 45 minutes or until doubled.

20 Preheat the oven to 190°C (375°F/Gas 5). Bake for 40–45 minutes until well browned.

21 The loaves should sound hollow when tapped on the base. Cool on a wire rack.

Classic Loaf variations

White Loaf

Mastering a classic white loaf should be a rite of passage for all amateur bakers. Nothing beats the taste of fresh, crusty white bread, still warm from the oven.

MAKES 1 LOAF | **20 MINS** | **40–45 MINS** | **UP TO 4 WEEKS**

Rising and proving time
2–3 hrs

Ingredients
500g (1lb 2oz) very strong white bread flour, plus extra for dusting
1 tsp fine salt
2 tsp dried yeast
1 tbsp sunflower oil, plus extra for greasing

Method
1 Put the flour and salt into a bowl. In a small bowl, dissolve the dried yeast in 300ml (10fl oz) warm water. Once it has dissolved, add the oil. Make a well in the centre of the flour. Pour in the liquid, stirring to form a rough dough. Use your hands to bring the dough together.

2 Turn the dough out onto a lightly floured work surface. Knead for 10 minutes until smooth, glossy, and elastic. Put the dough in a lightly oiled bowl, cover loosely with cling film and leave to rise in a warm place for up to 2 hours, until doubled in size.

3 When the dough has risen, turn it out onto a floured surface and knock it back to its original size. Knead it and shape it into the desired shape; I prefer a long, curved oblong shape known as a bloomer. Place the dough on a baking tray, cover it with cling film and a tea towel, and leave it in a warm place until well risen and doubled. This could take 30 minutes–1 hour. The bread is ready to bake when it is tight and well risen, and a finger poked into the dough leaves a dent which springs back quickly.

4 Preheat the oven to 220°C (425°F/Gas 7). Place one oven shelf in the middle of the oven, and one below it, close to the bottom of the oven. Boil a kettle. Now slash the top of the loaf 2 or 3 times with a knife on the diagonal. This will allow the bread to continue to rise in the oven. Dust the top with flour and place it on the middle shelf.

Place a roasting pan on the bottom shelf of the oven and then quickly pour the boiling water into it and shut the door. This will allow steam to be created in the oven and help the bread to rise.

5 Bake the bread for 10 minutes, then reduce to 190°C (375°F/Gas 5) and bake it for 30–35 minutes until the crust is golden brown and the bottom sounds hollow when tapped. Reduce to 180°C (350°F/Gas 4) if it is starting to brown too quickly. Remove the bread from the oven and leave to cool on a wire rack.

STORE Best eaten the day it is made, the loaf will store, wrapped in paper, in an airtight container overnight.

BAKER'S TIP
Tempting as it may be to taste the loaf as soon as it comes out of the oven, try to leave the bread to cool for at least 30 minutes before cutting. This will vastly improve the taste and texture of the finished loaf.

CLASSIC AND ARTISAN BREADS

Walnut and Rosemary Loaf

A perfect combination of flavours; the texture of the nuts is fabulous.

MAKES 2 LOAVES	20 MINS	30–40 MINS	UP TO 12 WEEKS

Proving time
2 hrs

Ingredients
3 tsp dried yeast
1 tsp granulated sugar
3 tbsp olive oil, plus 2 tsp extra for oiling and glazing
450g (1lb) strong white bread flour, plus extra for dusting
1 tsp salt
175g (6oz) walnuts, roughly chopped
3 tbsp finely chopped rosemary leaves

Method

1 Mix the yeast and sugar in a small bowl, then stir in 100ml (3½fl oz) lukewarm water. Leave for 10–15 minutes or until the mixture becomes creamy. Lightly oil a large bowl.

2 Put the flour in bowl with a pinch of salt and the olive oil, then add the yeast mixture and 200ml (7fl oz) lukewarm water. Mix the ingredients until they come together to form a dough. Knead the dough on a floured surface for 15 minutes. Knead in the walnuts and rosemary, then put the dough in the oiled bowl. Cover with a tea towel. Leave in a warm place for 1½ hours until doubled.

3 Knock the air out of the dough and knead for a few more minutes. Halve it, and shape each half into a 15cm (6in) round loaf. Cover with a towel and leave for 30 minutes to rise. Preheat the oven to 230°C (450°F/Gas 8) and oil a large baking sheet.

4 When the dough has doubled, brush with oil and place on the baking sheet. Bake on the middle shelf for 30–40 minutes until the loaves sound hollow when tapped on the base. Cool on a wire rack.

STORE Will keep for 1 day, wrapped in paper.

Pane di patate

Bread made with mashed potato has a soft crust and moist centre. In this recipe, the dough is coated in butter and baked in a ring mould.

MAKES 1 LOAF **50–55 MINS** **40–45 MINS** **UP TO 8 WEEKS**

Rising and proving time
1½–2¼ hrs

Special equipment
1.75-litre (3-pint) ring mould, or 25cm (10in) round cake tin and a 250ml (8fl oz) ramekin

Ingredients
250g (9oz) potatoes, peeled
  and cut into 2–3 pieces
2½ tsp dried yeast
125g (4½oz) unsalted butter,
  plus extra for greasing
1 large bunch of chives, snipped
2 tbsp sugar
2 tsp salt
425g (15oz) strong white bread flour,
  plus extra for dusting

Method

1 Place the potatoes in a saucepan with plenty of cold water. Bring to a boil and simmer until tender. Drain, reserving 250ml (8fl oz) of the liquid. Mash with a potato masher. Let them cool.

2 In a small bowl, sprinkle the yeast over 4 tablespoons lukewarm water. Leave for 5 minutes until dissolved, stirring once. Melt half the butter in a pan. Put the reserved liquid, mashed potato, dissolved yeast, and melted butter into a bowl. Add the chives, sugar, and salt, and mix together thoroughly.

3 Stir in half the flour and mix well. Add the remaining flour, 60g (2oz) at a time, mixing well after each addition, until the dough pulls away from the sides of the bowl. It should be soft and slightly sticky. Knead the dough on a floured work surface for 5–7 minutes until smooth and elastic.

4 Grease a large, clean bowl. Put the dough in the bowl, and flip it so the surface is lightly buttered. Cover with a damp tea towel and let the dough rise in a warm place for 1–1½ hours until doubled in size.

5 Grease the ring mould or cake tin. If using a tin, grease the outside of the ramekin and place it upside down in the centre. Melt the remaining butter. Turn the dough out onto a lightly floured work surface and knock back. Cover and let rest for 5 minutes. Flour your hands and pinch off walnut-sized pieces of dough, making about 30 pieces. Roll each piece of dough into a smooth ball.

6 Put a few balls into the dish of melted butter and turn them with a spoon until coated. Transfer the balls of dough to the prepared mould or tin. Repeat with the remaining dough. Cover with a dry tea towel, and let the loaf rise in a warm place for 40 minutes until the mould or tin is full.

7 Preheat the oven to 190°C (375°F/Gas 5). Bake the bread for 40–45 minutes until it is golden brown and starts to shrink away from the mould. Let it cool slightly on a wire rack, then carefully unmould. With your fingers, pull the bread apart while still warm.

STORE This bread is delicious still warm from the oven, but can be tightly wrapped in paper and kept for 2–3 days.

PREPARE AHEAD The dough can be made, kneaded, and left to rise in the refrigerator overnight. Shape the dough, let it come to room temperature, then bake as directed.

BAKER'S TIP
This is both a classic Italian and an American recipe, where it is known as "monkey bread". It is designed to be placed in the centre of the dinner table and for diners to pull apart the sections with their fingers – great for a large family gathering.

Dinner Rolls

You can shape the rolls however you like, though an assortment of different shapes looks very nice in a basket.

MAKES 16

45–55 MINS

15–18 MINS

8 WEEKS, UNBAKED

Rising and proving time
1½–2 hrs

Ingredients

150ml (5fl oz) milk
60g (2oz) unsalted butter, cubed,
  plus extra for greasing
2 tbsp sugar
3 tsp dried yeast
2 eggs, plus 1 yolk, for glazing
2 tsp salt

550g (1¼lb) strong white bread flour,
  plus extra for dusting
poppy seeds, for sprinkling (optional)

1 Bring the milk to a boil. Put 4 tablespoons into a small bowl and let cool to lukewarm.

2 Add the butter and sugar to the remaining milk in the pan until melted. Cool to lukewarm.

3 Sprinkle the yeast over the 4 tablespoons of milk. Leave for 5 minutes to dissolve. Stir once.

4 In a large bowl, lightly beat the eggs. Add the sweetened milk, salt, and dissolved yeast.

5 Gradually stir in the flour until the dough forms a ball. It should be soft and slightly sticky.

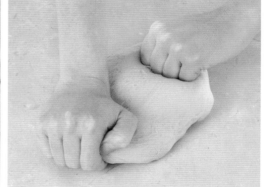

6 Knead the dough on a floured work surface for 5–7 minutes until very smooth and elastic.

7 Put in an oiled bowl. Cover with cling film. Put in a warm place for 1–1½ hours until doubled.

8 Grease 2 baking sheets. Put the dough on a floured work surface and knock it back.

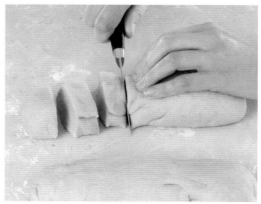

9 Cut in half, and roll each piece into a cylinder. Cut each cylinder into 8 equal pieces.

10 To shape round rolls, roll the dough in a circular motion so it forms a smooth ball.

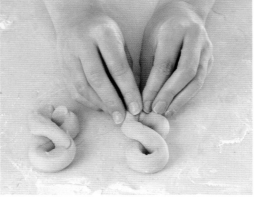

11 For a baker's knot, roll into a rope, shape into an 8, and tuck the ends through the holes.

12 For a snail, roll into a long rope and wind it around in a spiral, tucking the end underneath.

13 Put on the baking sheets. Cover with a tea towel. Leave in a warm place for 30 minutes.

14 Preheat the oven to 220°C (425°F/Gas 7). Beat the egg yolk with a tablespoon of water.

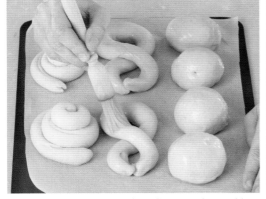

15 Brush the rolls with the glaze and sprinkle evenly with poppy seeds (if using).

16 Bake for 15–18 minutes until golden brown. Serve warm. **PREPARE AHEAD** These rolls can be frozen at the shaping stage, brought back to room temperature, then glazed and baked.

Bread Roll variations

Spiced Cranberry and Pecan Rolls

These sweetened, fragrant rolls were adapted from a basic white bread recipe. Try adapting your own dough with different combinations of dried fruit, nuts, seeds, and spices.

MAKES 8 ROLLS | **20 MINS** | **20–25 MINS** | **UP TO 4 WEEKS**

Rising and proving time
2–3 hrs

Ingredients
500g (1lb 2oz) very strong white bread flour, plus extra for dusting
1 tsp fine salt
1 tsp mixed spice
2 tbsp caster sugar
2 tsp dried yeast
150ml (5fl oz) whole milk
50g (1¾oz) dried cranberries, roughly chopped
50g (1¾oz) pecans, roughly chopped
1 tbsp sunflower oil, plus extra for greasing
1 egg, beaten, for glazing

Method

1 Put the flour, salt, mixed spice, and sugar into a large bowl. Dissolve the yeast in 150ml (5fl oz) warm water. Once it has dissolved, add the milk and oil. Pour the liquid into the flour mixture, stirring it together to form a rough dough. Use your hands to bring the dough together.

2 Turn the dough out onto a lightly floured work surface. Knead the dough for 10 minutes, until it becomes smooth, glossy, and elastic.

3 Stretch the dough out thinly, scatter the cranberries and pecans over the surface and knead for 1–2 minutes more until the added ingredients are well incorporated. Put the dough in an oiled bowl, cover with cling film, and leave to rise in a warm place for up to 2 hours until doubled.

4 Turn the dough out onto a floured work surface and gently knock it back. Knead it briefly and divide it into 8 equal-sized pieces. Shape each into a plump, round roll. Try and poke any bits of fruit or nut that are sticking out back into the rolls, as these may burn on baking.

5 Place the rolls onto a large baking tray, cover loosely with cling film and a clean tea towel, and leave them to rise in a warm place for 1 hour until almost doubled in size. Preheat the oven to 200°C (400°F/Gas 6). Gently slash the top of the rolls in the shape of a cross with a sharp knife. This will allow the rolls to continue to rise in the oven. Lightly brush the tops with beaten egg and place them on the middle shelf of the oven.

6 Bake for 20–25 minutes until golden brown and the bottoms sound hollow when tapped. Remove the rolls from the oven and leave to cool on a wire rack.

STORE These are best eaten the day they are made, but will store, well wrapped in paper, in an airtight container overnight.

BAKER'S TIP
These are a delightful alternative to plain rolls, great for breakfast. Try making double quantity White Loaf dough (see page 402) and using half of it to make these rolls. They are especially welcome on Christmas morning, with the festive colours of the cranberries and warming fragrance of spices.

Sesame Seed Buns

These soft bread rolls are very easy to make and great for picnics or packed lunches, or for sandwiching home-made burgers at a summer barbecue.

MAKES 8 BUNS | **30 MINS** | **20 MINS**

Rising and proving time
1½ hrs

Ingredients
450g (1lb) strong white bread flour, plus extra for dusting
1 tsp salt
1 tsp dried yeast
1 tbsp vegetable oil, sunflower oil, or light olive oil, plus extra for greasing
1 egg, beaten
4 tbsp sesame seeds

Method

1 Stir the flour and salt together in a bowl, then make a well in the middle. Dissolve the yeast in 360ml (12fl oz) warm water, then add the oil. Tip this liquid into the well and quickly stir together. Leave for 10 minutes.

2 Turn the dough out onto a floured surface. Knead for 5 minutes or until smooth. Shape into a ball by bringing the edges into the middle, then turn into a oiled bowl, smooth side up. Cover with oiled cling film and leave in a warm place for 1 hour or until doubled.

3 Meanwhile, dust a baking tray with flour. Scoop the dough onto a floured surface, dust with a little flour, then knead briefly. Pull the dough into 8 even-sized pieces, then shape into rounds. Place onto the floured baking tray, well spaced apart, then leave for 30 minutes or until larger and pillowy. Preheat the oven to 200°C (400°F/Gas 6).

4 Once risen, brush the buns with egg and sprinkle sesame seeds over each. Bake for 20 minutes or until golden, risen, and round. Cool on a wire rack.

STORE These are best eaten the day they are made, but will store, well wrapped in paper, in an airtight container overnight.

Wholemeal Fennel Seed Rolls

Fennel seeds and cracked black pepper make these savoury rolls perfect for smoked ham sandwiches, or as buns for chorizo or pork burgers. Try experimenting with different whole spices, such as caraway or cumin.

MAKES 6 ROLLS | **20 MINS** | **25–35 MINS** | **UP TO 12 WEEKS**

Rising and proving time
2 hrs

Ingredients
2 tsp dried yeast
1 tsp demerara sugar
450g (1lb) plain wholemeal flour, plus extra for dusting
1½ tsp fine salt
2 tsp fennel seeds
1 tsp black peppercorns, cracked
olive oil, for greasing
1 tsp sesame seeds (optional)

Method

1 Sprinkle the yeast into a small bowl, add the sugar, and mix in 150ml (5fl oz) lukewarm water. Leave for about 15 minutes for the mixture to become creamy and frothy.

2 Mix the flour with a pinch of salt in a bowl, then add the yeast mixture, and gradually add a further 150ml (5fl oz) of lukewarm water. Mix until it comes together (it may need a little more water if it is too dry). Transfer to a lightly floured board and knead for about 10–15 minutes until smooth and elastic, then knead in the fennel seeds and cracked black pepper.

3 Lightly grease a bowl with olive oil. Sit the dough in the prepared bowl, cover with a tea towel, and leave somewhere warm for 1½ hours until doubled in size.

4 Knock back the dough and knead for a few more minutes, then divide into 6 pieces and shape each into a roll. Place them on an oiled baking sheet, cover, and leave to rise again for about 30 minutes. Preheat the oven to 200°C (400°F/Gas 6).

5 Brush the rolls with a little water, then sprinkle with sesame seeds (if using) and bake for about 25–35 minutes until the rolls are golden and sound hollow when tapped on the base. Allow to cool on the baking sheet for a few minutes, then transfer to a wire rack to cool completely.

STORE These are best eaten the day they are made, but will store, well wrapped in paper, in an airtight container overnight.

Pão de queijo

These unusual miniature cheese rolls, crisp on the outside and chewy on the inside, are a popular Brazilian street food.

MAKES 16 | 10 MINS | 30 MINS | 8 WEEKS, UNBAKED

Special equipment
food processor with blade attachment

Ingredients
125ml (4fl oz) milk
3–4 tbsp sunflower oil
1 tsp salt
250g (9oz) tapioca (manioc or cassava) flour, plus extra for dusting
2 eggs, beaten, plus extra for glazing
125g (4½oz) Parmesan cheese, grated

Method

1 Put the milk, sunflower oil, 125ml (4fl oz) water, and salt in a small saucepan and bring it to a boil. Put the flour into a large bowl and quickly mix in the hot liquid. The mixture will be very claggy and stuck together. Set aside to cool.

2 Preheat the oven to 190°C (375°F/Gas 5). Once the tapioca mixture has cooled, put it into a food processor. Add the eggs and process until all the lumps disappear, and it resembles a thick, smooth paste. Add the cheese and process together until the mixture is sticky and elastic.

3 Turn the mixture out onto a well-floured work surface and knead for 2–3 minutes until it is smooth and pliable. Divide the mixture into 16 equal pieces. Roll each piece into golf ball-sized balls and place, spaced apart, on a baking sheet lined with baking parchment.

4 Brush the balls with a little beaten egg and bake in the middle of the oven for 30 minutes, until well risen and golden brown. Remove them from the oven and let them cool for a few minutes before eating. These are best eaten the same day they are made, preferably still warm from the oven.

PREPARE AHEAD These can be open frozen on the baking sheet at the end of step 3 and transferred to freezer bags. Simply defrost for 30 minutes and bake as usual.

BAKER'S TIP
These classic Brazilian cheese rolls are made from tapioca flour (also known as manioc or cassava flour), and are thus wheat-free. The flour clumps when mixed with the liquid at first, but the use of a food processor will help enormously here. You will find that it soon becomes a smooth mass.

Seeded Rye Bread

A crusty loaf accented by aromatic caraway seeds. Low-gluten rye is mixed with white flour to lighten it.

MAKES 1 LOAF | **35–40 MINS** | **50–55 MINS** | **UP TO 8 WEEKS**

Rising and proving time
2¼–2¾ hrs

Ingredients

2½ tsp dried yeast, dissolved in 4 tbsp lukewarm water
1 tbsp black treacle
1 tbsp caraway seeds
2 tsp salt
1 tbsp vegetable oil, plus extra for greasing
250ml (8fl oz) lager

250g (9oz) rye flour
175g (6oz) very strong white bread flour, plus extra for dusting
polenta (fine yellow cornmeal), for dusting
1 egg white, beaten until frothy, for glazing

1 Put the dissolved yeast, treacle, two-thirds of the caraway seeds, salt, and oil into a bowl.

2 Pour in the lager. Stir in the rye flour, and mix together well with your hands.

3 Gradually add the strong white flour until it forms a soft, slightly sticky dough.

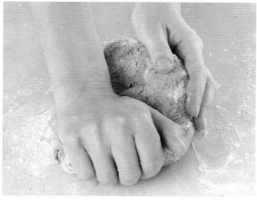

4 Knead for 8–10 minutes until the dough is smooth and elastic, and put in an oiled bowl.

5 Cover with a damp tea towel. Leave in a warm place for 1½–2 hours until doubled.

6 Sprinkle a baking sheet with polenta. Knock back the dough on a floured work surface.

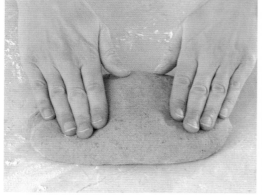

7 Cover and let it rest for 5 minutes. Pat the dough into an oval, about 25cm (10in) long.

8 Roll it back and forth on the work surface, exerting pressure on the ends to taper them.

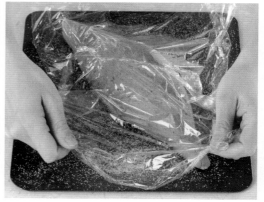

9 Transfer to the baking sheet. Cover and leave in a warm place for 45 minutes until doubled.

10 Preheat the oven to 190°C (375°F/Gas 5). Brush the beaten egg over the loaf to glaze.

11 Sprinkle with the remaining caraway seeds, and press them into the dough.

12 With a sharp knife, make 3 diagonal slashes, about 5mm (¼in) deep, on top.

13 Bake for 50–55 minutes until well browned. The bread should sound hollow when tapped on the base. Transfer to a wire rack and cool completely. **STORE** This loaf will keep, tightly wrapped in paper, for 2 days.

Rye Bread variations

Apricot and Pumpkin Seed Rolls

Rye flour is very dense, so mix it with white flour for a lighter texture.

MAKES 8 ROLLS	20 MINS	30 MINS	UP TO 4 WEEKS

Rising and proving time
up to 4 hrs

Ingredients
25g (scant 1oz) pumpkin seeds
2½ tsp dried yeast
1 tbsp black treacle
1 tbsp sunflower oil, plus extra for greasing
250g (9oz) rye flour
250g (9oz) very strong white bread flour, plus extra for dusting
1 tsp fine salt
50g (1¾oz) dried apricots, roughly chopped
1 egg, beaten, for glazing

Method
1 Toast the pumpkin seeds by dry-frying in a pan for 2–3 minutes, watching carefully to prevent them burning. Dissolve the dried yeast in 300ml (10fl oz) warm water. Add the treacle and oil and whisk to dissolve the treacle evenly. Put the 2 types of flour and the salt into a large bowl.

2 Pour the liquid into the flour mixture, stirring to form a rough dough. Turn the dough out on to a lightly floured work surface. Knead the dough for up to 10 minutes until smooth, glossy, and elastic.

3 Stretch the dough out thinly, scatter the apricots and pumpkin seeds over the surface, and knead for 1–2 minutes more until the added ingredients are well incorporated. Put into a oiled bowl, cover with cling film, and leave to rise in a warm place for up to 2 hours until well risen. This dough will not double in size as rye flour is very low in gluten, and rises slowly.

4 Turn it out on to a lightly floured work surface and gently knock it back. Knead it briefly and divide it into 8 equal-sized

pieces. Shape each into a plump, round roll. Try and poke any bits of fruit or seed that are sticking out back into the rolls, as these may burn on baking.

5 Place the rolls on a baking tray, cover with cling film and a tea towel, and leave them to prove in a warm place until well risen. This could take up to 2 hours. The rolls are ready to bake when they are tight and well risen, and a finger gently poked into the dough leaves a dent which springs back quickly.

6 Preheat the oven to 190°C (375°F/Gas 5). Brush the rolls with beaten egg and bake in the middle of the oven for 30 minutes until golden brown and the bottoms sound hollow when tapped. Remove the rolls from the oven and leave to cool on a wire rack.

STORE These are best eaten the same day, but will store overnight, well wrapped.

ALSO TRY...
Walnut Rye Bread Toast 75g (2½oz) walnuts by dry frying in a pan for 3–4 minutes. Rub in a clean tea towel to remove excess skin and roughly chop, then scatter the nuts over the thinly stretched dough, instead of the apricots and pumpkins. Once risen, shape into a single ball-shaped loaf by tucking the sides under the centre of the dough to get a tight, even shape, leaving the seam at the base; this is known as a boule. After it has risen a second time, bake for 45 minutes.

BAKER'S TIP
Here I have used apricot and pumpkin seeds, but dried cranberries, raisins, or blueberries would all work well too. As an alternative, you could also try other seeds, such as sesame or poppy seeds.

Pesto-filled Garland Bread

A loaf lightly flavoured with rye and spread with fragrant home-made pesto, this bread is perfect for serving at a buffet lunch or taking on a picnic, as the slices can be pulled off in individual portions. It also looks amazing!

MAKES 1 LOAF   **35–40 MINS**   **30–35 MINS**

Rising and proving time
1¾–2¼ hrs

Special equipment
food processor with blade attachment

Ingredients
2½ tsp dried yeast
125g (4½oz) rye flour
300g (10½oz) very strong white bread flour,
  plus extra for dusting
2 tsp salt
3 tbsp extra virgin olive oil,
  plus extra for greasing and glazing
leaves from 1 large bunch of basil
3 garlic cloves, peeled
30g (1oz) pine nuts, coarsely chopped
60g (2oz) freshly grated Parmesan cheese
freshly ground black pepper

Method
1 In a small bowl, sprinkle the yeast over 4 tablespoons taken from 300ml (10fl oz) lukewarm water. Let stand for about 5 minutes until dissolved, stirring once. Put the rye and white flour in a bowl along with the salt, and make a well. Combine the dissolved yeast and remaining water, pour into the well, and gradually draw in the flour. Mix well until it forms a soft, sticky dough.

2 Turn out the dough onto a floured surface and knead for 5 minutes until very smooth and elastic. Shape into a ball. Place in an oiled bowl. Cover with a damp tea towel and let rise in a warm place for 1–1½ hours until doubled in bulk.

3 Pulse the basil and garlic in the food processor with the garlic. Work until coarsely chopped. With the blades turning, gradually add 3 tablespoons oil until smooth. Transfer the pesto to a bowl and stir in the pine nuts, Parmesan, and plenty of black pepper.

4 Brush a baking sheet with oil. Place the dough onto a floured surface and knead to knock out the air. Cover and let rest for about 5 minutes. Flatten the dough, then roll it into a 40 x 30cm (16 x 12in) rectangle with a rolling pin. Spread the pesto evenly over the dough, leaving a 1cm (½in) border. Starting with a long end, roll up the rectangle into an even cylinder. Running the length of the cylinder, pinch the seam firmly together. Do not seal the ends.

5 Transfer the cylinder, seam-side down, to the prepared baking sheet. Curve it into a ring, overlapping and sealing the ends. With a sharp knife, make a series of deep cuts around the ring, about 5cm (2in) apart. Pull the slices apart slightly, and twist them over to lie flat. Cover with a dry tea towel, and let rise in a warm place for about 45 minutes until doubled in bulk.

6 Preheat the oven to 220°C (425°F/Gas 7). Brush the loaf with oil and bake for 10 minutes. Reduce to 190°C (375°F/Gas 5), and bake for 20–25 minutes until golden. Cool slightly on a wire rack. Serve the same day.

Multi-grain Breakfast Bread

This hearty bread combines rolled oats, wheat bran, polenta, wholemeal and strong white flours, with sunflower seeds for added crunch.

MAKES 2 LOAVES   **45–50 MINS**   **40–45 MINS**   **UP TO 8 WEEKS**

Rising and proving time
2½–3 hrs

Ingredients
75g (2½oz) sunflower seeds
425ml (14½fl oz) buttermilk
2½ tsp dried yeast
45g (1½oz) rolled oats
45g (1½oz) wheat bran
75g (2½oz) polenta or fine yellow cornmeal,
  plus extra for dusting
45g (1½oz) soft brown sugar
1 tbsp salt
250g (9oz) strong wholemeal bread flour
250g (9oz) strong white bread flour,
  plus extra for dusting
unsalted butter, for greasing
1 egg white, beaten, for glazing

Method

1 Preheat the oven to 180°C (350°F/Gas 4). Spread the seeds on a baking sheet and toast in the oven until lightly browned. Let cool, then coarsely chop.

2 Pour the buttermilk into a saucepan and heat until just lukewarm. Sprinkle the yeast over 4 tablespoons lukewarm water. Set aside for 2 minutes, stir gently, then leave for 2–3 minutes until completely dissolved.

3 Put the sunflower seeds, rolled oats, wheat bran, polenta, brown sugar, and salt in a large bowl. Add the dissolved yeast and buttermilk, and mix together. Stir in the wholemeal flour with half the strong white flour, and mix well.

4 Add the remaining strong white flour, 60g (2oz) at a time, mixing well after each addition, until the dough pulls away from the sides of the bowl in a ball. It should be soft and slightly sticky. Turn the dough out onto a floured work surface and knead for 8–10 minutes until it is very smooth, elastic, and forms into a ball.

5 Grease a large bowl with butter. Put the dough in the bowl, and flip it so the surface is lightly buttered. Cover with a damp tea towel and leave to rise in a warm place for 1½–2 hours until doubled in size.

6 Sprinkle 2 baking sheets with polenta. Turn the dough out onto a lightly floured work surface and knock back. Cover, and let it rest for 5 minutes. With a sharp knife, cut the dough in half. Shape each half into a thin oval. Cover with a dry tea towel and leave to rise in a warm place for 1 hour or until doubled in size again.

7 Preheat the oven to 190°C (375°F/Gas 5). Brush the loaves with egg white, and bake for 40–45 minutes until the base of the loaves sound hollow when tapped. Transfer the loaves to a wire rack to cool completely.

STORE This bread is best on the day of baking, but can be tightly wrapped in paper and kept for 2–3 days.

BAKER'S TIP
Buttermilk is a great ingredient for bakers. Try adding it to any baking recipe that calls for milk. Its mild acidity brings a slight tang of sourness, while its active ingredients will lighten and soften the texture of many baked goods. You can find it in most supermarkets.

Anadama Cornbread

This dark, sweet cornbread originally hails from New England. It is curiously sweet and savoury at the same time, and keeps very well.

MAKES 1 LOAF	25 MINS	45–50 MINS	UP TO 8 WEEKS

Rising and proving time
4 hrs

Ingredients
125ml (4fl oz) milk
75g (2½oz) polenta or fine yellow cornmeal
50g (1¾oz) unsalted butter, softened
100g (3½oz) black treacle
2 tsp dried yeast
450g (1lb) plain flour, plus extra for dusting
1 tsp salt
vegetable oil, for greasing
1 egg, beaten, for glazing

Method

1 Heat the milk and 125ml (4fl oz) water in a small saucepan. Bring to a boil and add the cornmeal. Cook for 1–2 minutes or until it thickens, then remove from the heat. Add the butter and stir until it is well mixed. Beat in the treacle, then set aside to cool.

2 Dissolve the yeast in 100ml (3½fl oz) warm water and stir well. Put the flour and salt into a bowl and make a well. Gradually stir in the cornmeal mixture, then add the yeast mixture to make a soft, sticky dough.

3 Turn the dough out onto a lightly floured work surface. Knead for about 10 minutes until soft and elastic. It will remain fairly sticky, but should not stick to your hands. Knead in a little flour if it seems too wet. Put the dough in a lightly oiled bowl, cover loosely with cling film, and leave to rise in a warm place for up to 2 hours. The dough will not double in size, but should be very soft and pliable when well risen.

4 Turn the dough out onto a lightly floured work surface and gently knock it back. Knead it briefly and shape it into a flattened oval, tucking the sides underneath the centre of the dough to get a tight, even shape. Place on a large baking tray, and cover loosely with cling film and a clean tea towel. Leave it to rise in a warm place for about 2 hours. The dough is ready to bake when it is tight and well risen, and a finger gently poked into the dough leaves a dent that springs back quickly.

5 Preheat the oven to 180°C (350°F/Gas 4). Place one oven shelf in the middle of the oven, and one below it, close to the bottom. Boil a kettle of water. Brush the loaf with a little beaten egg, and slash the top 2–3 times with a sharp knife on the diagonal. Dust the top with a little flour, if desired, and place it on the middle shelf. Place a roasting pan on the bottom shelf, then quickly pour the boiling water into it and shut the door.

6 Bake for 45–50 minutes until the crust is nicely darkened and the bottom sounds hollow when tapped. Remove from the oven and leave to cool on a wire rack.

STORE The bread will keep, well wrapped in paper, in an airtight container for 5 days.

BAKER'S TIP
Slashing the loaf allows the bread to continue rising in the oven, as does the steam from the pan of boiling water, which also helps to give the bread a good crust. Anadama tastes wonderful with Emmental or Gruyère, or simply buttered and topped with some good ham and a little mustard.

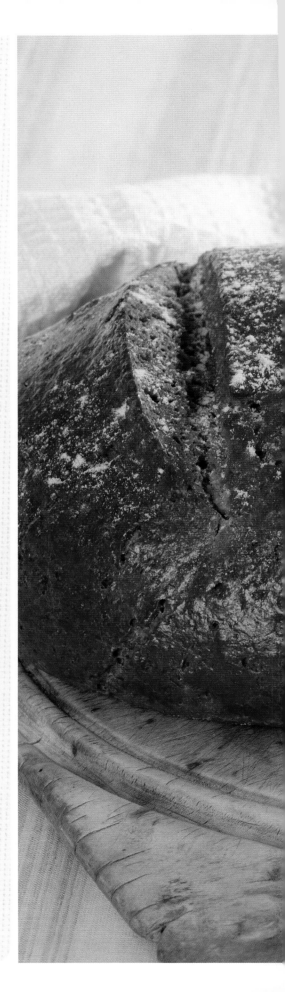

Rosemary Focaccia

A good-tempered dough that can be left in the refrigerator to rise overnight. Bring back to room temperature to bake.

SERVES 6–8 | **30–35 MINS** | **15–20 MINS**

Rising and proving time
1½–2¼ hrs

Special equipment
38 x 23cm (15 x 9in) Swiss roll tin

Ingredients
1 tbsp dried yeast
425g (15oz) strong white bread flour, plus extra for dusting
2 tsp salt
leaves from 5–7 rosemary sprigs, two-thirds finely chopped
90ml (3fl oz) olive oil, plus extra for greasing
¼ tsp freshly ground black pepper
sea salt flakes

1 Sprinkle the yeast over 4 tablespoons of warm water. Leave for 5 minutes, stirring once.

2 In a large bowl, mix the flour with the salt and make a well in the centre.

3 Add the rosemary, 4 tablespoons oil, yeast, pepper, and 240ml (8fl oz) lukewarm water.

4 Gradually draw in the flour and work it into the other ingredients to form a smooth dough.

5 The dough should be soft and sticky. Do not be tempted to add more flour to dry it out.

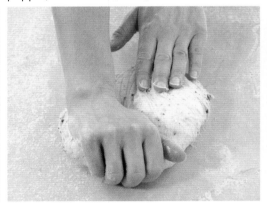

6 Sprinkle the dough with flour and knead for 5–7 minutes on a floured work surface.

7 When ready, the dough will be very smooth and elastic. Place in an oiled bowl.

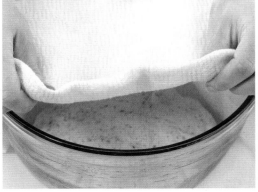

8 Cover with a damp tea towel. Leave to rise in a warm place for 1–1½ hours until doubled.

9 Put the dough on a floured work surface and knock out the air.

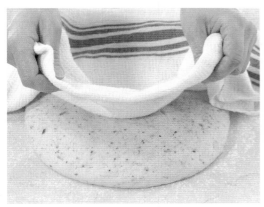

10 Cover with a dry tea towel and let it rest for about 5 minutes. Brush the tin with oil.

11 Transfer the dough to the tin. With your hands, flatten the dough to fill the tin evenly.

12 Cover with a tea towel and leave to rise in a warm place for 35–45 minutes until puffed.

13 Preheat the oven to 200°C (400°F/Gas 6). Scatter the reserved rosemary leaves on top.

14 With your fingertips, poke the dough all over to make deep dimples.

15 Pour spoonfuls of the remaining oil all over the dough and sprinkle with the salt flakes.

16 Bake in the top shelf for 15–20 minutes until browned. Transfer to a wire rack. **ALSO TRY...**
Sage Focaccia Omit rosemary and black pepper at step 3. Add 3–5 sage sprigs, chopped.

Focaccia variations

Blackberry Focaccia

A sweet twist on a classic bread, perfect for a late summer picnic.

SERVES 6–8 | 30–35 MINS | 15–20 MINS

Rising and proving time
1½–2¼ hrs

Special equipment
38 x 23cm (15 x 9in) Swiss roll tin

Ingredients
1 tbsp dried yeast
425g (15oz) strong white bread flour,
  plus extra for dusting
1 tsp salt
3 tbsp caster sugar
90ml (3fl oz) extra virgin olive oil,
  plus extra for greasing
300g (10½oz) blackberries

Method

1 In a small bowl, sprinkle the yeast over 4 tablespoons lukewarm water. Let stand for 5 minutes until dissolved, stirring once.

2 In a large bowl, mix the flour with the salt and 2 tablespoons of the sugar. Make a well in the centre and add the dissolved yeast, 4 tablespoons of the oil, and 240ml (8fl oz) lukewarm water. Draw in the flour and mix to form a smooth dough. The dough should be soft and sticky; avoid adding more flour to dry it out.

3 Flour your hands and the dough, and turn it out onto a floured surface. Knead for 5–7 minutes until smooth and elastic. Transfer to an oiled bowl and cover with a damp tea towel. Leave to rise in a warm place for about 1–1½ hours until doubled in bulk.

4 Generously brush the tin with olive oil. Turn out the dough and knock out the air. Cover with a dry tea towel and leave to rest for 5 minutes. Transfer to the tin, flattening with your hands to fill the tin. Scatter the blackberries over the surface of the dough, cover, and leave to prove in a warm place for 35–45 minutes until puffed.

5 Preheat the oven to 200°C (400°F/Gas 6). Brush the dough with the remaining oil and sprinkle over the rest of the sugar. Bake at the top of the oven for 15–20 minutes until lightly browned. Cool slightly on a wire rack, then serve warm.

PREPARE AHEAD After kneading, at the end of step 3, the dough can be loosely covered with cling film and left to rise in the refrigerator overnight.

Fougasse

Fougasse is the French equivalent of the Italian focaccia, most associated with the region of Provence. The traditional leaf effect is surprisingly easy to achieve and looks lovely.

MAKES 3 LOAVES · **30–35 MINS** · **15 MINS**

Rising and proving time
6 hrs

Ingredients
5 tbsp extra virgin olive oil, plus extra for greasing
1 onion, finely chopped
2 back bacon rashers, finely chopped
400g (14oz) strong white bread flour, plus extra for dusting
1½ tsp dried yeast
1 tsp salt
sea salt flakes, for sprinkling

Method

1 Heat 1 tablespoon of the oil in a frying pan. Fry the onion and bacon until browned. Remove from the pan and set aside.

2 In a small bowl, add 150ml (5fl oz) warm water and sprinkle over the yeast. Leave to dissolve, stirring once. Place 200g (7oz) flour in a bowl, make a well in the middle, pour the yeast mixture into the well and draw in the flour to form a dough. Cover and leave to rise and then fall again, for about 4 hours.

3 Add the remaining flour, 150ml (5fl oz) water, salt, and the remaining oil, and mix well. Knead to a smooth dough on a lightly floured surface. Return to the bowl to rise for 1 hour or until doubled in size.

4 Line 3 baking sheets with parchment. Punch down the dough, then tip on the onion and bacon. Knead and divide the dough into 3 balls. Flatten each ball to 2.5cm (1in) high with a rolling pin, shape into a circle, and place on the baking sheets.

5 To create the leaf shapes, cut each circle with a sharp knife, twice down the centre, then 3 times on either side on a slant. Cut all the way through the thickness of the dough, but not through the edges. Brush with olive oil, sprinkle with sea salt, and leave to rise for 1 hour or until doubled.

6 Preheat the oven to 230°C (450°F/Gas 8). Bake for 15 minutes until golden. Remove from the oven and cool before serving.

Ciabatta

One of the simplest breads to master, a good ciabatta should be well risen and crusty, with large air pockets.

MAKES 2 LOAVES | **30 MINS** | **30 MINS** | **UP TO 8 WEEKS**

Rising and proving time
3 hrs

Ingredients
2 tsp dried yeast
2 tbsp olive oil,
 plus extra for greasing
450g (1lb) strong white bread flour,
 plus extra for dusting
1 tsp sea salt

1 Dissolve the yeast in 350ml (11½fl oz) warm water, then add the oil.

2 Put the flour and salt in a bowl. Make a well, pour in the yeast, and stir to form a soft dough.

3 Knead on a floured surface for 10 minutes until smooth, soft, and somewhat slippery.

4 Put the dough in a lightly oiled bowl and cover loosely with cling film.

5 Leave to rise in a warm place for 2 hours until doubled. Turn out onto a floured surface.

6 Gently knock back the dough with your fists, then divide it into 2 equal pieces.

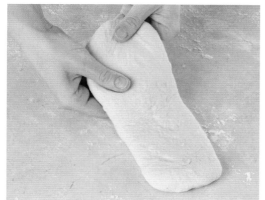

7 Knead them briefly and shape into traditional slipper shapes, around 30 x 10cm (12 x 4in).

8 Place each loaf on a lined baking sheet, with enough space around to allow it to expand.

9 Cover loosely with cling film and a tea towel. Leave for 1 more hour until doubled in size.

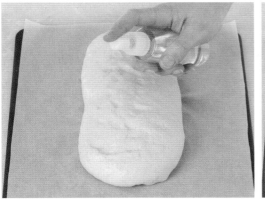

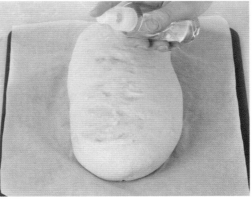

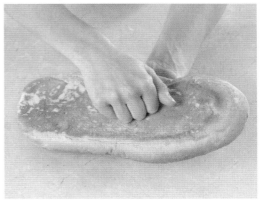

10 Preheat the oven to 230°C (450°F/Gas 8). Spray the loaves with a fine mist of water.

11 Bake on the middle shelf for 30 minutes, spraying them with water every 10 minutes.

12 It is cooked when the top is golden brown and the base sounds hollow when tapped.

13 When cooked, turn the loaves out onto a wire rack to cool for at least 30 minutes before cutting. **STORE** These are best eaten the same day, but can be stored overnight, wrapped in paper.

Ciabatta variations

Green Olive and Rosemary Ciabatta

Green olives and rosemary make a vibrant alternative to plain ciabatta.

MAKES 2 LOAVES | 40 MINS | 30 MINS | UP TO 8 WEEKS

Rising and proving time
3 hrs

Ingredients
1 quantity ciabatta dough,
 see page 424, steps 1–3
100g (3½oz) stoned green olives, drained,
 roughly chopped, and dried with kitchen paper
2 good sprigs of rosemary, leaves only,
 roughly chopped

Method

1 Once the dough has been kneaded for 10 minutes, stretch it out thinly on the work surface, scatter evenly with the olives and rosemary, and bring the sides together to cover the ingredients. Knead the dough until well incorporated. Put it in an oiled bowl, cover with cling film and leave to rise in a warm place for up to 2 hours until doubled.

2 Turn the dough out onto a floured work surface and knock it back. Divide it into 2 equal pieces. Knead the pieces and shape them into traditional slipper shapes, each 30 x 10cm (12 x 4in). Place each loaf on a lined baking sheet, with enough space around it to allow it to expand as it proves. Cover with cling film and a tea towel and leave for 1 hour until doubled in volume.

3 Preheat the oven to 230°C (450°F/Gas 8). Spray the loaves with a fine mist of water and bake in the centre of the oven for 30 minutes until golden brown; spray the loaves with water every 10 minutes. The bread is cooked when the underneath sounds hollow when tapped. Cool on a wire rack for 30 minutes before cutting.

STORE These are best eaten the same day. Can be stored overnight, loosely wrapped.

Ciabatta Crostini

Don't waste day-old ciabatta – slice it and bake the slices to make crostini, which will keep for days and can be used for snacks, canapés, or croutons. ▶

MAKES 25–30 | 15 MINS | 10 MINS

Ingredients
1 loaf day-old ciabatta bread,
 see pages 424–425
olive oil

For the toppings
100g (3½oz) rocket pesto, or
100g (3½oz) roasted red peppers, sliced
 and mixed with chopped basil, or
100g (3½oz) black olive tapenade topped
 with 100g (3½oz) goat's cheese

Method

1 Preheat the oven to 220°C (425°F/Gas 7). Slice the ciabatta into 1cm (½in) slices. Brush the tops with olive oil.

2 Bake them on the top shelf for 10 minutes, turning them after 5 minutes. Remove from the oven and cool on a wire rack.

3 Once cooled, top with any of the 3 suggested toppings, just before serving. If using the tapenade and goat's cheese topping, briefly grill before serving.

STORE The baked, unadorned crostini can be stored in an airtight container for 3 days. Add the topping just before serving.

Black Olive and Peppadew Ciabatta

Try using black olives and Peppadew peppers for a delicious ciabatta loaf studded with red and black. **PICTURED OVERLEAF**

MAKES 2 LOAVES | 40 MINS | 30 MINS | UP TO 8 WEEKS

Rising and proving time
3 hrs

Ingredients
1 quantity ciabatta dough,
 see page 424, steps 1–3
50g (1¾oz) stoned black olives, drained, roughly
 chopped, and dried with kitchen paper
50g (1¾oz) Peppadew red peppers, drained,
 roughly chopped, and dried with kitchen paper

Method

1 Once the dough has been kneaded for 10 minutes, stretch it out thinly on the work surface, scatter with the olives and peppers, and bring the sides together to cover the ingredients. Knead the dough briefly until they are incorporated. Put the dough in an oiled bowl, cover loosely with cling film and leave to rise in a warm place for up to 2 hours until doubled in size.

2 Turn the dough out onto a floured work surface and knock it back. Divide it into 2 pieces. Knead the pieces and shape them into 2 traditional slipper shapes, each 30 x 10cm (12 x 4in). Place each loaf on a lined baking sheet. Cover with cling film and a tea towel and leave for 1 hour until doubled.

3 Preheat the oven to 230°C (450°F/Gas 8). Spray the loaves with a mist of water and bake in the centre of the oven for 30 minutes until golden brown; spray the loaves with water every 10 minutes. The bread is cooked when the base sounds hollow when tapped. Cool for 30 minutes before cutting.

STORE Can be stored, wrapped, overnight.

BAKER'S TIP
Ciabatta dough should be wet and loose on kneading, as this will help to create the large air pockets traditionally found in the finished loaf. Wet doughs are easier to knead in a machine fitted with a dough hook, as they are a little sticky to manage well with your hands.

Grissini

Tradition has it that breadsticks should be pulled the length of the baker's arm – these are more manageable!

MAKES 32 | **40–45 MINS** | **15–18 MINS**

Rising time
1–1½ hrs

Ingredients
2½ tsp dried yeast
425g (15oz) strong white bread flour,
  plus extra for dusting
1 tbsp caster sugar
2 tsp salt
2 tbsp extra virgin olive oil
45g (1½oz) sesame seeds

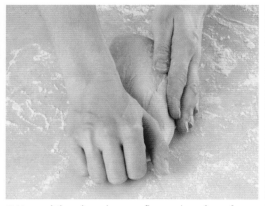

1 Sprinkle the yeast over 4 tablespoons warm water. Leave for 5 minutes, stirring once.

2 Put the flour, sugar, and salt in a bowl. Add the yeast and 250ml (8fl oz) lukewarm water.

3 Add the oil and draw the flour into the liquid, mixing to form a soft, slightly sticky dough.

4 Knead the dough on a floured surface for 5–7 minutes until very smooth and elastic.

5 Cover the dough with a damp tea towel and let it rest for about 5 minutes.

6 Flour your hands and pat the dough into a rectangle on a well-floured work surface.

7 Roll the dough out to a 40 x 15cm (16 x 6in) rectangle. Cover it with a damp tea towel.

8 Leave in a warm place for 1–1½ hours until doubled. Preheat oven to 220°C (425°F/Gas 7).

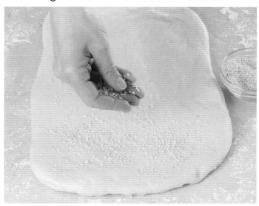

9 Dust 3 baking sheets with flour. Brush the dough with water. Sprinkle with sesame seeds.

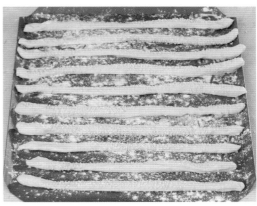

10 With a sharp knife, cut the dough into 32 strips, each about 1cm (½in) wide.

11 Stretch 1 strip to the width of a baking sheet. Set it on 1 of the baking sheets.

12 Repeat with the remaining strips, arranging them 2cm (¾in) apart.

13 Bake for 15–18 minutes until golden and crisp. Transfer to a wire rack and let cool completely.
STORE These will keep in an airtight container for 2 days.

Grissini variations

Spanish Picos

These miniature Spanish breadsticks are made by tying strips of dough in loops and are a great addition to a tapas meal.

MAKES 16 **40–45 MINS** **18–20 MINS**

Rising time
1–1½ hrs

Ingredients
½ quantity grissini dough,
  see page 430, steps 1–6
1½ tbsp sea salt

Method

1 Roll out the dough to a 20 x 15cm (8 x 6in) rectangle. Cover with a damp tea towel and leave to rise in a warm place for 1–1½ hours until doubled in size.

2 Preheat the oven to 220°C (425°F/Gas 7). Dust 2 baking sheets with flour. Cut the dough into 16 strips, then cut each strip into half. Take a half strip, loop it, and twist the ends in a single knot, and transfer to a prepared baking sheet. Shape the remaining strips in the same manner.

3 Lightly brush the loops with water and sprinkle with the sea salt. Bake the loops for 18–20 minutes until golden and crisp. Let cool as directed.

STORE The picos can be kept for 2 days in an airtight container.

Parmesan Grissini

Smoked paprika adds a depth of flavour to these cheesy grissini.

MAKES 32 **40–45 MINS** **10 MINS**

Rising time
1–1½ hrs

Ingredients
2½ tsp dried yeast
425g (15oz) strong white bread flour,
  plus extra for dusting
1 tbsp caster sugar
2 tsp salt
1½ tsp smoked paprika
2 tbsp extra virgin olive oil
50g (1¾oz) Parmesan cheese, grated

Method

1 Sprinkle the yeast over 4 tablespoons lukewarm water. Leave for 5 minutes until dissolved, stirring once. Put the flour, sugar, salt, and smoked paprika in a bowl. Pour in the oil, dissolved yeast, and 250ml (8fl oz) lukewarm water.

2 Draw in the flour to form a dough; it should be soft and sticky. Flour the surface and knead for 5–7 minutes until it is smooth and forms a ball. Cover with a damp tea towel and leave for 5 minutes. Flour your hands and pat the dough into a rectangle on a floured surface. Roll it out to a rectangle 40 x 15cm (16 x 6in). Cover with the tea towel, and leave for 1–1½ hours until doubled in size.

3 Preheat the oven to 220°C (425°F/Gas 7). Dust 3 baking sheets with flour and lightly brush the dough with water. Sprinkle with the Parmesan, pressing it down gently. With a sharp knife, cut the dough into 32 strips, each 1cm (½in) wide. Stretch 1 strip to the width of a baking sheet, and set on 1 of the prepared sheets. Repeat with the remaining strips, placing them 2cm (¾in) apart. Bake for 10 minutes until golden and crisp. Transfer to a wire rack to cool.

STORE These are best eaten fresh, but will keep in an airtight container for 2 days.

Parma Ham-wrapped Canapés

Try dipping these quick home-made canapés in herb mayo or salsa verde.

| MAKES 32 | 45 MINS | 15–18 MINS |

Rising time
1–1½ hrs

Ingredients
1 quantity grissini dough,
 see page 430, steps 1–8
3 tbsp sea salt
12 slices Parma ham

Method

1 Preheat the oven to 220°C (425°F/Gas 7) and dust 3 baking sheets with flour. Brush the rolled out dough with water and sprinkle with sea salt crystals.

2 With a sharp knife, cut the dough into 32 strips, each 1cm (½in) wide. Stretch each one to the width of the baking sheet and position 2cm (¾in) apart. Bake for 15–18 minutes until golden and crisp. Cool on a wire rack.

3 Cut each slice of Parma ham lengthways into 3. Wrap each grissini at one end with one-third of a slice of ham just before serving as a canapé.

PREPARE AHEAD The grissini can be made 1 day ahead and stored in an airtight container. Wrap with the Parma ham just before serving.

BAKER'S TIP
Home-made grissini are a lovely addition to a party menu. Experiment by adding flavour and texture, using items such as chopped olives, or smoked paprika, or your favourite cheeses; or leave them plain for a healthy and child-friendly snack. They will be at their best if eaten on the day they are baked.

GRISSINI VARIATIONS

Bagels

Making bagels is surprisingly simple. Try sprinkling with poppy or sesame seeds after brushing with egg.

MAKES 8–10	40 MINS	20–25 MINS	8 WEEKS, UNBAKED

Rising and proving time
1½–3 hrs

Ingredients
600g (1lb 5oz) strong white bread
  flour, plus extra for dusting
2 tsp fine salt
2 tsp caster sugar
2 tsp dried yeast
1 tbsp sunflower oil,
  plus extra for greasing
1 egg, beaten, for glazing

CLASSIC AND ARTISAN BREADS

1 Put the flour, salt, and sugar in a bowl. Mix the yeast in 300ml (10fl oz) warm water.

2 Add the oil and pour the liquid into the flour mixture, stirring together to form a soft dough.

3 Knead on a floured surface for 10 minutes until smooth. Transfer to an oiled bowl.

4 Cover loosely with cling film and leave to rise in a warm place for 1–2 hours until doubled.

5 Transfer to a floured surface, push it back to its original size, and divide into 8–10 pieces.

6 Take each piece of dough and roll it under your palm to make a fat log shape.

7 Using your palms, continue to roll it towards each end, until it is about 25cm (10in) long.

8 Take the dough and wrap it around your knuckles, so the join is underneath your palm.

9 Squeeze gently, then roll briefly to seal the join. The hole should still be big at this stage.

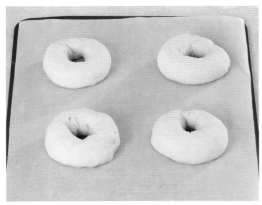

10 Transfer to 2 baking trays lined with baking parchment. Repeat to shape all the bagels.

11 Cover with cling film and a tea towel. Leave in a warm place for up to 1 hour until doubled.

12 Preheat the oven to 220°C (425°F/Gas 7), and set a large pan of water to boil.

13 Poach the bagels in gently simmering water for 1 minute on either side.

14 Remove them from the water with a slotted spoon. Dry them briefly on a clean tea towel.

15 Return the bagels to the baking trays and brush them with a little beaten egg.

16 Bake in the centre of the oven for 20–25 minutes until golden. Cool for 5 minutes on a wire rack before serving. **STORE** Best the day they are made, but still good toasted the next day.

Bagel variations

Cinnamon and Raisin Bagels

These sweet and spicy bagels are delicious fresh from the oven. Any leftovers can be trimmed of the crusts and turned into an alternative Bread and Butter Pudding (see page 92).

MAKES 8–10 | **40 MINS** | **20–25 MINS** | **8 WEEKS, UNBAKED**

Rising and proving time
1½–3 hrs

Ingredients
600g (1lb 5oz) strong white bread flour, plus extra for dusting
2 tsp fine salt
2 tsp caster sugar
2 tsp ground cinnamon
2 tsp dried yeast
1 tbsp sunflower oil, plus extra for greasing
50g (1¾oz) raisins
1 egg, beaten, for glazing

Method
1 Put the flour, salt, sugar, and cinnamon into a large bowl. Dissolve the dried yeast in 300ml (10fl oz) warm water, whisking gently to help it dissolve, then add the oil. Gradually pour the liquid into the flour mixture, stirring to form a soft dough. Knead on a well-floured work surface, until smooth, soft, and pliable.

2 Stretch the dough out thinly, scatter the raisins evenly over it, and knead briefly until well mixed. Put it in an oiled bowl, cover with cling film and leave to rise in a warm place for 1–2 hours, until nearly doubled.

3 Place the dough on a floured surface and gently push it down until it is back to its original size. Divide it into 8–10 equal pieces. Take each piece and roll it under your palm to make a fat log shape. Using both your palms, continue to roll the dough outwards towards each end, until it is about 25cm (10in) long.

4 Wrap the dough round your knuckles, so the join is underneath your palm. Squeeze gently, then roll the bagel briefly to seal the join. The hole should still be quite big at this stage. Transfer to 2 baking trays lined with baking parchment and cover loosely with cling film and a tea towel. Leave in a warm place for up to 1 hour, until well puffed up and doubled in size.

5 Preheat the oven to 220°C (425°F/Gas 7) and set a large pan of water to boil. Gently poach the bagels, in batches of 3 or 4, in the simmering water for 1 minute, then flip them over and poach for another minute. Remove with a slotted spoon, dry briefly on a tea towel, then return to the baking trays. Brush with the beaten egg. Bake in the centre of the oven for 20–25 minutes until golden brown. Remove from the oven and cool for at least 5 minutes on a wire rack before eating.

STORE The bagels are best served the same day, but good toasted the next day.

Mini Bagels

Great for parties, try serving halved and topped simply with cream cheese, a curl of smoked salmon, lemon juice, and a sprinkling of cracked black pepper. ▶

MAKES 16–20 | **45 MINS** | **15–20 MINS** | **8 WEEKS, UNBAKED**

Rising and proving time
1½–2½ hrs

Ingredients
1 quantity bagel dough, see page 434, steps 1–4

Method
1 When the dough has risen, place it on a floured work surface and gently knock it back. Divide it into 16–20 equal pieces, depending on the size of bagels you would like. Take each piece and roll it under your palm to make a log shape. Use both your palms to roll the dough outwards towards each end, until it is about 15cm (6in) long.

2 Take the dough and wrap it around the three middle fingers of your hand, so the join is underneath your palm. Pinch gently, then roll briefly to seal the join. The hole should still be quite big at this stage. Put the bagels on 2 baking trays lined with parchment, and cover loosely with cling film and a tea towel. Leave in a warm place for 30 minutes until well puffed up.

3 Preheat the oven to 220°C (425°F/Gas 7) and set a large pan of water to boil. Gently poach the bagels in batches of 6–8, poaching each side for just 30 seconds. Briefly dry the bagels with a tea towel, brush with the beaten egg, and bake for 15–20 minutes until golden brown. Remove from the oven and cool for at least 5 minutes on a wire rack before eating.

STORE These mini bagels are best served fresh the day they are made, but are also good toasted the next day.

BAKER'S TIP
The secret to cooking an authentic bagel is to poach the proven bagels briefly in simmering water before baking. It is this unusual step that helps to give them their classic chewy texture and soft crumb.

Pretzels

These German breads are great fun to make; the two-stage glazing method gives an authentic result.

MAKES 16	50 MINS	20 MINS	UP TO 8 WEEKS

Rising and proving time
1½–2½ hrs

Ingredients
350g (12oz) strong white bread flour, plus extra for dusting
150g (5½oz) plain flour
1 tsp salt
2 tbsp caster sugar
2 tsp dried yeast
1 tbsp sunflower oil, plus extra for greasing

For the glaze
¼ tsp bicarbonate of soda
coarse sea salt or 2 tbsp sesame seeds
1 egg, beaten, for glazing

1 Put the 2 types of flour, salt, and sugar into a large bowl.

2 Sprinkle the yeast over 300ml (10fl oz) warm water. Stir, leave for 5 minutes, and add the oil.

3 Gradually pour the liquid into the flour mixture, stirring to form a soft dough.

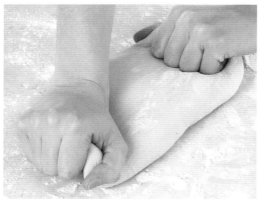

4 Knead for 10 minutes until smooth, soft, and pliable. Transfer to an oiled bowl.

5 Cover loosely with cling film and leave in a warm place for 1–2 hours until nearly doubled.

6 Turn the dough out onto a lightly floured work surface, and gently knock it back.

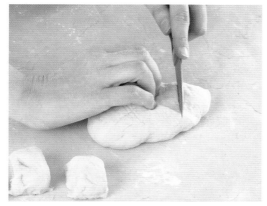

7 With a sharp knife, cut the dough neatly into 16 equal pieces.

8 Take each piece of dough and roll it under your palm to make a log shape.

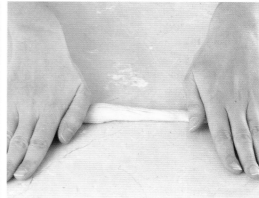

9 Using your palms, continue to roll the dough towards each end, until it is 45cm (18in) long.

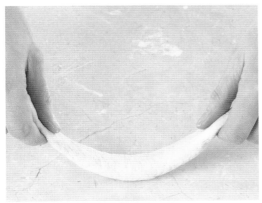

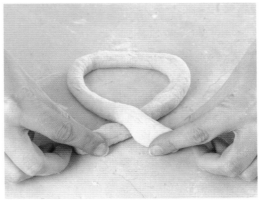

10 If difficult to stretch, hold by either end and rotate in a looping action, like a skipping rope.

11 Take each end of the dough and cross them over each other, forming a heart shape.

12 Now twist the ends around each other as though they had linked arms.

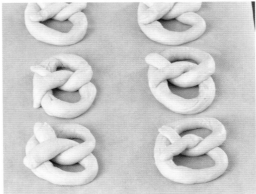

13 Secure the ends to the sides of the pretzel; it will appear quite loose at this stage.

14 Repeat to make 16 pretzels, placing them on baking sheets lined with parchment.

15 Cover with cling film and a tea towel. Leave in a warm place for 30 minutes until puffed up.

16 Preheat the oven to 200°C (400°F/Gas 6). Mix the soda in 2 tablespoons boiling water.

17 Brush the pretzels with the mixture. This gives them a dark colour and chewy exterior.

18 Scatter flakes of sea salt or sesame seeds over the brushed pretzels. Bake for 15 minutes.

19 Remove from the oven and brush with a little beaten egg. Bake for another 5 minutes.

20 Remove from the oven. The pretzels should be dark golden brown with a shiny finish.

21 Transfer to a wire rack and leave to cool for at least 5 minutes before serving.

PRETZELS

439

Pretzel variations

Sweet Cinnamon Pretzels

A delicious sweet alternative to plain pretzels, these are definitely best eaten straight from the oven.
Try toasting any leftover pretzels or gently reheating in a medium oven.

| MAKES 16 | 50 MINS | 20 MINS | UP TO 8 WEEKS |

Rising and proving time
1½–2½ hrs

Ingredients
1 quantity unbaked pretzels,
 see pages 440–441, steps 1–15

For the glaze
¼ tsp bicarbonate of soda
1 egg, beaten
25g (scant 1oz) unsalted butter, melted
50g (1¾oz) caster sugar
2 tsp ground cinnamon

Method

1 Preheat the oven to 200°C (400°F/Gas 6). Dissolve the bicarbonate of soda in 2 tablespoons boiling water and brush it all over the shaped and risen pretzels. Bake for 15 minutes. Remove from the oven, brush all over with egg, and return to the oven for 5 minutes until dark golden brown and shiny.

2 Remove the pretzels from the oven and brush each one with melted butter. Mix the sugar and cinnamon on a plate and dip the buttered side of the pretzels into the mix. Leave to cool on a wire rack for at least 5 minutes before serving.

STORE These can be stored in an airtight container overnight.

BAKER'S TIP
Pretzels get their traditional mahogany colouring and chewy texture from a quick dip in bicarbonate of soda before cooking. The dough can be tricky to handle at home, so be sure to brush twice: first with bicarbonate of soda solution, and later with beaten egg, for an easy way to perfect pretzels.

Hot Dog Pretzels

These pretzeldogs are guaranteed to go down a storm at a children's party and are simple to prepare.
They would make a great Bonfire Night treat, too. ▶

| MAKES 8 | 30 MINS | 15 MINS | UP TO 8 WEEKS |

Rising and proving time
1½–2½ hrs

Ingredients
150g (5½oz) strong white bread flour,
 plus extra for dusting
100g (3½oz) plain flour
½ tsp salt
1 tbsp caster sugar
1 tsp dried yeast
½ tbsp sunflower oil, plus extra for greasing
8 hot dogs
mustard (optional)

For the glaze
1 tbsp bicarbonate of soda
coarse sea salt

Method

1 Put the two types of flour, salt, and sugar into a bowl. Sprinkle the yeast over 150ml (5fl oz) warm water. Stir once, then leave for 5 minutes until dissolved. Once it has dissolved, add the oil.

2 Pour the liquid into the flour mixture, stirring it together to form a soft dough. Knead for 10 minutes on a floured work surface until smooth, soft, and pliable. Put in a lightly oiled bowl, cover loosely with cling film, and leave in a warm place for 1–2 hours until nearly doubled in size.

3 Turn the dough out onto a floured work surface and knock it back. Divide it into 8 equal pieces. Take each piece of dough and roll it under your palm to make a log shape. Use both your palms to continue to roll the dough outwards towards each end, until it is about 45cm (18in) long. If the dough is difficult to stretch, hold it by either end and gently rotate it in a looping action as you would a skipping rope.

4 Take each hot dog and, if you like mustard (and don't mind the mess) brush with a little mustard. Starting at the top, wrap the pretzel dough around it in a circular twisting motion, so that the hot dog is completely sealed in, with only the top and the bottom showing. Pinch the

dough together at the top and bottom to make sure it doesn't unwrap.

5 Place on baking sheets lined with baking parchment, cover with oiled cling film and a tea towel, and leave in a warm place for about 30 minutes until well puffed up. Preheat the oven to 200°C (400°F/Gas 6).

6 Dissolve the bicarbonate of soda in 1 litre (1¾ pints) boiling water in a pan. Poach the hotdogs, in batches of 3, in the simmering water for 1 minute. Remove with a slotted spatula, dry briefly on a tea towel, and return to the baking sheets.

7 Scatter with sea salt and bake for 15 minutes until golden brown and shiny. Remove from the oven and cool on a wire rack for 5 minutes before serving.

STORE These are best eaten while still warm, but can be stored in an airtight container in the refrigerator overnight.

English Muffins

First popular in the 18th century, this traditional English teatime bread crossed the Atlantic to become an American breakfast staple.

MAKES 10 **25–30 MINS** **13–16 MINS**

Proving time
1½ hrs

Ingredients

1 tsp dried yeast
450g (1lb) strong white bread flour,
  plus extra for dusting
1 tsp salt
25g (scant 1oz) unsalted butter, melted,
  plus extra for greasing
vegetable oil, for greasing
25g (scant 1oz) ground rice or semolina

Method

1 Pour 300ml (10 fl oz) lukewarm water into a bowl, sprinkle over the yeast, and leave for 5 minutes to dissolve, stirring once. Mix the flour and salt in a large bowl. Make a well and pour in the yeast mixture and melted butter. Gradually draw in the flour to form a soft, pliable dough.

2 Knead the dough on a lightly floured surface for 5 minutes. Shape it into a ball and place in a large greased bowl. Cover with oiled cling film and leave in a warm place for 1 hour or until doubled in size.

3 Lay a tea towel on a tray, and scatter with most of the ground rice. Turn the dough out onto a floured surface, knead briefly, and divide it into 10 balls. Place the balls on the

towel and press them into flattish rounds. Sprinkle with the rest of the ground rice, and cover with another tea towel. Leave to prove for 20–30 minutes until risen.

4 Heat a large, lidded frying pan and cook the muffins in batches. Cover with the lid and cook very gently for 10–12 minutes or until they puff up and the undersides are golden and toasted. Turn over and cook for 3–4 minutes or until golden underneath. Cool on a wire rack. Muffins are great split, toasted, and spread with butter and jam, or as the base for eggs Benedict.

BAKER'S TIP

Home-made muffins are far superior to anything you can buy, so it really is worth the extra effort of making them. Make the dough in the morning, and you can enjoy a freshly cooked batch for afternoon tea. Alternatively, leave to rise overnight, ready to bake for a leisurely breakfast.

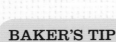

Hefezopf

This traditional German bread is similar to brioche. Like all yeasted sweet breads, it is at its best the day of baking.

MAKES 1 LOAF | **20 MINS** | **25–35 MINS** | **UP TO 8 WEEKS**

Rising and proving time
4–4½ hrs

Ingredients
2 tsp dried yeast
125ml (4fl oz) warm milk
1 large egg
450g (1lb) plain flour,
  plus extra for dusting
75g (2½oz) caster sugar
¼ tsp fine salt

75g (2½oz) unsalted butter, melted
vegetable oil, for greasing
1 egg, beaten, for glazing

CLASSIC AND ARTISAN BREADS

1 Dissolve the yeast in the warm milk. Let it cool, then add the egg and beat well.

2 Put the flour, sugar, and salt in a large bowl. Make a well and pour in the milk mixture.

3 Add the melted butter and gradually draw in the flour, stirring to form a soft dough.

4 Knead for 10 minutes on a floured surface until smooth, soft, and pliable.

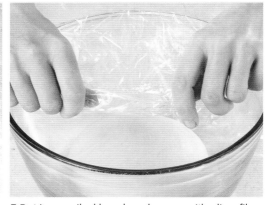

5 Put in an oiled bowl and cover with cling film. Keep it warm for 2–2½ hours until doubled.

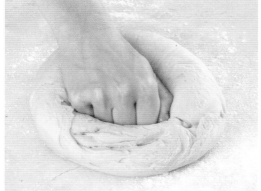

6 Put the dough on a floured work surface and gently knock it back. Divide into 3 equal pieces.

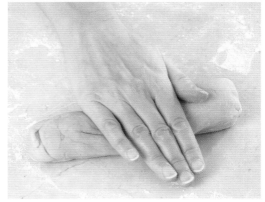

7 Take each piece of dough and roll it under your palm to make a fat log shape.

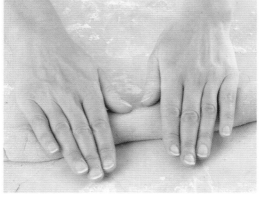

8 Using your palms, continue to roll it towards each end, until it is about 30cm (12in) long.

9 Pinch the tops of the 3 pieces together and tuck the join underneath to start the plait.

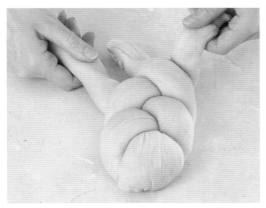
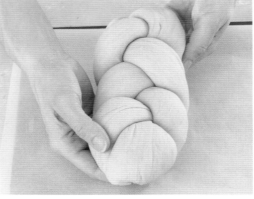

10 Loosely plait the dough, leaving room for it to rise. Pinch and tuck the ends underneath.

11 Put on a baking sheet lined with parchment. Cover with oiled cling film and a tea towel.

12 Leave in a warm place for 2 hours; it will not double now, but will rise on baking.

13 Preheat the oven to 190°C (375°F/Gas 5). Brush liberally with beaten egg.

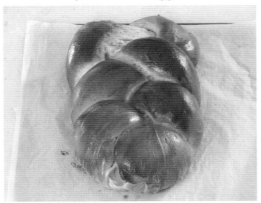

14 Bake for 25–30 minutes until golden. Check if undercooked where the plaits meet.

15 If undercooked, cover with foil and bake for 5 minutes. Cool for 15 minutes before serving.

STORE Wrap in cling film for up to 2 days. **ALSO TRY... Sultana and Almond Hefezopf** Add 75g (2½oz) golden sultanas at step 2 and scatter 2 tablespoons flaked almonds at step 13.

Hefezopf variations

Spiced Pecan and Raisin Hefezopf

The nuts and spices make this bread even tastier toasted.

MAKES 1 LOAF | 30 MINS | 25–35 MINS | UP TO 8 WEEKS

Rising and proving time
4–4½ hrs

Ingredients
3 x "logs" hefezopf dough, approx. 30cm (12in) long, see page 446, steps 1–8
50g (1¾oz) raisins
50g (1¾oz) pecans, roughly chopped
3 tbsp soft light brown sugar
2 tsp mixed spice

Method

1 Roll each "log" of dough out on its shorter edge, so that you have 3 pieces each 30 x 8cm (12 x 3¼in). The measurements do not have to be precise, but the pieces of dough should be roughly the same shape.

2 Mix together the raisins, pecans, sugar, and mixed spice. Scatter one-third of the mixture over each piece of dough, and press down with your palms firmly. Roll up each piece along its longest side, tucking the dough in firmly as you go. You should be left with three 30cm (12in) "ropes" of dough stuffed with the raisin and nut mix.

3 Pinch the tops of the 3 pieces of dough together and tuck the join underneath. Now loosely plait the dough together, leaving room for it to rise, and pinch and tuck the ends underneath.

4 Transfer the loaf to a baking sheet lined with baking parchment, cover with lightly oiled cling film and a tea towel, and leave in a warm place for a further 2 hours. This dough will rise, but not double in size. Preheat the oven to 190°C (375°F/Gas 5).

5 Brush the loaf with egg, making sure to get into the joins of the plait. Bake in the preheated oven for 25–30 minutes until well risen and golden brown. If the bread is undercooked where the plaits meet, but has browned well, cover loosely with foil and cook for a further 5 minutes. Remove from the oven and leave to cool on a wire rack for at least 15 minutes before serving.

STORE The loaf is best eaten the day it is made, but will store, wrapped in cling film, for 2 days.

BAKER'S TIP
Hefezopf is a sweet yeasted bread, traditionally plaited and baked at Easter all over Germany. It is quite similar to a brioche dough recipe, and can be baked plain or stuffed with a variety of dried fruits and nuts. Try experimenting with this recipe to include your favourites.

Challah

This traditional Jewish bread is baked for holidays and the Sabbath.

MAKES 1 LOAF | **45–55 MINS** | **35–40 MINS** | **UP TO 8 WEEKS**

Proving time
1¾–2¼ hrs

Ingredients
2½ tsp dried yeast
4 tbsp vegetable oil, plus extra for greasing
4 tbsp sugar
2 eggs, plus 1 yolk, for glazing
2 tsp salt
550g (1¼lb) strong white bread flour,
 plus extra for dusting
1 tsp poppy seeds, for sprinkling (optional)

Method

1 Put 250ml (8fl oz) of water into a pan and bring just to a boil. Pour 4 tablespoons into a bowl, and let cool to lukewarm. Sprinkle over the yeast and let stand, stirring once, for 5 minutes, until dissolved. Add the oil and sugar to the remaining water in the pan and heat until melted. Let cool to lukewarm.

2 In a large bowl, beat the eggs just until mixed. Add the cooled sweetened water, salt, and dissolved yeast. Stir in half the flour and mix well. Add the remaining flour gradually, until the dough forms a ball. It should be soft and slightly sticky.

3 Turn onto a floured work surface. Knead for 5–7 minutes until very smooth and elastic. Oil a large bowl. Put the dough in the bowl, and flip it. Cover with a damp tea towel and let rise in a warm place for 1–1½ hours until doubled in bulk.

4 Lightly brush a baking sheet with oil. Turn the dough on to a lightly floured work surface and knock back. Cut the dough into 4 equal pieces. Flour the work surface. Roll each piece of dough with your hands to a 63cm (25in) strand.

5 Line the strands up next to each other. Starting from your left, lift the first strand to cross over the second. Lift the third strand to cross over the fourth. Now lift the fourth

strand and lay it between the first and second strands. Finish plaiting the strands, pinching the ends together and tucking them under the plaited loaf.

6 Transfer the loaf to the prepared baking sheet. Cover with a dry tea towel and let rise in a warm place for about 45 minutes until doubled in bulk. Preheat the oven to 190°C (375°F/Gas 5). Make the glaze by beating the egg yolk with 1 tablespoon water until it looks frothy. Brush the loaf with the glaze, and sprinkle with poppy seeds, if you like.

7 Bake in the oven for 35–40 minutes until golden and the bread sounds hollow when the bottom is tapped.

STORE Challah is best eaten the day it is made, but will store, wrapped in cling film, for up to 2 days.

Pane al latte

This soft, slightly sweet Italian milk bread is perfect for small children – though adults will enjoy it for breakfast or afternoon tea as well!

MAKES 1 LOAF   30 MINS   20 MINS

Rising and proving time
2½–3 hrs

Ingredients
500g (1lb 2oz) plain flour, plus extra for dusting
1 tsp salt
2 tbsp caster sugar
2 tsp dried yeast
200ml (7fl oz) warm milk
2 eggs, plus 1 egg, beaten, for glazing
50g (1¾oz) unsalted butter, melted
vegetable oil, for greasing

Method

1 Put the flour, salt, and sugar into a bowl and mix well. Dissolve the yeast in the milk, whisking to help it dissolve. Once the liquid has cooled, add the eggs and beat well.

2 Gradually pour the milk mixture, then the butter, into the flour mixture, stirring it to form a soft dough. Knead the dough for 10 minutes on a floured work surface until smooth, glossy, and elastic.

3 Put the dough in a lightly oiled bowl, cover loosely with cling film, and leave to rise in a warm place for up to 2 hours until doubled in size. Turn the dough out onto a lightly floured work surface and gently knock it back. Divide it into 5 roughly equal pieces. Ideally, 2 should be slightly bigger than the rest.

4 Knead each piece briefly, and roll it out to a long, fat log shape – the 3 smaller pieces about 20cm (8in) long, and the 2 larger ones about 25cm (10in) long. Take the 3 shorter pieces and position them side by side on a baking sheet

lined with baking parchment. Place the 2 larger ones on each side and draw the tops and bottoms together around the central 3 to form a "circle". Pinch the top of the loaf together to ensure the dough does not come apart.

5 Cover it loosely with lightly oiled cling film and a clean tea towel, and leave it in a warm place to rise for 30 minutes–1 hour until almost doubled in size. Preheat the oven to 190°C (375°F/Gas 5).

6 Gently brush with a little beaten egg and bake for 20 minutes until golden brown. Remove from the oven and leave to cool for at least 10 minutes before serving.

STORE Best eaten still warm from the oven, the bread can be wrapped overnight and toasted the next day.

BAKER'S TIP
The use of eggs, milk, and sugar give this very soft Italian bread a sweet, gentle flavour and velvety texture. It toasts well, but is at its best served still warm with plenty of cold, unsalted butter and home-made strawberry jam. It is especially popular with children.

Sourdough Loaf

A true sourdough starter uses naturally occurring yeasts to ferment. Dried yeast is a bit of a cheat, but more reliable.

MAKES 2 LOAVES | **45–50 MINS** | **40–45 MINS** | **UP TO 8 WEEKS**

Fermenting time
4–6 days

Rising and proving time
2–2½ hrs

Ingredients

For the starter
1 tbsp dried yeast
250g (9oz) strong white bread flour

For the sponge
250g (9oz) strong white bread flour,
  plus extra for sprinkling

For the bread
1½ tsp dried yeast
375g (13oz) strong white bread flour,
  plus extra for dusting
1 tbsp salt
vegetable oil, for greasing
polenta or fine yellow cornmeal,
  for dusting

1 Make the starter 3–5 days ahead. Dissolve the yeast in 500ml (16fl oz) lukewarm water.

2 Stir in the flour, and cover. Let it ferment in a warm place for 24 hours.

3 Look at the starter; it should have become frothy and have a distinct, sour odour.

4 Stir, cover, and ferment for 2–4 days longer, stirring it each day. Then use, or refrigerate.

5 For the sponge, mix 250ml (8fl oz) starter with 250ml (8fl oz) lukewarm water in a bowl.

6 Stir in the flour and mix vigorously. Sprinkle with 3 tablespoons flour.

7 Cover with a damp tea towel and leave it to ferment overnight in a warm place.

8 For the bread, dissolve the yeast in 4 tablespoons warm water. Mix into the sponge.

9 Stir in half the flour and the salt, and mix well to combine all the ingredients.

10 Gradually add the remaining flour. Mix well, until the dough forms a soft, slightly sticky ball.

11 Knead for 8–10 minutes until very smooth, and elastic. Put in an oiled bowl.

12 Cover with a damp tea towel and let rise in a warm place for 1–1½ hours until doubled.

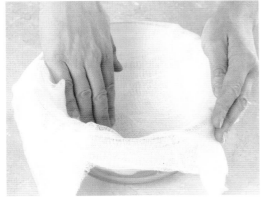

13 Line two 20cm (8in) bowls with pieces of cloth, and sprinkle generously with flour.

14 Knock back the dough on a floured surface, cut in half, and shape each half into a ball.

15 Place in the bowls, covering with tea towels. Keep warm for 1 hour until the bowls are full.

16 Put a tin in the oven. Heat to 200°C (400°F/ Gas 6). Sprinkle 2 baking sheets with polenta.

17 Place the loaves, seam-side down, on the baking sheets and remove the cloth.

18 With a sharp knife, make criss-cross slashes on the top of each loaf.

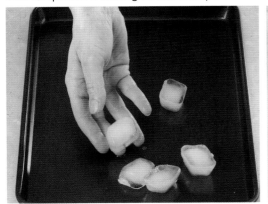

19 Put the loaves in the oven. Drop ice cubes into the roasting tin, then bake for 20 minutes.

20 Reduce to 190°C (375°F/Gas 5) and bake for another 20–25 minutes until well browned.

21 Transfer to a wire rack. **STORE** These can be kept for 2–3 days, tightly wrapped in paper.

Sourdough Bread variations

Sourdough Rolls

These pretty rolls are perfect for a picnic lunch.

| MAKES 12 | 45–50 MINS | 25–30 MINS | UP TO 8 WEEKS |

Fermenting time
4–6 days

Rising and proving time
2–2½ hrs

Ingredients
1 quantity sourdough bread dough,
see pages 452–453, steps 1–12

Method

1 Sprinkle 2 baking sheets with polenta. Knock the air out of the dough and cut it in half. Roll one piece into a cylinder 5cm (2in) in diameter. Cut into 6 and repeat with the remaining dough.

2 Lightly flour a work surface. Cup a piece of dough under the palm of your hand and roll to form a smooth ball. Repeat to shape the remaining dough. Set the rolls on the prepared baking sheets. Cover and let rise in a warm place for about 30 minutes until doubled in size.

3 Preheat the oven to 200°C (400°F/Gas 6). Lightly sprinkle each roll with flour, then with a sharp knife make criss-cross slashes in the middle of each roll. Place a roasting tin on the oven floor to heat up. Drop ice-cubes into the roasting tin, then place the rolls in the centre of the oven and bake for 25–30 minutes until golden and hollow-sounding when tapped.

STORE The rolls will keep for 2–3 days, tightly wrapped in paper.

PREPARE AHEAD These rolls can be frozen at the shaping stage, brought back to room temperature, then glazed and baked.

Fruit and Nut Sourdough Loaf

Raisins and walnuts are a great addition to a tangy sourdough loaf. Once you've learnt how to combine fruit and nuts into the dough, try experimenting with your own favourite combinations.

MAKES 2 LOAVES · **45–50 MINS** · **40–45 MINS** · **UP TO 8 WEEKS**

Fermenting time
4–6 days

Rising and proving time
2–2½ hrs

Ingredients
1 quantity starter and sponge,
   see page 452, steps 1–7

For the dough
2 tsp dried yeast
275g (10oz) strong white bread flour,
   plus extra for dusting
100g (3½oz) rye flour
1 tbsp salt
50g (1¾oz) raisins
50g (1¾oz) walnuts, chopped
vegetable oil, for greasing
polenta, for dusting

Method

1 Dissolve the yeast in 4 tablespoons lukewarm water. Leave for 5 minutes until frothy, then mix into the sponge. Combine the 2 types of flour and stir half the flour mix and all the salt into the sponge, mixing well. Add the remaining flour, mixing well, until the dough forms a soft, sticky ball.

2 Knead for 8–10 minutes on a floured surface, until smooth and elastic. Flatten the dough into a rough rectangle, scatter over the raisins and walnuts, and bring together, kneading in the fruit and nuts.

3 Place the dough in an oiled bowl, cover with a damp tea towel, and let rise in a warm place for 1–1½ hours until doubled in size. Line two 20cm (8in) bowls with pieces of cloth and sprinkle with flour. Knock back the dough on a floured surface, cut in half, and shape each half into a ball. Place in the bowls, cover with dry tea towels, and let rise in a warm place for 1 hour until the bowls are full.

4 Preheat the oven to 200°C (400°F/Gas 6) and heat a roasting tin on the oven floor. Sprinkle 2 baking sheets with polenta. Turn the loaves, seam-side down, onto the baking sheets. Make criss-cross slashes on the loaves using a sharp knife.

5 Drop ice cubes into the hot roasting tin, place the loaves in the oven, and bake for 20 minutes. Reduce to 190°C (375°F/Gas 5) and bake for another 20–25 minutes until well browned. Cool on a wire rack.

STORE The loaves will keep for 2–3 days, tightly wrapped in paper.

Pugliese

This classic Italian country loaf is flavoured and preserved with olive oil. Do not worry if the dough seems wet at first, as the looser the dough, the larger the air pockets in the finished crumb.

MAKES 1 LOAF · **30 MINS** · **30–35 MINS** · **UP TO 4 WEEKS**

Fermenting time
12 hrs or overnight

Rising and proving time
up to 4 hours

Ingredients

For the biga
¼ tsp dried yeast
100g (3½oz) strong white bread flour
olive oil, for greasing

For the dough
½ tsp dried yeast
1 tbsp olive oil, plus extra for greasing
300g (10½oz) strong white bread flour,
   plus extra for dusting
1 tsp salt

Method

1 For the biga, dissolve the yeast in 100ml (3½fl oz) warm water, whisking. Add the liquid to the flour and bring it together to form a dough. Place in an oiled bowl, cover with cling film and put in a cool place to rise for at least 12 hours, or overnight.

2 For the dough, dissolve the yeast in 140ml (4¾fl oz) warm water, then add the oil. Put the biga, flour, and salt into a bowl. Add the liquid. Stir it to form a rough dough. Knead for 10 minutes on a well-floured surface until smooth and elastic.

3 Put the dough in an oiled bowl, cover with cling film, and leave to rise in a warm place for up to 2 hours until doubled. Turn it out onto a floured surface. Knock it back and knead it into a shape; I like a rounded oblong.

4 Place the dough on a baking sheet, cover with oiled cling film and a tea towel, and leave in a warm place for up to 2 hours until doubled in size. The bread is ready to bake when it is tight and well risen, and a finger gently poked into the dough leaves a dent that springs back quickly. Preheat the oven to 220°C (425°F/Gas 7).

5 Slash the the loaf in a slightly off centre line. Dust with flour, spray with water, and place on the middle shelf. Bake for 30–35 minutes. For a crisper crust, spray with water every 10 minutes. Remove from the oven and cool.

STORE The loaf will keep for 2–3 days, tightly wrapped in paper.

Baguette

Master this basic recipe and you can shape it to produce baguettes, ficelles, or bâtards whenever you like.

MAKES 2 | **30 MINS** | **15–30 MINS** | **UP TO 4 WEEKS**

Fermenting time
12 hrs or overnight

Rising and proving time
3½ hrs

Ingredients

For the sponge
⅛ tsp dried yeast
75g (2½oz) strong white bread flour
1 tbsp rye flour
vegetable oil, for greasing

For the dough
1 tsp dried yeast
300g (10½oz) strong white bread
  flour, plus extra for dusting
½ tsp salt

1 Dissolve the yeast in 75ml (2½fl oz) warm water and add to the 2 types of flour.

2 Form a sticky, loose dough and place in an oiled bowl, with room for it to expand.

3 Cover with cling film and put in a cool place to rise for at least 12 hours.

4 To make the dough, dissolve the yeast in 150ml (5fl oz) warm water, whisking.

5 Put the risen sponge, flour, and salt into a large bowl and pour in the yeast liquid.

6 Stir it all together with a wooden spoon to form a soft dough.

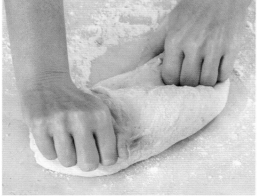

7 Knead for 10 minutes on a floured surface until smooth, soft, glossy, and elastic.

8 Place in an oiled bowl, cover with cling film, and leave to rise in a warm place for 2 hours.

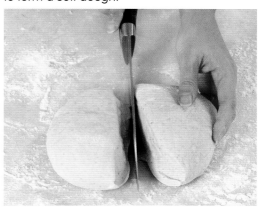

9 Place it on a floured surface. Knock it back. Divide into 2 for baguettes or 3 for ficelles.

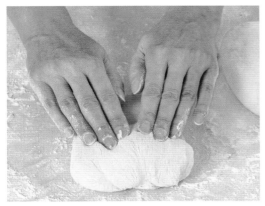

10 Knead briefly and shape each piece into a rectangle. Tuck one short edge into the centre.

11 Press down firmly, fold over the other short edge, and press firmly again.

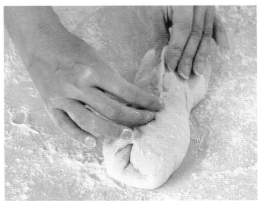

12 Shape the dough into a rounded oblong. Pinch to seal and turn seam-side down.

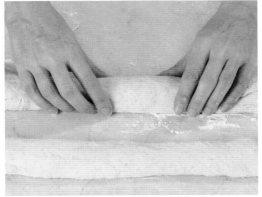

13 Shape into a long, thin log. A baguette is 4cm (1½in) wide, a ficelle 2–3cm (¾–1¼in).

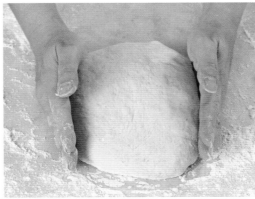

FOR A BÂTARD LOAF Knead all the dough briefly and shape it into a rough rectangle.

Tuck the furthest edge into the centre, press it, then do the same with the nearest edge.

Turn it over to tuck the seam underneath and gently shape it so it tapers at the ends.

14 Place the loaves on baking trays and cover with oiled cling film and a clean tea towel.

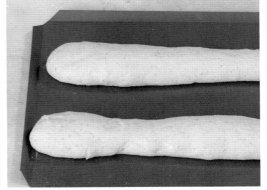

15 Keep warm for 1½ hours until doubled. Preheat the oven to 220°C (425°F/Gas 7).

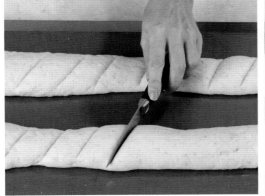

16 Slash the loaf deeply on the diagonal along the top, or criss-cross for a bâtard.

17 Dust with a little flour, spray it with water, and place on the middle shelf of the oven.

18 Bake for 15 minutes for a ficelle, 20 for a baguette, and 25–30 for a bâtard. Let it cool.

BAGUETTE

Baguette variations

Pain d'épi

This attractive variation on the baguette gets its name from its resemblance to wheat ears, *"épi"* in French. The wheat-ear effect is not too difficult to achieve and looks very decorative.

MAKES 3 | **40–45 MINS** | **25–30 MINS**

Rising and proving time
4–5 hrs

Ingredients
2½ tsp dried yeast
500g (1lb 2oz) strong white bread flour,
  plus extra for dusting
2 tsp salt
unsalted butter, melted, for greasing

Method
1 Sprinkle the yeast over 4 tablespoons lukewarm water. Let it stand for 5 minutes until dissolved, stirring once.

2 Put the flour on a work surface with the salt. Make a well in the centre and add the dissolved yeast and 365ml (12fl oz) lukewarm water. Draw in the flour to form a dough. It should be soft and slightly sticky.

3 On a floured surface, knead the dough for 5–7 minutes until very smooth and elastic. Place the dough in a large bowl brushed with butter. Cover with a damp tea towel and leave to rise in a warm place for 2–2½ hours until tripled in size.

4 Turn the dough out onto a lightly floured work surface and knock back. Return to the bowl, cover, and leave to rise in a warm place for 1–1½ hours until doubled in size.

5 Sprinkle a cotton cloth with flour. Turn the dough onto a floured surface and knock back. Cut the dough into 3 equal pieces. Cover 2 pieces of dough while shaping the other. Flour your hands and pat the third piece into an 18 x 10cm (7 x 4in) rectangle.

6 Starting with a long side, roll the rectangle into a cylinder, pinching and sealing it with your fingers. Roll the cylinder, stretching it until it is a stick shape about 35cm (14in) long. Put the shaped loaf on the floured cloth. Repeat to shape the remaining dough, pleating the cloth between the pieces of dough.

7 Cover with a dry tea towel and let rise in a warm place for about 1 hour until doubled in size. Preheat the oven to 220°C (425°F/Gas 7). Set a roasting tin to heat on the floor of the oven. Sprinkle 2 baking sheets with flour. Roll 2 loaves onto 1 baking sheet, placing them 15cm (6in) apart. Roll the third loaf on to the other baking sheet.

8 Make a V-shaped cut about halfway through 1 of the loaves, 5–7cm (2–3in) from the end. Pull the point to the left. Make a second cut 5–7cm (2–3in) from the first, pulling the point to the right. Continue like this, shaping each loaf like "wheat ears". Drop ice cubes into the hot roasting tin and bake the loaves for 25–30 minutes until well browned and hollow-sounding when tapped. Leave to cool and eat the same day.

Wholemeal Baguette

Try this healthier, high-fibre alternative to a white baguette.

MAKES 2 | **20 MINS** | **20–25 MINS** | **UP TO 4 WEEKS**

Fermenting time
12 hrs or overnight

Rising and proving time
3½ hrs

Ingredients
1 quantity sponge, see page 458, steps 1–3, substituting wholemeal for the white bread flour

For the dough
½ tsp dried yeast
100g (3½oz) strong wholemeal bread flour
200g (7oz) strong white bread flour, plus extra for dusting
½ tsp salt

Method

1 To make the dough, dissolve the yeast in 150ml (5fl oz) warm water. Put the risen sponge, 2 types of flour, and salt into a large bowl. Gradually pour in the dissolved yeast, stirring together to form a dough.

2 Knead for 10 minutes on a floured work surface until smooth, glossy, and elastic. Put the dough in a lightly oiled bowl, cover loosely with cling film, and leave in a warm place for up to 1½ hours until doubled.

3 Turn the dough out onto a floured surface and knock it back. Divide into 2 equal pieces. Knead each piece and shape it into a rough rectangle. Use your hands to tuck the furthest edge of the dough into the centre, pressing it down with your fingertips, then do the same with the nearest edge. Fold the dough in half to make a long, thin oblong and press down to seal the edges.

4 Turn the dough over so the seam is underneath and use your hands to gently stretch and roll it into a long, thin log shape, no more than 4cm (1¾in) wide. Don't roll it longer than the length of a baking sheet, and bear in mind it will expand.

5 Place the loaves on 2 large baking sheets and cover loosely with oiled cling film and a tea towel. Leave in a warm place until well risen and almost doubled in size. This could take up to 2 hours. The bread is ready to bake when it is tight and well risen, and a finger gently poked into the dough leaves a dent that springs back quickly. Preheat the oven to 230°C (450°F/Gas 8).

6 Take a sharp knife and slash the top of the loaves deeply on the diagonal all along the top. This will allow the bread to continue to rise in the oven. Dust the tops with a little flour, if liked, spray with water, and place on the middle shelf of the oven. Bake for 20–25 minutes. For a crisper crust, spray the loaves with water every 10 minutes during baking. Remove the bread from the oven and cool on a wire rack.

STORE The baguettes can be stored, loosely wrapped in paper, overnight.

Artisan Rye Bread

Breads made with rye flour are very popular in central and eastern Europe. This version uses a starter.

MAKES 1 LOAF   **25 MINS**   **40–50 MINS**

Fermenting time
overnight

Rising and proving time
1½ hrs

Ingredients

For the starter
150g (5½oz) rye flour
150g pot live natural yogurt
1 tsp dried yeast
1 tbsp black treacle
1 tsp caraway seeds, lightly crushed

For the dough
150g (5½oz) rye flour
200g (7oz) strong white bread flour,
  plus extra for dusting
2 tsp salt
1 egg, beaten, for glazing
1 tsp caraway seeds, to decorate

1 In a bowl, mix all the starter ingredients together with 250ml (8fl oz) tepid water.

2 Cover and leave overnight. When you look at it the next day, it should be bubbling.

3 For the dough, mix the flours together with the salt, then stir into the starter.

4 Mix to make a dough, adding a little extra water if required.

5 Turn out onto a floured surface and knead for 5–10 minutes or until smooth and springy.

6 Shape into a ball, put into an oiled bowl, and cover loosely with cling film.

7 Leave in a warm place for 1 hour or until doubled in size.

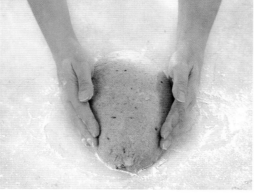

8 Flour a baking tray. Lightly knead the dough again, then form it into a rugby-ball shape.

9 Lift onto the tray, re-cover it loosely, and leave to rise again for another 30 minutes.

10 Preheat the oven to 220°C (425°F/Gas 7). Brush the dough with the egg.

11 Immediately sprinkle evenly with the caraway seeds; they should stick to the egg.

12 Slash the loaf along its length. Bake for 20 minutes, then reduce to 200°C (400°F/Gas 6).

13 Bake for 20–30 minutes until dark golden. Cool on a wire rack. **STORE** Keeps well, wrapped, for 2–3 days. **ALSO TRY... Seeded Rye Bread** Knead in 100g (3½oz) mixed seeds, such as pumpkin, sunflower, sesame, poppy seeds, and pine nuts, at the end of step 5.

Artisan Rye Bread variations

Hazelnut and Raisin Rye Bread

The hazelnuts and raisins in this version add a little sweetness and crunch to the bread. Try experimenting with different combinations of your own favourite nuts and dried fruit.

| MAKES 1 LOAF | 25 MINS | 40–50 MINS | UP TO 8 WEEKS |

Fermenting, rising, and proving time
overnight, plus 1½ hrs

Ingredients

For the starter
150g (5½oz) rye flour
150g pot live natural yogurt
1 tsp dried yeast
1 tbsp black treacle

For the dough
150g (5½oz) rye flour
200g (7oz) strong white bread flour,
　plus extra for dusting
2 tsp salt
50g (1¾oz) hazelnuts, toasted,
　and roughly chopped
50g (1¾oz) raisins
vegetable oil, for greasing
1 egg, beaten, for glazing

Method

1 In a bowl, mix all the starter ingredients together with 250ml (8fl oz) tepid water. Cover and leave overnight. When you look at it the next day, it should be bubbling.

2 For the dough, mix the flours together with the salt, then stir into the starter. Mix to make a dough, adding extra water if required. Turn out onto a floured surface and knead for 5–10 minutes or until smooth and springy.

3 Stretch out the dough to a rough rectangle, scatter the hazelnuts and raisins on top, fold it over, and knead gently to incorporate. Shape the dough into a ball and place in an oiled bowl, covered with cling film. Leave in a warm place for 1 hour, until doubled.

4 Flour a baking tray. Lightly knead the dough again, then form it into a rugby-ball shape. Lift onto the tray, cover loosely with cling film, and leave to rise again for another 30 minutes.

5 Preheat the oven to 220°C (425°F/Gas 7). Brush the loaf with egg and slash along its length. Bake for 20 minutes. Reduce to 200°C (400°F/Gas 6) and bake for 20–30 minutes until dark golden. Cool on a wire rack.

STORE This rye bread will keep, wrapped in paper, for 2–3 days.

BAKER'S TIP

Rye bread makes a healthy alternative to sandwich bread. It is denser in the crumb and makes a more substantial bite. The addition of a variety of seeds, nuts, and dried fruit add crunch, extra nutrition, and texture to the finished bread. It is especially delicious with salt beef and pickles, or with cheese.

Pumpernickel

The unlikely inclusion of cocoa and coffee powder add depth of flavour.

| MAKES 1 LOAF | 20 MINS | 30–40 MINS | UP TO 8 WEEKS |

Fermenting time
12 hrs or overnight

Rising and proving time
4½ hrs

Special equipment time
1-litre (1¾ -pint) loaf tin

Ingredients

For the starter
½ tsp dried yeast
75g (2½oz) rye flour
30g (1oz) live natural yogurt

For the dough
½ tsp dried yeast
1 tsp coffee powder
1 tbsp sunflower oil, plus extra for greasing
130g (4½oz) strong wholemeal bread flour, plus extra for dusting
30g (1oz) rye flour
½ tbsp cocoa powder
1 tsp salt
½ tsp caraway seeds, lightly pounded

Method

1 To make the starter, dissolve the yeast in 100ml (3½ fl oz) warm water. Put the rye flour, yogurt, and yeasted liquid in a large bowl and stir well to combine. Cover with cling film and keep in a cool place to rise for at least 12 hours, or overnight.

2 To make the dough, dissolve the yeast in 3–4 tablespoons warm water. Add the coffee powder and stir until dissolved, then add the oil. Mix the starter, flours, cocoa powder, salt, and caraway seeds in a large bowl. Add the liquid.

3 Stir the ingredients, and when it seems a little stiff, use your hands to bring the dough together. Knead for 10 minutes on a lightly floured work surface until smooth, glossy, and elastic.

4 Put the dough in a lightly oiled bowl, cover loosely with cling film, and leave to rise in a warm place for up to 2 hours

until doubled in size. Turn it out onto a lightly floured work surface and gently knock it back. Shape it into a ball again, return to the bowl, and cover. Leave for 1 hour while it rises again.

5 Turn it out onto a lightly floured work surface and knock it back again. Knead it briefly and shape it into an oblong shape. Put it into a lightly oiled loaf tin, cover loosely with oiled cling film and a clean tea towel, and leave it to prove in a warm place for another 1½ hours until almost

doubled in size. It is ready to bake when it is tight and well risen, and a finger gently poked into the dough leaves a dent that springs back quickly. Preheat the oven to 200°C (400°F/Gas 6).

6 Bake in the centre of the oven for 30–40 minutes until risen and with a dark brown crust. Leave to cool on a wire rack.

STORE This keeps well, wrapped in paper, for 3 days.

Pane siciliano

This rustic semolina bread from Sicily toasts particularly well and makes deliciously crunchy bruschetta.

MAKES 1 LOAF | **20 MINS** | **25–30 MINS** | **UP TO 4 WEEKS**

Fermenting time
12 hrs or overnight

Rising and proving time
2½ hrs

Ingredients

For the starter
¼ tsp dried yeast
100g (3½oz) fine semolina or semolina flour
vegetable oil, for greasing

For the dough
1 tsp dried yeast
400g (14oz) fine semolina or semolina flour, plus extra for dusting
1 tsp fine salt
1 tbsp sesame seeds
1 egg, beaten, for glazing

Method

1 To make the starter, dissolve the yeast in 100ml (3½fl oz) warm water. Add the liquid to the semolina, and bring together to form a rough, loose dough. Place the dough in a lightly oiled bowl, with plenty of room for it to expand. Then cover it with cling film, and keep it in a cool place to rise for at least 12 hours or overnight.

2 To make the dough, dissolve the yeast in 200ml (7fl oz) warm water. Put the risen starter, flour, and salt into a large bowl. Add the dissolved yeast to the mixture.

3 Stir the ingredients with a wooden spoon and, when it seems a little stiff, use your hands to bring the dough together. Knead for up to 10 minutes on a floured work surface, until smooth, glossy, and elastic.

4 Put the dough in a lightly oiled bowl, cover loosely with cling film and leave to rise in a warm place for up to 1½ hours, until doubled in size.

5 Turn the dough out onto a floured work surface and gently knock it back. Knead it briefly, and mould it into the desired shape; traditionally a tight boule shape (see page 414, Walnut Rye Bread, for how to shape a boule). Place it on a large baking tray, and cover it loosely with oiled cling film and a clean tea towel. Leave it to prove in a warm place for 1 hour until almost doubled in size. The bread is ready to bake when it is tight and well risen, and a finger gently poked into the dough leaves a dent, which springs back quickly.

6 Preheat the oven to 200°C (400°F/Gas 6). Brush the top of the bread with the beaten egg, and scatter the sesame seeds over it. Bake the bread in the centre of the oven for 25–30 minutes until well risen and golden brown. Remove from the oven and transfer to a wire rack to cool for at least 30 minutes before serving.

STORE The bread can be stored, loosely wrapped in paper, for 2 days.

BAKER'S TIP

This bread can be made using either fine semolina or semolina flour. Semolina is made from durum wheat, so this bread is not wheat-free, but the semolina does give a deliciously rustic texture, similar to that of polenta or cornmeal. It is good on the side with an oil-rich tomato salad.

Schiacciata di uva

This sweet Italian "squashed" bread is very similar to a sweetened focaccia, and can be served cold or while still warm.

MAKES 1 LOAF | **25 MINS** | **20–25 MINS**

Rising and proving time
3 hrs

Special equipment
20 x 30cm (8 x 12in) Swiss roll tin

Ingredients

For the dough
700g (1lb 9oz) strong white bread flour, plus extra for dusting
1 tsp fine salt
2 tbsp caster sugar
1½ tsp dried yeast
1 tbsp olive oil, plus extra for greasing

For the filling
500g (1lb 2oz) small red seedless grapes, washed
3 tbsp caster sugar
1 tbsp finely chopped rosemary (optional)

Method

1 Put the flour, salt, and sugar into a large bowl. Dissolve the yeast in 450ml (15fl oz) warm water, then add the oil.

2 Gradually pour the liquid into the flour mixture, stirring together to form a soft dough. Knead for 10 minutes on a floured work surface, until smooth, glossy, and elastic. This dough should remain soft.

3 Put the dough in a lightly oiled bowl and cover it loosely with cling film. Leave it to rise in a warm place for up to 2 hours until doubled in size. Turn the dough out onto a floured work surface and gently knock it back. Knead it briefly and divide it into 2 portions, with roughly one-third of the dough in one and two-thirds in the other. Lightly oil the Swiss roll tin.

4 Take the largest piece of dough and roll it out roughly to the size of the tin. Place it in the tin and stretch it out to fill the tin, using your fingers to mould it to the sides.

Scatter two-thirds of the grapes over the surface, and sprinkle with 2 tablespoons of the caster sugar.

5 Roll out the smaller piece of dough to fit on top of the grapes, stretching it with your hands if necessary. Scatter the remaining grapes, and the chopped rosemary (if using) on the surface. Place the dough on a large baking tray, and cover it loosely with lightly oiled cling film and a clean tea towel. Leave it to prove in a warm place for up to 1 hour until well risen and almost doubled in size. Preheat the oven to 200°C (400°F/Gas 6).

6 Scatter the remaining tablespoon of caster sugar on top of the risen dough. Bake for 20–25 minutes until well risen and golden brown. Remove from the oven and allow to cool for at least 10 minutes before serving.

STORE Best eaten the day it is made, but will store, well wrapped in paper, overnight.

BAKER'S TIP
This unusual Italian flat bread is traditionally served to celebrate the grape harvest in the Tuscany region of Italy. It is best eaten the day it is made, and more or less sugar can be added to taste. Great with cheese and, of course, with Italian red wines.

flat breads

Four Seasons Pizza

If you prepare the sauce the day before and leave the bread to rise overnight, these are very quick to assemble.

MAKES 4 PIZZAS **40 MINS** **40 MINS**

Rising time
1–1½ hrs

Ingredients
500g (1lb 2oz) strong white bread
  flour, plus extra for dusting
½ tsp salt
3 tsp dried yeast
2 tbsp olive oil, plus extra for greasing

For the tomato sauce
25g (scant 1oz) unsalted butter
2 shallots, finely chopped

1 tbsp olive oil
1 bay leaf
3 garlic cloves, crushed
1kg (2¼lb) ripe plum tomatoes,
  deseeded and chopped
2 tbsp tomato purée
1 tbsp caster sugar
sea salt and freshly ground pepper

For the toppings
175g (6oz) mozzarella, thinly sliced
115g (4oz) mushrooms, thinly sliced
2 tbsp extra virgin olive oil
2 roasted red peppers, thinly sliced
8 anchovy fillets, halved lengthways
115g (4oz) pepperoni, thinly sliced
2 tbsp capers
8 artichoke hearts, halved
12 black olives

1 Mix the flour and salt. Dissolve the yeast in 360ml (12fl oz) tepid water, in a separate bowl.

2 Add the oil to the yeast mix, then combine with the dry ingredients. Mix to form a dough.

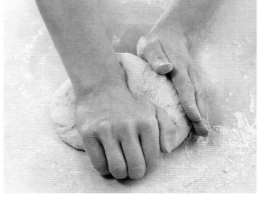

3 Knead on a floured surface for 10 minutes, or until the dough is smooth and elastic.

4 Roll the dough into a ball and place in an oiled bowl covered with oiled cling film.

5 Leave in a warm place for 1–1½ hours, until doubled; or store in the refrigerator overnight.

6 For the sauce, put a pan over low heat. Add the butter, shallots, oil, bay leaf, and garlic.

7 Stir, cover, and sweat the ingredients together for 5–6 minutes, stirring occasionally.

8 Add the tomatoes, tomato purée, and sugar. Cook for 5 minutes, stirring.

9 Now pour in 250ml (8fl oz) water, bring to a boil, and reduce the heat to a simmer.

FLAT BREADS

10 Cook for 30 minutes, stirring, until reduced to a thick sauce. Season to taste.

11 Using a wooden spoon, press the sauce through a sieve. Cover and chill until needed.

12 To bake, preheat the oven to 200°C (400°F/Gas 6). Transfer the dough to a floured surface.

13 Knead lightly, divide into 4, and roll or press out into 23cm (9in) rounds.

14 Grease 4 baking sheets and carefully lift a pizza base onto each sheet.

15 Spread the sauce over the bases, leaving a 2cm (¾in) border around the edge of each.

16 Place any leftover sauce in a small freezer-safe container and freeze for later use.

17 Top the pizzas with mozzarella, dividing it equally between the bases.

18 Arrange the mushroom slices on a quarter of each pizza and brush with the olive oil.

19 Pile the roasted pepper slices on another quarter with the anchovy fillets on top.

20 Use pepperoni and capers for the third and artichokes and olives for the fourth quarter.

21 Bake at the top of the oven, 2 at a time, for 20 minutes or until golden brown. Serve hot.

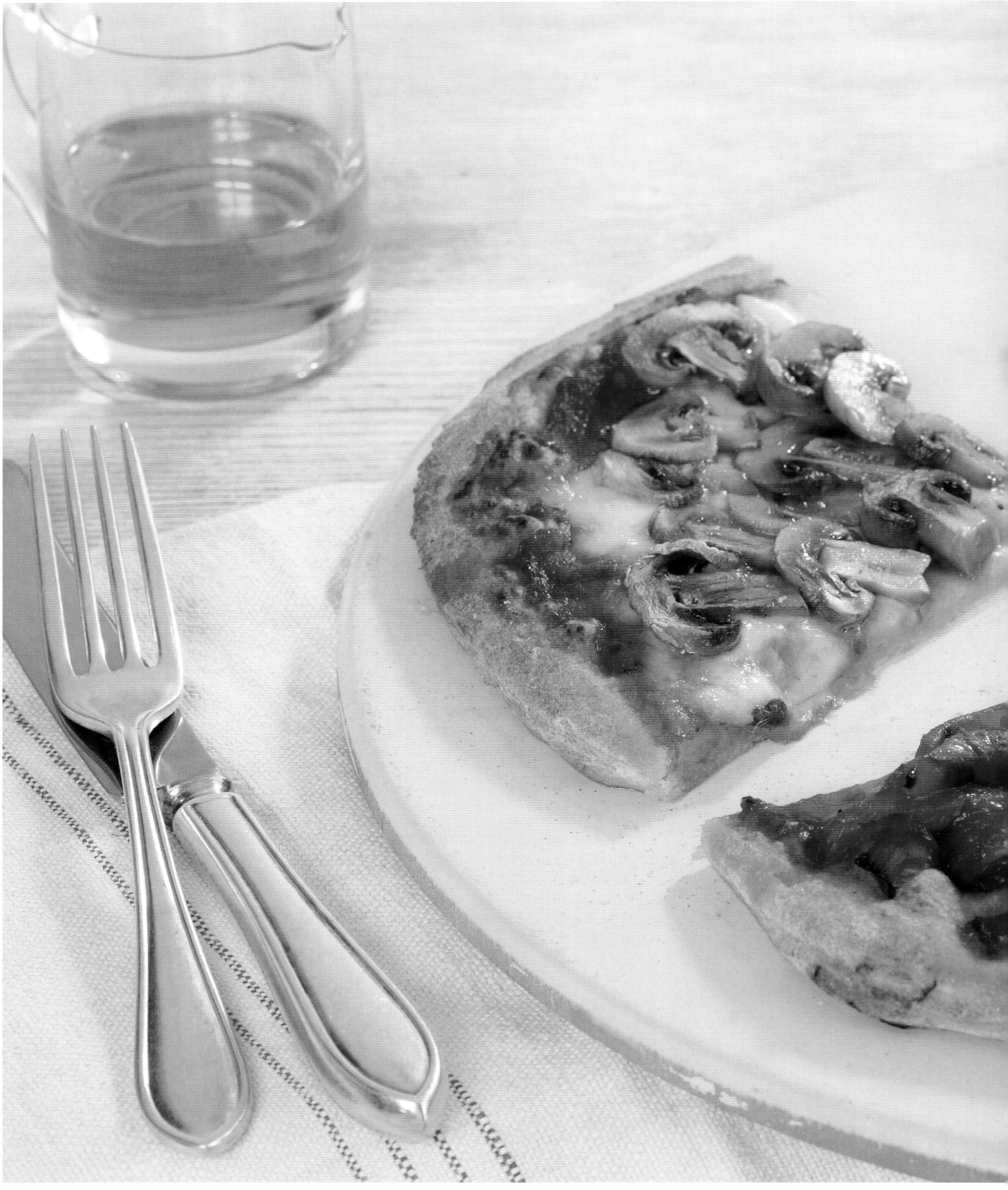

Pizza variations

Pepper Calzone

"Calzone" means "trouser leg" in Italian, perhaps due to a resemblance or because this pizza turnover could be stuffed into a roomy trouser pocket!

MAKES 4 CALZONE | **25 MINS** | **15–20 MINS**

Rising and proving time
1½–2 hrs

Ingredients
1 quantity pizza dough, see pages 472–473, steps 1–5
4 tbsp extra virgin olive oil, plus extra to serve
2 onions, thinly sliced
2 red peppers, cored and cut into strips
1 green pepper, cored and cut into strips
1 yellow pepper, cored and cut into strips
3 garlic cloves, finely chopped
1 small bunch of any herb, such as rosemary, thyme, basil, or parsley, or a mixture, leaves finely chopped
sea salt
cayenne pepper, to taste
175g (6oz) mozzarella cheese, drained and sliced
plain flour, for dusting
1 egg, beaten, for glazing

Method

1 Heat 1 tablespoon oil in a pan, add the onions. Cook for 5 minutes until soft but not brown. Transfer to a bowl and set aside.

2 Add the remaining oil to the pan, followed by the peppers, garlic, and half the herbs. Season with salt and cayenne pepper. Sauté for 7–10 minutes, stirring, until soft but not brown. Add to the onions, and let cool.

3 Knock back the dough and divide into 4 equal pieces. Roll and pull each piece into a square about 1cm (½in) thick. Spoon the pepper mixture onto a diagonal half of each square, leaving a 2.5cm (1in) border.

4 Arrange the mozzarella on top. Moisten the edge of each square with water, and fold one corner over to meet the other, forming a triangle. Pinch the edges together. Put on a floured baking sheet. Let rise for 30 minutes. Preheat the oven to 230°C (450°F/Gas 8).

5 Whisk the egg with ½ teaspoon salt, and brush over. Bake for 15–20 minutes, until golden brown. Brush with a little olive oil before serving.

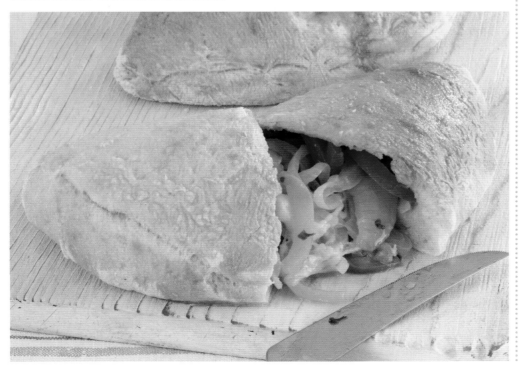

Chicago Deep-pan Pizza

A hearty pizza, dating back to 1940s Chicago.

SERVES 4 | **35–40 MINS** | **20–25 MINS**

Rising and proving time
1 hr 20 mins–1 hr 50 mins

Special equipment
2 x 23cm (9in) cake tins

Ingredients

For the dough
2½ tsp dried yeast
500g (1lb 2oz) strong white bread flour, plus extra for dusting
2 tsp salt
3 tbsp extra virgin olive oil, plus extra for greasing
2–3 tbsp polenta or cornmeal

For the sauce
375g (13oz) mild Italian sausage
1 tbsp olive oil
3 garlic cloves, finely chopped
2 x 400g cans chopped tomatoes
freshly ground black pepper
leaves from 7–10 flat-leaf parsley sprigs, chopped
175g (6oz) mozzarella cheese, torn into chunks

Method

1 In a small bowl, sprinkle the yeast over 4 tablespoons lukewarm water. Let it stand for 5 minutes, stirring once, until dissolved. In a large bowl, mix the flour with the salt and make a well in the centre. Add the dissolved yeast, 300ml (½ pint) lukewarm water, and the oil. Draw in the flour and work it into the other ingredients to form a smooth dough. It should be soft and slightly sticky.

2 Lightly flour a work surface, and knead the dough for 5–7 minutes until very smooth and elastic. Brush a large bowl with oil. Put the dough in the bowl and flip it so the surface is lightly oiled. Cover with a damp tea towel and let rise in a warm place for 1–1½ hours until doubled in size.

3 Slit the side of each sausage and push out the meat, discarding the casing. Heat the oil in a sauté pan. Add the sausage meat, and fry over medium-high heat, breaking up the meat with the wooden spoon, for 5–7 minutes until cooked. Reduce the heat to medium, remove the meat from the pan, and pour off all but 1 tablespoon of the fat.

4 Stir the garlic into the pan and fry for about 30 seconds. Return the sausage and stir in the tomatoes, salt, pepper, and all but 1 tablespoon of the parsley. Cook, stirring occasionally, for 10–15 minutes until thickened. Remove from the heat, taste for seasoning, and let cool completely.

5 Brush the tins with oil. Sprinkle the polenta into the tins, and turn it to coat the bottom and sides, then turn upside down and tap to remove the excess. Turn out the dough onto a lightly floured work surface and knock back. Shape the dough into 2 loose balls. With a rolling pin, roll the balls into rounds to fit your tins. Working carefully, wrap the dough around the rolling pin and drape it over each tin. With your hands, press the dough into the bottom of the tins, and 2.5cm (1in) up the sides, to form a rim. Cover with a dry tea towel and let rise for about 20 minutes. Preheat the oven to 230°C (450°F/Gas 8). Heat a baking sheet in the oven.

6 Spread the sauce over the dough, leaving a border. Sprinkle over the cheese and remaining parsley. Bake for 20–25 minutes until crisp and golden.

Pizza Bianca

This version is made without tomato sauce, kept moist with olive oil instead and packed with fresh Mediterranean flavours.

MAKES 4 PIZZAS · **25 MINS** · **20 MINS**

Rising time
1–1½ hrs

Ingredients
4 pizza bases, see pages 472–473, steps 1–5 and 12–14
4 tbsp extra virgin olive oil, plus extra for greasing
140g (5oz) Gorgonzola cheese, crumbled
12 slices Parma ham, torn into strips
4 fresh figs, each cut into 8 wedges, and peeled
2 tomatoes, deseeded and diced
115g (4oz) wild rocket leaves
freshly ground black pepper

Method
1 Preheat the oven to 200°C (400°F/Gas 6). Place the pizza bases on greased baking trays. Brush them with half the olive oil and scatter the cheese over the surface.

2 Bake in the oven for 20 minutes or until the bases are crisp and turning golden. Remove from the oven.

3 Arrange the ham, figs, and tomatoes on top. Then return to the oven for another 8 minutes or until the toppings are just warmed and the bases are golden brown.

4 Scatter over the rocket, season with plenty of black pepper, and serve at once, drizzled with the rest of the olive oil.

BAKER'S TIP
Pizzas are delicious with or without tomato sauce. However you like it, always remember that the toppings should be spread evenly over the base, and enough moisture added – either from tomato sauce, cheese, or extra virgin olive oil – to ensure the toppings remain well lubricated and appetizing.

Pissaladière

This French version of the Italian pizza derives its name from *pissala*, a paste made from anchovies.

SERVES 4 **20 MINS** **1 HOUR 25 MINS** **UP TO 12 WEEKS**

Rising time
1 hr

Special equipment
32.5 x 23cm (13 x 9in) Swiss roll tin

Ingredients

For the base
225g (8oz) strong white bread flour, plus extra for dusting
sea salt and freshly ground black pepper

1 tsp soft brown sugar
1 tsp dried yeast
1 tbsp olive oil, plus extra for greasing

For the topping
4 tbsp olive oil
900g (2lb) onions, finely sliced
3 garlic cloves
sprig of thyme
1 tsp herbes de Provence (dry mix of thyme, basil, rosemary, and oregano)
1 bay leaf
100g jar anchovies in oil
12 black pitted niçoise olives, or Italian olives

Method

1 For the base, mix the flour, 1 teaspoon salt, and black pepper to taste in a large bowl. Pour 150ml (5fl oz) lukewarm water into a separate bowl, and use a fork to whisk in the sugar, then the yeast. Set aside for 10 minutes to froth, then pour into the flour with the olive oil.

2 Mix together to form a dough, adding 1–2 tablespoons lukewarm water if it looks too dry. Turn the dough out onto a lightly floured surface and knead for 10 minutes or until smooth and elastic. Shape it into a ball, put in a lightly oiled bowl, and cover with a tea towel. Leave in a warm place for 1 hour or until doubled in size.

3 For the topping, put the oil in a saucepan over very low heat. Add the onions, garlic, herbs, and bay leaf. Cover and sweat gently, stirring occasionally, for 1 hour or until the onions look like a purée. Be careful not to let the onions catch; if they begin to stick, add a little water. Drain well and set aside, discarding the bay leaf.

4 Preheat the oven to 180°C (350°F/Gas 4). Knead the dough briefly on a lightly floured surface, and roll it out so it is thin and large enough to fit in the Swiss roll tin. Press the dough into the tin and prick it with a fork.

5 Spread the onions over the base. Drain the anchovies, reserving 3 tablespoons oil, and slice the fillets in half lengthways. Embed the olives in rows in the dough and drape the fillets in a criss-cross pattern on top of the onions. Drizzle with the reserved anchovy oil and sprinkle with pepper.

6 Bake for 25 minutes or until the crust is brown. The onions should not brown or dry out. Remove and serve warm, cut into rectangles, squares, or wedges, or allow to cool before serving.

BAKER'S TIP

All the elements of pissaladière are very simple, so it is imperative that you use the best-quality ingredients for the finest result. Take care when selecting the anchovies, and make sure they are packed in good-quality oil. When you can find them, smoked anchovies make an amazing substitution.

FLAT BREADS

Pita Bread

This pocket bread is delicious stuffed with salad and other fillings, or cut up and eaten with dips.

MAKES
6

20–30
MINS

5
MINS

UP TO 8
WEEKS

Rising and proving time
1 hr–1 hr 50 mins

Ingredients
1 tsp dried yeast
60g (2oz) strong wholemeal
 bread flour
250g (9oz) strong white bread flour,
 plus extra for dusting
1 tsp salt
2 tsp cumin seeds
2 tsp olive oil, plus extra for greasing

1 In a bowl, mix the yeast with 4 tablespoons lukewarm water. Leave 5 minutes, then stir.

2 In a large bowl, mix together the 2 types of flour, salt, and cumin seeds.

3 Make a well and pour in the yeast, 190ml (6¾fl oz) lukewarm water, and oil.

4 Combine the flour mix with the wet ingredients, mixing to form a soft, sticky dough.

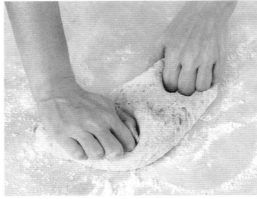

5 Turn the dough onto a floured work surface and knead until very smooth and elastic.

6 Place the dough in a lightly greased bowl and cover with a damp tea towel.

7 Leave to rise in a warm place for 1–1½ hours until doubled in size. Flour 2 baking sheets.

8 Turn the dough onto a lightly floured work surface, and knock back.

9 Shape the dough into a cylinder 5cm (2in) wide, then cut into 6 pieces.

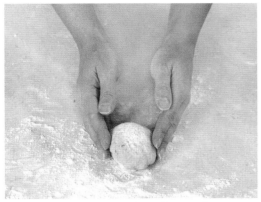

10 Take 1 piece of dough and leave the rest covered with a tea towel as you work.

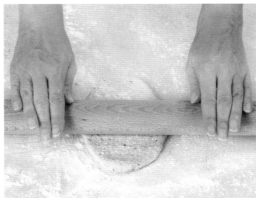

11 Shape the dough into a ball, then roll into an 18cm (7in) oval.

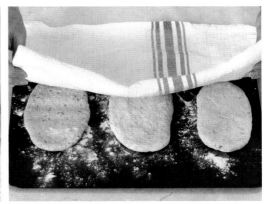

12 Transfer to a baking sheet. Repeat to shape the remaining pitas. Cover with a tea towel.

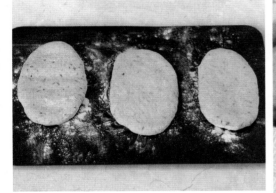

13 Leave in a warm place for 20 minutes and preheat the oven to 240°C (475°F/Gas 9).

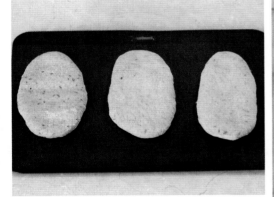

14 Place another baking sheet in the oven. Once hot, transfer half the pitas to the sheet.

15 Bake for 5 minutes. Transfer to a wire rack and brush the tops lightly with water.

16 Bake the remaining rounds, transfer to the rack, and brush with water.
STORE Best eaten warm from the oven, pitas can be stored overnight in an airtight container.

Spiced Lamb Pies

Snacks such as these are found all around the Middle East.

MAKES 12 **40–45 MINS** **10–15 MINS**

Rising and proving time
1 hr–1 hr 50 mins

Ingredients

1 quantity pita dough, see pages 480,
  steps 1–8, omitting the cumin seeds
2 tbsp extra virgin olive oil
375g (13oz) lamb mince
sea salt and freshly ground black pepper
3 large garlic cloves, finely chopped
1cm (½in) piece of fresh root ginger,
  peeled and finely chopped
1 onion, finely chopped
½ tsp ground coriander
¼ tsp ground turmeric
¼ tsp ground cumin
large pinch of cayenne pepper
2 tomatoes, peeled, deseeded, and chopped
leaves from 5–7 coriander sprigs, finely chopped
Greek yogurt, to serve (optional)

Method

1 Heat the oil in a frying pan. Add the lamb, season, and stir over medium-high heat until evenly browned. Transfer to a bowl with a slotted spoon. Reduce the heat to medium, and pour off the fat, reserving 2 tablespoons. Add the garlic and ginger, and fry for 30 seconds. Put in the onion and stir until soft, then add the coriander, turmeric, cumin, cayenne pepper, lamb, and tomatoes. Cover and cook for 10 minutes until thickened.

2 Remove the pan from the heat. Stir in the chopped coriander leaves and taste for seasoning. Let the filling cool, then taste again: it should be well seasoned, so adjust if necessary.

3 Cut the dough in half. Shape 1 piece into a cylinder, 5cm (2in) in diameter. Cut into 6 pieces, and cover. Repeat to shape and divide the remaining dough. Shape 1 piece of dough into a ball. Roll out into a 10cm (4in) round. Spoon some lamb into the centre, leaving a 2.5cm (1in) border. Lift

the dough up and over the filling, to form a triangular parcel. Pinch the edges to seal. Place the pie on a baking sheet. Repeat to shape and fill the remaining dough.

4 Cover the pies with a tea towel and let rise in a warm place for 20 minutes. Preheat the oven to 230°C (450°F/Gas 8). Bake for 10–15 minutes, until golden brown. Serve warm, with Greek yogurt, if you like.

STORE The pies will keep in an airtight container overnight.

PREPARE AHEAD The lamb filling can be prepared, covered, and refrigerated 1 day ahead.

Spiced Chickpea Pitas

These are good chargrilled, and best eaten on the day they are made.

MAKES 8 · **25 MINS** · **15 MINS**

Rising time
1 hr

Ingredients
1 tsp dried yeast
1½ tsp cumin seeds, plus more for sprinkling
1½ tsp ground coriander
450g (1lb) strong white bread flour, plus extra for dusting
1 tsp salt
small bunch of coriander, roughly chopped
200g can chickpeas, drained and crushed
150g (5½oz) plain yogurt
1 tbsp extra virgin olive oil, plus extra for greasing

Method

1 Sprinkle the yeast over 300ml (10fl oz) lukewarm water and allow to dissolve, stirring once. Toast the cumin and ground coriander in a dry pan for 1 minute. Mix the flour and salt in a bowl. Stir in the spices, coriander, and chickpeas, then make a well in the middle. Pour in the yogurt, oil, and yeast liquid, and bring together to form a sticky dough. Set aside for 10 minutes.

2 Turn the dough out onto a floured surface, and knead it for 5 minutes, shaping it into a ball. Place the dough in an oiled bowl, cover it with oiled cling film, and leave it to rise in a warm place for 1 hour or until doubled.

3 Dust 2 baking trays with flour. Preheat the oven to 220°C (425°F/Gas 7). Turn the dough out onto a floured surface. Cut into 8 pieces.

4 Using a rolling pin, flatten them out into ovals, each about 5mm (¼in) thick. Place them on the baking trays, brush with oil, and scatter over cumin seeds. Bake for 15 minutes or until golden and puffed up.

STORE The pitas will keep in an airtight container overnight.

Pita Crisps

Serve these simple home-made pita crisps as part of a range of meze or starters for a healthier alternative to potato crisps.

SERVES 8 · **10 MINS** · **7–8 MINS**

Ingredients
6 pita breads, shop-bought, or see pages 480–481
extra virgin olive oil, for brushing
sea salt, for sprinkling
cayenne pepper, for sprinkling

Method

1 Preheat the oven to 230°C (450°F/Gas 8). Divide the pita breads in half, by separating the 2 layers of bread. Brush the bread on both sides with olive oil, then sprinkle them with salt and cayenne pepper.

2 Stack the bread pieces on top of each other in piles of 6, and cut them into large triangles. Lay the cut crisps on large baking sheets in a single layer, making sure they do not overlap.

3 Bake on the top shelf of the oven for 5 minutes or until the bottoms start to brown. Turn them over and cook for 2–3 minutes until they are browned and crisp. Leave to cool on kitchen paper before serving.

STORE The crisps will keep in an airtight container for 2 days.

BAKER'S TIP
These simple snacks go well with home-made dips and salsas, or even chilli con carne. They are an inexpensive alternative to crisps, and much healthier too! To make them even more nutritious, bake wholemeal pita crisps instead.

Naan Bread

This familiar Indian flat bread is traditionally cooked in a tandoor oven but this recipe uses a conventional oven.

MAKES 6 NAAN · **20 MINS** · **8 MINS** · **UP TO 12 WEEKS**

Rising time
1 hr

Ingredients

500g (1lb 2oz) strong white bread
 flour, plus extra for dusting
2 tsp dried yeast
1 tsp caster sugar
1 tsp salt
2 tsp black onion (nigella) seeds
100ml (3½fl oz) full-fat plain yogurt
50g (2oz) ghee, or butter, melted

1 Heat the ghee or butter in a small saucepan until melted. Set aside.

2 In a large bowl, mix together the flour, yeast, sugar, salt, and onion seeds.

3 Make a well. Add 200ml (7fl oz) lukewarm water, the yogurt, and the melted ghee.

4 Draw in the flour and mix gently with a wooden spoon to combine.

5 Keep mixing for 5 minutes until it forms a rough dough.

6 Cover and keep warm until doubled; about 1 hour. Preheat the oven to 240°C (475°F/Gas 9).

7 Place 2 baking trays in the oven. Knock back the dough.

8 Knead the dough on a floured surface until smooth. Divide into 4 equal pieces.

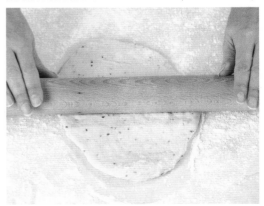

9 Roll each piece into an oval shape about 24cm (10in) long.

10 Transfer the bread to the preheated trays and bake for 6–7 minutes until well puffed.

11 Preheat the grill to its hottest setting. Transfer the bread to the grill pan.

12 Cook the naans for 30–40 seconds on each side or until they brown and blister.

13 When grilling, take care not to put the breads too close to the heat, to prevent burning. Transfer to a wire rack and serve warm.

ALSO TRY... Garlic and Coriander Naan Add 2 crushed garlic cloves and 4 tablespoons finely chopped coriander in step 2.

Naan variations

Feta, Chilli, and Herb-stuffed Naan

Try stuffing a simple naan bread dough with this herby feta mix for an unusual picnic dish, which brings together flavours of the Mediterranean with those of the Subcontinent.

MAKES 6 NAAN — **15 MINS** — **6–7 MINS**

Rising time
1 hr

Ingredients
500g (1lb 2oz) strong white bread flour, plus extra for dusting
2 tsp dried yeast
1 tsp caster sugar
1 tsp salt
2 tsp black onion (nigella) seeds
100ml (3½fl oz) full-fat plain yogurt
50g (2oz) ghee, or butter, melted
150g (5½oz) feta cheese, crumbled
1 tbsp finely chopped red chilli
3 tbsp chopped mint
3 tbsp chopped coriander

Method

1 In a bowl, mix together the flour, yeast, sugar, salt, and onion seeds. Make a well. Add 200ml (7fl oz) lukewarm water, the yogurt, and the ghee. Mix with a wooden spoon to combine. Mix for 5 minutes until it forms a smooth dough. Cover and keep warm for about 1 hour until doubled.

2 Make the stuffing by mixing together the feta, chilli, and herbs. Preheat the oven to 240°C (475°F/Gas 9) and place 2 large baking trays in the oven.

3 Divide the dough into 6 pieces, and roll each one out into a circle approximately 10cm (4in) in diameter. Divide the filling into 6 portions, and put a portion into the middle of each circle. Pull the edges up around the filling to form a purse shape. Pinch the edges to seal. Turn the dough over and roll out into an oval, taking care not to tear the dough.

4 Transfer the breads onto the preheated baking trays, and cook in the oven for 6–7 minutes or until well puffed. Transfer to a wire rack, and serve while still warm.

PREPARE AHEAD These can be stored overnight, wrapped in cling film. To reheat (from fresh or frozen), scrunch up a piece of greaseproof paper and soak it in water. Squeeze out the excess water and use to wrap the naan. Place them in a medium oven for 10 minutes until warm and soft.

Peshwari Naan

Children love these sweet, nutty stuffed naans, best eaten still warm from the pan, either as a dessert or a side dish to savoury curry. Try substituting finely chopped apple for the raisins and adding some cinnamon. ▶

MAKES 6 NAAN — **15 MINS** — **6–7 MINS** — **UP TO 8 WEEKS**

Rising time
1 hr

Special equipment
food processor with blade attachment

Ingredients
500g (1lb 2oz) strong white bread flour, plus extra for dusting
2 tsp dried yeast
1 tsp caster sugar
1 tsp salt
2 tsp black onion (nigella) seeds
100ml (3½fl oz) full-fat plain yogurt
50g (2oz) ghee, or butter, melted

For the stuffing
2 tbsp raisins
2 tbsp unsalted pistachios
2 tbsp almonds
2 tbsp dessicated coconut
1 tbsp caster sugar

Method

1 In a bowl, mix together the flour, yeast, sugar, salt, and onion seeds. Make a well. Add 200ml (7fl oz) lukewarm water, the yogurt, and the ghee. Mix with a wooden spoon to combine. Mix for 5 minutes until it forms a smooth dough. Cover and keep warm for about 1 hour until doubled.

2 Make the stuffing by whizzing together all the ingredients in a food processor, until finely chopped. Preheat the oven to 240°C (475°F/Gas 9) and place 2 baking trays in the oven.

3 Divide the dough into 6 pieces and roll each one out into a circle approximately 10cm (4in) in diameter. Divide the filling into 6 portions, and put a portion into the middle of each circle. Pull the edges up around the filling to form a purse shape. Pinch the edges together to seal.

4 Turn the dough over and roll out into an oval, taking care not to tear the dough or reveal any of the filling. Place on the preheated trays, and bake for 6–7 minutes or until well puffed. Transfer to a wire rack, and serve while still warm.

PREPARE AHEAD These can be stored overnight, wrapped in cling film. To reheat (from fresh or frozen), scrunch up a piece of greaseproof paper and soak it in water. Squeeze out the excess water and use to wrap the naan. Place them in a medium oven for 10 minutes until warm and soft.

BAKER'S TIP
Once you have mastered the art of stuffing and rolling out naan dough, there's no end to the number of things you can fill it with. Here the naan is stuffed with nuts, dried fruit, and coconut. Try a spiced lamb filling and serve with a minted yogurt dip.

FLAT BREADS

Stuffed Paratha

These stuffed flat breads are quick and easy to make. Try doubling the quantities, then freezing half stacked between layers of greaseproof paper.

MAKES 4 | 20 MINS | 15–20 MINS | UP TO 8 WEEKS

Resting time
1 hr

Ingredients

For the dough
300g (10½oz) chapatti flour
½ tsp fine salt
50g (1¾oz) unsalted butter, melted and cooled

For the stuffing
250g (9oz) sweet potato, peeled and diced
1 tbsp sunflower oil, plus extra for brushing
½ red onion, finely chopped
2 garlic cloves, crushed
1 tbsp finely chopped red chilli, or to taste
1 tbsp finely chopped fresh root ginger
2 heaped tbsp chopped coriander
½ tsp garam masala
sea salt

Method

1 To make the dough, sift the flour and salt together. Add the butter and 150ml (5fl oz) water, and bring the mixture together to form a soft dough. Knead for 5 minutes, then let the dough rest, covered, for 1 hour.

2 To make the stuffing, boil or steam the sweet potato for about 7 minutes until tender. Drain it well. In a frying pan, heat the oil over medium heat and fry the red onion for 3–5 minutes until soft but not golden. Add the garlic, chilli, and ginger, and continue to fry for 1–2 minutes.

3 Add the cooked onion mixture to the sweet potato, and mash well. You should not need extra liquid as the potato is quite moist and the oil from the onion mixture will help too. Add the coriander, garam masala, and a good seasoning of salt, and beat until smooth. Set aside to cool.

4 When the dough has rested, divide it into 4 pieces. Knead each piece and roll it out into a circle, around 10cm (4in) in diameter. Put a quarter of the stuffing in the middle. Pull the edges up around it, forming a purse shape.

5 Pinch the edges together to seal in the stuffing, turn the dough over, and roll it out into a circle, about 18cm (7in) in diameter, taking care not to roll too hard. If the filling bursts out, wipe it off and pinch the dough together to reseal the paratha.

6 Heat a large cast-iron frying pan or griddle (big enough to take the parathas) to medium heat. Fry the parathas for 2 minutes on each side, turning occasionally to make sure they are well cooked and browning in places. Once they have cooked on each side once, brush the surface with a little oil before turning them again. Serve immediately alongside a curry or as a light lunch dish with a green salad.

PREPARE AHEAD These can be stored overnight, wrapped in cling film. To reheat (from fresh or frozen), scrunch up a piece of greaseproof paper and soak it in water. Squeeze out the excess water and wrap in the paper. Place them in a medium oven for 10 minutes until warm and soft.

BAKER'S TIP

These Indian flat breads are made with traditional chapatti flour, but if you cannot find it easily, use plain wholemeal flour instead. Try stuffing them with a variety of fillings, including leftover vegetable curry, just make sure the ingredients are diced small so the stuffing is easily contained.

Tortillas

These classic Mexican flat breads are simple to make and far tastier than any shop-bought tortilla.

MAKES 8　　**10 MINS**　　**15–20 MINS**　　**UP TO 8 WEEKS**

Resting time
1 hr

Ingredients
300g (10oz) plain flour,
　plus extra for dusting
1 scant tsp salt
½ tsp baking powder
50g (1¾oz) lard or white vegetable
　fat, chilled and diced,
　plus extra for greasing

1 Put the flour, salt, and baking powder into a large bowl. Add the lard.

2 Rub the lard in with your hands until the mixture resembles fine crumbs.

3 Add 150ml (5fl oz) warm water. Bring the mixture together to form a rough, soft dough.

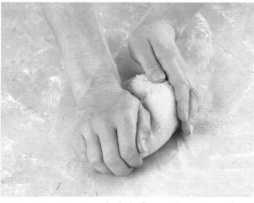

4 Turn it out onto a lightly floured work surface and knead for a few minutes until smooth.

5 Put the dough in a greased bowl and cover with cling film. Rest in a warm place for 1 hour.

6 Turn the dough out onto a floured work surface and divide it into 8 equal portions.

7 Take 1 piece and leave the others covered with cling film to prevent them from drying.

8 Roll each piece of dough out thinly to a circle about 20–25cm (8–10in) in diameter.

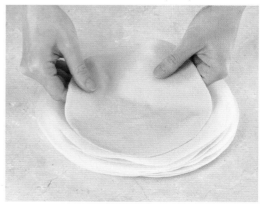

9 Stack the rolled tortillas in a pile. Place a piece of cling film or parchment between each.

FLAT BREADS

10 Heat a frying pan over medium heat. Take a tortilla and dry fry for 1 minute.

11 Turn it over and continue to fry until both sides are cooked and browned in places.

12 Transfer to a wire rack and repeat to cook all the remaining tortillas. Serve warm or cool.

PREPARE AHEAD Cooled tortillas can be stored overnight, wrapped in cling film. To reheat from fresh or frozen, scrunch up greaseproof paper and soak it in water. Squeeze out the excess, use to wrap the tortillas, and bake in a medium oven for 10 minutes.

Tortilla variations

Quesadillas

Almost any filling works for quesadillas: try substituting chicken, ham, Gruyère cheese, or mushrooms.

MAKES 1 OF EACH   5–10 MINS   30–35 MINS

Ingredients

For the spiced beef and tomato filling
1 tbsp extra virgin olive oil
150g (5½oz) beef mince
pinch of cayenne pepper
sea salt and freshly ground black pepper
handful fresh flat-leaf parsley, finely chopped
2 tomatoes, diced
50g (1¾oz) Cheddar cheese, grated

For the avocado and spring onion filling
4 spring onions, finely chopped
1–2 fresh hot red chillies, deseeded and chopped
juice of ½ lime
½ avocado, peeled, stoned, and sliced
50g (1¾oz) Cheddar cheese, grated

For the tortillas
2 tbsp vegetable oil
4 tortillas, see pages 490–491

Method

1 For the beef filling, heat the oil in a pan. Fry the beef with the cayenne pepper on medium heat for 5 minutes or until no longer pink. Reduce the heat and loosen with a little hot water. Season, and cook for 10 minutes until the beef is cooked through. Stir in the parsley.

2 For the avocado filling, place the spring onions, chillies, and lime juice in a bowl. Season and mix. Set aside for 2 minutes.

3 Heat half the oil for the tortillas in a non-stick frying pan. Fry 1 tortilla for 1 minute or until lightly golden. Spoon the beef mixture over. Scatter over the tomato and cheese, then top with the other tortilla, pressing it down with the back of a fish slice to sandwich the two. Scoop the quesadilla up, carefully turn it over, and cook the other side for another minute or until golden. Slice in halves or quarters, and serve.

4 Heat the remaining oil in the frying pan, then fry 1 tortilla for 1 minute, or until golden. Scatter over the avocado, leaving a little space around the edge, and spoon on the spring onion mixture, and sprinkle with the cheese. Continue as in step 3.

Kids' Hot Tortilla Sandwiches

A quick alternative to a sandwich lunch that kids love.

SERVES 2   10 MINS   8 MINS

Ingredients
4 tortillas, shop-bought, or see pages 490–491
4 thin slices of ham
ketchup, mild mustard, or chilli sauce (optional)
50g (1¾oz) grated cheese, such as Cheddar
carrots, peeled and chopped, to serve (optional)
cucumber, chopped, to serve (optional)

Method

1 Place 2 of the tortillas on the work surface. Place 2 slices of ham on each tortilla, trying to ensure that the ham covers the whole tortilla. Tear it a little and spread it out, if necessary.

2 Depending on your children's tastes, you could spread a little ketchup, mild mustard, or chilli sauce over the top of the ham. Sprinkle the grated cheese evenly over both the tortillas, and top with a second tortilla to make a sandwich.

3 Heat a large cast-iron frying pan or griddle (big enough to take the tortillas) to medium heat. Fry the tortillas one at a time for 1 minute on each side, until both sides are cooked and browned in places.

4 Cut each tortilla into 8 segments, as you would a pizza, and serve immediately, with some chopped carrot and cucumber for a quick lunch.

FLAT BREADS

Prawn and Guacamole Tortilla Stacks

These sophisticated Mexican-style canapés are simple to make.

MAKES 50 | **15 MINS** | **10–15 MINS**

Special equipment
3cm (1¼in) pastry cutter
piping bag with small plain nozzle

Ingredients
5 tortillas, shop-bought, or see pages 490–491
1 litre (1¾ pints) sunflower oil, for deep-frying
2 ripe avocados
juice of 1 lime
Tabasco sauce
4 tbsp finely chopped coriander
4 spring onions, trimmed and finely chopped
sea salt and freshly ground black pepper
25 cooked king prawns, peeled, deveined, and halved horizontally, or 50 prawns left whole

Method

1 Cut at least 100 disks out of the tortillas with the pastry cutter. Heat the oil in pan. Drop the tortillas into the oil, a handful at a time, and deep-fry until golden. Do not overcrowd the pan, or the tortillas will not crisp up properly. Remove them with a slotted spoon, and drain on kitchen paper. Cool.

2 In a bowl, mash the avocado with half the lime juice, dash of Tabasco, 3 tablespoons of the chopped coriander, chopped onions, and salt and pepper to taste.

3 When there are 30 minutes left before serving, marinate the prawns with the remaining lime juice and the rest of the chopped coriander.

4 Pipe a little guacamole on a tortilla, top it with another tortilla, pipe more guacamole on top, and finish with a curl of prawn. If the prawn is too big, twist it on the diagonal and stand it up in the guacamole.

PREPARE AHEAD The fried tortilla disks can be stored in an airtight container for 2 days.

quick breads & batters

Soda Bread

This has a light, cake-like texture. As an added bonus, it requires no kneading, so is a wonderfully effort-free loaf.

MAKES 1 LOAF   **10–15 MINS**   **35–40 MINS**

Ingredients

unsalted butter, for greasing
500g (1lb 2oz) stone-ground
   strong wholemeal flour,
   plus extra for dusting
1½ tsp bicarbonate of soda
1½ tsp salt
500ml (16fl oz) buttermilk,
   plus extra if needed

1 Preheat the oven to 200°C (400°F/Gas 6). Grease a baking sheet with butter.

2 Sift the flour, bicarbonate of soda, and salt into a large bowl, tipping in any leftover bran.

3 Mix thoroughly to combine and make a well in the centre.

4 Gradually pour the buttermilk into the centre of the well.

5 With your hands, quickly draw in the flour to make a soft, slightly sticky dough.

6 Do not overwork the dough. Add a little more buttermilk if it seems dry.

7 Turn the dough out onto a floured surface, and quickly shape into a round loaf.

8 Put the loaf on the baking sheet and pat it down into a round, about 5cm (2in) high.

9 Make a cross 1cm (½in) deep in the top of the loaf with a very sharp knife or scalpel.

10 Bake the loaf in the preheated oven for 35–40 minutes, until brown.

11 Turn the loaf over and tap the bottom. The bread should sound hollow.

12 Transfer the bread to a wire rack and let it cool slightly.

13 Cut the bread into slices or wedges and serve warm. Soda bread also makes very good toast. **STORE** The bread will keep, well wrapped in paper, in an airtight container, for 2–3 days.

Soda Bread variations

Skillet Bread

In this version, the dough is cut in wedges and cooked in a heavy frying pan or skillet, and the addition of white flour makes it a little lighter.

MAKES 8 WEDGES   **5–10 MINS**   **30–40 MINS**

Special equipment
lidded cast-iron frying pan

Ingredients
375g (13oz) stone-ground strong wholemeal flour
125g (4½oz) strong white bread flour,
  plus extra for dusting
1½ tsp bicarbonate of soda
1 tsp salt
375ml (13fl oz) buttermilk
unsalted butter, melted, for greasing

Method
1 Put the 2 types of flour, the bicarbonate of soda, and salt into a large bowl. Make a well in the centre of the flour mixture, and pour the buttermilk into the well. Using your fingertips, quickly draw the flour into the liquid to make a soft dough. It should be slightly sticky.

2 Turn the dough out onto a lightly floured work surface and quickly shape it into a round loaf. Pat the dough with the palms of your hands to form a round shape, about 5cm (2in) high. With a sharp knife, cut the dough into 8 wedges.

3 Heat a large cast-iron frying pan to medium-low. Brush the heated pan with melted butter. In 2 batches, put the dough into the pan, cover, and cook, turning the wedges frequently, for 15–20 minutes, until golden brown and puffed. Serve warm.

Griddle Cakes

These sweet cakes are crisp on the outside, moist in the centre.

MAKES 20 CAKES   **5–10 MINS**   **10 MINS**

Special equipment
griddle or large cast-iron frying pan

Ingredients
250g (9oz) stone-ground strong wholemeal flour
1½ tsp bicarbonate of soda
1½ tsp salt
90g (3oz) rolled oats
3 tbsp soft brown sugar
600ml (1 pint) buttermilk
unsalted butter, melted, for greasing

Method
1 Put the flour, bicarbonate of soda, and salt into a large bowl. Stir in the oats and sugar, and make a well in the centre. Pour the buttermilk into the well. Stir, gradually drawing in the dry ingredients to make a smooth batter.

2 Heat a griddle or a large cast-iron frying pan, to medium-low. Brush the heated griddle with melted butter. Using a small ladle, drop about 2 tablespoons of the batter onto the hot surface. Repeat to make 5–6 cakes. Cook for about 5 minutes until the underside of the cakes are golden brown and crisp. Turn and brown them on the other side for about 5 minutes longer.

3 Transfer to a platter, cover, and keep warm. Continue with the remaining batter, brushing the griddle with more butter as needed. Serve the cakes warm.

QUICK BREADS AND BATTERS

American Soda Bread

This classic sweet bread can be ready for an afternoon snack in no time.

**MAKES
1 LOAF** · **10–15
MINS** · **50–55
MINS** · **UP TO 8
WEEKS**

Ingredients
400g (14oz) plain flour, plus extra for dusting
1 tsp fine salt
2 tsp baking powder
50g (1¾oz) caster sugar
1 tsp caraway seeds (optional)
50g (1¾oz) unsalted butter, chilled and diced
100g (3½oz) raisins
150ml (5fl oz) buttermilk
1 egg

Method

1 Preheat the oven to 180°C (350°F/Gas 4). In a large bowl, mix together the flour, salt, baking powder, caster sugar, and caraway seeds (if using). Rub in the butter until the mixture resembles fine crumbs. Add the raisins and mix well.

2 Whisk the buttermilk and the egg. Make a well in the centre of the flour mixture and pour in the buttermilk mixture, slowly stirring until it is all incorporated. You will need to use your hands at the end to bring the mixture together to form a loose, soft dough.

3 Turn the dough out onto a lightly floured surface and knead it briefly until smooth. Shape it into a round, about 15cm (6in) in diameter, and slash the top with a cross to allow the bread to rise easily when baking.

4 Place the dough on a baking tray lined with baking parchment and cook in the middle of the oven for 50–55 minutes until well risen and golden brown. Transfer to a wire rack and let it cool for at least 10 minutes before serving.

STORE This bread is best eaten the day it is made, but will keep, well wrapped in paper, for 2 days. It makes great toast.

Quick Pumpkin Bread

The use of grated pumpkin ensures this quick bread keeps moist for days. A perfect accompaniment for soup.

MAKES 1 LOAF   **20 MINS**   **50 MINS**   **UP TO 8 WEEKS**

Ingredients

300g (10½oz) plain flour, plus extra for dusting
100g (3½oz) wholemeal self-raising flour
1 tsp bicarbonate of soda
½ tsp fine salt

120g (4¼oz) pumpkin or butternut squash, peeled, deseeded, and roughly grated
30g (1oz) pumpkin seeds
300ml (10fl oz) buttermilk

1 Preheat the oven to 220°C (425°F/Gas 7). In a bowl, mix the flour, bicarbonate, and salt.

2 Add the grated pumpkin and seeds, and stir well to combine so that no clumps remain.

3 Make a well in the centre and pour in the buttermilk. Stir together to form a dough.

4 Use your hands to bring the mixture together into a ball, then turn out onto a floured surface.

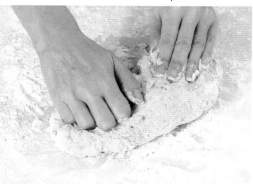

5 Knead the dough for 2 minutes until it forms a smooth mass. You may need to add flour.

6 Shape the dough into a round 15cm (6in) in diameter. Place on a lined baking sheet.

7 Use a sharp knife to slash a cross into the top. This helps the bread to rise when baking.

8 Cook for 30 minutes in the centre of the oven until risen. Reduce to 200°C (400°F/Gas 6).

9 Cook for a further 20 minutes. The base should sound hollow when tapped.

10 Transfer the bread to a wire rack and allow it to cool for at least 20 minutes before serving. **STORE** This will keep, well wrapped in paper, for 3 days. Cut the bread into wedges or slices and serve as an accompaniment to soups and stews.

Vegetable Quick Bread variations

Sweet Potato and Rosemary Rolls

The gentle scent of rosemary makes these rolls something special.

MAKES 8 ROLLS | **20 MINS** | **20–25 MINS** | **UP TO 8 WEEKS**

Ingredients
300g (10½oz) plain flour, plus extra for dusting
100g (3½oz) wholemeal self-raising flour
1 tsp bicarbonate of soda
½ tsp fine salt
freshly ground black pepper
140g (5oz) sweet potato, peeled and grated
1 tsp finely chopped rosemary
280ml (9fl oz) buttermilk

Method

1 Preheat the oven to 220°C (425°F/Gas 7). Line a baking sheet with parchment. In a bowl, mix the plain flour, wholemeal flour, bicarbonate of soda, salt, and pepper. Chop the grated potato to reduce the size of the shreds. Add it to the bowl, with the rosemary, mixing well.

2 Make a well in the centre of the dry ingredients and gently stir in the buttermilk, bringing the mixture together to form a loose dough. Use your hands to bring the mixture together into a ball, then turn it out onto a floured surface and knead for 2 minutes until it forms a smooth dough. You may need to add a little flour at this stage.

3 Divide the dough into 8 equal pieces, and shape them into tight rounds. Flatten the tops and cut a cross in the centre of each roll with a sharp knife to help the dough to rise in the oven.

4 Place the rolls onto the lined baking tray. Cook in the middle of the oven for 20–25 minutes until well risen and golden brown. Transfer to a wire rack and cool for at least 10 minutes before serving. These are particularly delicious eaten still warm.

STORE The rolls will keep, well wrapped in paper, for 3 days.

QUICK BREADS AND BATTERS

502

Courgette and Hazelnut Bread

Hazelnuts add taste and texture to this quick and easy bread.

MAKES 1 LOAF | **20 MINS** | **50 MINS** | **UP TO 8 WEEKS**

Ingredients

300g (10½oz) plain flour, plus extra for dusting
100g (3½oz) wholemeal self-raising flour
1 tsp bicarbonate of soda
½ tsp fine salt
50g (1¾oz) hazelnuts, roughly chopped
150g (5½oz) courgette, coarsely grated
280ml (9fl oz) buttermilk

Method

1 Preheat the oven to 220°C (425°F/Gas 7). Line a baking sheet with parchment. In a bowl, mix the plain flour, wholemeal flour, bicarbonate of soda, salt, and hazelnuts. Add the grated courgette, mixing it in well.

2 Make a well in the centre of the dry ingredients and stir in the buttermilk, bringing the mixture together to form a loose dough. Use your hands to bring the mixture together into a ball, then turn it out onto a floured surface and knead for 2 minutes until it forms a smooth dough. You may need to add a little extra flour at this stage.

3 Shape the dough into a round about 15cm (6in) in diameter. With a sharp knife, slash a cross in the top of the dough to help it to rise easily when baking.

4 Place the dough onto the baking sheet and cook in the middle of the oven for 30 minutes. Reduce to 200°C (400°F/Gas 6), and bake for 20 minutes until well risen, golden brown, and a skewer inserted into the middle emerges clean. Transfer to a wire rack and allow it to cool for at least 20 minutes before serving.

STORE The bread will keep, well wrapped in paper, for 3 days.

Parsnip and Parmesan Bread

A perfect combination of flavours to serve with a bowl of warming soup on a cold winter's day.

MAKES 1 LOAF | **20 MINS** | **50 MINS** | **UP TO 8 WEEKS**

Ingredients

300g (10oz) plain flour, plus extra for dusting
100g (3½oz) wholemeal self-raising flour
1 tsp bicarbonate of soda
½ tsp fine salt
freshly ground black pepper
50g (1¾oz) Parmesan cheese, finely grated
150g (5½oz) parsnip, coarsely grated
300ml (10fl oz) buttermilk

Method

1 Preheat the oven to 220°C (425°F/Gas 7). Line a baking sheet with parchment. In a bowl mix the plain flour, wholemeal flour, bicarbonate of soda, salt, pepper, and Parmesan. Roughly chop the grated parsnip to reduce the size of the shreds. Add it to the bowl, mixing it in well.

2 Make a well in the centre of the dry ingredients and gently stir in the buttermilk, bringing the mixture together to form a loose dough. Use your hands to bring the mixture together into a ball, then turn it out onto a floured surface and knead for 2 minutes until it forms a smooth dough. You may need to add a little extra flour at this stage.

3 Shape the dough into a round, about 15cm (6in) in diameter. With a sharp knife, slash a cross in the top of the dough to allow the bread to rise easily when baking.

4 Place the dough onto the baking tray and cook in the middle of the oven for 30 minutes to create a good crust. Reduce to 200°C (400°F/Gas 6), and bake for 20 minutes until well risen, golden brown, and a skewer inserted into the middle emerges clean. Transfer to a wire rack and allow it to cool for at least 20 minutes before serving.

STORE The bread will keep, well wrapped in paper, for 3 days.

Cornbread

Cornbread is a traditional American loaf that makes a quick and easy accompaniment to soups and stews.

SERVES **15–20** **20–25**
8 **MINS** **MINS**

Special equipment
23cm (9in) flameproof cast-iron
frying pan or similar-sized
loose-bottomed round cake tin

Ingredients
60g (2oz) unsalted butter or bacon
  dripping, melted and cooled,
  plus extra for greasing
2 fresh corn cobs, about 200g (7oz)
  weight of kernels
150g (5½oz) fine yellow cornmeal
  or polenta
125g (4½oz) strong white bread flour

50g (1¾oz) caster sugar
1 tbsp baking powder
1 tsp salt
2 eggs
250ml (8fl oz) milk

1 Preheat the oven to 220°C (425°F/Gas 7). Oil the pan with butter or dripping. Place in oven.

2 Cut away the kernels from the cobs and scrape out the pulp with the back of the knife.

3 Sift the polenta, flour, sugar, baking powder, and salt into a bowl. Add the corn.

4 In a bowl, whisk together the eggs, melted butter or bacon dripping, and milk.

5 Pour three-quarters of the milk mixture into the flour mixture and stir.

6 Draw in the dry ingredients, adding the remaining milk mixture. Stir just until smooth.

7 Carefully take the hot pan out of the oven and pour in the batter; it should sizzle.

8 Quickly brush the top with butter or bacon dripping. Bake for 20–25 minutes.

9 The bread should shrink from the sides of the pan and a skewer should come out clean.

QUICK BREADS AND BATTERS

504

10 Let the cornbread cool slightly on a wire rack. Serve warm, with soup, chilli con carne, or fried chicken. The cornbread does not keep well but leftovers can be used as a stuffing for roast poultry.

Cornbread variations

Corn Muffins with Roasted Red Pepper

In the spirit of the American West, sweet red pepper is roasted, diced, and stirred into a corn batter. Baking the cornbread in muffin trays makes it easily portable for a picnic, packed lunch, or buffet.

MAKES 12 | **20 MINS** | **15–20 MINS**

Special equipment
12-hole muffin tin

Ingredients
1 large red pepper
150g (5½oz) fine yellow cornmeal or polenta
125g (4½oz) strong white bread flour
1 tbsp caster sugar
1 tbsp baking powder
1 tsp salt
2 eggs
60g (2oz) unsalted butter or bacon dripping, melted and cooled, plus extra for greasing
250ml (9fl oz) milk

Method
1 Heat the grill on its highest setting. Set the pepper underneath and grill, turning as needed, until the skin blackens and blisters. Put the pepper in a plastic bag, close it, and let cool. Peel off the skin and cut out the core. Cut the pepper in half and scrape out the seeds and ribs. Dice the flesh finely.

2 Preheat the oven to 220°C (425°F/Gas 7). Generously grease the muffin tin and place it in the oven to heat up. Sift the polenta, flour, sugar, baking powder, and salt into a large bowl, and make a well in the centre.

3 In a bowl, whisk together the eggs, melted butter or bacon dripping, and milk. Pour three-quarters of the milk mixture into the well in the flour, and stir. Draw in the dry ingredients, adding the remaining milk mixture, and stirring until smooth. Stir in the diced pepper.

4 Remove the muffin tin from the oven and spoon the batter into the muffin holes. Bake in the oven for 15–20 minutes until they start to shrink from the sides of the holes and a metal skewer inserted in the centre comes out clean. Unmould the muffins and let cool.

PREPARE AHEAD Best served warm from the oven, these can be made 1 day ahead and kept tightly wrapped in paper. If possible, warm gently in the oven before serving.

Southern US-style Cornbread

This quick American cornbread is traditionally served as an accompaniment for a barbecue, soup, or stew. Some authentic Southern recipes omit the honey. ▶

SERVES 8 | **10–15 MINS** | **25–35 MINS**

Special equipment
18cm (7in) loose-bottomed round cake tin or similar-sized flameproof cast-iron frying pan

Ingredients
250g (9oz) fine cornmeal or polenta, ideally white cornmeal if you can get it
2 tsp baking powder
½ tsp fine salt
2 large eggs
250ml (8fl oz) buttermilk
50g (1¾oz) unsalted butter or bacon dripping, melted and cooled, plus extra for greasing
1 tbsp honey (optional)

Method
1 Preheat the oven to 220°C (425°F/Gas 7). Grease the cake tin or frying pan and place it in the oven to heat up. In a bowl, mix the cornmeal, baking powder, and salt. Whisk together the eggs and buttermilk.

2 Make a well in the centre of the cornmeal mixture and pour in the buttermilk mixture, stirring. Stir in the melted butter or bacon dripping, and honey (if using) and mix.

3 Remove the hot cake tin or frying pan from the oven and pour in the mixture. The tin or pan should be hot enough to make the batter sizzle as it goes in; this is what gives the cornbread its distinctive crust.

4 Bake in the middle of the oven for 20–25 minutes until it has risen, and is browning at the edges. Leave to cool for 5 minutes before turning out and slicing as a side dish.

PREPARE AHEAD Best served warm from the oven, the bread can be made 1 day ahead and kept tightly wrapped. Warm gently in the oven before serving.

ALSO TRY...

Chilli and Coriander Cornbread
Add 1 red chilli, deseeded and finely chopped, and 4 tablespoons finely chopped coriander at the same time as the honey.

> **BAKER'S TIP**
> Southern US-style cornbread gains a lot of its flavour from the use of melted bacon dripping in the batter, and a jar of collected leftover bacon grease is a common sight in kitchens across the Southern states of America – so start your own collection!

QUICK BREADS AND BATTERS

American Blueberry Pancakes

Dropping the blueberries on top of the half-cooked pancakes stops the juice leaking out into the pan and burning.

MAKES 30 | **10 MINS** | **15–20 MINS**

Ingredients
30g (1oz) unsalted butter,
  plus extra for frying and to serve
2 large eggs
200g (7oz) self-raising flour
1 tsp baking powder

40g (1¼oz) caster sugar
250ml (8fl oz) milk
1 tsp vanilla extract
150g (5½oz) blueberries
maple syrup, to serve

1 Melt the butter in a small saucepan and set aside to cool.

2 Crack the eggs into a small bowl and lightly beat with a fork until combined.

3 Sift the flour and baking powder into a bowl, lifting the sieve high above to aerate the flour.

4 Stir in the sugar until evenly mixed with the flour, so each pancake will be equally sweet.

5 In a jug, lightly beat together the milk, eggs, and vanilla extract until well blended.

6 With a spoon, form a well in the centre of the dry ingredients.

7 Pour a little of the egg mixture into the well and start to whisk it in.

8 Wait until each addition of egg mixture has been incorporated before whisking in more.

9 Finally, whisk in the melted butter until the mixture is entirely smooth.

10 Melt a knob of butter in a large, non-stick frying pan over a medium heat.

11 Pour 1 tablespoon of the batter into the pan, to form a round pancake.

12 Continue to add tablespoons of batter, leaving space between for them to spread.

13 As they begin to cook, sprinkle a few blueberries over the uncooked surface.

14 They are ready to turn when small bubbles appear and pop, leaving small holes.

15 Turn the pancakes over carefully with a palette knife.

16 Continue to cook for 1–2 minutes until golden brown on both sides and cooked.

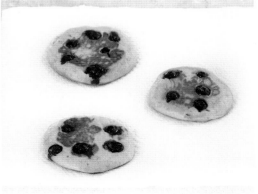

17 Remove the pancakes from the pan, and drain briefly on kitchen paper.

18 Place the pancakes on a plate and transfer to a warm oven.

19 Wipe out the frying pan with kitchen paper, and add another knob of butter.

20 Repeat for all the batter and wipe between batches. The pan should not get too hot.

21 Remove the pancakes from the oven. Serve warm in piles, with butter and maple syrup.

AMERICAN BLUEBERRY PANCAKES

American Pancake variations

Cinnamon Pancakes

Transform any leftover pancakes with this quick topping.

| MAKES 8 | 10 MINS | 5 MINS |

Ingredients
1 tsp ground cinnamon
4 tbsp caster sugar
8 leftover American pancakes,
  see pages 508–509
25g (scant 1oz) unsalted butter, melted
Greek yogurt, to serve (optional)

Method
1 Preheat the grill on its highest setting. Mix the cinnamon and sugar together, and tip out onto a plate. Brush each cold pancake on both sides with melted butter, and press each side into the sugar and cinnamon mixture, shaking off the excess sugar.

2 Place the pancakes on an oven tray, and cook under the hot grill until the sugar is bubbling and melted. Leave the sugar to set for 1 minute before turning them over and grilling on the other side. Serve immediately with Greek yogurt or just plain as an afternoon snack.

BAKER'S TIP
American pancakes are a great standby, and the recipe is easy to remember once you have cooked it a few times. They can be served as breakfast or dessert, with strawberries, chocolate sauce, or banana and yogurt. Make the toppings as decadent or as healthy as you like.

Drop Scones

So-called because the batter is dropped onto a frying pan.

| MAKES 12 | 10 MINS | 15 MINS | UP TO 4 WEEKS |

Ingredients
225g (8oz) plain flour
4 tsp baking powder
1 large egg
2 tsp golden syrup
200ml (7fl oz) milk, plus extra if needed
vegetable oil

Method
1 Place a flat griddle pan or large frying pan over medium heat. Fold a tea towel in half and lay it on a baking tray.

2 Sift the flour and baking powder into a bowl. Make a well in the centre and add the egg, golden syrup, and milk. Whisk well to make a smooth batter with the consistency of thick cream. If the mixture is too thick, beat in a little more milk.

3 Test that the griddle pan is hot enough by sprinkling a little flour on the hot surface; it should brown slowly. If it burns, the pan is too hot and needs to cool a little. When the temperature is right, dust off the flour and rub a piece of kitchen towel dipped in cooking oil lightly over the surface. Use oven gloves to protect your hands.

4 Drop a tablespoon of batter from the tip of the spoon onto the pan to make a nice round shape. Repeat, leaving enough room for them to rise and spread.

5 When bubbles appear on the surface of the pancakes, gently flip with a palette knife to cook the other side, pressing lightly with the flat knife to ensure even browning. Place cooked pancakes inside the folded towel to keep them soft, while you fry the rest of the batch.

6 Carefully oil the hot pan after each batch and watch the heat. If the pancakes are cooking too pale, increase the heat; if they brown too quickly, reduce it. Best eaten fresh and warm.

Banana, Yogurt, and Honey Pancake Stack

Try stacking pancakes for a luxurious breakfast treat. ▶

| SERVES 6 | 10 MINS | 15–20 MINS |

Ingredients
200g (7oz) self-raising flour
1 tsp baking powder
40g (1¼oz) caster sugar
250ml (8fl oz) whole milk
2 large eggs, beaten
½ tsp vanilla extract
30g (1oz) unsalted butter, melted
  and cooled, plus extra for frying
2–3 bananas
200g (7oz) Greek yogurt
runny honey, to serve

Method
1 Sift the flour and baking powder into a large bowl, and add the sugar. In a jug, whisk together the milk, eggs, and vanilla extract. Make a well in the centre of the flour mixture and whisk in the milk mixture, a little at a time. Finally, whisk in the butter until the mixture is entirely smooth.

2 Melt a knob of butter in a large, non-stick frying pan. Pour tablespoons of the batter into the pan, leaving space between them for the pancakes to spread. The pancakes should spread to approximately 8–10cm (3¼–4in) in diameter. Cook the pancakes over medium heat. Turn them over when small bubbles appear on the surface and pop. Cook for another 1–2 minutes until golden brown and cooked through.

3 Slice the bananas on the diagonal to produce 5cm (2in) long strips. Place one warm pancake on a plate, and top with a spoonful of Greek yogurt and some slices of banana. Top with another pancake, more yogurt, and honey. Finish the stack with a third pancake, topped with a spoonful of yogurt and drizzled over generously with runny honey.

Buttermilk Biscuits

A favourite dish of the American South, where they are eaten for breakfast spread with something sweet or to accompany sausage and gravy.

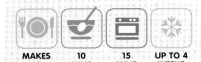

MAKES 12 | 10 MINS | 15 MINS | UP TO 4 WEEKS

Special equipment
6cm (2½in) pastry cutter

Ingredients
250g (9oz) self-raising flour
1 tsp baking powder
½ tsp fine salt
100g (3½oz) unsalted butter, softened
100ml (3½fl oz) buttermilk, plus extra for brushing
1 tbsp runny honey

Method

1 Preheat the oven to 200°C (400°F/Gas 6). Sift the flour and baking powder into a bowl and add the salt. With your fingertips, rub the butter into the dry ingredients until the mixture resembles fine crumbs.

2 Make a well in the centre and pour in the buttermilk and honey. Work the mixture together to form a rough dough, then turn it out onto a lightly floured work surface and bring it together into a smooth ball. Do not over handle it or the biscuits may harden (see Baker's Tip).

3 Roll out the dough to a thickness of 2cm (¾in) and cut 6cm (2½in) biscuits out of it with the pastry cutter. Gather up the remaining dough, re-roll it, and cut out biscuits until all the dough is used up.

4 Place the biscuits on a non-stick baking sheet and brush the tops with buttermilk, to give them a golden finish. Bake in the top third of the oven for 15 minutes until golden brown and well risen. Remove from the oven and cool for 5 minutes on a wire rack before serving, still warm.

STORE The biscuits can be kept in an airtight container for 1 day and warmed up again in the oven before serving.

BAKER'S TIP
Buttermilk biscuits have a tendency to harden and taste tough if overhandled. To avoid this, bring the mix together gently and stop as soon as it forms a dough. When rolling gently, try to cut out as many biscuits from the first rolling as possible, as biscuits from subsequent rollings will be tougher.

Crumpets

Eaten for breakfast or at teatime, toasted crumpets are great with both sweet and savoury toppings.

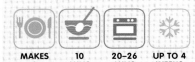

MAKES 8	10 MINS	20–26 MINS	UP TO 4 WEEKS

Special equipment
4 crumpet rings or 10cm (4in) metal pastry cutters

Ingredients
125g (4½oz) plain flour
125g (4½oz) strong white bread flour
½ tsp dried yeast
175ml (6fl oz) tepid milk
½ tsp salt
½ tsp bicarbonate of soda
vegetable oil, for greasing

Method

1 Mix together the 2 types of flour and yeast. Stir in the milk and 175ml (6fl oz) lukewarm water, and leave for 2 hours or until the bubbles have risen and then started to fall again. Sprinkle the salt and bicarbonate of soda over 2 tablespoons lukewarm water, and whisk into the batter. Set aside for about 5 minutes.

2 Oil the crumpet rings or pastry cutters. Lightly oil a large, heavy frying pan and place the rings in the pan.

3 Pour the batter into a jug. Heat the pan over medium heat, and pour batter into each ring to a depth of 1–2cm (½–¾in).

Cook the crumpets for 8–10 minutes until the batter has set all the way through or holes appear in the top. If no bubbles appear, the mixture is too dry, so stir a little water into the remaining batter.

4 Lift the rings off the crumpets, turn them over, and cook for another 2–3 minutes, or until just golden. Repeat with the remaining batter. Serve the crumpets warm, or toast to reheat if serving them later.

BAKER'S TIP
The holes on top of crumpets are their unique selling point, making them the perfect repository for butter, jam, or marmalade. The leavening creates bubbles as they cook, which burst to produce these holes. Home-made crumpets tend to have fewer holes, but are no less tasty or absorbent for it.

QUICK BREADS AND BATTERS

Crêpes Suzette

In this most classic of French desserts, crêpes are flambéd just before serving. A sure way to create culinary drama.

SERVES 6

40–50 MINS

45–60 MINS

Standing time
30 mins

Ingredients

For the crêpes
175g (6oz) plain flour, sifted
1 tbsp caster sugar
½ tsp salt
4 eggs

375ml (13fl oz) milk,
  plus extra if needed
90g (3oz) unsalted butter, melted
  and cooled, plus extra if needed

For the orange butter
175g (6oz) unsalted butter,
  at room temperature
30g (1oz) icing sugar

3 large oranges, 2 finely grated
  and 1 pared with a vegetable
  peeler, then cut into julienne strips
1 tbsp Grand Marnier

For flaming
75ml (2½fl oz) brandy
75ml (2½fl oz) Grand Marnier

QUICK BREADS AND BATTERS

1 Mix the flour, sugar, and salt. Make a well in the centre. Add the eggs and half the milk.

2 Whisk, drawing in the flour, to make a batter. Whisk in half the butter until smooth.

3 Add milk to give a batter the consistency of single cream. Cover and leave for 30 minutes.

4 For the orange butter, cream together the butter and icing sugar with an electric whisk.

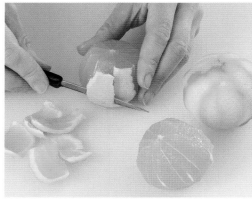

5 With a sharp knife, cut the pith and skin from all 3 oranges.

6 Slide the knife down both sides of each segment to cut it free. Set aside.

7 Add the zest and 2 tablespoons juice to the butter with the Grand Marnier. Whisk well.

8 Add the julienned orange strips to a pan of boiling water, simmer for 2 minutes. Drain.

9 Add a little melted butter to a small frying pan and heat over medium-high heat.

10 Ladle 2–3 tablespoons of the batter into the pan, tilting the pan so the base is covered.

11 Fry for 1 minute. Gently loosen with a palette knife. Turn and cook for 30–60 seconds.

12 Repeat to make 12 crêpes, adding butter only when they start to stick.

13 Spread the orange butter over 1 side of each crêpe. Heat the pan over medium heat.

14 Add 1 crêpe at a time, butter-side down. Cook for 1 minute and fold into quarters.

15 Arrange the crêpes in the hot frying pan. Heat the alcohol, then pour over the crêpes.

16 Stand back. Hold a lighted match to the side of the pan. Baste until the flames die down.

17 Divide the crêpes among warmed plates, and spoon the sauce from the pan over them.

18 Decorate with orange segments and strips, and serve. **PREPARE AHEAD** The plain crêpes can be made 3 days ahead, layered with parchment, and stored, wrapped, in the refrigerator.

Crêpe variations

Buckwheat Galettes

These savoury pancakes are popular in the Brittany region of France, where the local cuisine is defined by rich, rustic flavours

SERVES 4 | 25 MINS | 25–30 MINS | 12 WEEKS, UNFILLED

Resting time
2 hrs

Ingredients

For the galettes
75g (2½oz) buckwheat flour
75g (2½oz) plain flour
2 eggs, beaten
250ml (8fl oz) milk
sunflower oil, for greasing

For the filling
2 tbsp sunflower oil
2 red onions, thinly sliced
200g (7oz) smoked ham, chopped
1 tsp thyme leaves
115g (4oz) Brie, cut into small pieces
100ml (3½fl oz) crème fraîche

Method

1 Sift the flour into a large bowl, make a well in the centre, and add the eggs. Gradually beat the eggs into the flour using a wooden spoon, then add the milk and 100ml (3½fl oz) water to make a smooth batter. Cover and let it stand for 2 hours.

2 Heat the oil for the filling in a small frying pan, add the onions, and fry gently until softened. Add the ham and thyme, then remove from the heat and set aside.

3 Preheat the oven to 150°C (300°F/Gas 2). Heat a large frying pan and grease lightly. Spoon in 2 tablespoons of the batter and swirl so it coats the base of the pan. Cook for about 1 minute or until lightly browned underneath, then flip over and cook for another minute or until browned on the other side. Make 7 more galettes, re-greasing the pan as necessary.

4 Stir the Brie and crème fraîche into the filling, and divide it between the crêpes. Then roll or fold them up, and place them on a baking sheet. Heat through in the oven for 10 minutes before serving.

PREPARE AHEAD Make the batter a few hours in advance and leave to stand until ready to cook. If it thickens too much, stir in a little water before using.

Spinach, Pancetta, and Ricotta Pancake Bake

Try making with shop-bought pancakes for a speedy supper.

SERVES 4 | 30 MINS | 35 MINS | 12 WEEKS, UNBAKED

Special equipment
25 x 32cm (10 x 12¾in) shallow ovenproof dish

Ingredients

For the batter
175g (6oz) plain flour
½ tsp fine salt
250ml (8fl oz) whole milk, plus extra if needed
4 eggs
50g (1¾oz) unsalted butter, melted and cooled, plus extra for frying and greasing

For the filling
50g (1¾oz) pine nuts
2 tsp extra virgin olive oil
1 red onion, finely chopped
100g (3½oz) diced pancetta
2 garlic cloves, crushed
300g (10½oz) baby spinach, washed and dried
250g (9oz) ricotta
3–4 tbsp double cream
sea salt and freshly ground black pepper

For the cheese sauce
350ml (12fl oz) double cream
60g (2oz) Parmesan cheese, finely grated

Method

1 To make the pancakes, mix the flour and salt in a large bowl. In a separate bowl, whisk together the milk and eggs. Make a well in the centre of the flour mixture and whisk in the milk mixture, a little at a time, until it is all incorporated. Add the butter and whisk until entirely smooth. The mixture should be the consistency of pouring cream. Add a little extra milk if needed. Transfer the batter to a jug, cover with cling film, and leave it to rest for 30 minutes.

2 To make the filling, dry-fry the pine nuts in a large frying pan for a couple of minutes over medium heat, turning them often until they are golden brown in places. Set aside.

3 Add the olive oil to the pan and sauté the onion for 3 minutes until softened, but not browned. Add the pancetta and fry it over medium heat for another 5 minutes until golden brown and crispy. Add the garlic and cook for another minute. Add the baby spinach in handfuls. The spinach will wilt very quickly, so cook only until it begins to wilt, then remove the pan from the heat.

4 Tip the spinach mixture into a sieve, and press down with the back of a spoon to remove excess water. Tip it into a bowl, add the pine nuts, and mix it all with the ricotta and the cream. Season well and set aside.

5 Melt a knob of butter in a large, non-stick frying pan, and when it begins to sizzle wipe away any excess with a piece of kitchen paper. Pour a ladleful of the pancake mixture into the frying pan and then tip the pan to cover with a thin layer of the batter. Cook for 2 minutes on each side, turning them when the first side is golden brown. Set the cooked pancakes aside and continue until all the batter has been used up, adding a knob more butter when necessary. This should make 10 pancakes.

6 Preheat the oven to 200°C (400°F/Gas 6). Lay a pancake out flat. Put 2 tablespoons of filling into the middle of the pancake. Use the back of the spoon to spread it out into a thick line, then roll the pancake up around it. Grease the dish, and lay the pancakes side by side in the dish.

7 For the sauce, heat the double cream until nearly boiling. Add nearly all the Parmesan. Whisk until the cheese melts, then bring to a boil and simmer for a couple of minutes until it thickens slightly. Season to taste and pour over the pancakes. Top with the reserved cheese.

8 Bake at the top of the oven for 20 minutes until golden brown and bubbling in places. Remove from the oven and serve at once.

PREPARE AHEAD This can be made up to the end of step 6, covered, and refrigerated for up to 2 days, before finishing with the sauce and baking as described.

Swedish Pancake Stack Cake

Make sure you use only the thinnest of crêpes for this sumptuous dessert – a perfect summer birthday cake and a children's favourite.

| SERVES 6–8 | 10 MINS | 15 MINS |

Ingredients

6 pancakes, made using ½ quantity crêpe batter, see pages 518–519, steps 1–3 and 10–12
200ml (7fl oz) double cream
250ml (8fl oz) crème fraîche
3 tbsp caster sugar
¼ tsp vanilla extract
250g (9oz) raspberries
icing sugar, to serve

Method

1 Whip the double cream to form stiff peaks. Mix the cream, crème fraîche, caster sugar, and vanilla extract, and whisk until well blended. Reserve about 4 tablespoons to decorate the top of the cake.

2 Set aside a handful of the raspberries. Lightly crush the remaining fruit with a fork, and add them to the remaining cream mixture, folding them through roughly to create a rippled effect.

3 Place 1 pancake on a platter, spread one-fifth of the cream over it, and top with a second pancake. Continue to layer until all the pancakes and cream are used up.

4 Decorate the top with the reserved cream mixture, scatter the remaining raspberries over the top, dust with icing sugar and serve.

BAKER'S TIP

This stack cake is extremely versatile. Try using chopped strawberries or blueberries, which will make an equally delicious cake. In Sweden, lingonberry jam (similar to sweet cranberry sauce) is often used as a substitute for the fresh fruit. Look for the jam in Scandinavian delicatessens.

Staffordshire Oatcakes

These oat pancakes can have sweet or savoury fillings, can be folded in half, rolled up, or cooked on top of each other, then sliced in quarters.

MAKES 10   10 MINS   15 MINS

Resting time
1–2 hrs

Ingredients
200g (7oz) fine oatmeal
100g (3½oz) wholemeal flour

100g (3½oz) plain flour
½ tsp fine salt
2 tsp dried yeast
300ml (10fl oz) milk
unsalted butter, for frying

For the filling
250g (9oz) cheese, such as Cheddar
   or Red Leicester, grated
20 slices streaky bacon

Method

1 Sift together the fine oatmeal, wholemeal flour, plain flour, and salt. Add the dried yeast to 400ml (14fl oz) warm water and whisk well until it is completely dissolved. Add the milk. Make a well in the centre of the dry ingredients, and stir in the milk and water mixture.

2 Whisk the mixture together until the batter is completely smooth. Cover and set aside for 1–2 hours until small bubbles start to appear on the surface of the batter.

3 Melt a knob of butter in a large, non-stick frying pan and when it begins to sizzle, wipe any excess away quickly with a piece of kitchen paper.

4 Pour a ladleful of the oatcake mixture into the centre of the frying pan, and then tip the pan to allow the batter to spread all around. The idea is to cover the surface of the pan as quickly as possible with a thin layer of the oatcake batter.

5 Cook the oatcakes for 2 minutes on each side, turning them when the edges are cooked through and the first side is golden brown. Set the cooked oatcakes aside in a warm place and continue until all the batter has been used up.

6 Meanwhile, preheat the grill on its highest setting, and grill the streaky bacon. Sprinkle a handful of grated cheese all over the surface of an oatcake.

7 Place it under the grill for 1–2 minutes until the cheese has completely melted. Place 2 slices of grilled streaky bacon on top of the melted cheese to one side of the oatcake, roll it up, and serve.

BAKER'S TIP
These traditional oatcakes are really savoury pancakes, though a little more wholesome, and make a fantastic breakfast treat every once in a while. For an even quicker breakfast, the batter can be made the night before and stored, covered, in the refrigerator overnight.

QUICK BREADS AND BATTERS

Blinis

These buckwheat-based pancakes originated in Russia. Try serving them as canapés, or larger topped with smoked fish and crème fraîche for lunch.

MAKES 48 BLINIS · **20 MINS** · **15 MINS** · **UP TO 8 WEEKS**

Resting time
2 hrs

Ingredients

½ tsp dried yeast
200ml (7fl oz) warm milk
100g (3½ oz) soured cream
100g (3½oz) buckwheat flour
100g (3½oz) strong white bread flour
½ tsp fine salt
2 eggs, separated
50g (1¾oz) unsalted butter, melted and
  cooled, plus extra for frying
soured cream, smoked salmon, chives, and
  freshly ground pepper, to serve (optional)

Method

1 Mix the yeast with the warm milk, and whisk until the yeast dissolves. Whisk in the soured cream and set aside.

2 In a large bowl, mix together the 2 types of flour and the salt. Make a well in the centre and gradually whisk in the milk and soured cream. Add the egg yolks and continue to whisk. Finally, add the butter and whisk until smooth.

3 Cover the bowl with cling film and keep in a warm place for at least 2 hours until bubbles appear all over the surface.

4 In a clean bowl, whisk the egg whites to form soft peaks. Add the egg whites to the batter and gently fold them in using a metal spoon or spatula, until they are well combined and there are no lumps of egg white. Transfer the batter to a jug.

5 Heat a knob of butter in a large, non-stick frying pan. Pour the batter into the pan, 1 tablespoon at a time, to form small blinis, about 6cm (2½in) in diameter. Cook the

blinis for 1–2 minutes over medium heat until bubbles start to appear on the surface. When the bubbles begin to pop, turn and cook for another minute on the second side. Transfer the blinis to a warm plate, cover with a clean tea towel, and continue to cook them until all the batter is used up. Add another knob of butter to the pan occasionally, if it gets dry.

6 Serve the blinis soon after cooking or while still warm, with soured cream and smoked salmon, seasoned with plenty of black pepper and topped with snipped chives, for delicious canapés. They can also be wrapped in foil and gently reheated in a medium oven for 10 minutes before serving.

PREPARE AHEAD The blinis can be made up to 3 days ahead of time and kept in an airtight container in the refrigerator. Reheat from fresh or frozen as in step 6.

BAKER'S TIP

Blinis are simple to make, but can be difficult to get perfectly circular and small enough to serve as a canapé. Remember to pour the batter directly into the centre of the blini and use a spoon to catch any drips from the jug as you finish pouring.

Cherry Clafoutis

This French dessert combines sweetened egg custard and ripe fruit, baked until set and the fruit is bursting.

SERVES 6 · **12 MINS** · **35–45 MINS**

Resting time
30 mins

Special equipment
25cm (10in) tart tin or ovenproof dish

Ingredients
750g (1lb 10oz) cherries
3 tbsp Kirsch
75g (2½oz) caster sugar
unsalted butter, for greasing
4 large eggs
1 vanilla pod or 1 tsp vanilla extract
100g (3½oz) plain flour

300ml (10fl oz) milk
pinch of salt
icing sugar, for dusting
thick cream, crème fraîche,
  or vanilla ice cream, to serve
  (optional)

QUICK BREADS AND BATTERS

1 Toss the cherries with the Kirsch and 2 tablespoons sugar. Leave for 30 minutes.

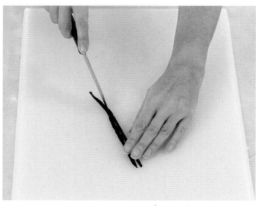

2 Preheat the oven to 200°C (400°F/Gas 6). Butter the flan tin, and set aside.

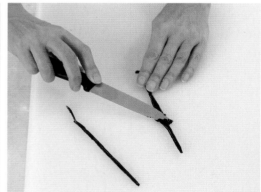

3 Strain the Kirsch from the cherries into a large bowl. Set the cherries aside.

4 Beat the eggs and vanilla extract (if using) into the Kirsch, until thoroughly combined.

5 With a sharp knife, split the vanilla pod (if using) vertically down the middle.

6 Run the tip of the knife down the middle of each half to scrape out all the seeds.

7 Add the seeds to the egg and Kirsch mixture and mix well to distribute.

8 Add the remaining sugar and beat well to combine.

9 Sift the flour into a large bowl, lifting the sieve high to aerate the flour as it floats down.

10 Beat the flour into the egg mixture, whisking after each addition, to make a smooth paste.

11 Pour in the milk, add the salt, and whisk until it makes a smooth batter.

12 Arrange the cherries in 1 layer in the flan dish. They should fill the dish.

13 Slowly pour the batter over the top of the cherries, trying not to displace the cherries.

14 Bake for 35–45 minutes or until the top is browned and the centre is firm to the touch.

15 Allow to cool on a wire rack, then remove from the tin and dust with icing sugar.

16 Serve warm or at room temperature, with plenty of thick cream or crème fraîche for spooning over, or with vanilla ice cream.

Clafoutis variations

Toad in the Hole

This savoury British version of clafoutis is perfect comfort food.

SERVES 4 · **20 MINS** · **35–40 MINS**

Standing time
30 mins

Special equipment
Roasting tin or shallow ovenproof dish

Ingredients
125g (4½oz) plain flour
pinch of salt
2 eggs
300ml (10fl oz) milk
2 tbsp vegetable oil
8 good-quality sausages

Method

1 To make the batter, put the flour into a bowl with the salt, make a well in the centre, and add the eggs with a little of the milk. Whisk together, gradually incorporating the flour. Add the remaining milk and whisk to make a smooth batter. Leave to rest for at least 30 minutes.

2 Preheat the oven to 220°C (425°F/Gas 7). Heat the oil in a roasting tin or shallow ovenproof dish. Add the sausages and toss them in the hot oil. Bake for 5–10 minutes or until the sausages are just coloured and the fat is very hot.

3 Reduce the oven temperature to 200°C (400°F/Gas 6). Carefully pour the batter around the sausages and return to the oven for a further 30 minutes or until the batter is risen, golden, and crisp. Serve immediately.

PREPARE AHEAD The batter can be made 24 hours in advance. Keep chilled and whisk briefly just before using.

Apricot Clafoutis

This French favourite can be enjoyed warm or at room temperature. Tinned apricots taste just fine, when fresh are out of season.

SERVES 4 · **10 MINS** · **35 MINS**

Special equipment
shallow ovenproof dish

Ingredients
unsalted butter, for greasing
250g (9oz) fresh ripe apricots, halved and pitted
  or 1 tin of apricot halves, drained
1 egg, plus 1 egg yolk
25g (scant 1oz) plain flour
50g (1¾oz) caster sugar
150ml (5fl oz) double cream
¼ tsp vanilla extract
thick cream or crème fraîche, to serve (optional)

Method

1 Preheat the oven to 200°C (400°F/Gas 6). Lightly grease the dish; it should be big enough to fit the apricots in a single layer. Place the apricots cut-side down in a single layer in the dish; there should be space between them.

2 In a bowl, whisk together the egg, egg yolk, and the flour. Whisk in the caster sugar. Finally, add the cream and vanilla extract, and whisk thoroughly to form a smooth custard.

3 Pour the custard around the apricots, so the tops of a few are just visible. Bake in the top shelf of the oven for 35 minutes until puffed up and golden brown in places. Remove and let cool for at least 15 minutes. It is best served warm, with thick cream or crème fraîche.

PREPARE AHEAD The clafoutis is best freshly baked and served warm, but can be cooked up to 6 hours ahead and served at room temperature.

Plum and Marzipan Clafoutis

This stunning version is equally good made with damsons or cherries, but instead of putting the marzipan in the fruit cavities, dot little pieces between each fruit.

SERVES 6 · **30 MINS** · **50 MINS**

Special equipment
shallow ovenproof dish

Ingredients

For the marzipan
115g (4oz) ground almonds
60g (2oz) caster sugar
60g (2oz) icing sugar, plus extra for dusting
few drops of almond extract
½ tsp lemon juice
1 egg white, lightly beaten

For the clafoutis
675g (1½lb) plums, halved and stoned
75g (2½oz) butter
4 eggs and 1 egg yolk
115g (4oz) caster sugar
85g (3oz) plain flour, sifted
450ml (15fl oz) milk
150ml (5fl oz) single cream

Method

1 Preheat the oven to 190°C (375°F/Gas 5). Mix the marzipan ingredients together with enough of the egg white to form a stiff paste. Push a tiny piece of the paste into the cavity in each plum half.

2 Grease a shallow, ovenproof dish, large enough to hold the plums in a single layer, with 15g (½oz) of the butter. Arrange the plums cut-side down in the dish, with the marzipan underneath. Melt the remaining butter and leave to cool.

3 Add any leftover egg white from the marzipan to the eggs and egg yolk. Add the sugar and whisk until thick and pale. Whisk in the melted butter, flour, milk, and cream to form a batter. Pour over the plums and bake in the oven for about 50 minutes until golden and just set. Serve warm, dusted with icing sugar.

PREPARE AHEAD The clafoutis is best freshly baked and served warm, but can be cooked 6 hours ahead and served at room temperature.

> **BAKER'S TIP**
> Clafoutis is basically a sweetened custard, baked around any type of seasonal fruit. As a storecupboard standby, try this version with tinned apricots, but in season, you can use cherries, blackberries, plums, and black, white, or redcurrants.

Plum Clafoutis

This is a satisfying autumn dessert to make when the plums are at their peak. You can substitute the Kirsch for plum or ordinary brandy, if preferred. **PICTURED OVERLEAF**

SERVES 6–8 · **20–25 MINS** · **30–35 MINS**

Special equipment
shallow ovenproof dish

Ingredients
unsalted butter, for greasing
100g (3½oz) caster sugar,
    plus extra for baking dish
625g (1lb 5oz) small plums, halved and pitted
45g (1½oz) plain flour
pinch of salt
150ml (5fl oz) milk
75ml (2½fl oz) double cream
4 eggs, plus 2 egg yolks
3 tbsp Kirsch
2 tbsp icing sugar
whipped cream, to serve (optional)

Method

1 Preheat the oven to 180°C (350°F/Gas 4). Grease the baking dish. Sprinkle over some sugar, and turn it around to coat the bottom and sides evenly. Tip out any excess. Spread the plums, cut-side up, in an even layer.

2 Sift the flour and salt into a bowl. Make a well in the centre, and pour in the milk and cream. Whisk, drawing in the flour, to make a smooth paste. Add the eggs, egg yolks, and caster sugar, and whisk to make a smooth batter.

3 Just before baking, ladle the batter over the plums, then spoon over the Kirsch. Bake for 30–35 minutes until puffed up and beginning to brown. Just before serving, sift over the icing sugar. Serve warm or at room temperature, with whipped cream.

PREPARE AHEAD The clafoutis is best freshly baked and served warm, but can be cooked 6 hours ahead and served at room temperature.

Waffles

These easy-to-make and versatile waffles are perfect for breakfast, a light snack, or dessert.

MAKES 6–8
10 MINS
20–25 MINS
UP TO 4 WEEKS

Special equipment
waffle maker or waffle iron

Ingredients
175g (6oz) plain flour
1 tsp baking powder
2 tbsp caster sugar
300ml (10fl oz) milk
75g (2½oz) unsalted butter, melted
1 tsp vanilla extract
2 large eggs, separated
maple syrup, jam, fresh fruit, sweetened cream, or ice cream, to serve (optional)

Method

1 Place the flour, baking powder, and caster sugar in a bowl. Make a well in the centre, and pour in the milk, butter, vanilla extract, and egg yolks. Gradually whisk in the flour.

2 Preheat the waffle maker or iron. In a clean large bowl, whisk the egg whites until soft peaks form. Fold into the batter with a metal spoon.

3 Preheat the oven to 130°C (250°F/Gas ½). Spoon a small ladleful of the batter onto the hot iron (or the amount recommended by the waffle maker manufacturer) and spread almost to the edge. Close the lid and bake until golden.

4 Serve immediately, with maple syrup, jam, fresh fruit, sweetened cream, or ice cream, or keep warm in a single layer in the oven until all are ready.

PREPARE AHEAD Although best eaten as fresh as possible, you can make waffles 24 hours in advance and reheat them in a toaster.

BAKER'S TIP
Whenever a recipe calls for the addition of melted butter, as here, make sure it is completely cooled before adding to a batter. Warm or hot butter can curdle a mixture, starting to cook it before time, or forming lumps of cooked eggs within it. So do not skip the vital step of cooling melted butter.

QUICK BREADS AND BATTERS

Index

Page numbers in **bold** indicate step-by-step illustrations of recipes or techniques. Page numbers in *italics* indicate Baker's Tips.

About the author

After spending years as an international model, Caroline Bretherton dedicated herself to her passion for food, founding her company, Manna Food, in 1996.

Her fresh, light, and stylish cooking soon developed a stylish following to match, with a catering clientele that included celebrities, art galleries, theaters, and fashion magazines, as well as cutting edge businesses. She later expanded the company to include an all-day eatery called Manna Café on Portobello Road, in the heart of London's Notting Hill.

A move into the media has seen her working consistently in television over the years, appearing as a guest on and presenting a wide range of food programs for local and cable broadcasters.

More recently Caroline has worked increasingly in print, becoming a regular contributor to *The Times on Saturday*, and writing her first book *The Kitchen Garden Cookbook*.

In her spare time, Caroline tends her beloved community garden near her home in London, growing a variety of fruits, vegetables, and herbs. When she can, she indulges her passion for wild food foraging, both in the city and the country.

She is married to Luke, an academic, and has two boys, Gabriel and Isaac, who were more than happy to test the recipes for this book.

Acknowledgments

The author would like to thank
Mary-Clare, Dawn, and Alastair at Dorling Kindersley for their help and encouragement with this massive task, as well as Borra Garson and all at Deborah McKenna for all their work on my behalf. Lastly I would like to thank all my family and friends for their tremendous encouragement and appetites!

Dorling Kindersley would like to thank
The following people for their work on the photoshoot:

Art Directors
Nicky Collings, Miranda Harvey, Luis Peral, Lisa Pettibone

Props Stylist
Wei Tang

Food Stylists
Kate Blinman, Lauren Owen, Denise Smart

Home Economist Assistant
Emily Jonzen

Baking equipment used in the step-by-step photography kindly donated by Lakeland. www.lakeland.co.uk; 011 44 15394 88100.

Caroline de Souza for art direction and setting the style of the videos and presentation stills photography.

Dorothy Kikon for editorial assistance and Anamica Roy for design assistance.

Jane Ellis for proofreading and Susan Bosanko for indexing.

Thanks to the following people for their work on the US edition:

Consultant
Kate Curnes

Americanizers
Nichole Morford and Jenny Siklós

Thanks also to Steve Crozier for retouching.

Useful Information

Oven temperature equivalents

For a fan-assisted oven, reduce the temperature by at least 10°C / 25°F.

CELSIUS	FAHRENHEIT	GAS	DESCRIPTION
110°C	225°F	¼	Cool
130°C	250°F	½	Cool
140°C	275°F	1	Very low
150°C	300°F	2	Very low
160°C	325°F	3	Low
180°C	350°F	4	Moderate
190°C	375°F	5	Moderately hot
200°C	400°F	6	Hot
220°C	425°F	7	Hot
230°C	450°F	8	Very hot
240°C	475°F	9	Very hot

Volume equivalents

Note that 1 teaspoon measures 5ml and 1 tbsp measures 15ml.

METRIC	IMPERIAL	METRIC	IMPERIAL
30ml	1fl oz	450ml	15fl oz
60ml	2fl oz	500ml	16fl oz
75ml	2½fl oz	600ml	1 pint
100ml	3½fl oz	750ml	1¼ pints
120ml	4fl oz	900ml	1½ pints
150ml	5fl oz (¼ pint)	1 litre	1¾ pints
175ml	6fl oz	1.2 litres	2 pints
200ml	7fl oz (⅓ pint)	1.4 litres	2½ pints
240ml	8fl oz	1.5 litres	2¾ pints
300ml	10fl oz (½ pint)	1.7 litres	3 pints
350ml	12fl oz	2 litres	3½ pints
400ml	14fl oz	3 litres	5¼ pints